BEAUTY AND THE NATION

Beauty and the Nation

WOMEN, CULTURE, AND THE NATIONAL IMAGE
IN INTERWAR VIETNAM

Christina E. Firpo

Columbia University Press
New York

Columbia University Press
Publishers Since 1893
New York   Chichester, West Sussex
cup.columbia.edu

Copyright © 2026 Columbia University Press
All rights reserved

Library of Congress Cataloging-in-Publication Data
Names: Firpo, Christina Elizabeth author
Title: Beauty and the nation : women, culture, and the national image in interwar Vietnam / Christina E. Firpo.
Description: New York : Columbia University Press, 2025. | Includes bibliographical references and index.
Identifiers: LCCN 2025021165 | ISBN 9780231208864 hardback | ISBN 9780231208871 trade paperback | ISBN 9780231557665 ebook
Subjects: LCSH: Women—Vietnam—Social conditions—20th century | Beauty, Personal—Vietnam—History—20th century | Feminine beauty (Aesthetics)—Vietnam—History—20th century | National characteristics, Vietnamese | Sex role—Vietnam—History—20th century | Social change—Vietnam—History—20th century | Vietnam—History—1945–1975
Classification: LCC HQ1750.5 .F57 2025
LC record available at https://lccn.loc.gov/2025021165

Cover design: Elliott S. Cairns
Cover image: Trần Bình Lộc, "Silence," *Ngày Nay* newspaper, issue 35 cover illustration.

GPSR Authorized Representative: Easy Access System Europe, Mustamäe tee 50, 10621 Tallinn, Estonia, gpsr.requests@easproject.com

I dedicate this book to Chiara and my mother, who are beautiful people, both inside and out. Of course, I won't forget Mike, Ezra, and my dad!

CONTENTS

ACKNOWLEDGMENTS ix
NOTE ON NAMES AND TRANSLATIONS xiii

Introduction 1

Chapter One
The Dissemination of Beauty Trends 35

Chapter Two
Fashion 75

Chapter Three
Cosmetics 113

Chapter Four
Physique 153

Chapter Five
Beauty Contests 192

Conclusion 223

NOTES 233
BIBLIOGRAPHY 293
INDEX 313

ACKNOWLEDGMENTS

I would like to open and close these acknowledgments by thanking my family. I began researching this book at the beginning of the COVID-19 pandemic, which was undeniably difficult for everyone. This book became my outlet—dare I say my escape—from the constant bad news of the pandemic. I arose each morning at 4 A.M. and worked until around 7 A.M., when my daughter Chiara (two-and-a-half-years-old) quietly joined me at her "work desk" and solved Disney-themed puzzles. We paused for breakfast when my son Ezra (ten months old) and my husband Mike awoke. The four of us would spend the rest of the day together, typically listening to the *Frozen* soundtrack while Mike and I tried to work. Occasionally I fled to the beach, where I opened the hatch of my car and wrote from the trunk while enjoying the waves. I must admit that at the time I thought the shutdown was a nightmare, with the constant anxiety, the sting of hand sanitizer, the separation from extended family, and the impossibility of two adults working in a small space with young children. However, as I reflect on the days spent writing this book, I sometimes unexpectedly find myself nostalgic for that truly bizarre time and thankful for the silliness and levity that my family brought to it.

The difficulties we all experienced during the pandemic render me extra grateful to those who helped bring this book into print. My students at Cal Poly University in San Luis Obispo were understanding when Chiara wanted to join in my zoom office hours, or when Ezra demanded milk as I zoomed my World History lecture. Once we returned to campus, the rich discussions in my classes—"Gender and Consumerism," "History of Beauty," and "Vietnamese History"—inspired many of the ideas in this book. I have always been happy at Cal Poly, but the pandemic made me especially grateful for the university's family-friendly environment. The History Department chairs—Kate Murphy, Tom Trice, and Joel Orth, and associate chair Farah Al-Nakib—used all their strength to support faculty during this rough period. Although teaching is the primary mission of the California State University system, I am grateful to the vice president for research Dawn Neill, and the college of liberal arts dean Kate Murphy for encouraging and protecting faculty research. Denna Zamarron is the backbone of our department, and nothing could be accomplished without her help. And I owe a special thanks to the CLA librarian Brett Bodemer and the staff of the Interlibrary Loan office for sourcing books from Vietnam and France.

At Columbia University Press, I would like to express my deep appreciation to the faculty board, as well as the incredibly patient Caelyn Cobb, Monique Laban, and Marisa Lastres. And I am grateful to Kay Mikel, who copyedited the manuscript, and Ben Kolstad at KGL, who managed the project.

Over the last twenty-four years of researching in Vietnam, I have been fortunate to work with wonderful colleagues and friends. I am appreciative of the National Library of Vietnam, and its director Nguyễn Xuân Dũng and the associate director Nguyễn Ngọc Anh. At the National Archives, I thank Hoàng Hằng for more than twenty years of friendship. One of my first professors in Hanoi was the renowned historian Đặng Thị Vân Chi, who welcomes me into her home with every visit to Hanoi. I am grateful to the hard work of Alain Léger, the director of the archives of Les entreprises colonial françaises, and Hillary Belzer of the Makeup Archives. I also thank Sheon Montgomery from Texas Tech University, who helped me find the rare newspapers that informed many of the stories in this book.

I am grateful for the rich network of colleagues in the Association of Asian Studies, the Vietnam Studies Group, the French Colonial History Society, and the Cosmetics Network. I owe a tremendous debt to Peter Zinoman, Hayden Cherry, Chris Goscha, Nora Taylor, Jennifer Boittin, Hillary Belzer, and Kate Murphy for giving me valuable feedback on the book proposal and the manuscript. Marie-Agathe Simonetti and David Del Testa graciously shared images and documents with me. I am also thankful for feedback from the Center for Southeast Asian Studies at UCLA, where

ACKNOWLEDGMENTS

I presented a draft of chapter 4, and the History Department at Harvard University, where I presented chapter 5 of this book.

I thoroughly enjoyed long conversations with colleagues across the globe, from Hawaii to Boston, Ithaca to Paris, Leiden to Hanoi, and Tai Pei. Thank you to David Ambaras, Barbara Watson Andaya, David Biggs, Hong An Ly, Kristen Brennan, Brad Davis, David Del Testa, Claire Edington, Chiara Formichi, Holly Grout, Judith Henchy, Hòang Lan Hường, Tom Hoogervorst (who plays a killer game of Connect Four), Charles Keith, Xiorong Li, Shawn McHale, Martina Nguyen, Dịu Hương Nguyễn, Nguyễn Thị Hoa, Nguyễn Thị Hông Hạnh, Thao Nguyen, Kate Norberg, Philippe Peycam, Johanna Ramsmeier, Lucy Santos, Marie Agathe Simonetti, Ron Spector, Michelle Thompson, Ben Tran, and Mike Vann. As I've said in previous books, Jennifer Boittin and Elisa Camiscioli are the sharpest minds in history—and outstanding friends.

In addition to my colleagues from the field, I would like to thank the colleagues and friends back at home: Reggie Allen, Jane Lehr, Kate Murphy and Preston Moon, Devin and Don Kuhn-Choi, Julie and Jay Bettergarcia, Tom Trice, Andrew Morris, Andrea Oñate-Madrazo, Farah Al-Nakib, Matt Hopper, Thanayi Jackson, Elizabeth Sine, Liz Adan, Denise Isom, Dawn Neill and Justin Cooley, Maggie and Brett Bodemer, Pat Lin, Suzy Smith, Aly Holob, Meme Lobecker, Heather and Jeff Goldman, Marissa Araujo, Melissa Edwards, Jason Hilford, Jayan Kalathil, and Shereen Langrana. I am forever grateful to my loving family: my parents Kathy and John, my sisters Patrice and Erica and their respective families, my in-laws David and Cecelia Chen, Andrew and Su Wen Chen and their children, and my extended family, Laura Lofaro, Jim Freeman, June and Ross Stoddard, the Sangiacomos, and my late uncle Sal.

We've come a long way since the pandemic. Ezra, now six years old, is playing soccer and quickly learning to read. Chiara, almost eight years old, is sewing her own dresses from old bed sheets, reading Harry Potter, and dominating on the jujitsu mat. Although one might assume that parenting would make writing more difficult, on the contrary, my children enrich my intellectual life and enhance my writing. But this book could not have been completed without the love, patience, and support of my husband, Mike. He brightens every day, reminds me to have fun, and moves mountains to get me to Grateful Dead shows. He's my sunshine daydream and the love of my life.

NOTE ON NAMES AND TRANSLATIONS

Today the word *hiện đại* is the most commonly used term for "modern," but sources from the interwar years used terms such as *mới* (literally "new") to describe Modern Girls (*gái mới, đàn bà mới*), pursuit of a modern lifestyle (*theo mới*), or modernity (*cái mới, sự thích mới*). Sources also drew from the Sino-Vietnamese lexicon with the term *tân thời*, which translated literally means "a new era" and was used to refer to things that were modern or trendy. Two additional terms often associated with interwar era modernity are *văn minh*, which I translate as "civilized," and *lịch sự*, which I translate as "polite."

While female voices are difficult to find in early twentieth-century Vietnamese sources, women's opinions are crucial to this history of beauty. I was lucky to find a plethora of women-authored articles and letters published in the Vietnamese-language newspapers. When appropriate in the text, I point out those sources that are written by women. Many more female journalists can be found—though their gender not specified—in the footnotes.

Readers will notice that throughout the manuscript I use the name Vietnam, which did not exist as a country during the interwar years. The first official use of the name Vietnam to refer to the territory spanning from to Hà Giang to Cà Mau occurred in 1802, but the country of Vietnam would be split apart half a century later when France laid claim to the southern provinces. What I refer to as Vietnam consisted of the two French protectorates of Tonkin, Annam, and the colony of Cochinchina. These three *pays*—each a separate administrative unit—were governed under the French colony of Indochine, which also included Cambodia, Laos, and Kouang-Tchéou-Wan. Although Vietnam was not a political entity during this period, authors of the majority of my primary sources saw themselves as addressing an imagined community of Vietnamese-language speakers, for whom the geo-body of Vietnam maintained a firm place in their conscious and political aspirations.

BEAUTY AND THE NATION

INTRODUCTION

"Miss Anna . . ." the article begins, as though the narrator is searching for a suitable name. "Miss Anna Phiếm," it continues. "A Western wife." The name is a play on words: "Anna" to highlight the subject's affinity for French culture and "Phiếm," a play on the word "*phù phiếm,*" meaning vain or frivolous. The article appeared in 1938 in Vịt Đực, a satirical newspaper famous for its biting humor—specifically in a running column called "*Mốt,*" a Vietnamization of the French word *mode* meaning trend or fashion. Mốt regularly targeted women's fashion, often with a misogynist slant.[1]

"Let's look at this modern woman from head to toe," the narrator continues, with faux gravitas, and proceeds to dissect "Anna's" looks with a checklist of modern fashion cliches:

> The bun hairstyle
> the white teeth
> the powder on cheeks, lipstick on lips
> the smoothly flowing áo dài
> the high-heeled shoes
> carrying an umbrella
> carrying a purse
> riding a bike

Anna Phiếm is, in short, a caricature of the Vietnamese woman who slavishly followed every fashion trend of the 1930s, many of them Western. That she is married to a Western man hints at the association often made by critics between the embrace of Western fashion trends and a penchant for licentiousness. The narrator continues in the same lightly mocking tone: "Whenever such a new trend appears, the ladies purse their lips in scorn— 'Such a whore!'" Whereupon he performs the final skewering of his target: "but they are the ones who are foolish. Because it's they in particular who copy the trends so foolishly."[2] His point is that the women who criticized the Anna Phiếms of colonial Vietnam were hypocritically succumbing to the very same fashion trends themselves.

As the caricature of Anna Phiếm exemplifies, perspectives on women's beauty underwent a radical transformation in Vietnam during the interwar years—a transformation that had social, economic, and political implications. Young, mainly urban women coming of age after World War I looked and behaved very differently from their mothers and grandmothers. Whereas women of generations past had worn dark, loose-fitting clothing that concealed their lithe figures, young women in the interwar years experimented with bright colors, textured fabrics, and silhouettes cut to accentuate their curves. Some even donned bathing suits at the beach, allowing the sun to kiss the skin that their mothers had worked so hard to keep white. The mothers had carefully parted their long hair in the middle and twisted it up into a turban; their daughters chopped their hair above their shoulders and parted it seductively on the side. The mothers had pursed their lips in small tight smiles that hid their blackened teeth; their daughters brightened their eyes with black mascara and slicked on red lipstick to highlight their dazzling white smiles. Day after day they leaned close to their vanity mirrors, painstakingly applying their makeup, artfully transforming their faces from plain to pretty.

Young women's relationship to social norms also changed. While growing up, their mothers had been constantly reminded to adhere to the Confucian doctrines of the Threefold Dependencies (*tam tòng*) on the father, husband, and sons[3] and the Four Virtues (*tứ đức*) of proper work (*công*), comportment (*dung*), eloquence (*ngôn*), and virtue (*hạnh*). These mothers had been raised to revere the so-called *khuê các* maiden, a reference to the boudoirs in which daughters of upper-class families in Chinese feudal times had remained sequestered until marriage. (Of course, by the late nineteenth and early twentieth centuries, the khuê các maiden was more of an ideal than a reality as few families could afford not to draw on the labor of their daughters.) As for the urban middle-class young women coming of age after World War I, they turned away from the Three Dependencies, the Four Virtues, and the khuê các ideal, opting instead to openly participate in the public sphere. They played sports, rode the tram across town, and watched the latest films at the cinema, often leaning in close to—or even kissing—their date under the cover of the dark theater. In the 1930s, dance halls opened their doors to pretty young women who allowed their well-dressed and pampered bodies to be touched by sweaty young men. Some women even entered themselves in beauty pageants with the hope that audiences and judges alike would find them beautiful.

While urban middle-class young women comprised the majority of this new generation, the new beauty and lifestyle trends they followed were hardly limited to one demographic. Women's looks and comportment were changing in the countryside as well as in the big cities. Notwithstanding their more conservative bent, rural women may have embraced beauty trends more enthusiastically than the surviving sources would suggest, given that their risqué indulgences could be quickly hidden with a mere change of outfit or washing of the face. Many of the new fashion and beauty trends of that era originated in rural areas among *me tây*, women involved in romantic relationships with French and Foreign Legion soldiers stationed in rural military bases. Rural women—even those not in a relationship with Westerners—were further exposed to new trends through local newspapers, whose pages contained images of dazzling beauty queens, how-to articles on cosmetics application, and patterns for the latest dress styles. Traveling cinemas regularly circulated through the provinces, setting up a projector and screen in a field and inviting audiences to gaze at starlets in slinky dresses under the stars. State-organized fairs staged in rural areas attracted huge crowds eager to witness the latest innovations in consumer goods and catch a glimpse of the ubiquitous beauty contest. The rural-urban cultural divide was further blurred by migrations in both directions—some permanent, others temporary—driven in large part by the turbulent interwar economy, new educational opportunities, and transportation innovations such as automobiles and trains. Rural dwellers went to cities seeking work or school, and middle-class urbanites visited relatives in the countryside or vacationed in coastal and mountain towns, bringing cosmopolitan culture with them.

The new beauty trends spanned class strata as well as the rural-urban divide, often in surprising ways. No longer was pretty clothing enjoyed solely by the upper class. Middle-class wives and daughters, whose ranks expanded greatly during the interwar years, happily shopped for fashion and cosmetics with newly acquired disposable income. In new professions as shop girls, telephone operators, teachers, and journalists, young women earned money that they now dared to spend on themselves instead of saving it for the family coffers per the Confucian virtue of proper work. These middle- and upper-class women comprised the majority of the beauty market, but lower-class women consumed beauty and fashion products as well. After all, many beauty practices popular during the interwar years required little to no investment. One could cut one's hair for the price of a pair of scissors; lipstick could double as blush; breasts could be easily unbound; and exercises targeting certain areas of the body could be learned from a newspaper article or a friend. Thanks to the arrival of mass production, cosmetics and, to a lesser extent, clothing were sold at low enough price points to enable a fair number of lower-class women to purchase them on occasion. Even women unable to afford trendy clothing or a full palette of makeup could acquire an occasional tube of lipstick or mascara. Sex workers, whose ranks swelled during the Great Depression, constituted a distinct category of impoverished consumers who paradoxically could not afford such products yet relied on them to perform their jobs. While researching my previous book on Tonkin's interwar-era sex industry, I found that many brothel owners issued cash advances to enable sex workers to pay for the fashionable—and even sexy—clothing and dramatic makeup deemed necessary to attract customers.[4]

Although the new fashion and beauty trends were embraced primarily by younger women, middle-aged women also delighted in fashion and beautification. In the 1920s, when schoolgirls began arriving in class wearing brightly colored tunics with white pants—the latest craze—and faces painted with makeup, women in their twenties, thirties, and forties soon followed suit. Mothers—once considered past their prime and tasked with devoting themselves entirely to their family, often to the point of sacrificing their personal needs—now turned their focus to their own looks. This transformation was most salient among a new demographic group that emerged during the interwar years: middle-class housewives. These urban women—some newlyweds, others middle-aged—did not need to work thanks to their husbands' middle-class income. Unlike their rural counterparts who labored over crops or sold produce at the market to help their families survive, housewives—supported by an army of servants to cook, clean, and watch the children—enjoyed a fair amount of leisure time. Much of it was spent socializing, enjoying recreational activities, and tending to their appearance. Indeed, beauty advice columns from the interwar period addressed housewives directly, teaching them how to maintain their appearance so their husbands did not stray, how to bounce back after having a baby, how to dress more youthfully, and how to avoid appearing like a harried housewife even when they felt like one. Middle-aged women's embrace of the trend marked a decisive shift in their identity and, in many cases, in their role in society. Until the interwar era, older Vietnamese women had once garnered respect, or at least harbored a sense of dignity, from their advanced age. Now, however, they took pains to prevent the appearance of further aging—dying their hair, concealing or minimizing their wrinkles, and choosing whatever color nail polish had been deemed most "youthful."

These changes in beauty norms and female comportment shocked the nation. Some men and women, especially those of older generations, began defending the merits of Confucian dictates for women's behavior. They grew suspicious of women's sudden desire to subvert their "natural" looks with science's new cosmetic concoctions, which they believed—often correctly—to be literally poisonous. They were repulsed, and in some cases secretly titillated, by the show of skin, the curvier silhouettes, and even the newly toned musculatures. Critics were also shocked by the amount of time and money devoted to something as frivolous as cosmetics and embarrassed by the mismatched, attention-seeking outfits that seemed to confirm colonizers' assumptions that Vietnamese people did not understand *taste*. And they worried about the long-term implications of these trends, fearing that younger generations would care more about the pleasures of sexual passion than procreating to continue the ancestral line.

It would be easy to dismiss dress patterns and lip-lining tutorials as frivolous. Yet I take beauty culture seriously because it commanded the attention of so much of Vietnam's female population. Female customers purchasing beauty products drove the market; female entrepreneurs built businesses around this market; female journalists reported on and shaped the trends. Beauty culture, defined as the choices women make about their appearance and public reaction to those choices, thus proves to be a rich historical source. This is especially true in the context of interwar Vietnam, where few types of conventional historical sources speak to the multifarious experiences of a generation of women. Conversely, the sheer volume of beauty-related sources that appeared in the Vietnamese press during the interwar years—and the degree of consternation they caused among detractors—makes them impossible to ignore and reveals much about interwar Vietnamese society and politics. The way Vietnamese women dressed, painted their faces, styled their hair, and showed off their bodies in public were nonverbal ways of participating in society. As Kathy Peiss shows in the case of twentieth-century American beauty culture, women used makeup to express both their selfhood and their social role.[5] Similarly, in the case of interwar Vietnam, beauty trends tell us about women's feelings and opinions, their economic choices, their artistic expression, and their interactions with the new media and technologies of the time. These fresh *looks* were, in short, a way for Vietnamese women to express their new roles in this rapidly changing world. Of course, historians should take care not to overinterpret their choices. Not every eyeshadow color or dress style is a deliberate form of political expression—that would be exhausting for the wearer! But it is important to examine the choices women make as an aggregate to understand how they interact with the broad social, political, economic, and technological forces at play during their particular era. In this study of beauty culture during the interwar years, I take seriously Vietnamese women's bodily expressions of beauty, the way women wrote about them, and the public reaction to them—not least because women themselves took these matters seriously.

Further underscoring the significance of beauty culture as a historical source of women's expression, Vietnamese women were taking a significant risk when they wore trendy outfits and experimented with makeup. Although there is certainly an element of conformity associated with fashion and beauty, the changes undertaken by the women of Vietnam's interwar years left women vulnerable to critique or even ridicule. Indeed, the transformation of women's appearance in Vietnam was much more pronounced than any concurrent changes happening in Europe or the United States, both of which arguably saw a degree of continuity with beauty practices dating back even before the Industrial Revolution. Women of interwar Vietnam broke from the past as well as from Confucian norms governing society by wearing clothing and makeup that expressed an individualist spirit, vivaciousness, financial impulsivity, and frank sexuality. As a result, new beauty choices came with serious consequences: social ostracization, punishment at school, disgrace upon their family, accusations of prostitution, or rejection by marital prospects—all of which we see anecdotally in a range of the documents from the interwar years. That women were willing to take these kinds of risks consciously or unconsciously speaks volumes about the importance of treating Vietnam's interwar beauty culture as a historical source.

Indeed, the small personal risks women incurred in wearing white pants with a colorful tunic or parting their hair on the side would, in the aggregate, play an important role in shaping the kind of nation Vietnam would become in the modern world. Among the many political, social, and economic movements that influenced Vietnam's quest to redefine its national identity, three were specifically relevant to the revolution in Vietnamese women's beauty culture. These three movements are discussed in detail here: (1) the increasing influence of the French colonizer on Vietnamese culture, a development that would eventually be known as the "Europeanization" movement; (2) the Vietnamese modernist movement, which sought to forge a distinct national identity that was a break with tradition, yet uniquely Vietnamese; and (3) and a Neo-Confucian backlash against both of these trends that sought to return Vietnam to the values and traditions of its Confucian past. It should be noted that while these three movements represented distinct approaches, they often overlapped in their agendas. The movements should not be construed as anything like political parties; indeed, it wasn't uncommon for actors in the beauty movement to draw from different aspects of Europeanization, Vietnamese modernism, and neo-Confucianism simultaneously.

The first movement that influenced beauty culture began with *La Mission Civilisatrice* to bring French language and culture to colonized people, which would, by World War I, become the "Europeanization movement" (*phong trào âu hóa*), promoted by Vietnamese whose livelihood often depended on collaborating with the French. Multiple sociocultural developments drove the Europeanization movement, including the development of the colonial school system, which educated Vietnamese girls for the first time and imparted French cultural values through the curriculum; the increased importation of French goods and resulting consumerist mentality; and a growing urban Vietnamese middle class that pursued a European way of life. One cannot underestimate the influence of European culture, European consumer goods, and the Europeanization trend on the women of Vietnam during the interwar period. Young women, seduced by Western individualism, casually ignored family obligations; spent their money freely on fashion and cosmetics under the spell of Western materialism; and freed by Western morality even dared to steal away for a weekend vacation with a paramour.

A second movement, Vietnamese modernism, formed in opposition to both French colonial rule and the Vietnamese monarchy. The movement was pioneered at the turn of the century by a group of Confucian reformers (nationalists at heart) who condemned the Vietnamese monarchy for capitulating to the French and regarded as illegitimate the succession of emperors hand-picked by the colonial state. Although the early Vietnamese modernists were themselves educated in Confucianism—the philosophy that permeated the legal system, educational system, and the political and social order—they dismissed Confucianism as an outdated philosophy that hindered the progress they deemed essential to the modernization of the Vietnamese nation. They also denounced mandarins—the Confucian scholar-bureaucrats who served the monarchy—most of whom had been bribed with positions of political power in the colonial administration or land concessions (property seized by the French from rebel Vietnamese villages).[6] Vietnamese modernists developed a vision for a modern Vietnam that was influenced by the Japanese Meiji Restoration, Western republican values, and the politics of Chinese reformers Liang Qichao and Kang Youwei—republicans who, among other things, called for female education to strengthen the nation. The vision of a modern Vietnam put forth by these Vietnamese reformers was to eliminate the existing monarchy and mandarin bureaucracy and replace it with a government that would grant individual rights and educate the entire Vietnamese population, including women and peasants. Only through participation by all classes and both genders would Vietnamese society become strong and independent, Vietnamese modernists avowed. Male and female modernists championed not just women's education but women's participation in the public sphere and women's right to determine their own destiny, notably in the matter of marital choice. Consequently, women all over Vietnam took their place in the classroom, initially as students then as teachers themselves; scored goals on the soccer field and rode their bicycles around town; and asserted their opinions on the pages of newspapers. These very acts, which called into question traditional expectations for women's role in family and society, sent shock waves throughout Vietnam's social structure.

Yet Vietnamese modernism was not accepted by all. A third movement that shaped beauty culture, Neo-Confucianism, emerged as a backlash to the rapid pace of cultural change in Vietnamese society brought about by French colonization and Vietnamese modernism. Neo-Confucianism as expressed in Vietnam was part of a larger trend sweeping East Asia, most notably China, during this era. Although Confucian philosophy has a long and complicated history in Vietnam, it is not my intent to present early twentieth-century Vietnam as a uniformly "Confucian society"; to do so would elide the country's incredible intellectual diversity.[7] Neo-Confucian ideology was, however, invoked during the interwar years as a discursive tool with which to critique women's beauty culture—a sharp contrast to Korea, where Neo-Confucianists encouraged women to beautify themselves. In Vietnam, Neo-Confucianists warned that the collective morality was being compromised by the individualism, materialism, and sexual promiscuity brough about by Europeanization and Vietnamese modernism, with beauty culture exemplifying all of the above. Facing such rapid social upheaval, Neo-Confucianists looked to the past as a source of stability. The conservative intellectuals who led the movement called to strengthen Vietnam by returning it to its "national essence" (quốc túy), largely defined by Confucian dictates. In their quest to reorganize society in order to counteract the growing European influence as well as the Vietnamese modernist social order, this group of male and female Neo-Confucianists drew from ancient Confucian texts and what they claimed were Vietnamese traditions. One of the foci of Neo-Confucianists during the interwar years was a call to restore a "traditional" gendered order that was derived from both real and apocryphal historic precedent.[8] They exhorted women to adhere to the Three Dependencies and the Four Virtues, celebrated the ideal of the khuê các sequestered maiden, and encouraged women to remain chaste until marriage and after widowhood. The tensions that developed among the respective proponents of Europeanization, Vietnamese modernism, and Neo-Confucianism had far-reaching political, cultural, and social implications, especially for Vietnamese women.

In this book I contend that interwar Vietnamese beauty culture, including beauty practices and the discourse surrounding them, was shaped by the tensions playing out among Europeanization, Vietnamese modernism, and Neo-Confucianism during that era. Within the context of these three developing movements, beauty practices (and the debates they triggered) became a powerful expression of how women (and onlookers) attempted to make sense of their rapidly changing world. Understood this way, beauty culture reveals anxieties about the tumultuous political, economic, social, and cultural changes transforming Vietnam during the interwar years. Women's faces and bodies, in short, became a vigorously debated site for envisioning what it meant to be Vietnamese in a modern world.

Debates about fashion trends, as you will see in chapter 2, were framed in terms of national respectability. Cosmetics, chapter 3 will show, came to represent far more than tools with which to beautify the face: they also heralded the rise of individualism and the changing role of women in the family and society. Women's more developed musculature, the topic of chapter 4, made manifest the health and strength of the Vietnamese people, and their voluptuous bodies reflected the influence of Europeanization. Meanwhile beauty contests, the subject of chapter 5, shattered the Confucian notion that women should remain sequestered until marriage and keep their beauty hidden. In short, a vast array of actors—intellectuals opining about women's fashion; housewives writing impassioned letters to newspapers; male artists happily taking on advisory roles; and female entrepreneurs claiming their share of the consumer market—held women responsible for representing the Vietnamese nation, not necessarily as political participants but as powerful visual symbols.

While this book focuses on women, I had originally set out to write about gender and beauty more widely. Among other things, I had hoped to find examples of men experimenting or crossing boundaries into what was considered the feminine beauty world. Although I did not find such stories in these primary sources, I direct the reader to Richard Tran's fascinating research on the spectrum of gender expressions that existed in early twentieth-century Vietnam.[9] As for men's fashion during the interwar years, important changes arose in hair, clothes, and body type, all of which carried political, social, and cultural implications. Certainly, the history of men's appearance in interwar Vietnam deserves a book of its own. However, given the preponderance of sources specifically addressing women's beauty,

INTRODUCTION

the intensity of the debates on this issue, and the implications for the profound transformation of women's role in society during this era, I decided to keep this study focused on the subject of women's beauty. That being said, I will heed Martina Nguyen's assertion that female fashion cannot be studied without understanding male fashion trends, and I make comparative references to such trends throughout the book.[10]

THE HISTORY OF INTERWAR BEAUTY CULTURE

The discourse on beauty that developed in the late colonial period was embroiled in debates about "tradition" and "modernity." The cultural shift toward "modernity" was a gradual process set in motion by *La Mission Civilisatrice* and early French administrative policies that weakened the political power of the monarchy and the cultural power of the scholarly ruling class. After a series of military battles and treaties, French forces took southern Vietnam, establishing the colony of Cochinchina in 1867. As a direct colony, Cochinchina was governed by a French administration and subject to French law. The consequences for Vietnamese political and cultural power were manifold. The Vietnamese emperor lost his claim to rule in the South; Vietnamese legal codes ceased to apply in the region; Vietnamese mandarins were replaced with French civil servants; and the Confucian educational system was replaced by a French one. Although the population of French colonists in Cochinchina never exceeded twenty thousand residents, most of whom lived in the cities, such political and bureaucratic changes substantially influenced urban Vietnamese culture in Cochinchina. Moreover, as French and French Foreign Legion troops were stationed throughout the countryside to quell rebellions,[11] European ideas on women's beauty began to seep into rural areas as well. In the late nineteenth century, *me tây* (Vietnamese women involved in sexual relationships with European troops) began appearing with white teeth and unbound breasts, per the tastes of their military lovers. These two trends, which would later become widely popular, were at first embraced solely by the me tây population and—like their Western lovers—were considered a gross violation of Vietnamese social and gender norms.[12] Given its cosmopolitan cities and intense military occupation, it is not surprising that Cochinchina would be the region most receptive to foreign fashion and beauty trends.

The middle and northern regions of Vietnam remained under the jurisdiction of the emperor, but in 1883 they became the French protectorates of Annam and Tonkin. Protectorate status, which brought minimal French cultural influence, allowed for indirect colonial rule, such that the Vietnamese emperor continued to rule the two regions, the Vietnamese legal code prevailed,[13] and the emperor's mandarins governed at the local level. Yet the French government nonetheless achieved gradual political predominance. It did so by controlling royal succession via the deposing of emperors and selection of successors; appointing a French Resident Superior to both Tonkin and Annam; establishing the Resident Superior of Annam as the head of the two regions' royal council; and stripping the emperor's ministers of most governing powers. The result was a considerable erosion of the political power previously enjoyed by the Vietnamese monarchy and the scholarly mandarin class.[14]

From the very early days of colonialism, the French government had met with armed resistance. In the second half of the nineteenth century, such rebellions, the most famous of which was the Cần Vương movement—literally meaning Save the King—were, for the most part, focused on bolstering the monarchy, restoring the line of succession, and looking to "traditional" institutions as a means of saving the country. But by the end of the century, Vietnamese intellectuals began to lose confidence in the monarchy as a whole, given the succession of French-appointed emperors, the French influence on the royal court, and the unscrupulousness of local mandarins, who had become embroiled in repeated scandals involving corruption or collaboration with the French.[15]

At the turn of the century a new resistance movement arose. The resistance was comprised largely of Confucian reformers who were classically trained scholars who had come to view the current implementation of Confucianism as outdated and were beginning to look to foreign influences for solutions to Vietnam's problems. They were frustrated by recent scandals involving the Vietnamese emperor Thành Thái and influenced by the major political movements sweeping Asia in the late nineteenth and early twentieth century.[16] The wildly successful Meiji Restoration and 1905 Japanese victory over Russia inspired Phan Bội Châu and Prince Cường Để to establish the Việt Nam Duy Tân Hội (Modernization Association) movement in 1904 to restore Vietnamese independence.[17] Although members of the Duy Tân Hội worked closely with the Vietnamese royal family and the Cần Vương movement, they began to look to the Japanese model of modernization. The group also founded the Đông Du movement (1906–07), which encouraged Vietnamese students to travel to Japan and study the Japanese modernization model. Meanwhile, the 1898 Hundred Days Reform movement in China and subsequent 1911 Revolution that took down four thousand years of dynastic rule in the Middle Kingdom were exposing the weakness of traditional ruling institutions.

Vietnamese modernists expressed their political ideology to a great extent through their appearance, marking a major change in male fashion during the colonial period. The changes embraced by Vietnamese modernists—short hair and a three-piece suit—were originally introduced to Vietnam by French colonists, but the styles ironically became popular in Vietnam only by way of Japan. In the aftermath of the Meiji Restoration and the defeat of Russia, Japan—where men had been wearing Western-style suits and cutting their hair short since the 1890s—had become a revered model of Asian modernity.[18] In 1906, the Vietnamese reformer Phan Châu Trinh returned to his homeland from Japan—where he had been involved in the Duy Tân anticolonial movement—sporting the new short haircut. Phan Khôi, a fellow reformer, met with Phan Châu Trinh shortly after the latter's return from Japan.[19] Phan Khôi initially found his friend's haircut shocking, a clear rejection of the Confucian dictum prohibiting men from cutting their long hair, which was seen as both an important part of the body and a symbol of loyalty to the Vietnamese monarch.[20] But Phan Châu Trinh encouraged Phan Khôi to cut off his own bun, and within a few days most of their reformist-minded associates in the village and Duy Tân movement had likewise trimmed their tresses. Although the group was initially met with laughter and scorn, by 1908 the trend had spread throughout Annam. That year, when male peasants sporting short hair revolted against the colonial administration, the French dubbed it the head-shaving movement (*movement de tonsure*) and claimed that the modernists were forcing the peasants to cut their hair, something Phan Khôi denied.[21]

The history of the three-piece Western suit in Vietnam is less documented but follows the same trajectory. Popular in the West since the late nineteenth century, the three-piece suit was introduced to Vietnam by French colonists. It did not catch on initially, even among most Vietnamese interpreters or other collaborators with the colonial government; indeed, images from the late nineteenth century show these men donning traditional tunics.

By the turn of the century, only a few among the collaborating class wore Western-style closed-toe shoes under their tunic or experimented with the three-piece suit. The trend in three-piece suits was likely popularized among Vietnamese after Phan Châu Trinh brought the style home from Japan, where three-piece suits were worn by men who embraced the modernization movement.[22] Phan Châu Trinh himself often wore three-piece suits in public and photographs, although he never fully abandoned the traditional tunic, which he wore on official and religious occasions. The sartorial trend spread easily because suits were the uniform of French men, and the infrastructure for popularizing the style was already in place to accommodate the colonizers: suit fabric had been imported, local tailors in urban areas were familiar with the sewing pattern, and department stores already carried dress shirts and ready-made suits. By 1908, three-piece suits had become commonplace among middle-class Vietnamese men in Hanoi and in the urban areas of Cochinchina, but men in rural areas continued to wear variations of the traditional tunic or dark silk pants with a button-down short tunic.[23]

Although it was the Europeanization trend that brought short hair and three-piece suits to Vietnam, it would be the Vietnamese modernists who popularized both trends. It is important to note that most Vietnamese men wore short hair and three-piece suits not to imitate the colonizer but to express their commitment to nationalist and modernist ideals. As Christopher Goscha has shown with the case of Nguyễn Văn Vĩnh, Vietnamese modernists were tapping into a global fashion trend to demonstrate that the Vietnamese were just as civilized as French colonizers and citizens of other nations.[24] This tactic speaks to Homi Bhabha's work on mimicry in the colonial context: the act of dressing like the colonizer subverted—wittingly or unwittingly—the power of the colonizer by blurring the distinction between the "civilized" colonizer and "uncivilized" colonized.[25] The political impact of this strategy dissipated within a few years, when short hair and three-piece suits had become popular among not just Vietnamese modernists but colonial collaborators as well. As for Vietnamese women, they would have to wait until the late 1920s for short hair and Western-style clothing to be accepted—and not without considerable initial controversy.

Spreading new fashion trends was not, however, the main focus of Vietnamese modernists. Reformist Confucian scholar Phan Châu Trinh called for new ways of educating Vietnamese youth because the traditional

Confucian scholar system was in the process of being gutted by colonial policies.²⁶ Phan Châu Trinh, heavily influenced by Chinese reformers Kang Youwei and Liang Qichao, argued that mass education—including peasants and women—was essential for strengthening a nation. In 1907, he and some of his cohort had founded the Tonkin Free School (*Đông Kinh Nghĩa Thục*), which aimed to modernize the country through the teaching of Western scientific methods and technology among other things. The school instructed students in *quốc ngữ*, the Romanized phonetic script that was much easier for students to learn than *chữ nôm*, the character-based writing system used in the traditional Confucian educational system.²⁷ The school encouraged students to follow the aesthetic of Vietnamese modernism by cutting their hair and long fingernails, which had traditionally been associated with mandarin status.

Among its more radical acts, the Tonkin Free School welcomed female students. At the school, female students learned to read quốc ngữ and other subjects, including Vietnamese history, for the first time in Vietnamese formal education. The school encouraged female students not to blacken their teeth, a traditional Vietnamese practice, and taught them principles of Western hygiene in hopes that the young women would reproduce the knowledge at home. Although the Tonkin Free School would be shut down after only a year in operation, its impacts on Vietnamese history were manifold. In addition to instilling a nationalist and modernist vision among students, as well as teaching them in quốc ngữ, the school played a vital role in developing a female intelligentsia, however small in number. Many of the female students educated at the Tonkin Free School would go on to become prominent intellectuals and journalists, later known as New Women. And male and female students alike left the school with a new understanding of women's role in the nation.²⁸

Widespread changes in women's clothing and hair would not arrive in Vietnam until after World War I. However, the beauty industry of the interwar years that is examined in this book developed out of the capitalist economy introduced by the French in the late nineteenth century. Whereas precolonial Vietnam had operated on subsistence agriculture, the export-oriented capitalist economy instituted with French colonial rule operated on cash and wage labor.²⁹ The result was both a highly impoverished class (in worst-case scenarios) and a class with disposable income (in best-case scenarios). A nascent capitalist, consumer economy was thus developing, and a merchant class of small-scale entrepreneurs expanded to fill the gaps in the new colonial consumer market, particularly after the crisis in maritime trade brought about by World War I.[30]

As France was unable to supply its colonies during the war, local industry developed to supply the Vietnamese market and trade within other Asian nations and colonies. With the exception of a brief postwar economic dip in 1920, the ensuing decade was marked by a rapid economic boom in Indochina. After the war, when the French franc depreciated, metropolitan investors rushed to capitalize on the relative stability of the Indochinese piaster. Between the foreign investment flooding Vietnam and the high price at which rubber and rice were selling on the international market, Vietnam's economy boomed during the 1920s. The local cement, rubber, rice, and textile industries flourished, as did the wage-labor working class that manned the factories.[31]

A significant portion of the money that flowed into Vietnam after World War I was invested in urban infrastructure, which in turn promoted the growth of big cities. Urban areas saw new amenities such as running water, sewer systems, and electric lights. Improved roads accommodated the cars and bicycles that were now being imported to the colony. Tram systems in Saigon and Hanoi brought customers downtown, where they could shop in the district's new department stores and elegant boutiques. The demand for construction workers attracted male and female migrants from the countryside, further boosting urban population numbers. Cities doubled or tripled in size under colonial rule, becoming the colony's economic centers and home to the middle class.[32]

Colonial industrialization and the economic boom of the 1920s led to a remarkable expansion of both the bourgeois and lower-middle classes in urban areas.[33] The lower-middle class developed as the wage labor force swelled to meet postwar demands for production, and the upper echelons of the middle class expanded as small- and medium-size businesses likewise profited from the economic demand. Meanwhile, the colonial educational system churned out graduates well equipped to take their place in the upper-middle class. Recognizing the political threat posed by the Tonkin Free School of the prewar days, the colonial government expanded the Franco-Annamite educational system with the aim of establishing a Franco-Viet school in every village. In the schools, students learned to read quốc ngữ and studied a French curriculum. In 1919, Governor General

Sarraut instituted universal education and increased the variety of professional schools for aspiring low-level colonial clerks, lawyers, teachers, doctors, pharmacists, midwives, and journalists. All of these professions guaranteed a comfortable salary, for women as well as men, that allowed for discretionary spending.[34]

Indeed, spending was what marked the middle class, and they developed a distinct class consciousness during the interwar period. Similar to Thorstein Veblen's findings on the middle class of the late nineteenth century United States, educated middle-class Vietnamese urbanites were eager to distinguish themselves from their rural counterparts, and conspicuous consumption proved to be a felicitous expression of class identity.[35] Class affect was another important way for the middle class to maintain their status. Although the middle class was thriving during the 1920s—especially relative to their peasant compatriots—their position was precarious. Whereas the wealthy class had staked their claim to large landholdings, which preserved long-term wealth through equity, a middle-class individual would likely have owned no more than a medium-sized house in the city and depended on income generated from wages. Wages were, of course, subject to the whims of one's boss and a volatile economy. As many in the middle class had come from the peasantry, they were well aware that the new social mobility meant that they could slip down the social ladder as easily as they had risen. Consequently, many within the middle class looked for ways to maintain their precarious social position—a position inherently lower for colonized people than for any of their French friends. Many within the middle class preserved their status by socializing with those above them and cultivating an identity through carefully curated possessions and activities. The middle class traveled by bicycle, tram, or automobile rather than by foot. Middle-class Vietnamese men were easily recognizable in their Western-style suits, with their hair slicked back in the "tango" style; their female counterparts donned brightly colored tunics or dresses made of imported fabrics and high-heeled shoes purchased at department stores or boutiques in big cities or provincial capitals. With middle-class jobs that allowed for a weekend respite, they spent their leisure time at the local Circle Sportif playing tennis or descended upon seaside resorts to lounge by the pool.[36] As the economy prospered in the mid-1920s, the middle class grew wealthier, giving it tremendous purchasing power—and cultural power as well.

During the interwar period, Vietnam's middle class became more oriented toward Western culture than toward the Confucian-based culture of their parents' generation, a shift that would set the course for fashion throughout the era. As you shall see, this shift in orientation can be traced to French policies that gradually eliminated civil servant exams, thereby eroding the proliferation of the Confucian scholarly gentry and, by extension, the influence of Confucian morality on post–World War I Vietnamese society.[37] The fall of the scholarly gentry and the ensuing shift in orientation toward Western culture manifested in multiple ways. During the precolonial period, passing the traditional civil service exam had conferred status by enabling the pursuit of a prestigious career as a government administrator or scholar; during the colonial period, however, a French education and the middle-class status associated with it became the new marker of status.[38] Once regarded as society's intellectual gatekeepers, Confucian scholars were humiliated during the interwar years when Vietnamese women, trained in Franco-Annamite schools, replaced them as teachers and taught a French curriculum.

As the importance of Confucian and Chinese intellectual precepts dwindled, so too did the importance of traditional Chinese aesthetics—and Western aesthetics became ascendant. New expressive movements self-consciously turned away from the Chinese and Confucian realm of influence, instead embracing elements of Western culture. The 1920s saw the rise of Western-style spoken theater (*kịch nói*) in Hanoi and reform theater (*cải lương*) in Cochinchina;[39] Western-style novels and short stories, written in Romanized font (quốc ngữ) and replete with French syntax; and the 1926 opening of Hanoi's École des Beaux Arts de l'Indochine, which trained a generation of professional painters in French technique.[40] In the 1930s, newspapers began experimenting with realism journalism (*phong sự*);[41] the New Poetry (*Thơ Mới*) movement replaced the Chinese metrical pattern of verse with Western-influenced verse;[42] the New Music movement (*Tân Nhạc*) set Vietnamese lyrics to French tunes; and Indochinese style architecture, a mixture of French and Asian-inspired themes, graced the streets of big cities. Women's fashion and beauty expression—which I consider yet another of these artistic movements—likewise drew from Western elements, as you will see in the chapters of this book.

The scope and diversity of change in so many of the arts have led historians to recognize Vietnam's interwar era as a cultural revolution.[43] Although there was a sense at the time that French artistic expressions were supplanting Vietnamese culture, it would be a mistake to assume that these new artistic movements represented a wholehearted embrace of Western culture.[44] Instead, such movements should be understood within the context of a new generation of Vietnamese modernism, one that embraced selected elements of Western culture but maintained a very Vietnamese—and often nationalist—perspective. As you will see in chapters 2 and 4, the aesthetic paradigm shift that occurred in Vietnam during the interwar years played out not just in new styles of dress but in new ways of perceiving and defining beautiful bodies.

New cultural and technological developments in the post–World War I era gave rise to the new trend of Europeanization (*âu hóa*), which was most popular among urban middle-class Vietnamese. Most significant, new forms of media transmitted Western culture to Vietnam, including newspapers and books, gramophones and photographs, and art and cinema. The students who graduated from the colony's Franco-Annamite schools were trained in the French curriculum, leaving them well-versed in French language, literature, philosophy, and culture. Those who took jobs in the colonial administration were further exposed to the French way of life, including the professional clothing they wore to work and the French-style leisure activities they enjoyed during their vacation time—yet another concept introduced by the French. The Europeanization trend was embraced with particular fervor by members of the Constitutionalist Party, who simultaneously collaborated with the colonial government and demanded greater rights for Vietnamese within the French empire. The Vietnamese students who studied in the metropole and the roughly one hundred thousand military *tirailleurs* who aided the French effort during World War I returned home from Europe with a newfound taste for French wine, food, and fashion—and even a penchant for the scent of French perfume on their lover's skin.[45] The nation was shocked in 1932 when Emperor Bảo Đại returned to Vietnam as an enthusiastic proponent of materialism, individualism, and romantic marriage. With his hair cut short and slicked back in the "tango" style, his tailored Western suit and oxford brogue shoes, he seemed the very embodiment of the Europeanization trend.

Beyond aesthetics and day-to-day cultural practices, Europeanization facilitated a broader trend toward individualism during the interwar years, calling into question key aspects of the traditional Vietnamese social structure and ushering in a spirit of personal liberation and independence. Individualism was a global trend that began in the late nineteenth century and was playing out in France as a movement against the Catholic Church, and in China as a tenant of the May Fourth Movement.[46] The rise of individualism in Vietnam can be attributed to multiple trends dating back to nineteenth-century colonial policies that led to the breakdown of family life and the decline of the village. In Cochinchina, a direct colony, the French dissolved the model of local governance that had allowed villages to operate more or less autonomously. French administrators—rather than village heads—ruled the inhabitants of the village as individuals. Land, previously owned communally, was now divided into parcels that were individually owned. Taxes, once paid by the village, were now collected from individuals. Annam and Tonkin underwent similar changes, although to a lesser extent. Throughout the Vietnamese *pays* of Indochina, the colonial state shifted the tax burden from the village to the individual. Moreover, much of the village land was sold off or seized by the colonial state, resulting in large-scale peasant tenancy.[47]

By World War I, landless peasants seeking work were migrating en masse, with many making their way into the colony's rapidly growing cities. In the city, the media and Franco-Annamite school curriculum disseminated ideas about individualism and egalitarian ideas about society and nation. The Franco-Annamite educational system, with its French curriculum and teaching of quốc ngữ writing, eroded the Confucian family system insofar as children were no longer required to study texts about Confucian family values. Many graduates of colonial schools went on to earn salaries that were paid to them individually rather than to their family or village, as had been the practice of past generations. Even the way people spoke about themselves during the interwar years reflected this trend. Whereas members of the elder generation referred to themselves as "*ta*," a pronoun that translates to both the collective "we" as well as "I," members of the younger generation used "*tôi*," an exclusive first-person singular pronoun. Literary and realist writers, as well as poets of the New Poetry (Thơ Mới) movement, explored themes of individualism and referenced to the individual (*cá nhân*) and stature (*vóc dáng*), both of which are often found in discussions of women's beauty during this era. Not surprisingly, the trend in individualism was reflected in the politics of the interwar years with the wild popularity of Nguyễn An Ninh, followed, in the mid-1930s, with the Self Reliant Literary movement (*Tự Lực văn đoàn*) calling for "individual freedom."[48]

INTRODUCTION

The trend toward individualism and the weakening of the family and village structure in turn led to a reconsideration of gender roles among the generation of young women who came of age after World War I. Young women began rejecting arranged marriages and demanded the right to choose their own husbands.[49] Daughter-in-laws began protesting abuse from their husband's family, and widows pleaded for the right to remarry. A new movement of New Women insisted on girls' right to an education, and young women generally insisted on participating in public life—sports, dancing, and time at the beach. Although women's experience with individualism in the interwar years was more limited than that of men, that women did experiment in following their own needs and questioned their role in society was a threat to traditionalists.

The post–World War I Europeanization trend that was sweeping Vietnam's urban areas met with resistance in the form of a Neo-Confucian revival. The origins of this revival were complex. Most obvious, Vietnamese Neo-Confucianism drew from the contemporaneous Neo-Confucian movements in Korea and China.[50] In Vietnam, Neo-Confucianism was also a reaction to the Europeanization and modernism movements that were gaining popularity and specifically to the social displacement that accompanied the erosion of the Vietnamese mandarin system. Although colonial officials made significant efforts to dismantle the Confucian educational system and render mandarin scholars politically and socially impotent, they paradoxically came to see a political value in certain aspects of Confucian philosophy. Confucianism's emphasis on loyalty, submission, social hierarchy, and social control would prove useful to encourage subordination among the colonized; the colonial government thus attempted to "re-Confucianize the past and strip Confucianism of any subversive content."[51] In the 1920s, the Franco-Annamite school curriculum introduced lessons on morality and etiquette, billed as Confucian philosophy but heavily interpreted through a French lens. Lessons for girls included the Four Virtues and the Three Dependencies.[52] In 1932, the public intellectual Trần Trọng Kim published the first comprehensive volume on Confucianism in Vietnam in quốc ngữ, making it easier to read and hence accessible to the general public.[53]

The Confucian revival that arose in interwar Vietnam was in part a reaction to the changing role of women during this period. As bright young women, trained in the Franco-Annamite system, replaced Confucian scholars as educators, they appropriated what had been a masculine space and role.[54] Meanwhile, teacher income in the colonial school system greatly surpassed that of mandarin scholars and other male professions.[55] Neo-Confucian thinkers attempted to reassert their relevance (and assuage their sense of scholarly emasculation) by debating the issue of "national essence" (*quốc túy*), often in reaction to issues concerning women.[56] In interwar-era discussions of beauty and fashion, for example, Confucian principles were invoked to challenge the supposed immorality and alien nature of the new trends, which detractors claimed ran counter to Vietnamese identity.[57] As you will see in chapters 4 and 5, Neo-Confucian principles were also invoked to protest women's participation in sports and beauty contests.

Newspapers of the interwar years published debates about morality in colonial Vietnamese society, notably debates about women's role in society.[58] Neo-Confucianists, from prominent intellectuals such as Phạm Quỳnh to ordinary citizens, dashing off letters to local newspapers, considered—and reconsidered—the Three Dependencies (Tam Tòng) and the Four Virtues (Tứ Đức). The Three Dependencies called for women to defer to the guidance of their father, husband, and sons; the Four Virtues referred to household labor (*công*), physical appearance (*dung*), polite speech (*ngôn*), and proper behavior (*hạnh*).[59] As women's chastity was an important cultural value, Vietnamese society idealized the khuê các woman. Also known as the *khuê-môn* ideal (閨閣 *gui-ge*), this drew from the Chinese literary tradition in which unmarried daughters were sequestered in the khuê các, a boudoir, until marriage.[60] (The reality, as Hue Tam Ho Tai points out, was hardly one of gender segregation because the communal nature of village living meant that boys and girls inevitably interacted.[61]) During the interwar years, the *gái khuê các* image was often invoked as a rhetorical foil in debates about female education, the choice of marriage partners, the treatment of daughters-in-law, the fidelity of widows, female participation in sports, and women's comportment. These last two issues in turn touched on multiple beauty-related issues, as you will see in chapters 4 and 5, respectively.

Notwithstanding the pushback from Neo-Confucianists, Vietnam saw an undeniable decline in Confucian precepts and a concomitant rise in Western ideas about individualism and consumerism.[62] Out of this massive cultural shift, a new generation of middle-class Vietnamese women emerged. Among other things, this was the first generation of Vietnamese

INTRODUCTION

women to be fully educated in the French colonial system. They were literate in quốc ngữ, the Vietnamese Romanized script, and their colonial education oriented them more toward French culture than that of East Asia.[63] In school, they had read French romantic literature—no doubt a major factor in their rejection of arranged marriages in favor of romantic love. These young women were out and about in society and, as Liz Connor argues, this "feminine visibility" had significant political consequences.[64] Young women went to school, migrated to urban areas for work, and crisscrossed the city on the public tram. They eagerly embraced Western forms of leisure, riding bicycles, playing tennis, drinking coffee with friends at street cafés, and they vacationed at Đồ Sơn beach and Cap Saint Jacques, where they frolicked in bathing suits. Now that women were so publicly visible, they wanted to look good.

Meanwhile, women—especially urban middle-class women—were becoming an important consumer class with considerable purchasing power. Those women who came from middle-class families already had disposable income to spend. For those who did not, the colonial educational system offered pathways to class mobility. Educated women found jobs as teachers, journalists, and French-trained midwives, the earnings from which allowed for the occasional new dress and lipstick to match. Such purchases were encouraged by the many beauty- and fashion-oriented newspaper articles and advertisements that targeted this new literate class. Young women with less or no education could find work as telephone operators or shopgirls, both of which professions not only offered women pocket money, but also encouraged employees to meet certain standards of appearance. As for impoverished women, increasing numbers were migrating to cities, where some of them moonlighted as taxi girls or clandestine sex workers and purchased clothing and beauty products to attract customers.

This new generation of young women became a powerful consumer market just as the Western beauty industry was growing into a global business during the late 1920s—and international beauty companies made every effort to target this consumer class. Imperial economic networks began flooding the Vietnamese market with fashion and cosmetics from Europe, the United States, or Japan. New ideas about beauty spread through newspaper images, cinema, and beauty contests. Elegant department stores in Hanoi, Hải Phòng, Saigon, and Huế offered luxurious European creams and cosmetics from their glass counters; import companies advertised stylish ready-to-wear clothing and products from exclusive French companies; and local tailors copied the French styles.

In the late 1920s, Vietnam's economy crashed. Rubber and rice markets were saturated, limiting Indochina's profits and slowing its economy; crop failures in the Red River Delta resulted in widespread malnourishment; and after a series of policy failures on the part of the French government and Bank of Indochina, the Indochinese piaster depreciated in 1929.[65] That same year, the global economy plummeted into the Great Depression, the effects of which, combined with a series of natural disasters in the Tonkin and Annam throughout the 1930s, left the countryside reeling in poverty for most of the decade.

Yet not even the Great Depression could slow the demand for clothing and beauty items. As was the case in the United States, the beauty industry in colonial Vietnam continued strong throughout the economic crisis—something economists have come to describe as the Lipstick Effect.[66] In this phenomenon, consumers continue to spend money on small indulgences such as cosmetics even during periods of economic recession; indeed, they are drawn to small indulgences rather than to expensive purchases. Lipstick—and other forms of cosmetics and fashion—provided an affordable little pick-me-up to women and enhanced their looks, thus increasing their chances of finding a mate or securing employment during a time of scarcity. The case of interwar Vietnam adds another dimension to the Lipstick Effect. Makeup—merely a minor indulgence for middle-class women—became a virtual necessity for a growing class of impoverished women. As I have shown in my past work, during the Great Depression a trend developed among peasant women in northern Vietnam of moonlighting as sex workers to supplement their earnings between harvests. To attract clients, they had to invest in their looks. They spent what little money they had on new clothing and makeup to beautify themselves and attract customers, and in many cases entered debt bondage agreements to afford what they needed. For such women, makeup and clothing were an occupational investment.[67] With a customer base drawing from both the middle and impoverished classes, the beauty industry was one of the few industries in Vietnam that flourished during the Great Depression.

With the Vietnamese middle class recovering quickly from the economic crisis, the trend in consumerism bounced back. The French government, attempting to stimulate the metropolitan industrial economy, dumped unsold manufactured goods into Vietnam's market.[68] By 1933, these French manufactured goods were being bought by Vietnam's urban middle class, which was showing not just early signs of recovery from the economic crisis but a voracious appetite for European trends.

Vietnamese modernists—and even nationalists—came to see materialism and consumerism more generally as essential to the success of the Vietnamese nation, Martina Nguyen argues. Originally founded as a literary collective in 1932, the Self-Reliant Literary Association (Tự Lực Văn Đoàn) and other Vietnamese modernists promoted materialism as a valuable means of improving the nation's quality of life and enhancing its image in the world.[69] Although they were certainly empathetic to the exploited peasant population, the members of the literary group and their colleagues aimed to transform the image of Vietnam from impoverished colony to a bourgeois nation. In crasser terms, they sought to rehabilitate its land of downtrodden peasants and vulgar women in mismatched Western clothes. This, after all, was the era of the Modern Girl, a global construction of the advertising and entertainment industries, infamous for her sexually suggestive Western clothing, her atrocious fashion sense, and her lack of decorum. Vietnamese modernists were deeply embarrassed by Modern Girls and, influenced by recent cultural reforms in Turkey and Siam, endeavored to make women (and the nation) look more respectable.[70] They drew from what Pierre Bourdieu would later recognize as cultural capital to set the standards for good *taste* and revamp the national image.[71] As you will see in the chapters of this book, Vietnamese modernists from this group promoted new hybrid fashions, lent their expertise as judges for beauty contests, and published extensive fashion and cosmetic tutorials.

To sum it up, looks mattered. As increasingly visible and economically relevant members of colonial Vietnamese society, women began to be held responsible—at least by journalists and intellectuals—for representing the nation. This occurred at a time when the colony was grappling with difficult questions about nationalism and anticolonialism, and cultural forms of nationalism carried an important weight. It is not surprising that this new generation of young women who were spending so much time, energy, and money on their appearance faced a backlash from multiple quarters. Newspapers published heated debates authored by men and women accusing urban young women of being superficial and extravagant (*xa xỉ*). Discussions about cosmetics devolved into bitter arguments about the morality of manipulating "natural" beauty with modern science. In reaction to women's sartorial experiments, male nationalists working with Vietnamese artists and fashion designers took control over the rapidly Westernizing fashion landscape and created a uniquely (and perhaps somewhat artificially) Vietnamese national dress that would reflect a "civilized" Vietnamese nation. Advice columns about exercise, health, and dieting promoted curvaceous bodies that would give birth to healthy young citizens. In violation of Confucian codes on modesty, the era's ubiquitous beauty contestants displayed enticing (or scandalous, depending on one's perspective) new concepts of fashion, cosmetics, and the female body for all to judge. The beauty industry, in short, became an arena for developing modern female consumers who would represent the nation—not as political participants but as visual ambassadors. The many debates about women's appearance and the image of the woman in colonial Vietnam shed light on vital questions of what a society is and what it wants to be.

BEAUTY SOURCES

Beauty and the Nation explores the role of women's faces and bodies in defining Vietnamese identity during a critical period in Vietnamese history (1920–1940). Drawing from large datasets, I investigate the broad political, cultural, and economic trends in Vietnam that contributed to this process. My work was influenced by Sebastian Conrad, who calls for a global perspective in World History that highlights how societies interact and diverse peoples adopt and modify global trends. Following Conrad, I delve into the global dynamics of Vietnamese beauty culture. Rather than focusing on the foreign beauty trends themselves, I focus on how Vietnamese women and critics engaged with these trends—embracing, critiquing, modifying, or outright rejecting them.

As the interwar years marked the peak of colonial capitalism and Vietnam's burgeoning consumer economy, businesses were motivated to invest in consumer outreach to capitalize on the emerging market of female consumers. I draw from internal business documents from trading companies, department stores, hotels, and cinemas in Vietnam to provide insights into these businesses' marketing strategies and how they perceived their target customers.

INTRODUCTION

French- and Vietnamese-language newspapers, whose readership exploded during the interwar era thanks to rapidly rising literacy rates—especially among women—provide the richest data on Vietnamese beauty culture on many levels. Realizing there was money to be made from the colony's expanding market of literate women, newspapers generated content specifically designed to appeal to female readers. Indeed, many of these newspapers employed female journalists, providing future historians with an abundance of women's voices. Child-rearing and family relations were, of course, popular topics, as were fashion and cosmetics. As sports became increasingly trendy during the late 1920s, newspapers covered stories by and about female sports stars, their physical accomplishments, the outfits they wore, and the controversies they generated. By the 1930s, most major newspapers ran regular columns by male and female journalists on fashion, dieting, exercise regimes, cosmetics application, and directions for making homemade beauty products. New looks debuted by Vietnamese and foreign style icons frequently made a splash in the news, and as the motion picture industry grew more popular in Vietnam, newspapers regularly reviewed French and Hollywood films and reported gossip about starlets' lives.

Images of women likewise proved quite lucrative for newspapers. Newspapers printed photographs of local and international beauty queens; indeed, for some readers the newspaper was the only medium through which they could catch a glimpse of such beautiful women. Newspapers themselves even staged beauty contests to attract readership and generate income. In many cases, these efforts were less about cultivating a wholesome appreciation of beauty than about catering to more prurient interests. By the 1930s, newspapers were printing lurid images of beautiful women caught in wardrobe malfunctions or other embarrassing positions, or misogynistic cartoons featuring comically sexy modern girls or outrageously buxom women.

It was thus not surprising that newspaper coverage of beauty-related issues generated a fair amount of controversy. Male and female readers from the city and countryside alike wrote letters to editors protesting beauty contests, supporting or denouncing female athletes, voicing their opinions on new fashions, and criticizing Modern Girls and me tây looks. The same feminist New Woman journalists who wrote articles encouraging women to cut their hair, participate in sports, or wear the famous Lemur Tunic joined conservatives in denouncing many other beauty-related trends as frivolous and distracting. Neo-Confucianists went so far as to accuse women's fashion, cosmetics, and participation in beauty contests and leisure activities of blaspheming the morals and very essence of the nation.

Beauty businesses took advantage of the explosion in newspaper's female readership to reach prospective customers via print advertisements. Major international beauty companies, local Vietnamese and ethnic Chinese beauty entrepreneurs, French- and Vietnamese-owned beauty institutes, salons, dentists, and tailors all purchased print space in newspapers. More than just fetching images, these advertisements educated readers about the ingredients of various products, proper application methods, and where to buy them. The ads generated revenue for the newspapers that printed them, but they also attracted ever-greater numbers of female readers.

Of course, beauty-related content was not generated solely by the media. Vietnamese entrepreneurs produced not just beauty products but also manuals teaching women how to improve their looks. Self-styled experts, mostly women, published books and guides teaching readers cosmetics application and skin-care regimes. So-called experts on nutrition and fitness offered exercise routines and diet tricks to transform readers' body shapes. Artists-cum-designers guided women through sartorial choices, often highlighting their own creations. As it turned out, many of these "experts" were nothing more than charlatans eager to take advantage of desperate or insecure customers.

Beauty-related content found more highbrow expression in the literature of the era, with women's looks serving as a powerful literary tool for Vietnamese authors. Male novelists and short fiction writers rhapsodized about beautiful women and drew on imagery of modern fashion and cosmetics and quirks of female behavior to speak to larger themes about the human condition during interwar Vietnam. Likewise, nonfiction authors (*phóng sự*) often cited women's fashion, cosmetics, body shape, and behavior as illustrative of the broad social and economic problems facing Vietnamese society.

Only recently has the rich discourse on women's beauty—not just in colonial Vietnam but throughout the world—been taken seriously by historians. In the early 1980s, Lois K. Banner introduced the study of beauty in American history and influenced a generation of scholars who studied fashion, cosmetics, physique, and beauty contests.[72] In the late 1990s,

INTRODUCTION

business historians identified the historical market for beauty products and the women who consumed them as a rich field of analysis. Most notably, Kathy Peiss's work on the early American beauty industry uncovered the role of female entrepreneurs during the late nineteenth century and early twentieth century.[73] And Geoffrey Jones went on to apply Peiss's model to a global context, tracing the historic rise of major beauty corporations, their sourcing from the colonies, and their sales throughout the world, including back to the colonies.[74]

In the field of Asian Studies, Cho Kyo's longue-durée comparative cultural history of beauty in China and Japan is a classic.[75] Antonia Finnane and Toby Slade focus on the history of fashion in early twentieth-century China and Japan.[76] While exploring the discourse on modernity and new forms of womanhood—housewives, working women, and modern girls—in the context of interwar Japanese consumer culture, Barbara Sato's work naturally covers fashion, cosmetics, and beauty care.[77] Similarly, in her books on New Women and Modern Girls in Korea, Hyaeweol Choi explores fashion and beauty as part of the changing landscape of women's role in early twentieth-century Korea.[78] Most recently, Chiara Formichi's book on women in interwar Indonesia and Charles Sullivan's dissertation address the role of women's fashion and body culture in nation building.[79]

As an analysis of beauty discourse, much of which originated in the metropole, *Beauty and the Nation* owes a debt to the rich scholarship on fashion and beauty in interwar France. Holly Grout analyzes the history of the French beauty industry during the interwar period.[80] Mary Lynn Stewart investigates Third Republic efforts to increase French birth rates by promoting hygiene and beauty culture.[81] In a subsequent book, Stewart examines the role of the fashion industry in creating an image of the modern French woman, and the role of ordinary middle-class French women in popularizing Haute Couture fashion silhouettes.[82] Additionally, articles and book chapters by David Pomfret, Elizabeth Ezra, and Aro Valmet explore the history of beauty contests in the empire.[83]

The secondary scholarship on beauty culture in Vietnam originated within the field of anthropology. Studies of Vietnamese beauty practices began appearing in the early twentieth century, mostly in the context of Orientalist studies. Henri Joseph Oger's 1908 study on material culture in Vietnam recorded techniques for handicraft, including jewelry-making and textile weaving and dying.[84] Eugène Langlet's ethnography of the people and customs of Vietnam detailed women's fashion and hairstyles on the eve of World War I.[85] And in 1948, Dr. Pierre Huard drew from his medical training to explore the custom of teeth blackening in Vietnam.[86] Most comprehensive, however, were works by Vietnamese-language writers. The most thorough of such studies is the journalist Phan Kế Bính's seminal 1915 study of contemporary Vietnam customs, which included sections on beauty practices, fashion, dermatology, and even beauty-related proverbs.[87] Drawing from Phan Kế Bính's methodology, in 1970 Nhất Thanh also published a historical approach to the customs of Vietnam, including beauty culture.[88]

The subsequent study of beauty in Vietnam focused for the most part on historical sartorial trends. The field of fashion studies in Vietnam opened with Nguyễn Ngạc and Nguyễn Văn Luận's study of nineteenth- and twenty-century changes in dress.[89] Most Vietnamese-language studies of fashion take a long durée approach to investigating the evolution of clothing. The art historian Đoàn Thị Tình analyzes images of sartorial trends by class, gender, age, and occasion dating from 200 BCE to the present.[90] Trần Quang Đức traces the state edicts and broader social changes influencing the dress of both elites and commoners over a millennium.[91] And the anthropologist Ngô Đức Thịnh has conducted a comparative survey of clothing among Vietnam's fifty-four officially recognized ethnic groups.[92]

More recently, scholars have taken an interest in the history of Nguyễn Cát Tường's Lemur Tunic, the original iteration of the modern-day *áo dài* known today as the national dress of Vietnam. Articles and book chapters by Ann Marie Leshkowich, Martina Nguyen, and Trần Thị Phương Hoa investigate the history and evolution of the Lemur Tunic, now known as the áo dài dress.[93] But it is Phạm Thảo Nguyên who most thoroughly explores the rapidly changing political and cultural climate that led Nguyễn Cát Tường to design his "modern" Lemur Tunic—and the backlash that followed.[94]

As the history of beauty in Vietnam has been dominated by studies of fashion, there is little work on other aspects of beauty. Phan Kế Bính and Nguyễn Văn Ký both devote chapters to changes in hair and cosmetics during the early twentieth century.[95] Dinh Trong Hieu draws from literature, cultural anthropology, history, and philosophy to take a truly fascinating interdisciplinary approach to studying body culture during the colonial period.⁹⁶ Sociologists and anthropologists such as Hong-Kong Nguyen, Lisa Drummond, Nina Hien, and Ann Marie Leshkowich explore the changes in beauty culture that have transpired since the 1986 Đổi Mới reforms opened Vietnam's economy to international markets and led to a flood of foreign goods and ideas into local markets.⁹⁷ Most recently, Thuy Linh Nguyen Tu conducted a groundbreaking study of the Vietnam War's influence on dermatology and modern cosmetics in Vietnam.⁹⁸

Although the history of beauty in Vietnam is woefully understudied in academic circles, it is richly explored in modern-day popular Vietnamese culture. The online fashion-business magazine *Style-Republik* regularly publishes meticulously researched Vietnamese-language articles about historical fashion and cosmetics trends.⁹⁹ Social media has proven to be an excellent collective for those interested in beauty history. There are Facebook pages, Instagram accounts, and YouTube channels devoted exclusively to the history of the áo dài, once known as the Lemur Tunic. Social media users have provided great assistance to professional historians by posting images of their mothers and grandmothers throughout the twentieth century, particularly under the Republic of Vietnam (1955–1975), when women had access to a variety of fashion styles. These photos are scrutinized for what they reveal not just about historical fashion choices but also makeup trends. Indeed, cosmetologists dissect these images on social media, posting videos that teach users how to reproduce various historical looks.

Drawing on the important extant scholarship on fashion and beauty in Vietnamese history, this book explores the discourse around beauty trends that were popular during the interwar years. Sources from the interwar era were flooded with images of striking new sartorial styles, vividly made-up faces, voluptuous and scantily clad bodies, and statuesque beauty contestants, and they linked these groundbreaking images to political, social, and cultural issues that were being hotly debated in the public sphere—particularly issues related to the changing role of women in society. Following their lead, I have organized this book topically to reflect the main debates about women that arose during the interwar years.

Beauty and the Nation begins with a study of the cultural apparatuses through which beauty knowledge was disseminated during the interwar years. The first chapter traces the development of commercial infrastructure, the rising popularity of leisure activities, the emergence of new communication technologies, and the ascendence of trendsetters within Vietnamese popular culture to highlight the networks through which trends spread.

Chapter 2 analyzes the dramatic changes in women's sartorial choices during the interwar period. In the early 1920s, young women attending Franco-Annamite schools set off a literal color revolution by wearing brightly colored tunics over white pants. After this point, the once-ubiquitous black and brown tunics of the prewar days began to be considered a bit passé, at least among the colony's cultural cognoscenti. Meanwhile, department stores and boutiques began importing ready-to-wear Western clothing that was snatched off the racks by eager Vietnamese customers. By the end of the decade, Western fashion—once associated with promiscuous women—was now regularly seen on the streets of Saigon, Hanoi, Hải Phòng, and many of the provincial capitals. In the early 1930s, concerned that Vietnamese women's choice of clothing would reflect negatively on the image of the nation, a small coterie of mostly male journalists called for a clothing reform campaign. This chapter traces the development of a new relationship between Vietnamese women and their clothing, in which fashion became the political responsibility of the wearer and women's sartorial choices were now a matter of public debate.

Chapter 3 explores the explosive rise of cosmetics usage among Vietnamese women as a global beauty industry emerged after World War I. The transformation—faces awash in pink blush, mauve eyeshadow, thick black mascara, and glossy red lipstick—was shocking to many onlookers. Pencils, powders, and brushes manipulated women's features to make their eyebrows appear arched and their nose bridge heightened. Young women rejected long-standing traditions of black lacquered teeth—and by implication, their parents' values—in favor of Western-style white teeth, and they cut their long tresses into short styles parted seductively on the side. The cosmetics industry owed its spectacular success not only to persuasive advertising and affordable price points but also to its ability to capitalize on a significant cultural shift—the new trend of individualism. Among the most enthusiastic devotees of this trend were the many women—young and middle-aged—who began questioning their obligations to family and society and embraced cosmetics as a means of self-expression and asserting their independence. Critics were inclined to regard cosmetics as an express of something more akin to rebellion—something to deplore rather than celebrate.

INTRODUCTION

Chapter 4 investigates how notions about the ideal female physique and comportment changed during the interwar years. Before World War I, a beautiful body was described as a "willow leaf": its thin physique, weak musculature, and hunched-over posture resembled the lithe leaves and branches of a willow tree. In the 1920s, new ways of thinking about the relationship between the body and the strength of the nation led Vietnamese proponents of eugenics to embrace colonial programs to promote personal health and teach physical education in schools. Vietnamese feminists seized on this discourse to claim women's contribution to the nation. They argued that female participation in sports would strengthen the race—and promote women's liberation. By the end of the decade, public discourse about women's bodies celebrated a strong, athletic female physique with erect posture. During the 1930s, as urban middle-class women embraced leisure activities such as swimming, tennis, and dancing, they began exposing their bodies in new ways. The result was a new beauty ideal that emphasized a well-toned musculature and a voluptuous—especially buxom—physique.

Chapter 5 examines the history of beauty contests in interwar Vietnam, using this topic as a lens through which to examine changing attitudes about how women should conduct themselves in public. When beauty contests were first introduced to Vietnam in the mid-1920s, there was a widespread backlash, as public displays of women's bodies and beauty—for competition, no less—violated the khuê các ideal as well as Confucian norms governing women's behavior. During the following decade, public opinion began to change, in large part due to the expanding economic and cultural influence of Vietnam's urban middle class. Heavily influenced by French bourgeois culture, middle-class urbanites had begun to embrace a variety of leisure activities in which women were prominent—the most salient being beauty pageants. The widespread popularity of beauty pageants made it acceptable not only for women to show off their beauty but for the public to openly consume it.

The book follows Vietnamese beauty trends through 1940, when life in Vietnam changed dramatically. The maritime hostilities of World War II all but halted the import of foreign consumer goods into Vietnam; foreign cosmetics, French fashion magazines, and Western ready-made clothing eventually disappeared from store shelves by the end of the war. When the Japanese military marched through northern Vietnam that September, the country's larger textile factories in Nam Định and Chợ Lớn redirected production toward the military effort. As the war progressed, middle-class leisure activities and beauty contests grew less frequent, and fewer women were spending money on clothing and cosmetics. With limited imports, redirected textile production, and wartime privations, Vietnamese women were steered toward more austere looks. The public no longer focused as much on how women looked, and the once contentious discourse about beauty and the nation quieted down. Women, of course, would still be expected to represent the nation, but now as mothers sacrificing for the nation or younger women as warriors for national independence.

Chapter One

THE DISSEMINATION OF BEAUTY TRENDS

During the two decades between World War I and World War II, new trends in beauty and fashion whipped through Vietnam. At the end of World War I, schoolgirls in Saigon began showing up in brightly colored tunics and white pants, a look that would spread throughout the colony's urban areas by the end of the decade. Young women abandoned the traditional practice of lacquering their teeth black and now flashed bright white smiles, a trend that began with *me tây* (wives and girlfriends of Western men) and quickly spread to French-educated young women. The end of the 1920s saw New Women in Hanoi cut their long hair short and part it on the side; within a few years the trend caught on in Saigon and eventually in Huế. The sporting movement that took Vietnam by storm in the late 1920s led French-educated middle-class women to abandon traditional beauty ideals such as the thin, frail, willow leaf figure and stooped crane neck in favor of erect posture and a strong athletic physique. By the mid-1930s, some women stopped binding their breasts and even sought to augment their curves through targeted exercises and padding. Modern Girls sporting Western clothing and made up like Hollywood starlets strutted down the streets of major cities or flirted with Western soldiers stationed at rural bases. In 1934 Nguyễn Cát Tường introduced his Lemur Tunic in the pages of the *Ngày Nay* newspaper, and within a year it became the daily uniform of fashionable young women, beauty queens, and even the empress Nam

Phương. The magnitude and speed with which these new beauty trends caught on was remarkable.

In this chapter I investigate the avenues by which trends spread throughout Vietnam during the interwar years. The dissemination of information on fashion, makeup, body image, and beauty contests occurred in tandem with the development of "colonial modernity," which in turn promoted a consumerist mentality. Transportation innovations enabled products to travel to Vietnam from Europe, the United States, and Japan. Trading companies, department stores, and elegant shopping districts popped up to meet consumer demand. Leisure activities, popularized via colonial contact, necessitated new forms of clothing and brought people together, thereby facilitating the spread of ideas and images. New media technologies introduced after World War I disseminated beauty trends across local, provincial, and even national borders. Self-proclaimed experts and entrepreneurs came out of the woodwork to capitalize on women's lust for beauty tips. Global fashion archetypes, notably the New Woman and the Modern Girl, arrived on the streets of Vietnam, and fashion icons including beauty queens, the empress, and movie stars reigned as national celebrities. Beauty trends swept Vietnam, adapting to meet the needs and interests of local women and the particular sociocultural issues with which they were grappling. Investigating the avenues through which beauty ideas spread in Vietnam during the interwar years illustrates more broadly the ways that such ideas diffuse across time, space, and social groups.

BEAUTY COMMERCE AND INTERNAL DISTRIBUTION NETWORKS: A STORY OF COLONIAL DEVELOPMENT

The story of Vietnam's modern beauty industry begins with early consumerism and trading companies. Almost immediately after France colonized Cochinchina in the 1850s, metropolitan trading companies seized on the twin opportunities of exporting resources from the colony and importing goods from the metropole on the return trip to Vietnam. The natural resources extracted from Vietnam's rich land were shipped to the metropole on a fleet of ships run by import-export trading companies. The ships unloaded in Marseille, where they were restocked with comfort items such as pith helmets, canned French vegetables, Marseille soaps, and liqueurs from Provence. Their routes of commerce linked the metropole to colonies, protectorates, concessions, as well as other famous trading ports outside the French empire.[1]

As most industrially produced cosmetics and ready-to-wear garments were initially imported from abroad, Vietnam's beauty culture and consumer market grew out of the colony's new and expanding transportation infrastructure. The colony's transportation network was built to facilitate not just the extraction of raw materials from Vietnam to be sold on the global market but also the importation and distribution of mass-produced industrialized goods from the metropole. Industrial goods arrived on steamships from France, England, Germany, Japan, and other parts of the world and were unloaded at ports and reloaded onto trains;[2] or they were sent off on smaller steam and later diesel boats, dispatched to urban areas, and eventually dispersed into the countryside. After World War I, the colony's growing fleets of trucks and cars helped transport goods from the cities out to the provincial capitals, where itinerant vendors dragged rickety carts or pedaled bicycles to deliver the small luxuries to local neighborhood markets.

Trading companies selling imported European goods typically opened stores in colonial cities. Hanoi was home to Agents L. Rondon Company Limited; Maron, Rochat, and Company; and Comptoire Commercial, among others. Saigon was the Far-East base for the Companie de Commerce et de Navigation d'Extrême Orient and for the Indochine Import Agent C. Huchet. The Morin Frères trading company, whose original shop was located in Tourane, quickly opened stores throughout Annam before moving into the hotel and movie theater business. Reflecting the changing demographics of the colonial venture, trading companies stocked products targeting the colony's rapidly growing population of French women, including baby formula, furniture, household appliances, and lipstick.[3] With the French military stationed in the countryside, trading companies set up storefronts near permanent military bases. The Rochat et Beaumont company capitalized on the heavy military presence in Tuyên Quang to establish a shop frequented by soldiers and their Vietnamese paramours, known as me tây.[4] As you will see, me tây would become early adapters of Western fashion, makeup, and body trends in Vietnam. By the interwar years, French trading companies could count middle-class Vietnamese with a taste for French-made products among their customers.

Glamorous shopping streets debuting the latest Parisian fashions along with other products from the metropole developed around the showrooms of higher-end trading companies. Most famous was Rue Catinat, Saigon, often compared to the celebrated Le Canebière in Marseille. Its strategic location between the port and post office was ideal for a trading company. In 1887, Rue Catinat was home to Aux Nouveautés Catinat, where homesick French men and women picked up cognac, Loire Valley wine, lavender oils, and other products from the homeland. The trading company quickly became popular among upper-class urban me tây, who typically enjoyed a European lifestyle, as well as wealthy Vietnamese and Chinese seeking exotic European luxuries. Upscale boutiques opened along the tree-lined street, supplying the city with imported ascot ties, diamond necklaces, and perfumes. The colony's growing Indian population began to settle on and around Rue Catinat, opening boutiques that sold stylish calicos and brightly colored silks, and Indian money lenders, with operations in the alleyways off Rue Catinat, offered to finance expensive purchases or underwrite small businesses. By 1923, the electric tram that connected Saigon to the surrounding provinces was routed through the city center, with a stop on Rue Catinat at Place de Frances Garnier, near the opera house.[5]

Hanoi had its own stretch of consumable elegance running along the south end of Hoàn Kiếm lake, beginning at Rue Paul Bert and terminating at the city's municipal opera house on Rue de France. Like Saigon's Rue Catinat, Hanoi's Rue Paul Bert to Rue de France shopping district began with a few well-placed trading companies. Most notable were the Maison Goddard and the Comptoire d'Extrême Orient, around which a bevy of high-end shops emerged. Located just around the corner from the Metropole Hotel at the northern end of the French quarter, the district catered to wealthy hotel guests and colonists from the metropole.[6]

Although Hải Phòng and Huế had smaller populations of French residents than Hanoi, they too had elegant streets and shops selling lavish French imports. As a port city with a high turnover of French sailors and military personnel, Hai Phòng was well stocked with accoutrements imported from the metropole. Debeaux Frères trading company opened at the turn of the century and helped transform Boulevard Amiral Beaumont into a posh shopping district. At the intersection of Rue Paul Bert, residents enjoyed their share of trading companies, elegant cafés, and an opera house. After World War I, department stores were added. Infamous for crime, Hai Phòng had a thriving black market of stolen imports that were resold in local market stalls or by itinerant vendors who easily dodged city police. Seven hundred kilometers to the south, Huế's Rue Jules Ferry was home to Morin Frères trading company and hotel, where one could find such rarities as Marquis de Bergey champagne, Coty powders, Crème Siamoise face cream, and Guerlain perfume.[7]

By World War I, most Vietnamese cities had been bestowed with the crown jewels of late nineteenth- and twentieth-century commerce: department stores. The metropolitan department store business model emerged out of the Industrial Revolution, which had enabled the mass production of goods and the growth of capitalism and urbanization. This gave rise to a middle class who were quickly amassing spending power. Department store shopping became a way for middle-class consumers to publicly assert their class status through the purchase of luxury goods. Shopping at department stores was not just about consuming, however. It was the entire shopping *experience* that department stores marketed to customers. Customers were invited to stroll from department to department, trying on ready-to-wear dresses in the store's fitting rooms, testing electric irons on cotton sheets, sampling perfume, and applying the latest shade of rouge. Shopping became not just a practical endeavor but a leisure activity.[8]

The department store business model was transnational, spreading throughout Europe and North and South America. By the interwar years, refined department stores were commanding consumer attention in most major Asian cities. European entrepreneurs certainly dominated the department store industry, but Chinese and *Hua Quiao* businessmen opened stores in China, Hong Kong, and Singapore.[9] In Japan, local entrepreneurs transformed the aesthetic of Japanese fashion and households by introducing Western ideas, style, and home appliances, thus establishing a "key site for the constitution of Japanese modernity," as Tomoko Tamari writes.[10] Japanese entrepreneurs brought this business model and modernity culture to colonies in Taiwan in 1932, when they opened the famed Kikumoto department store in Taipei and Hayashi department store in Tainan,[11] and to Korea with the sophisticated Mitsukoshi, Chōjiya, Minakai, and Hirata department stores.[12]

At the turn of the century, some of the more successful trading companies in Vietnam gradually converted their businesses into elegant department stores. Hanoi's Godard trading company became the Maison Godard department store, later known as the Maison Réunis;[13] the Comptoir d'Extrême Orient became the Société Poinsard et Veyret. During the interwar years, as French women increasingly migrated to the colony with their families in tow, department stores opened in all of the colony's major cities to take advantage of the new clientele. By the 1920s, Hanoi was home to the Société Poinsard et Veyret, and the Grands Magasins Réunis, mentioned previously, as well as the Magasin Chaffanjon. Saigon saw the opening of the Grands Magasins Charner and Les Établissements Boy Landry. In Hải Phòng, French and middle-class Vietnamese as well as ethnic Chinese enjoyed strolling around the Grands Magasins de la Société Bordelaise Indochinoise, Magasins du Godelu, and Magasins Girodolle. And Huế was known for the Grands Magasins Chafagnon-Colombani and the Grands Magasins Morin Frères, the former trading company that also opened department stores in Quy Nhơn, Tourane, and Bà Nà.[14]

During the interwar years, customers from all over Vietnam came to admire the colony's splendid department stores and shop for the latest imports from the metropole. Outside car parks valeted the private automobiles of wealthier customers, and rickshaw drivers stood by to assist customers burdened with heavy loads. Passersby gazed in awe at the ornate domed architecture and stained-glass windows of these "cathedrals of consumption."[15] Stores such as Hanoi's Grands Magasins Réunis were modeled after the Bon Marché and Printemps stores in Paris, known to bedazzle even the wealthiest Europeans. In Saigon, the Grands Magasins Charner occupied more than half a city block (figure 1.1), and Hải Phòng's Grands Magasins de la Société Bordelaise Indochinoise was home to an entire movie theater. Stores featured stately staircases and mirrored walls. Linking entertainment and consumption, many housed gourmet restaurants and ballrooms so elegant that they served as venues for charity fundraiser dinner dances and beauty contests.[16] Displays in bay windows seduced customers with seafoam-colored chiffon dresses, darted blouses, and slinky backless gowns in majestic shades of purple. In December, windows showcased the latest toys that *Père Noel* promised to bring to local children.[17]

The colony's department stores symbolized not just luxury but European modernity. With their modern lighting and electric ceiling fans whirring to the backbeat of mechanized cash registers, department stores exuded the technological sophistication of twentieth-century life. And, of course, they sold a broad spectrum of the most up-to-date industrialized products, household appliances, sewing machines, cameras, gramophones, and radios.[18]

THE DISSEMINATION OF BEAUTY TRENDS

FIGURE 1.1. Grands Magasins Charner department store in Saigon c. 1930.
Source: Wikimedia commons.

Although they sold a distinctly European vision of modernity, the colony's department stores catered to a decidedly Vietnamese clientele. In 1928, the Grands Magasins Réunis in Hanoi hired its first Vietnamese floor manager to better connect with the local customer base and promised to treat Vietnamese women shoppers "the way they should be treated."[19] The message here was not just that these young women would be indulged and pampered; there was also a tacit admission that such women had not always been treated well in the colony's French social spaces. In a more direct reference to race and class, the Grands Magasins Charner in Saigon issued assurances that "Vietnamese women of all classes would be welcome to the store."[20]

Whereas department stores in the metropole suffered setbacks during the interwar years, those in Vietnam prospered, likely due to an emerging Vietnamese middle class that was gaining consumer power and eagerly participating in conspicuous consumption.[21] Although department stores projected an image of upper-class exclusivity, they were open to all classes. The clever marketing strategy was to set prices low enough for middle-class (and eventually lower-class) women to afford while simultaneously promoting the illusion that it was a privilege to shop there. Strategically located close to tram, bus, and rail stops, the stores targeted customers from afar, including those from less affluent neighborhoods and suburbs. The stores typically propped open their glass double doors, inviting any passersby to enter. Prices were discounted at holiday sales to celebrate Christmas and Tết.[22] Department stores thus "democratized" luxury by making the *experience* of luxury—and at least some of the products themselves—accessible to all.[23] Moreover, department stores simplified the experience of shopping in new and unexpected ways. They offered fixed prices, a respite from the haggling traditionally required in Vietnamese markets and shops; offered home delivery; and eliminated the risk associated with costly purchases by allowing customers to return them for a refund.

As Holly Grout has noted in the case of the metropole, "department stores allowed women of all classes to envision themselves as part of a bourgeois world at the same time that [they] encouraged consumers to indulge in their most intimate, personal fantasies." In fitting rooms, customers twirled around, admiring themselves in floor-to-ceiling mirrors and soliciting advice from salesclerks. Jewelry departments, which evoked the magic of "the dreamlands described in Arabian nights," offered gold monogram necklaces, pearl drop earrings, celluloid broches, and diamond and sapphire engagement rings, per the European style.[24] Customers fogged up the glass with their breath as they peered into the dazzling cases.[25] Meanwhile, store security kept an eye out for shoppers with sticky fingers. In-house detectives arrested shoplifters and investigated rumors of employee-led theft rings.[26]

Essential to department stores were their vast and opulent cosmetics departments. Women tried the latest coral-hued lipstick, tested Forvil creams, and matched powder to their skin tone. Salesclerks hired for their pretty faces offered tips on application, shading, and technique. Customers were encouraged to compare Coty perfume with brands such as Houbigant, Piver, and Gellé Frères.[27] Thanks to a setting that exuded refinement, department stores rehabilitated the once-vulgar image of cosmetics.[28]

Outside of department stores women found the latest fashion trends in a variety of new venues that had emerged as a by-product of colonialization.

THE DISSEMINATION OF BEAUTY TRENDS

As mentioned previously, high-end boutiques situated on fancy shopping streets sold ready-to-wear clothing imported from Europe and the United States. The colony's growing population of Indian traders quickly dominated the silk industry, opening "Bombay shops" that offered vibrant prints not found in European or local textiles. Factories in Nam Định or Chợ Lớn, where Chinese women had been imported as cheap labor, produced inexpensive ready-to-wear clothing.[29] And local designs were stitched together in the backrooms of tailor shops.

Tailor shops large and small transformed bolts of fabric into garments custom-made to fit their customers. Customers admired their new outfits in full-length mirrors and in back an army of tailors hunched over sewing machines, churning out garments. The owners of such shops—including Nguyễn Cát Tường, about whom you will learn more later—created designs that would dramatically change the course of modern Vietnamese fashion history. Medium-sized tailor businesses often copied the styles of famous designers and altered customers' clothing to flatter their body shapes. For customers who could not afford expensive alterations, unmarried women ran tailoring businesses out of their own small apartments, sometimes selling sex on the side to make ends meet.[30]

Like shopping, beautification became a pleasurable—and public—experience during the interwar era. The most notable venues for beauty-related services were beauty institutes modeled on those in Paris. French-owned institutes such as the Kéva Institute or the Vietnamese-owned Institute de Beauté Madeleine opened in elegant urban districts and catered to wealthy French, Vietnamese, and Chinese women, who enjoyed facials, hair treatments, manicures and pedicures, antiaging treatments or skin-lightening treatments, makeup tutorials or eyebrow tattoos, weight loss treatments, and electric shock treatments for fat loss. Some local women opened their own salons, offering Vietnamese as well as European treatments and products and in many cases catering to a less affluent clientele.[31]

The 36 Streets section of Hanoi was home to smaller beauty vendors. The Phúc Thịnh shop on Hàng Đậu carried face powder, the French perfume Houbigant, and Kéva powder.[32] The Quảng Hưng Long on Hàng Bồ in Hanoi advertised imported goods including perfume, scented soap, and lipsticks of all hues.[33] And pharmacies such as the Nhà Thuốc Phùng Gia Viên on Paris Street in Chợ Lớn sold local beauty products.[34] To entice customers to venture into the stores, some pharmacies such as the

Western-medicine pharmacy Khương-bình Tịnh in Can Thơ offered free low-quality beauty products with purchases.[35]

During the interwar years, local markets—vast collections of stalls once located outdoors and then moved into stately colonial buildings—also catered to women's beauty needs. Shoppers snapped up deals at the Đồng Xuân market and Hôm Market in Hanoi, the Sát Market in Hải Phòng, the Đông Ba market in Huế, the New Market (Bến Thành market) in Saigon, and the Bình Tây market in Chợ Lớn. They bargained for low-end ready-to-wear clothing or fabric produced in Nam Định—which in its heyday of the 1920s employed no less than six thousand workers, earning it the nickname "The Manchester of Tonkin"[36]—and sometimes scored impossibly low prices on what were actually stolen luxury goods. Shoppers could even get their hair shampooed while relaxing to a brief massage. As you will see in chapter 5, some markets went so far as to stage their own beauty contests.

APPLIED BEAUTY: LEISURE ACTIVITIES

From the early days of French colonization, as part of the "mission to civilize" Vietnam as well as to cater to French residents, state and private organizations introduced French cultural and leisure activities. Plazas and sports clubs served as venues for athletic competitions; fairs and philanthropic events offered nonstop entertainment; and hotels sprang up along the coast to cater to urban vacationers. The new forms of leisure facilitated the visible participation of women in public life. Initially only French women partook publicly, but during the interwar years as European-style leisure became a marker of middle-class status Vietnamese women joined in. Because leisure activities were generally performed in highly visible ways and connoted class status, participants wanted to look good doing them. Leisure thus became fundamental to the spread of fashion and beauty trends.

French urban planners of the late nineteenth century redesigned Vietnam's cities with an abundance of appealing leisure activities in mind.[37] Residents of Saigon enjoyed relaxing strolls in the city's zoo, music pavilion, and adjacent thirty-acre botanical garden. Hanoi residents escaped the sun's blistering rays at the serene pavilion at Paul Bert Square and bet on horses at the hippodrome. The turn of the century saw the opening of *Cercles Sportifs* in Saigon as well as Huế, where Europeans and a handful of wealthy Vietnamese and Chinese businessmen mingled and struck deals while hitting tennis balls, shooting billiards, or, by the 1930s, relaxing by the pool.[38] In Hải Phòng, people strolled the city's canals, which earned the city the moniker "the Venice of Tonkin," and flocked to its opulent opera house.

As Phyllis Martin details with regard to the French colony of Brazzaville (now the Republic of Congo), colonial life changed the way urban colonized people perceived and organized time.[39] In Vietnam, French colonization introduced the notion of school days and workdays, and wrist or pocket watches kept wearers accountable for daily tasks. Whereas rural farmers remained responsible for their crops day in and day out, many members of Vietnam's new middle class ended their workweek on Friday afternoons and enjoyed an unprecedented two-day weekend of free time. Many of these workers seized on this to assert their class identity via what Thorstein Veblen described as "conspicuous leisure": leisure activities performed for the sake of displaying wealth, often mimicking the activities of the upper class.[40] In a 1934 critique of the practice, *Phụ Nữ Tân Văn* newspaper noted wryly: "People cheered that the Annam women were civilized, because they were modern people who came to play at the beach, went to the dance hall, and sat down for aperitifs at coffee shops."[41]

It is not surprising that the young women partaking in the new middle-class leisure activities of the 1930s wanted to look good doing so. As Tobe Slade found in the case of interwar Japan, "the development of leisure made for social spaces, such as dancing, movies, or resorts, where modernity was performed," often through fashion.[42] In Vietnam, such social spaces were also marked by sartorial expressions of modernity. Women donned knee-length gaberdine skirts and strappy high heels for a trip to the cinema, colorful silk Bombay dresses for a night at the dance hall, and bias-cut silk evening gowns for philanthropic charity events. Indeed, writing about his fashion inspirations, the designer Nguyễn Cát Tường cited the influence of leisure activities on women's fashion: "At market fairs, mornings at church, or afternoons dancing, we often meet a lot of young women in new, colorful outfits."[43]

New leisure activities involved new ways of using the body, thereby altering expectations for the female physique and fashion.[44] Footwork on the tennis court necessitated shorts or knee-length tennis dresses, and swimming called for skin-baring bathing suits. Bicycling clubs for women encouraged members to wear hip-length shirts over pants or long shorts.

More and more women chopped off their long hair and embraced shoulder- or chin-length bobs to suit their active lifestyles. As you will see in chapter 4, the former ideal of a thin, weak, willowy physique was replaced by a curvier, more athletic one.

In the evenings, young urbanites and suburbanites gathered at dance halls. Dance halls were an international fad that took Asia by storm in the 1930s.[45] At Tourane's Caravelle and Hải Phòng's Hotel de Paix, young women relaxed in the gentle embrace of their male partners while stepping to the foxtrot—or shed all inhibitions to dance the sensual tango. Dancing, like sports, required clothing that allowed for unconstrained movement, so Western fashion accompanied Western music. Pleated knee-length skirts allowed high-heeled shoes to kick up flirtatiously, showcasing the wearer's shapely calves. Lighter fabrics, shorter sleeves, and spaghetti straps helped female dancers stay cool on the hot, sweaty dance floor. In the event that a wild dance move offered a sneak peek of their nether regions, dancers made sure to wear their prettiest floral-print or lace underwear. Some women even enhanced their figure with falsies: rubber or cotton pads tucked into their Western-style bras. As dance halls were prime flirtation zones, young women did their best to stand out in the dim light. Eyeshadow and mascara made their eyes appear bigger, and lipstick lured men into a kiss—or at least sparked a desire to kiss the pretty young woman who wore it.

Philanthropic events, discussed in chapter 5, also played an important, if unlikely, role in disseminating new notions of female beauty. Organized to raise funds for the poor, such events also served as a new form of socializing during the interwar years. As such, they showcased new fashions, and the sophisticated locations at which they were held—theaters, hotels, upscale restaurants, and department store ballrooms—were themselves integral to the propagation of beauty trends. More important, though, the posh philanthropic fundraisers lent a certain bourgeois respectability to items and activities associated with beauty—most notably beauty contests—that until only recently had been shunned. The older, more conservative crowds that attended such events wore understated Western-style attire made of high-quality fabric. After 1934, most ladies arrived in a silk Lemur Tunic, walking arm in arm with their husbands, who donned Western-style suits. At these fundraiser events, couples enjoyed sumptuous Franco-Vietnamese fusion dishes, ballroom danced, and—for the evening's climatic event—watched young women in elegant Western-style gowns or Lemur Tunics and pink lipstick sashay across the stage as competitors in a beauty contest.[46]

THE DISSEMINATION OF BEAUTY TRENDS

The form of consumptive leisure with perhaps the widest participation in interwar Vietnam—spanning all economic classes—was fairs and expositions. Given their vast and diverse array of visitors, fairs were central to the spread of beauty trends. A wildly popular phenomenon around the world during the early twentieth century, the events were typically state-sponsored and staged for the triple purpose of showcasing national grandeur (particularly of an imperial nature), promoting modernity via evidence of industrial prowess, and stimulating economies by promoting consumer products. To lure attendees, the events featured athletic competitions, air shows, dancing, fashion shows, and the ubiquitous beauty contests. Although they were not designed with the aim of disseminating beauty trends, that became yet another of their functions.

During the first half of the twentieth century, fairs and expositions were staged at local, national, and international levels. International expositions even became a site of contest among nations, with each host vying to show off its imperial conquests and superior technological innovations.[47] Fairs and expositions attracted audiences eager to catch a glimpse of the unveiling of cutting-edge modern consumer products. Beauty products were among the "modern" products showcased. As a testament to their significance, the 1939 World Fair in New York even housed a pavilion—designed in the shape of a powder compact—dedicated to Coty cosmetics. Inside, women could admire the company's new case designs and application technologies, test new shades and formulas of makeup, and even enjoy a professional makeover.[48]

In France, as Shanny Peers shows, fairs and expositions "conveyed the values of the modern era, extolling the virtues of industry and progress in rationalized urban society" while promoting the cult of consumerism.[49] After World War I, French expositions included elaborate and expensive exhibits showcasing the colonial empire. French (and universal) fairs and expositions have been well studied by Dana Hale, Panivong Norindr, and others who show that they served multiple performative functions: to enhance the imperial prestige of France, to disseminate positive ideas about the French empire, and to "stage the idea of Indochina."[50]

Scant research has been done on the fairs held in the colonies, particularly Vietnam.[51] During the interwar era at least a dozen local or regional fairs organized by the colonial state or charity groups were held in Vietnam each year. Newspapers promoted the events weeks in advance, covered opening ceremonies and sporting events minute-by-minute, interviewed fairgoers, and published photos of beauty pageant winners. Most fairs and expositions were staged in Annam, the seat of Vietnamese imperial power, which amounted to a stamp of approval from "traditional" authority (the emperor) for "modernity" (the products showcased at the fair). The local fairs and expositions were popular among both French and Indigenous people, and their low price of entry—typically just five cents per day and ten cents for night activities—made them accessible to all. The 1936 Faifoo (Hội An) fair brought in more than ten thousand people a day, and in its three-day run the Huế fair welcomed 103,000 people in 1936 and 110,000 in 1937.[52]

With large audiences hailing from different social classes, fairs were the ideal environment to promote not just the latest consumer goods but also pro-colonial propaganda. The message was clear: colonialism with its modern technology would uplift the colonized. Indeed, the French colonial government used fairs as a way to "stage modernity" and promote the idea of imperial prowess.[53] Said to be a "true Franco-Vietnamese collaboration," fairs included local forms of entertainment and leisure, such as bonsai competitions and cock fighting, as well as blatant displays of French modernity and the Mission Civilisatrice.[54] Fair programs from the interwar years reflect the colonial push for sanitation and hygiene education, which normalized public discussions of intimate parts of the body (see chapter 4). At exhibits, fairgoers tested new kinds of antiseptics and admired displays of bathrooms with running water, bathtubs, and showers, all intended to be installed in the privacy of the home interior.

From the opening ceremony (broadcast on the radio) to the concluding show, advertising was at the forefront of fairs, and images of women were an essential part of the advertising strategy. The cover of the program for the 1938 Huế fair featured a beautiful woman with darkened cupid's bow lips and a sultry gaze. The 1935 Hà Đông fair opened with a procession of motor floats that advertised, among other things, Fhantasia shoes and the Hop Thanh Silk and Tailor Shop. Some float decorations were quite elaborate; one representing the province of Hà Đông showcased a beauty queen high atop a throne, smiling and waving at the adoring crowd below. Even more elaborate was the float from the Chương Mỹ district, which carried a piano along with the glamorous female musician and trendsetter Ái Liên, discussed at length below, who sang a few *nhạc mới* tunes. The fairgrounds themselves abounded with still more ravishing women, many of whom had been secretly hired by local tailors to model their latest designs; as instructed, the women handed out business cards to admirers.[55]

Much of the entertainment staged at fairs influenced the spread of beauty trends in the colony. Audiences were captivated not just by the singing competitions and musical performances but by the stylishly coiffed and outfitted performers themselves. At cycling races, soccer games, and badminton matches, audiences marveled at the coordination and strength of the athletes, female as well as male.[56] At dance competitions, crowds gathered to admire splendidly attired couples performing the breathtakingly sensual tango—with some couples even bounding up from the audience to join in. Beautiful modern women charmed fairgoers in fashion shows and beauty pageants, which were often the most anticipated attraction at fairs.[57]

From the most celebrated guests to the humblest visitors, fairgoers had a profound influence on fashion and beauty. The dashing emperor Bảo Đại and exquisite empress Nam Phương appeared at many local fairs, the empress in a pleated drop-waist dress and high-heeled brogue shoes, her shoulder-length hair parted to the side and topped with a beret; the emperor in a pinstripe suit, hair slicked back.[58] It was not uncommon to see fairgoers themselves dressed to impress. Many young men wore three-piece Western-style suits, and Modern Girls sported Western dresses with shoulder pads and cinched waists.[59] Other young women stuck with trendy Vietnamese styles, notably brightly colored tunics with white pants. No matter what their fashion bent, high heels and made-up faces were *de rigeur*.[60] It was the trendy young women at the 1933 Lạc Thiện fair who served as muses for Nguyễn Cát Tường when he designed the Lemur Tunic, which in turn made its in-person debut at that very same fair the following year. The *Ngày Nay* magazine chronicled his process of inspiration and the subsequent popularization of the tunic: "Hội An women hit the streets [of the fair] wearing high heels, colored shirts, scarves, hair done up in modern style. . . . A year later, [Nguyễn] Cát Tường debuted his style. . . . This year, thousands of audience members were wearing Cát Tường's [tunic] dress."[61]

Fairgrounds quickly developed a reputation as a place to pick up comely women. Young men, *Tràng An* newspaper claimed, went to the fair to see "not one, but ten, hundreds of beautiful girls." Shopkeepers hired pretty women to hang around their stalls and attract customers. Young men would poke around, pretending to buy, but really just hoping for a shot at talking to the girls.[62] Savvy restauranteurs invited beauty queens to sip

THE DISSEMINATION OF BEAUTY TRENDS

FIGURE 1.2. Cartoon of fair published in *Vịt Đực* newspaper, November 16, 1938.

drinks at their booths to attract male customers.[63] In his 1936 novel, *Vỡ Đê*, Vũ Trọng Phụng spoke of the sultrier side of fairs: "Young women whose modern clothes were sometimes polite, sometimes very ridiculous, and sometimes provocatively exposing their skin . . . women wearing push-up bras and tighter shirts showing off their breasts, leaving two round circles that would make any sane person want to use two hands [to fondle them]." As for the dance floors at the fairs, he wrote, they were "just an excuse for adultery, fornication, prostitution."[64]

"Whoever has a family should not use the excuse of going to the fair to commit adultery," a 1938 edition of the *Vịt Đực* newspaper warned readers.[65] An accompanying cartoon in the same issue illustrated the point (figure 1.2). In the foreground of the cartoon, a modern man with short hair and a dapper suit hungrily eyes a modern girl in a Lemur Tunic, high heels and earrings, her hair parted on the side; in return she gives him a meaningful glance and a hint of a seductive smile. Another man, dressed in traditional clothing, tosses confetti at her—a 1930s way of telling a woman she was beautiful. Behind the flirtatious pair in the foreground, a more unsavory scene is playing out. Another woman, dressed more traditionally than the other and holding what appears to be an umbrella, is bending down while—unbeknownst to her—a grinning, lecherous old man snaps a photo of her shapely bottom. Meanwhile, a father hurries his young son past the inappropriate display. The sardonic caption reads: "Progress at the fair."[66]

Vacationing, the quintessence of leisure, also played a key role in transforming how women's bodies were used and displayed in interwar Vietnam. Further academic research needs to be done on the topic of vacation travel in Vietnam, but during the precolonial era, when much of the population was beholden to the needs of an agrarian economy, vacations were for the most part limited to visiting family or ancestral homelands during holidays such as Tết or between growing seasons. After all, leisure travel not only cost money but took time away from the tilling of crops, which had to be performed on a schedule dictated by the weather. It was not until French colonization that leisure vacations—and the infrastructure to support them—were introduced in Vietnam.

French culture had a history of vacationing, although it had long remained a luxury enjoyed strictly by the aristocracy. It was not until the late nineteenth century that vacationing became popular among the middle class thanks to the transportation innovations of the Industrial Revolution (including trains, steamships, automobiles, and later airplanes) as well as improved roads and bridges, all of which made mass tourism immensely popular. During the interwar years, taking time off for vacations became a hot political topic in Europe, and by the mid-1930s it was at the forefront of French political consciousness.[67]

The growing Vietnamese middle class, armed with disposable income, quickly embraced the vacation time that was now being offered by their employers, particularly the colonial government and most French businesses, just as it was in metropolitan France. Before long vacationing had become yet another form of conspicuous consumption. Vietnamese urbanites packed their automobiles with suitcases containing enough items of brightly colored clothing to last an entire summer. Vacationers spent their days off frolicking in the water, with most women unabashedly sporting bathing suits cut to the thigh. A few lucky vacationers might even be invited to compete in a swimsuit competition at a local hotel. Beach resorts also hosted sports tournaments, outdoor movie screenings, restaurant tastings, and beauty contests. At night, well-heeled guests donned ball gowns to attend charity balls in the dining room of the Grand Hotel de Đồ Sơn, a famous playground for the wealthy. At other elegant hotels, local bands covered songs such as Tino Rossi's "Amapola" or played *nhạc mới* (Western songs set to Vietnamese lyrics).[68]

Most of Vietnam's early vacation resorts developed out of the infrastructure of early French naval bases, weather stations, and colonial sanitariums, which colonists used as a refuge from the tropical heat. Resort towns were built in the cool mountain air of Tam Đảo, Chapa [Sapa], Dalat, Bà Nà, and Bạch Mã, as well as coastal spots such as Đồ Sơn, Sầm-Sơn, Nha Trang, Quy Nhơn, Phan Thiet, and Cap Saint Jacques. Other popular beach vacation spots in Vietnam included Phan Thiết and Nha Trang, both in Annam. The automobile, introduced to Vietnam at the turn of the century and popularized after World War I, enabled middle-class drivers to reach beach destinations with ease—and clad in stylish "car clothes."[69] In Annam, where even Westernized bourgeois were more modest, middle-class women covered themselves with one of Nguyễn Cát Tường's chic "beach pajamas," also known as palazzo pants, as they explored the grounds of one of the Morin Hotels dotting the protectorate's coastline. By the interwar years, tourism in Annam came to be dominated by the Morin Frères company, which owned resorts in Nha Trang, Quy Nhơn, and mountain hotels in Bà Nà and Bạch Mã. As discussed earlier, the company began its operations importing French products before expanding into department stores and cinemas. As the Morin Frères company had a long history of catering to the stylish middle class, it is no surprise that its hotels and resorts became associated with high fashion. Chic vacationers posed for photographs enabled by technological advances such as affordable lightweight cameras, roll film, and simplified developing processes. Such photos were a means not only of sharing one's adventures with family and friends, but of preserving the precise details of one's "look," thereby inviting scrutiny and revision over time.

The ultimate symbol of stylish middle-class vacationing excess was Cap Saint Jacques, roughly one hundred kilometers from Saigon. Originally a colonial naval base, a sanitarium was soon built for colonists looking to convalesce, and by the turn of the century the beach town had become a popular beach resort.[70] By the 1930s, Cap Saint Jacques was a bustling spot with luxury hotels (Le Grand Hotel Mottet was the most splendid of all), cinemas, and shops. In one of its many efforts to cultivate Emperor Bảo Đại and Empress Nam Phương, the colonial state gifted them the luxurious former vacation home of the governor of Cochinchina, known as Villa Blanche, which to this day remains one of the town's main tourist attractions. The posh royal couple's presence increased the prestige of the beach resort and attracted vacationers eager to be seen looking good among the colony's modern elite. The beach town even achieved an international status, with foreign cruise ships stopping in port during tours of Southeast Asia.[71]

As more and more urbanites descended upon coastal towns long inhabited by fishermen and farmers, class tensions began to escalate. The material luxuries and behavioral indulgences middle-class Vietnamese vacationers considered their prerogative were viewed as scandalous and even reprehensible by longtime local residents. In a scathing 1940 reportage about the famed Sầm-Sơn vacation resort, Tùng-Hiệp chronicled how vulgar Vietnamese middle-class urbanites flooded into the town, littering the streets and graffitiing rocks and trees with carvings of their initials. Their new vacation villas displaced local fishermen and other villagers, who were forced to resettle in the pine forest above the shore and subsist on meager servings of rice, corn, potatoes, and whatever tiny fish had not been sold to vacationers.[72] Their resulting resentment would fuel decades of class warfare in Vietnam during the second half of the twentieth century. In hindsight, it is easy to understand how outrage and hatred toward the middle class eventually propelled the Communist Party to power.

COMMUNICATED BEAUTY: NEW FORMS OF MEDIA

The emergence of mass media during the interwar years enabled beauty knowledge to spread rapidly throughout Vietnam, including into the countryside.[73] New forms of media developed with the support of the colonial state. The state used the press, radio, and cinema as a "modern propaganda machine" to promote the ideals of Franco-Vietnamese collaboration and spread French culture throughout the colony.[74] These new forms of communication exposed Vietnamese women to international frames of reference for their fashion and cosmetics knowledge, including those of Japan, China, the United States, and Turkey.

Print Media

Newspapers were the most effective vehicle for disseminating beauty knowledge. Increased literacy rates due to the teaching of quốc ngữ, the country's Romanized script, led to an explosion of readership—especially among young women who were being educated thanks to French policies that opened schools to female students.[75] This newly literate female population was eager for beauty knowledge. Airplanes shipped in syndicated columns from popular French magazines such as *Femina, Paris Soir Dimanche, Eve, Almanach d'Eve, Journal de la Femme,* and *Miroir du Monde*, which were translated and published in Vietnamese newspapers.

Many newspapers ran regular columns on fashion or related issues. Throughout the interwar period, *La Dépêche d'Indochina* delighted readers with commentary on the latest Western styles for women and children.[76] In 1932, *Hà Thành Ngọ Báo* published a column called "Ways to Dress" (Lối phục). The Self-Reliant Literary Group, which embraced material goods as agents of modernization, taught women the rules of fashion etiquette in its 1934 column "Women's Fashion" (Y phục của phụ nữ), published in the *Phong Hóa* newspaper, as well as the 1936 column "Social Relations: Behavior and Dress" (Xã Giao: Phép xử thế, Phục Sức), published in the *Ngày Nay* newspaper. It was across the pages of *Phong Hóa* that Nguyễn Cát Tường had laid out his preliminary sketches of the Lemur Tunic in 1934. In 1939, the *Đàn-Bà* newspaper ran a weekly column titled "Beautiful and Beautiful" (Đẹp và Đẹp), written by a variety of female journalists. Beyond these columns, newspapers published articles offering critiques of the latest fashions along with advice on cosmetic application, decorum, and calisthenics designed to shape the body. Some female journalists made their names sharing beauty advice. In 1928, Phan Thị Bạch Vân shared makeup tips in the pages of *Hà Thành Ngọ Báo*; in 1936 Miss Duyên taught women cosmetics application in *Ngày Nay*; and throughout the late 1930s Song Nguyệt Phạm thị Lan Khanh Mỹ-Chânall offered fashion and makeup know-how in the *Đàn-Bà* newspaper.[77] Cosmetics advertisements—by firms as diverse as the French brand Coty, the Japanese brand Toshiko, and the Vietnamese brand Trường Xuân Milk—not only provided revenue for Vietnamese language newspapers but also transmitted beauty knowledge to their readers.

Pictures of well-known beauties, such as Empress Nam Phương and the singer Aí Liên regularly graced the pages of Vietnamese-language newspapers, which quickly became one of Vietnam's main sources of female imagery. In the 1930s, the results of Miss Europe, Miss Universe, and local beauty contests were typically front-page news, accompanied by prominent pictures of the winners. But not all the images were polite. As notions about the ideal women's physique began to change during the 1930s, newspapers published voyeuristic and sometimes punishing images of unsuspecting female beachgoers and wardrobe malfunctions.

Such images, along with the glut of articles earnestly offering advice on beauty and fashion minutiae, prompted more than a few misogynistic sniggers in the press. Cartoons in *Ngày Nay* and *Phong Hóa* overtly mocked women with large breasts. In 1938, the *Vịt Đực* newspaper published scores of articles lambasting women for being materialistic, for obsessively following trends, and for squandering money on beauty and hair treatments.[78] The writers further accused women of being sexually promiscuous, tempting elderly men, cheating on husbands, or naively allowing lewd men to touch them at beauty institutes.[79] The paper also ran a satirical column called "Trends" (Mốt), a parody of beauty advice and fashion columns whose author—"Miss Ngã"–was probably a man.[80]

Many self-proclaimed beauty experts advised women on beauty topics with the intention of selling their products. Lệ Chi published a book teaching women tricks for slimming down, and "Mademoiselle Mộng Khanh" published the beauty manual "Want to Be Beautiful"(*Muốn Đẹp*).[81] Most influential, however, was Nguyễn Cát Tường, best known for his redesigning of the classic Vietnamese tunic. Born in 1912 in Sơn Tây, at the age of sixteen he entered the prestigious École des Beaux Arts in Hanoi, where he studied oil painting from 1928 to 1933. The school opened in 1925 and taught both Western art and Far Eastern traditions and undoubtedly had a profound influence on Nguyễn Cát Tường's asthetics. His classmates Lê Phổ, Tô Ngọc Vân, and Lê Thị Lựu would go on to become some of Vietnam's most celebrated artists, and at times they were called upon to put their discriminating eye to use as judges at beauty contests.[82]

Nguyễn Cát Tường burst onto the scene almost immediately after graduation and began dispensing fashion and beauty advice in regular articles in the *Ngày Nay* newspaper. *Ngày Nay* was the organ of the Self-Reliant Literary Group (*Tự Lực Văn Đoàn*), whose philosophy was to improve the nation by raising the standard of living through material goods and architecture, as Martina Nguyen has shown in a recent study. The group identified material reform as the vehicle through which Vietnamese civilization would "evolve"; clothing, specifically, was considered an effective means of rehabilitating the image of the Vietnamese people. Although Nguyễn Cát Tường was not an official member of the Self-Reliant Literary Group, he was in close alignment with its agenda.[83]

In early 1934, Nguyễn Cát Tường began a series of articles intended to help Vietnamese women update their *look* and, by extension, improve Vietnam's international reputation. In February 1934, Nguyễn Cát Tường published his first sketches of the Lemur Tunic. "Lemur" was taken from "*le mur*," a French translation of the last word of his name, Tường, which, if separated from the two-syllable name Cát Tường (good omens), means "The Wall." The French influence did not stop there. The Lemur Tunic itself was disparaged by other artists as a mere Frenchification of the traditional Vietnamese tunic. Complaints notwithstanding, the design proved wildly popular among Vietnamese women, who rushed to their local tailor to have the design copied. By 1935, the Lemur Tunic had become the uniform of beauty pageant contestants, middle-class women, and even Empress Nam Phương herself.

Nguyễn Cát Tường's impact extended well beyond the Lemur Tunic. Throughout the mid-1930s, Nguyễn Cát Tường taught Vietnamese women how to be beautiful in almost every way. So pervasive was his influence that remarks about his beauty advice appear in every chapter of this book. He guided women on how to select colors for each season and how to select patterns to flatter each body type. In 1934, together with former classmate and fellow artist Lê Phổ, he published a catalogue of designs for dresses, pants, shoes, beach attire, and jewelry to outfit the nation's women.[84] He taught women how to apply eye makeup, how to select powder to match their skin, and how to identify lipstick colors to enhance a youthful smile. Even nail polish did not escape his scrutiny. There was a proper color for every dress and every occasion, and plenty of taboos as well (by no means should a woman wear red nail polish to a funeral). Insisting that a toned, healthy body was as important as the clothes that adorned it, he taught women how to do stretches to make themselves taller, exercises to cinch their waist, and even movements to augment their breasts.

Cinema

As was the case throughout the world, cinema became the "great diffuser of fashion" in Vietnam.[85] Film technology initially arrived in Vietnam at the turn of the century as part of the French effort to entertain troops and spread propaganda. Traveling cinemas set up in fields in rural areas drew large audiences. As early as 1911, a cinema opened in the spacious Morin Frères department store in Tourane. After a screening, women inspired by a cinema starlet could make a beeline to the store's cosmetics counter or dress department to replicate her look for themselves. Wealthy Vietnamese and Chinese businessmen began opening cinemas showcasing films from Hong Kong, China, and Japan, and by 1920 theaters welcomed moviegoers throughout the Cochinchina countryside. In 1932 there were twenty-seven public movie theaters in Tonkin, eleven in Annam, and thirteen in Cochinchina; by 1940 there were more than one hundred cinemas in Vietnam.[86] Mobile movie carts continued to bring the latest films to the Cochinchina countryside, enabling rural women to absorb beauty trends from around the world.[87]

As a visual medium, cinema had a revolutionary influence on beauty culture. In the years of silent film, actresses applied extravagant amounts of mascara to emphasize the movements of their eyes, their main form of expression. Female moviegoers around the world copied the look, creating a new and enthusiastic market for mascara. Women also copied Myrna Loy's tight curls, Danielle Darrieux's bow lips, and Florelle's painted eyebrows, as well as fashion trends such as puffed sleeves blouses, dresses with shoulder pads, high-waisted sailor pants, and skirt-like shorts.

Audiences were also exposed to new ideas about sexuality. During the interwar years, films, especially Hollywood films, were sexually charged. Nancy F. Cott observes that "a new cultural apparatus formed around the revelation that sexual expression was a source of vitality and personality . . . and that female sexual desire was there to be exploited."[88] Although the more explicitly sexual films likely did not make it past colonial censors, even tamer films hinted at women's sexuality. Blocking techniques highlighted the subtle physicality between actors and actresses; costuming revealed women's curves and showed their skin; and makeup enhanced sexual desirability.

The film industry's influence extended beyond the theater doors. The very act of going to the movies inspired Vietnamese women to dress up. Young women Marcel curled their hair, careful not to burn their hands on the electric iron, before catching an evening showing at Hải Phòng's Ciné Club. Couples sporting fur-lined winter jackets walked arm in arm to purchase tickets for Le Majestic cinema on chilly December evenings in Hanoi. Young ladies arrived at the Eden Center Theater in Saigon dressed in smart scalloped skirts, chiffon blouses, and Oxford shoes.

Newspapers closely followed film releases, as well as the lives and looks of actresses. In the mid-1930s, *Hà Thành Ngọ Báo* regularly covered movies, advertising upcoming films, publishing reviews, discussing the business of cinema, spreading Hollywood gossip, and critiquing starlets' latest looks. French stars such as Meg Lemonnier, Henri Garat, Henriette Tripette, and Marie Glory, as well as Hollywood stars including Ginger Rogers, Jean Harlow, and Clark Gable, appeared regularly in gossip and fashion pages.[89] Film stars even appeared in back-page product advertisements touting French, British, and American soaps and creams.

Cinema's influence on beauty culture and women in Vietnam did not go unnoticed by critics. In 1931, *Hà Thành Ngọ Báo* translated an article by "Doctor Dekobra," who warned that Hollywood "eats every person who comes there, from young maidens in childhood to sly girls who use beauty to seduce people. . . . [The movie industry] fascinates foolish young girls, tempts dreamers with fantasies . . . it releases them, it buries them in the pit of annihilation to teach them that fame comes to an end."[90] In 1934, a Vietnamese journalist by the nom de plume of WanCaln denounced the Hollywood business model that mass produced beauties: "Like Ford, which makes cars, the Penhoët factory [manufactures] the train, the province of Lyon that weaves silk . . . Hollywood produces women."[91] Huynh, the fictional protagonist of Vũ Trọng Phụng's 1938 novel *To Whore* (Làm Đĩ), blamed the influence of Hollywood for her descent into what was then considered licentious sexuality: "My brain was infected with the influence of newspapers that spoke loudly every day about the glittering stars, about European and American makeup, the way to draw eyebrows. Marlène Deitrich, [Joan] Crawford's [erotic essence] that people keep writing about innocently and without shame is sex appeal. . . . I also [wanted to] show off my sex appeal!"[92]

ARCHETYPES AND ICONS

Newspapers and movies introduced dazzling images that captured people's imaginations, but these images existed only on paper or celluloid. Department stores, shopping streets, and tailors supplied the goods, but their promotions had a limited reach. It was the women of Vietnam themselves who exerted the greatest influence on the *look* of the nation—simply by strolling down a boulevard, side-stepping at a dance club, or frolicking on the beach. Most were ordinary women who embodied one of several popular archetypes; a few rarefied others—most notably Empress Nam Phương—garnered widespread admiration for their singular beauty and taste.

Archetypes

The group most widely credited—and blamed—in the primary sources as being the first trendsetters of Western-style beauty in Vietnam were me tây: Vietnamese women in relationships with Western men who began embracing European fashion and beauty trends around the turn of the century.[93] French men and Vietnamese women had engaged in romantic relationships since the earliest contact between the two groups, although such exogamous relationships were frowned upon by Vietnamese society.[94] By the turn of the century, two classes of me tây had emerged. One was a privileged, primarily upper-class group of Vietnamese women, many of them the daughters of government administrators or wealthy landowners. In the mid-nineteenth century, many exogamous marriages were the result of shrewd business or political deals. Wealthy Vietnamese fathers looking to secure their place in the new colonial social, political, and economic order sought to marry off their daughters to French administrators, businessmen, or professionals who, for their part, were looking to make insider connections within the Vietnamese community. The fathers, many of them collaborators with the colonial government, saw to it that the weddings were official colonial state ceremonies. The families thus created, known as métis (mixed-race) families, were middle- or upper-class and tended to live in well-to-do urban neighborhoods. They enjoyed evenings at the opera, joined the Cercle Sportif—the wives surveying the children's tennis lessons while their husbands socialized for business—and went on annual vacations to France to visit the husband's family. Although the women in these marriages certainly faced discrimination from Vietnam's French community, the high social status of their husbands allowed them, for the most part, to integrate into European social circles, socialize with French and other métis families, and live according to French cultural norms.

The other class of me tây were women romantically or sexually involved with lower-income European men, typically soldiers stationed at temporary military bases in the countryside or poor whites (*petits blancs*) in the cities. As with their upper-class counterparts, the social status of this group of me tây was defined largely by their partners, whose reputation in this case was rather grim. For one thing, the soldiers had meager incomes and hence a lower standard of living. Moreover, they were often Foreign Legion soldiers: foreign recruits who had joined the French military to gain French citizenship. Legionnaires, whose ranks included criminals who had fled prosecution in their home country, were known to be a rowdy bunch. The reputations of these soldiers' female partners were further sullied by the fact that few of the couples were legally married. Their cohabitation tended to be temporary, lasting only a few months to a year, when the battalion moved to another area of Indochina.

Many of the unions between this second class of me tây and soldiers resulted in children, and the me tây were frequently left to raise these children as single mothers. Moreover, assuming the parents never married, their mixed-race children were considered illegitimate under colonial law and shunned by French and Vietnamese society alike. Once their French partners had left town, many me tây found themselves without a means of child support or even survival—so they waited around the military barracks for the arrival of the next battalion and flirted with new arrivals until they found another partner. Me tây were widely assumed to be sex workers, and some of them did indeed sell sex on the side.[95] It was this archetype of me tây as sex workers, single mothers, and lovers of low-class European men who dominated the cultural landscape in Vietnam during the interwar years.

As early adopters of French beauty norms, both upper- and lower-class me tây quickly developed a recognizable look. Given that their French lovers were known to be put off by the Vietnamese custom of blackened teeth—mistakenly associated with poor hygiene—me tây became the first demographic group in Vietnam to adopt the Western style of natural white teeth.[96] And to accommodate their lovers' preference for voluptuousness, me tây did not bind their breasts. Their bright Parisian dresses fluttered above their lower calves, cinched their waists, and showcased their unbound bosoms. They greeted strangers with an unabashed dazzling white smile, often framed with red lipstick.

THE DISSEMINATION OF BEAUTY TRENDS

As the Western-style beauty trend spread beyond me tây to other Vietnamese women, it continued to carry a whiff of licentiousness—even though many of the me tây who had originated the trend were considered proper married ladies. The flash of a white smile was enough to get neighborhood aunties accusing a cheery young woman of prostitution. Flowy French dresses hinted at nights spent in dance halls. And unbound breasts—or even naturally full breasts—struck some onlookers as vulgar and suggestive, irrespective of their owner's intentions. Yet the me tây look was undeniably influential. With their Western-style fashions made of high-quality fabrics and carefully crafted accessories, upper-class me tây set the bar for European chic. As for lower-class me tây, most of whom lived in the countryside, they familiarized rural women with Western-style clothing, cosmetics, and white smiles.

After World War I, a new trendsetting archetype arrived on the scene in the urban areas of Vietnam. Known in Vietnam as *phụ nữ tân tiến, tân nữ lưu*, or *đan bà mới*, this archetype corresponded closely with the global phenomenon of the New Woman, who appeared in Europe and the United States in the late nineteenth century and in China, Japan, and Korea around the turn of the century.[97] New Women were bourgeois, educated, independent, and outspoken—especially about political and social causes, women's education, women's health, and women's rights in society.

It was no coincidence that New Women—typically middle- or upper-class urbanites—appeared just as the first generation of women to have been fully educated graduated from the French colonial school system. In colonial colleges and lycées, Vietnamese girls began their days doing Western-style calisthenics as their French teacher barked commands.[98] Under her tutelage, the first generation of literate young women learned French language and quốc ngữ, studied French culture and history, and read French novels with determined female protagonists. Most elite colonial schools were in urban areas, but roughly half of their student populations came from the provinces and boarded in dormitories. On holidays, these students traveled back to the countryside, bringing with them new ideas about romance, athletics, and fashion.

Upon graduating, a freshly minted generation of New Women strode onto the scene. Educated in colonial schools, and undoubtedly influenced by the international women's movement including influential feminists who toured Vietnam, the New Woman broke from traditional expectations about what she wore, how she behaved, and what she believed.[99] New Women wore colorful tunics with white pants, modest French dresses, and after 1934 they wore the Lemur Tunic. Famous New Women such as Huỳnh Thị Bảo Hoà, Trịnh Thục Oanh, and Bạch Liên made waves with practical shoulder-length haircuts.[100] They kept their teeth white, powdered their faces, and on special occasions wore red lip gloss. Like her global counterparts, the Vietnamese New Woman began riding a bicycle, projecting an image of the female body as something strong and dynamic. The female journalist Mỹ Chân made the case that in strengthening women's bodies athletics would strengthen the Vietnamese race.[101] New Women Hồ Thị Lích and Nguyễn Thị Kế, tennis star Miss Ất, and long-distance walker Miss Hoàng Việt Nga were renowned not just for their athleticism but their willingness to defy Confucian norms.[102] New Women advocated for women's participation in sports, journalism, and philanthropy and were outspoken in their support for nationalism, poverty relief, women's education, and women's health issues. Indeed, New Women were known more for their sharp intellect and participation in society than for their beauty, style, or sexuality. Yet they undeniably paved the way for their less erudite counterpart, the Modern Girl.

New Women were, for the most part, portrayed favorably in the progressive Vietnamese-language press, notably the wildly popular progressive women's newspaper *Phụ Nữ Tân Văn*, published in Saigon from 1929 to 1934.[103] Along with articles by the husband-wife duo of founder Cao Thị Khanh and her husband and the director Nguyễn Đức Nhuận, the paper published pieces by the New Poetry movement leader Nguyễn Thị Kiêm (also known as Nguyễn Thị Manh Manh); Đà Nẵng Women's Union president Huỳnh Thị Bảo Hoà; the school mistress and fiction author Trịnh Thục Oanh; and the journalist Mme Bạch Liên.[104] The paper also included an impressive lineup of male political thinkers, including Phan Bội Châu, Phan Khôi, and Hồ Biểu Chánh. Newspaper images show the New Women of *Phụ Nữ Tân Văn* dressed in tunics and white pants, their short hair parted to the side, their lips darkened with lipstick. Their male collagues stand beside them unapologetically wearing Western suits.[105]

Like their international counterparts, New Women in Vietnam argued that women's participation in society was key to strengthening the nation. *Phụ Nữ Tân Văn* drew on nationalist symbols and icons, reviving historical heroines such as the Trưng Sisters and Bà Triệu, who were celebrated for fighting the Chinese during the first millennium. Like many New Women, the newspaper's journalists challenged Confucian norms; they opposed arranged marriages, polygamy, chastity for widows, and abusive mothers-in-law; and advocated for sanitary birthing, childcare, and physical fitness. These journalists denounced the khuê các ideal of the sequestered maiden, calling upon readers to support female education and women in the workforce while upholding their respect for marriage and the family. The cosmopolitan New Woman as presented in the pages of *Phụ Nữ Tân Văn* was connected to a global community of activist women in France, Japan, China, and India and inspired by the reformist politics of the male Chinese intellectual Lian Quichao.[106]

The New Woman was perhaps best exemplified by the protagonist of Hồ Biểu Chánh's 1937 novel *Tân Phong nữ sĩ*. The story opens with the protagonist Hai Tân's parents searching for her. In a shocking display of independence for a young Vietnamese woman living in the Mekong Delta, Hai Tân has driven the family car by herself up to Saigon. Her parents fear that she will be late for her date to meet Vĩnh Xuân, a dapper young man recently returned from medical school in Paris, whom they long ago arranged for her to marry. When the betrothed pair finally meet for the first time since childhood, Vĩnh Xuân is repulsed by Hai Tân's independence and outspokenness—qualities cultivated during her education in colonial schools. Vĩnh Xuân calls off the engagement and eventually finds himself a "traditional" woman, Ngọ, who will presumably live by the Confucian Three Dependencies and Four Virtues.[107]

The protagonist moves to Saigon, where she lives alone and changes her name to Tân Phong. She starts a newspaper, *Tân Phụ Nữ*, modeled after the real-life *Phụ Nữ Tân Văn* where Hồ Biểu Chánh, the author, was himself a staff writer. The fictional paper rails against traditional marriage and promotes women's education, health, and rights. As her paper becomes increasingly successful, Tân Phong attends high-society parties and vacations at a beach resort with male and female friends. True to the New Woman image, she is comfortable in both sharply tailored Lemur Tunics and dainty French dresses. She wears her hair short, powders her face, and adds a touch of lipstick for evening occasions. Tân Phong is pursued by many men, yet her experience with Vĩnh Xuân has led her to swear off marriage—a testament to her devotion to helping women.[108]

Like many members of the era's progressive intelligentsia, author Hồ Biểu Chánh presents the New Woman archetype as essential to the modernization of Vietnam. In *Tân Phong nữ sĩ*, he juxtaposes the New Woman and the traditional wife. Vĩnh Xuân calls off his engagement to Tân Phong because of her modern ways and instead marries Ngọ, a traditional girl. But as the story unfolds, the reader learns that Ngọ is uneducated, superstious, and terribly jealous—even refusing to allow her husband, a doctor, to see his patients. Vĩnh Xuân eventually realizes his mistake and divorces Ngọ. Their failed marriage warns readers that Vietnam cannot progress without embracing women's education and independence. Vĩnh Xuân eventually reunites with Tân Phong—not realizing (due to her name change) that she is the fiancé he rejected—and falls in love with her.[109] The story's ending thus underlines the idea that the New Woman is Vietnam's future.

In the early 1930s, a third archetype arrived on the scene: the Modern Girl (*gái tân-thời, gái mới, gái theo mới, thị tân, thiếu nữ tân thời*). The Modern Girl was another international phenomenon, strutting down city streets from New York to Cairo, Bombay to Rangoon, Tokyo to Tonkin. Various iterations existed from country to country—the American analogue was the flapper—but Modern Girls shared certain characteristics around the world. Like the New Woman, the Modern Girl was independent, wore her hair short, drove automobiles, and played sports. But she differed in many ways. Unlike the ambitious and erudite New Woman, the Modern Girl was materialistic, individualistic, and self-indulgent. Instead of caring for the poor, she concerned herself with the latest fashion trends; instead of uplifting the status of women, she went out dancing, flirted with men, and most scandalously subscribed to a new set of sexual mores.[110] Modern Girls craved the limelight and dressed accordingly, in provocative Western clothing, high heels, and sultry makeup.

As a potent means of seducing a new generation of young women to surrender to the global cult of consumerism, the Modern Girl may have been more of a marketing dream—or a figment of social imagination—than a real-life phenomenon. As Barbara Sato writes about Modern Girls in Japan, the new archetype "existed more as an object than a self-defining subject."[111] Conservatives everywhere, shocked by the idea if not the reality of young women acting independently and dressing provocatively, publicly and emphatically denounced the archetype as one of the many negative consequences of "modernity." However, a cross-cultural study by the Modern Girl Around the World Working Group shows that the public uproar over their supposed vanity, materialism, and promiscuity was, in many cases, an overreaction.[112] Moreover, it is entirely possible that the hype surrounding the Modern Girl was driven in no small measure by men—including many conservatives—who found her titillating.

By the end of World War I, the Modern Girl had made her debut in Asia, where she scandalized the more conservative members of society. Her look and behavior, says Sumei Wang, "[signified] a separation from traditional Confucian influences and a progression toward global capitalism that involved high political and economic tension between East and West."[113] The most famous fictional portrayal of the Modern Girl in Asia was Jun'ichiro Tanizaki's wildly popular 1924 novel *Naomi*, whose depiction of *modan gaaru*, or *moga*, shocked a generation.[114] The archetype spread to Japan's colonies in Korea and Taiwan, as well as to China, Hong Kong, Singapore, Burma, and India.[115]

It was not until the early 1930s that the Modern Girl trend appeared in Vietnam. It was made possible by the breakdown of Confucian expectations for women, the rise of individualism, and increased exposure to Western culture. The Great Depression also played a role in furthering the trend. To escape the despair associated with economic downturn, some young women dreamed of a more edgy and glamorous version of themselves, and young men escaped into sexual fantasies. To a large extent, the Modern Girl at the heart of these male and female fantasies dwelled in the ethereal realm of media images, novels, and cinema. But she also manifested more concretely. Some rural young women desperate to support their families between harvests moonlighted as Taxi Girl sex workers in dance halls; others got a thrill simply out of dressing up for the night, whether in provocative western-style clothing or more modest (yet still alluring) Lemur tunic. With their flirtatious banter and sexy clothes, these young women must have seemed the epitome of the Modern Girl. Yet this was a fluid, transitory, and in many cases even fanciful identity. Most Modern Girls were likely just playing a role to sell—or luxuriate in—a sexualized image of modernity. Paradoxically, even the fulfillment of the fantasy was still a fantasy.[116]

Vietnamese Modern Girls were easily recognizable on the street. Their faces were caked with white powder, their eyes lavished with mascara and mauve eyeshadow, and their eyebrows plucked and arched; their chin-length hair was artificially waved and tucked under a felt cloche hat pulled low to create an air of mystery. They wore Western-style garments, and after 1934 the Lemur Tunic, both of which cut a slim yet curvy figure with bold shoulders, cinched waists, and darts to emphasize the breasts. Their blouses, sometimes made of chiffon so scandalously transparent that the wearer's camisole-like undergarment was plainly visible, were cut to showcase their décolletage. Other garments, most of them brightly colored, were made of shimmering fabric or even glittering sequins. Dresses and skirts stopped at mid-calf, revealing shapely legs punctuated by strappy high-heels, and toenails and fingernails were painted to match coral-colored lips. Dressed to impress, Modern Girls walked with their heads held high and a sway in their hips.

Modern Girls provoked controversy in Vietnamese society.[117] Their penchant for leisure activities such as sports, dancing, swimming, and sunbathing led them to use—and show off—their bodies in new and often scandalous ways. Frolicking in tiny bathing suits at a crowded beach or parading before an audience in beauty contests clearly violated Confucian edicts. Moreover, their love of low-cut dresses, flashy jewelry, and the latest model of handbag made it easy to dismiss them as vain, materialistic, and frivolous (xa xỉ). Their flirtations with men—most visible on the dance floor—fueled suspicions not only about their chastity but about the possibility that they engaged in part-time sex work. They also came under fire for their individualism, for refusing to submit to arranged marriages, and for living on their own.

Modern Girls were also an object of disdain for mainstreaming a style associated with me tây, Vietnamese women in a relationship with European men. "In the past, shaving black teeth, wearing white pants, wearing [Western] dresses—unconventional gestures—seemed to be the duty of Western wives. . . . They go first, then [the rest of the girls] follow,"[118] lamented the *Tràng An Báo* newspaper. The *Hà Thành Ngọ Báo* newspaper made a similar connection between me tây and Modern Girls:

> in most countries there is a vanguard of women who lead fashion reforms, usually upper-crust. In England it's the royals, in China it's the oligarchs or the international students. They are a model for all the women in the country to follow. In our country, who are the vanguard of women? The *me tây*. They profoundly influence the spirit of modern girls [*gái mới*]. They wear a hat, bring an umbrella, they wear a corset and white pants and a

cotton shirt, a coat, a fox fur. Then there's the hairdo, side parting, the white teeth, the purse, the dress . . . who knows whether tomorrow you'll cut your hair, wear a sleeveless shirt or a Shanghai dress. . . . [It is these women who] are the vanguard of our country's Europeanization.[119]

Notwithstanding the ubiquitous talk of Modern Girls in the press, films, novels, commercial advertisements, and fashion columns, they represented only a small portion of Vietnam's urban female population.[120] As the *Phụ Nữ Tân Văn* newspaper reminded readers, Modern Girls were hardly the norm; the vast majority of Vietnamese women were struggling to survive and had neither the time nor the money to keep up with fashion trends or indulge in leisure activities.[121]

Yet the Modern Girl made frequent appearances in media and literature, some of which are discussed elsewhere in this book. In the opening vignette of this book's introduction, the fictional Miss Anna Phiếm, mocked by the satirical Vịt Đực newspaper, was a Modern Girl. As you will see in chapter 3, Kếu, the protagonist of a short story by Nguyễn Công Hoan, who defied her conservative parents by sneaking out in makeup and colorful clothing, lived a fantasy life as a Modern Girl.[122] The Modern Girls in Nguyễn Đình Lạp's novel *Depraved Youth* wear slinky dresses and allow men to grope them at dance halls.[123] Hiền, the protagonist of Khái Hưng's novel *Trống Mái*, takes up with a fisherman, Vọi—a scandalous liaison given that she is an upper-class urbanite. Even more scandalous is her overt sexual desire portrayed through her obsession with Vọi's body, described as that of a "Greek god."[124]

Icons

Real-life icons likewise captured the public's imagination. The movie industry introduced Hollywood starlets, such as Greta Garbo and Marlene Deitrich, to audiences from Hanoi to Hà Tiên, and beauty pageants crowned the international sensation Agnes Souret, winner of France's first national beauty pageant in 1920, and local beauty queens such as Phung Thi Phat, winner of the 1936 beauty contest at the Faifoo (Hội An) fair.[125] Most iconic, however, was Vietnam's royal couple, particularly Empress Nam Phương, arguably Vietnam's first national celebrity, with her arresting beauty and cutting-edge style. These traditional monarchs were strikingly modern and thoroughly attuned to French culture.

THE DISSEMINATION OF BEAUTY TRENDS

In 1932, the nineteen-year-old Emperor Bảo Đại returned to Vietnam from Paris, where he had spent a decade studying at elite schools, to assume his official royal duties. When only nine years old, the young royal had been sent to the metropole as part of a larger colonial plan for Franco-Vietnamese collaboration. In Paris, the colonial government had done its best to cultivate—and manage—him, putting him up in a grand mansion on Avenue de Lamballe under the supervision of the former Resident Superior of Annam, Jean Charles and his wife.[126] Their efforts were successful, and the young Vietnamese emperor easily acclimated to French culture. Not only did he speak French without an accent, but he cut a fine figure in Western clothes, wore his hair short and slicked back, and left his teeth pearly white. He listened to French music on his grammaphone, played tennis with classmates, and romanced the young women Madame Charles—and others of her ilk—had handpicked for him. Upon leaving the metropole, Bảo Đại told the *Le Petit Parisien* newspaper that he owed his "intellectual formation" to France, and the metropolitan paper smugly noted that the Vietnamese emperor "has been conquered by modern ideas."[127]

In 1932, the colonial government quickly ushered Bảo Đại back to his home country, where they hoped he would provide an innocuous political alternative to the nationalist and communist movements that had recently gained traction.[128] Indeed, from a French perspective, he seemed to offer the best of both worlds: ostensible continuity with Vietnamese tradition along with adherence to the colonial project. Upon returning to Vietnam, the emperor was heralded by French- and Vietnamese-language newspapers as the "sincere spirit of Franco-Annamite collaboration," "un ami de la France," and the "modern emperor" (*vua tân thời*).[129] The colonial government sent the monarch on tours of Vietnam with state photographers documenting his every move. Although the young emperor initially donned the royal tunic, embroidered with a dragon and phoenix, he quickly changed his style and often wore a Western three-piece double breasted suit and brogue Oxford shoes, with his hair cut short and slicked down. He quickly developed a reputation for shirking his palace responsibilities in favor of tennis, golf, hunting, and vacationing—all leisure activities picked up in the metropole.[130]

In January 1933, at a dinner held at his Art Deco palace in Đà Lạt, the emperor was stunned by the arrival of a certain eighteen-year-old guest

THE DISSEMINATION OF BEAUTY TRENDS

FIGURE 1.3. Empress Nam Phương, c. 1934.
Source: Wikimedia commons.

in a bias-cut black silk dress. Paris-educated, the grand-niece of a wealthy Cochinchinese planter named Lê Phát Đạt, her name was Nguyễn Hữu Thị Lan but she was introduced to the emperor as Mariette Jeanne. Mariette was seated across from the emperor at the banquet table, where the two young adults conversed in French over dinner. Afterward, the emperor invited her to join him on the dance floor and was delighted by her ability to waltz and tango.[131]

On March 9, 1934, the royal palace officially announced the couple's engagement (figure 1.3). The emperor explained to his subjects that he had been searching for a woman who, like him, moved fluently between French and Vietnamese culture and gushed that his fiancée "reconciled the fine culture of Europe and the glorious spirit of East Asia." Yet the public was shocked by his choice. Instead of a young woman from one of the noble families in Huế, he had chosen a commoner from Cochinchina who was, moreover, entirely too Frenchified in the opinion of many Vietnamese. Most controversial of all was her Catholicism. Educated in a convent, she was likely to raise her children—including the future Vietnamese emperor—as Catholic.[132] Bảo Đại's royal advisors had objected to Mariette's religion and French cultural upbringing, but the emperor had shunned their counsel. Rumors swirled as to the true motivations behind the match. Had the young emperor actually rebuffed his royal advisors? Had the marriage been arranged by the colonial government to ensure that the empress would be a close ally of France? Or was the match a power play orchestrated by the governor of Cochinchina and Mariette's uncle for their own personal political gain?[133]

Soon after the royal couple's engagement, the *Phụ Nữ Tân Văn* newspaper—known for being very pro–New Woman—voiced its concerns about the royal couple's proclivities. The emperor, it asserted, was a playboy who would be more devoted to French leisure activities than to ruling his country, which was suffering through the Great Depression. As for the empress-to-be, her French education and embrace of French culture and Catholicism made it likely that she would eschew Vietnamese royal tradition as well as Confucian rites and Buddhist ceremonies.[134] However, *Phụ Nữ Tân Văn* went on to defend the emperor's decision to marry Mariette. It noted with approval that the engagement marked a victory for the Free Love movement, which championed the right of young adults to choose their own spouses rather than be forced into an arranged marriage. "Love is love, religion is religion," the paper concluded. "In marriage only love is important."[135]

The wedding took place on March 20, 1934. Mariette took the name Nam Phương, meaning "fragrance of the South." The streets of Huế were clogged with locals seeking a glimpse of the nineteen-year-old bride, who smiled at the crowd amid glittering camera flashes. The press delighted in reporting on the many sumptuous creations she wore at the four-day event, the likes of which commoners rarely encountered: embroidered silk tunics of the highest quality, hand sewn for the empress-to-be according to the traditions of the Nguyễn dynasty.[136] Perhaps most stunning of all was a silk five-panel dress hand painted with flowers. Arguably an appropriation of Vietnamese tradition, the dress was made with a technique recently developed at Hanoi's École des Beaux Arts and inspired by the silk watercolors on ceremonial scrolls.[137]

As the *Phụ Nữ Tân Văn* newspaper had predicted, Emperor Bảo Đại, and to a lesser extent Empress Nam Phương, quickly gained a reputation for indulging in French leisure activities—to excess in the opinion of many. They were rarely seen at the palace in Huế, preferring instead to hop around

THE DISSEMINATION OF BEAUTY TRENDS

what would become a collection of vacation homes gifted to them by the French government, presumably to secure Bảo Đại's loyalty.[138] The young emperor and empress were impressively sporty. His backhand was said to rival that of the tennis professionals Nhánh and Nữa, and he established the Cúp Bảo Đại tennis tournament to encourage his people to take up the game. He was frequently seen driving a swank Lincoln Model K to the golf course he had commissioned in Giạ Lê village, flying a plane over the Langbian plateau, or hunting tigers and elephants in the highlands.[139] As for the empress, she delighted fairgoers lucky enough to catch a glimpse of her marking the opening ceremonies of a local exposition. A belt highlighted her slim waist and butterfly cap sleeves showcased her arms; her head was adorned with a cloche hat decorated with felt flowers; and her feet sported high-heeled spectator shoes that matched those of her dapper husband (figure 1.4). Guests at royal banquets at Bảo Đại's vacation home in Đà Lạt swooned when the empress stepped out in a silvery silk evening dress with a draped neckline, cut on the bias to highlight her curves. Upon the debut

FIGURE 1.4. Emperor Bảo Đại and Empress Nam Phương c. 1934. *Source*: Wikimedia commons.

of the Lemur Tunic, the empress was said to have had a personal fitting with the designer himself, and it became her preferred style.[140] The press followed the empress's every fashion move through the fall of 1935, when her pregnancy with the future Prince Bảo Long began to show, at which point her image shifted from modern woman to mother.

Images of less celebrated icons shared news spreads. In the early 1930s, as New Women began cutting their hair and stepping out into society, the *Phụ nữ Tân Văn* newspaper ran stories on Huỳnh Thị Bảo Hoà and Bạch Liên. The intent of the articles was to present short haircuts as a means of supporting feminism, but they had the additional effect of glamorizing these two women.[141] The *Ngày Nay* newspaper transformed Trịnh Thục Oanh, a school mistress and public intellectual, into a fashion icon after interviewing her about her observations on fashion and the Lemur Tunic in particular.[142]

In the mid-1930s, a regular fixture on the Saigon social scene was Madeleine Bùi Quang Chiêu, the charming daughter of Bùi Quang Chiêu, a wealthy naturalized French citizen, an influential member of the Constitutionalist Party, and the director of the widely read *La Tribune Indochinoise* newspaper. Born in Cochinchina, Madeleine spent much of her early childhood in France, and when the family returned to the colony, she was educated in elite French colonial schools. She began her career as an accomplished pianist before traveling back to France, where she earned a certificate from the elite Klytia Beauty Institute. In 1934 she returned to the colony, and the following year she opened the posh Institute de Beauté Madeleine with the goal of bringing French beauty knowledge and high-quality metropolitan products to the women of Vietnam (see chapter 3). She owed her modest fame not just to her winning personality but to exhaustive press coverage from her father's publication.[143]

In the mid-1930s, Vietnam fell in love with Ái Liên. It was a love affair that would last all the way through the twentieth century (figure 1.5). Born in Hải Phòng in 1918, Ái Liên grew up in a musical family in Tonkin. She studied New Theater (Cải Lương) and as a young girl mastered both traditional Vietnamese and Western musical instruments. In 1934, then sixteen-year-old Ái Liên wowed the people of Tonkin with her dramatic and musical talents. She became the lead actress with *La Scène Tonkinois*, a theater group in Tonkin, scored a record deal with Beka Records, and by the late 1930s her "New Music" songs (featuring Vietnamese lyrics set to Western tunes) were played regularly on Saigon's radio station. Ái Liên

THE DISSEMINATION OF BEAUTY TRENDS

FIGURE 1.5. Winner of Hanoi beauty contest, Ái Liên, wearing a Lemur Tunic. In 1935, Ái Liên was already a famous Cải Lương actress and part of the La Scène Tonkinoise acting troup. She would go on to be a star of the tân nhạc music trend and even recorded for the Béka record label.
Source: Hà Thành Ngọ Báo newspaper, February 12, 1935.

became a celebrated member of the era's "new" arts movements. But it was her twinkling eyes, glamorous white smile, and girl next door looks that made her Vietnam's sweetheart. In 1935, she won a beauty contest at a fundraiser fair for victims of the floods in Annam and modeled the latest fashions at a fundraiser fair in Hà Đông. Newspapers tracked her performances all over Vietnam and even Cambodia and Laos. She eventually became the subject of a play about her own life—"The Story of Miss Ái Liên" (Truyện cô Ái Liên)—that recounted her rise to stardom and lovelorn male fans.[144]

It was largely the colonial modernization project promoting consumerism that enabled the dissemination of new beauty trends in Vietnam. Vietnamese women could now access global trends and make them their own. They admired the stylishly coiffed hair of beauty queens, copied the eye makeup of Hollywood starlets, researched the latest antiaging technologies, and clipped sketches of the Lemur Tunic from newspapers so their local tailor could reproduce them. They bought the styles displayed on department store mannequins and showed them off at the fair or on beach vacations. Modern Girls cast flirty glances at male passersby and New Women voiced strong opinions in the newspaper. Schoolgirls revered icons such as Nam Phương and Aí Liên and studiously followed the advice of the "experts" Nguyễn Cát Tường and Cô Duyên. The following chapters explore the historical development of the era's provocative new trends in fashion, cosmetics, body image, and beauty contests.

Chapter Two

FASHION

In 1932, the journalist Lang-Quê, writing for *Trung Lập Báo*, recalled a troubling encounter with a Frenchman outside Saigon's New Market (Bến Thành market). New to the colony, the Frenchman stood enrapt by the bustling city. From his perch he surveyed the chaos of cars and bicycles merging into the traffic circle at Place Eugène-Cuniac, laborers unloading goods at the Halles Centrales, and passengers boarding cars at the Chemins de fer de l'Indochine train station. But one thing in particular caught the Frenchman's attention. "What country's people wear sleep shirts [pajamas] . . . on the street?" he asked Lang-Quê incredulously.[1]

Pajama sets had indeed become a popular form of streetwear in Vietnam during the year before Lang-Quê's article was published. It is easy to see why. European pajamas were undeniably feminine and flattering, with their pastel colors, calico flowers, eyelet trim, and little fabric roses strategically placed at the dip of the neck. The light floaty fabric skimmed a woman's curves, hinting at her breasts, and the flutter sleeves showcased the upper arms. The empire waist, falling loosely under the bust, elongated the wearer's frame. Typically made of soft airy cotton, the pajamas were comfortable even in the tropical heat. The wide-leg palazzo-style pants even fit similarly to those worn under the familiar *áo bà ba*.

The Frenchman's remark about pajamas shook Lang-Quê to the core with embarrassment. The wearing of pajamas—however comfortable and flattering—on a busy city street was a violation of the new grammar of fashion that had developed in the West, particularly France, and was making its way to Vietnam. As industry modernized late in the Industrial Revolution, factories in Europe and the United States rushed to churn out high volumes and unprecedented varieties of ready-to-wear clothing. Inspired by nineteenth-century French preoccupations with the separation of private and public life, rules emerged dictating what specific articles of clothing should be worn in what particular contexts. These rules developed symbiotically with the concurrent rise of leisure activities among the middle class in the west. Tennis dresses were to be worn when chasing balls on the court, Spencer jackets were donned at special events and ceremonies, and evening dresses made appearances at balls or evenings at the opera. Pajamas, of course, were to be worn strictly within the intimate confines of one's own home or a hotel room. Fluency in this new grammar of fashion quickly came to be considered the mark of a modern person. However, as the Frenchman's remark highlighted, many Vietnamese had yet to understand the new rules—evidence that they were neither "modern" nor "civilized." The misuse of pajamas reflected on the nation as a whole, and Lang-Quê concluded: "Improper dress shows us that the Vietnamese people [barely have] a taste of Western civilization; instead, we are a primitive people, a nation eager to imitate.... What's the point of self-respect?"[2]

Lang-Quê belonged to a loosely affiliated coterie of journalists who were deeply concerned about the astonishing changes in women's fashion that were sweeping the nation during the years following World War I. These changes originated from the margins of society: me tây, women in relationships with Western men; a new generation of high school-educated girls; and rebellious young women, known as Modern Girls. These diverse groups popularized an equally diverse array of fashion trends, from brightly colored tunics and white pants to Western clothing that jarred many onlookers. In addition to the kinds of fashion faux pas mentioned by Lang-Quê, journalists were horrified by the vast sums of money being spent on fashion during the depths of the Great Depression and by the materialistic trend that was developing among young women even as the rest of the nation struggled to make ends meet.

Critics, mostly male, called for a "fashion reform campaign" (*cuộc vận động canh cải y phục*) of women's clothing, effectively commandeering a movement that had originated among marginalized women. The artist

Nguyễn Cát Tường stepped up to the plate and released his designs for a new national dress, the wildly popular Lemur Tunic. Newspapers published prescriptive articles teaching women the rules of fashion, including the types of clothing suitable for particular occasions, the colors appropriate for a certain hour of the day or season of the year, and silhouettes that best suited specific body types.

In this chapter, I argue that a new relationship developed between Vietnamese women and the clothing they put on their bodies during the interwar years. Journalists—many of them male proponents of Vietnamese Modernism—took it upon themselves to design a national Vietnamese dress and enforce the grammar of Western fashion. The time and place in which women wore certain articles of clothing either bespoke a certain cosmopolitan bourgeois savoir-faire or, if done improperly, resulted in a humiliating fashion faux pas. The stakes of a woman's fashion choices were higher than ever now that she was expected to represent her nation, a nation that was fighting to improve its image in a degrading colonial context.[3] Her personal taste and fluency in the new grammar of fashion, directed and critiqued by journalistic authority figures, were deemed a political responsibility. In sum, one of the most intimate acts, the dressing of one's own body, was now a matter of public debate.

SARTORIAL HISTORY

In the early twentieth century, the most common garments for women were four- and five-panel tunics, as well as the áo bà ba, a long-sleeved shirt with no collar that fell to the waist and buttoned down the front, all worn over pants. A nuanced pre-twentieth-century history of those garments is regretfully underexplored in Vietnamese studies.[4] In its earliest iteration, the four-panel tunic (*áo tứ thân*) appeared during the Lý-Trần period (1009–1400). This multipaneled tunic developed as a result of limitations in the weaving technology in Vietnam at the time.[5] The tunic, comprised of four panels sewn together along three vertical seams, was wrapped in front of the body and belted at the waist. The front and back of the tunic were stitched together only from the armpits to just below the waist, creating two flaps on either side below the waist. The length of the tunic varied over time, but for the most part it fell just above or just below the knees. The sleeves of the tunic fit snugly down to the wrists. In Tonkin and northern Annam, most commoners dyed their tunics various shades of brown or light purple using brown yam (*Dioscorea cirrhosa*), but some women in Cochinchina and southern Annam wore more colorful tunics. Noble women and members of the royal family wore yellow silk tunics that were painted or embroidered. Historically, the tunic was worn over a long skirt that covered the ankles. As the four-panel tunic created an opening across the front of the body, women covered their breasts with a *yếm*, a diamond-shaped piece of fabric in which straps from the top point were tied around the neck just below the throat and straps from the two side points were tied under the arms and around the back. Upper-class women embroidered the top of their yếm and braided the straps. By the late nineteenth century, women were adding a hint of color to their outfit by dying both the yếm and the belt bright colors.[6]

In the late eighteenth century, women began wearing a five-panel tunic (*áo ngũ thân*). The trend can be traced to the mid-eighteenth century when Võ Vương (Lord Nguyễn Phúc Khoát) enacted a series of reforms to distinguish the culture of the Nguyễn-controlled lands in the South from that of the Trịnh-controlled lands in the North.[7] Among those reforms was a 1744 decree introducing the áo ngũ thân for both men and women in Nguyễn-controlled land. Influenced by both Chinese and Cham fashion, the tunic included a flap that extended across the chest and a high-neck collar. The fifth flap crossed over the body and was held in place by a row of buttons that ran from the base of the neck to the underarms. The sleeves were relatively narrow and tapered to fit snuggly at the wrist. As the fifth flap covered the chest, it eliminated the need for a yếm, the diamond shaped fabric worn under the four-panel tunic designed to hold the breasts and cover the décolletage.[8] The short, raised collar of the five-panel tunic was typically worn open. The five-panel tunic, designed to hang loosely on the body without a sash, cut a slightly boxy silhouette. Like the four-panel tunic, the seams connecting the front and back panels ended below the waist, creating flaps that swished when the wearer walked. Women had traditionally worn the four-panel tunic over a skirt, but they wore the five-panel tunic over pants. During the Tây Sơn Rebellion (1770–1802) and resulting large-scale migrations, the popularity of the five-panel tunic spread. By the time of unification in 1802, the five-panel tunic had become the garment of choice in the North, but women in the South continued to wear both the five- and four-panel tunics.[9]

In the mid-nineteenth century, Vietnamese women began wearing pants under their tunics, a style that has endured into the twenty-first century. In 1802, Emperor Gia Long embarked on a campaign to modernize the newly unified Vietnam according to the Chinese model. His successor, Ming Mạng, followed suit, aiming for large-scale cultural reform that also followed the Chinese model. The edicts, issued between 1828 and 1837, outlawed skirts, which were associated with the old order and deemed scandalous for providing inadequate coverage of the female groin. Pants, held up with a drawstring waist, were baggy with straight legs and typically fell to the ankle. Women rolled them up while working in the wet rice paddies. As Alexander Woodside points out, however, only urban women were likely to follow these edicts; pants were too expensive for peasant women to purchase, and some of these women continued to wear skirts through the mid-twentieth century.[10] The pants worn by urban women were typically dark brown or navy. The exception was wealthy women in the central region near Huế, typically wives of court officials who lived a life of leisure and could afford to wear white pants, which required extra care and laundering.

Four- and five-panel tunics continued to dominate the Vietnamese landscape through the end of World War I. Loom technology developed to allow for eighty centimeter panels, enabling a three-panel tunic (*áo dài ba thân*) as well.[11] The five-panel tunic was mostly popular in urban areas, and the four-panel wrap dress belted at the waist could still be seen in the countryside. Also popular among both men and women in urban and rural areas was the áo bà ba, a collarless long-sleeved shirt that buttoned down the front. It fell to the hips and had pockets and split sides. Little is known about the garment's history, but it is believed to have originated in Penang.[12]

Until the interwar period, Vietnamese women's tunics continued to be made of dark-colored fabric, typically brown. Those wearing four-panel tunics continued to accent their outfit with colorful belts or yếm.[13] Women occasionally wore brighter-colored tunics for holidays and ceremonies, and white tunics were reserved for funerals and anniversaries of deaths. Only sex workers wore bright colors such as red or blue. "You certainly didn't see bright colors like butterflies or garden flowers among the women of the North," groused the journalist female Phan Thị Nga.[14] Both the four- and five-panel garments were worn by men and women alike, with similar silhouettes and only slight differences in length and width. The pants worn underneath the five-panel tunic were typically made of black satin (*lĩnh thâm*) or maroon or brown crepe (*nhiễu*); as was the case in the past, white pants were worn only by wealthy women in the country's central region.[15]

Women of the pre–World War I period accessorized with a wide-brimmed flat round hat (*nón quai thao*) tied under the chin with a sash, sandals that curved up at the toe, multistranded necklaces of jade or glass beads, and three or four gold bracelets on the wrist.[16] They carried small belongings—coins, betel seed, tobacco—in a satchel or a bamboo paper wrapper tucked into a pocket in the seam of their belt.[17]

THE CHANGING FASHION LANDSCAPE

The first major changes in the colonial Vietnamese fashion landscape occurred with men's clothing. In the late nineteenth and early twentieth centuries, middle-class men throughout the urban areas of Asia began to adopt elements of Western dress and cut their hair in the Western style. The male suit, which had gained popularity in the West during the 1890s, was adopted by urban elite men in Japan, China, the Philippines, Burma, and Siam in the early twentieth century.[18] Western clothing, Nguyễn Văn Vĩnh writes, first appeared among a small subset of Vietnamese men who served in the colonial military or bureaucracy. Western clothing, he explains, was functional: jackets warmed men in the winter, pith helmets shaded their eyes better than the hat made of latanier palm leaves, and leather shoes protected their feet from cold and humidity more so than traditional shoes.[19]

As discussed in the introduction of this book, Western-style suits would not become popular among Vietnamese men until nationalist leaders promoted them. Inspired by trends in Japan, in 1906 reformist mandarins Phan Châu Trinh and Nguyễn Quyền called on Vietnamese men to cut their hair and wear Western-style suits. The trend immediately caught on among urban and upper-class men. By 1907, even Emperor Thành Thái was wearing Western clothing.[20] By the eve of World War I, it was not uncommon to see Vietnamese men strolling down the streets of Hanoi, Hải Phòng, or Saigon in three-piece suits. The Western suit had become the uniform among urban middle- and upper-class Vietnamese men by the 1930s.[21]

Vietnamese women's fashion during this period evolved in quite a different manner. Whereas the changes in men's fashion trickled down to the masses from on high, the changes in women's fashion developed more organically, exemplifying what fashion historians identify as trickle-up theory. Rather than the intelligentsia, it was instead a variety of unlikely, low-status populations—me tây, schoolgirls, and rebellious young women known as Modern Girls—who led the female fashion revolution.

Me Tây Style

As discussed in chapter 1, the first women to embrace Western fashion were me tây, women involved in sexual relations with Western men. In the late nineteenth century, a few me tây began to appear on the scene sporting white teeth, unbound breasts, and a hint of French perfume. For the most part, me tây continued to wear four- and five-panel tunics, a decision influenced as much by their own modesty as by their paramours' taste for "exotic" women. By the eve of World War I, however, me tây fashion had become a popular trend, inspired by the growing number of French women migrating to the colony. In both the city and rural areas, me tây began appearing in brightly colored or even white Western dresses with cinched waists. But because mixed-race relationships between Vietnamese women and the colonizer—even high-society marriages—were few in number and, more important, taboo in Vietnamese culture, me tây's Western fashion trends remained countercultural and hence potentially risky.[22] Women who dressed in the me tây style—whether they had Western lovers or not—could face accusations of sexual promiscuity or even prostitution.

White Pants and Colorful Tunics

After World War I, a visually arresting change in palette emerged in urban areas among female wearers of the five-panel tunic. A new trend, dubbed the "movement to shave teeth white, wear white pants," developed in which women swapped their traditional black and brown attire for white pants and a colorful tunic.[23] Dark pants had long been the trend in part because they proved functional in an agrarian society, where peasant women worked in the dirt and often ended the day with mud stains on their pants.[24] Since plowing the fields was not a concern for these urbanites, they were comfortable in more delicate colors. As mentioned previously, the exception was in Huế, the old imperial capital, where indigo tunics and white crepe pants had long been popular among the wealthy, who could afford the regular laundering they required.[25]

Historians know very little about the origins of the white pants and colorful tunics.[26] The trend likely commenced with the 1915 opening of the Collège des jeunes filles indigènes in Saigon, which required a uniform of white pants and a purple tunic, earning it the nickname "Purple Shirt School" (*trường áo tím*). Soon girls from schools throughout Cochinchina were wearing white pants and had moved beyond purple to brighter colors, which was likely influenced by French fashion. It is hardly surprising that the trend would commence with schoolgirls who were the first generation of young women to be exposed to French culture and art on a regular basis. But other factors likely bolstered the trend. The first decades of the twentieth century saw a proliferation of "Bombay shops," like the Pohoomull Frères and Nihalchand Bros. on Rue Catinat, which sold bright-colored fabrics imported from India.[27] Meanwhile, per the instructions from the minister of colonies, French women donned crisp white linens. They also sported their own style of colorful and patterned dresses, though more muted and demure than the Indian equivolents.[28] This style was not entirely foreign to Vietnam, because wealthy women in Huế had historically worn white pants. It is important to note that this new fashion trend was only a change in color palette; neither the form nor the function of the traditional garments was altered. By the end of the decade, the trend had spread to young women in urban areas of Cochinchina and Annam, but it was not yet widespread in Tonkin.[29]

By the late 1920s, white pants and colorful tunics had become more than just a pretty outfit. Proponents of the new look claimed that it would improve the international image of Vietnam, whose traditional black pants and dark tunics had long given the country what they considered a dreary look. Yet detractors clung to their disapproval, and even fear, of the outfit—understandably, given that white was traditionally worn at funerals and was thus associated with death and mourning. An article in *Hà Thành Ngọ Báo* reassured leery readers that Chinese regarded white as the most beautiful color and that Europeans associated white with purity.[30] Indeed, it was black, not white, that Europeans wore to funerals. While the Vietnamese were debating the meaning of the color white, the French underwent a remarkably similar rethinking of the color black, also associated with funerals and death. Like Vietnam's white pants and colorful tunics,

FASHION

Coco Chanel's Little Black Dress—intended to be worn at cocktail parties or formal dinners—instigated a veritable liberation from rigid and long-standing cultural confines of mourning.[31] By the early 1930s, proponents of Vietnam's new look had found another argument with which to justify it. Drawing from the new rhetoric about bodily hygiene (see chapter 4), they claimed that white pants were "more hygienic" than traditional black or brown pants because dirt had nowhere to hide amid the pristine white fibers.[32] The exception was during menses, when women were still expected to wear black pants to hide the color of blood because menstruation was seen as a form of defilement.[33]

By the mid-1930s, white pants and colorful tunics had become ubiquitous in urban areas. With the 1934 release of Nguyễn Cát Tường's Lemur Tunic and the wild popularity that it enjoyed, white pants became normalized and even came to be considered as respectable as the more traditional dark pants.[34]

As white pants grew in popularity throughout the 1930s, the color of women's pants became a marker of class, locale, and degree of cosmopolitanism. White pants came to be associated with modernity, with one reporter remarking that it was easy to distinguish between "modern" Hanoi women and those from the countryside. The Hanoi women wore white pants with pink, purple, or blue tunics; those from outside the city wore brown tunics and brown pants.[35] Black pants developed a negative image as they came to be associated with the peasants who worked long days in the rice fields and were considered dirty.[36]

The trend of white pants and colorful tunics nonetheless had its detractors. A 1929 article in *Hà Thành Ngọ Báo* reported that some considered white pants vulgar.[37] Even in 1934, many women in Tonkin still found themselves on the receiving end of sneering whispers when they ventured out in white pants.[38] As late as 1936, the journalist Hoàng-Đạo noted the hypocrisy of the many male detractors: "Men let their teeth go white, cut their top knot, and ditch their tunics for neat, Western clothing. People thought that was an improvement, but when women started wearing white pants they flew into a passion, called in an army of opposition . . . [the women] were met by a reactionary conservative army."[39]

Most controversial of all was the fact that young women drew attention to themselves when wearing white pants and bright tunics. During an era in which intellectuals struggled with the rise of individualism among the youth, such showiness was frowned upon. Moralists even feared that the bright colors adorning the young women would excite lecherous men.[40] Indeed, in his 1937 novel *To Be a Whore* (*Làm đĩ*), Vũ Trọng Phụng associates white pants with a loss of virtue. Huyền, the protagonist, traces her decent into prostitution to the moment when she began wearing white pants. She explains to the reader that white pants—originally worn only by the colony's dubious population of me tây—have come to be associated with a carefree lifestyle of going to the theater, the fair, and dance halls. She faces backlash from her teachers, her mother, and her aunties, all of whom urge her to stick with the dark pants that make her appear virtuous. Yet Huyền enjoys feeling fashionable and appreciates the glamorous set of new friends she has made while sporting the new style. Reflecting on her decent into sex work, she identifies this seemingly simple change in wardrobe as what led her into sex work. To Huyền, "the white pants are representative of all vanity and loss."[41]

Western Clothing

A second major shift in the Vietnamese fashion scene occurred in the late 1920s: Vietnamese women—not just me tây—began wearing Western clothing. As French women were moving to the colony in increasing numbers, department stores and ready-to-wear clothing stores rushed to cater to their fashion whims with garments imported from the metropole. During the interwar years, Vietnam was flooded with Western garments and accessories, each with its own designated function. Perhaps the two biggest changes in Vietnamese fashion during the interwar years were the sheer variety of pieces (day dresses, evening dresses, smoking jackets, and evening jackets) and the range of specific occasions on which they were to be worn. The market for Western clothing expanded beyond French women to the emergent middle-class Vietnamese female consumers.

Skirts, day dresses, and evening gowns transformed the plainest women into graceful icons of Western femininity (figure 2.1). Thin Bombay dresses comprised of brightly colored silk slinked over the curves of dancing girls. Trousers and button-down blouses designed for women flirted with the limits of gender-appropriate clothing. New silhouettes differentiated women from men, whereas the five-panel tunic had given men and women the same silhouette. In the 1920s, knee-length skirts showed off women's

FIGURE 2.1. Evening dresses.
Source: La Depeche Indochinoise, March 7, 1929.

legs; in the 1930s, hemlines went down but clothing began hugging women's curves. Western corsets cinched women's waists, brassieres shaped and uplifted their breasts, and padding augmented the breasts and buttocks of less endowed women.[42]

Certain garments fostered a new sense of privacy or intimacy in the wearers. Pajamas, bathrobes (*robes de chambre*), and indoor coats (*vestons d'interieur*) provided both luxury and comfort in the privacy of one's home. Camisoles and nightgowns in pastel shades of silk or chiffon were cut on the bias and featured spaghetti straps and plunging necklines that showcased the décolletage. In 1934, the actress Claudette Colbert wore men's pajamas in the Hollywood film *It Happened One Night* and single-handedly launched a gender-bending alternative trend.[43]

In the late 1920s, the "sporting movement" sparked a new market for athletic clothing (see chapter 4). To enable greater mobility, sporting attire

FIGURE 2.2. Tennis jumpers.
Source: *La Depeche Indochinoise*, June 30, 1932.

featured shorter sleeves, stretchy, tighter-fitting fabrics, and in some cases shorts and skirts that threatened to reveal naked knees. Bathing suits, squash shorts, and Lacoste tennis dresses flew off the racks of Maison Giao Sports, the main supplier of Cochinchina's sporting craze, and women stocked up on clothing "suitable for a strong and agile gait."[44] Shorts allowed women to jump or lunge to catch a badminton birdie or pedal their bicycles without their longer traditional Vietnamese pants getting caught in the gears. At the beach or swimming pool, tight-fitting swimsuits may literally have been lifesaving, sparing women the anguish of being pulled down by the voluminous tunics they had worn in the water and drowning.[45] White dresses and pleated skirts bounced around tennis courts and short-sleeved shirts freed women to extend their arms and slam a serve (figure 2.2). Sneakers, often manufactured with Vietnam's own rubber products, gave women speed on the court.[46]

Sneakers were just one of many new shoe styles to appear in Vietnamese stores during the interwar period. Self-important leather-laced shoes completed men's three-piece suits. High heels elongated the female leg, which was only now being revealed to the public. Lower kitten heels teased onlookers with their more demure sex appeal. Bare toes, their nails painted a flirtatious pink, peeked out of open-toe strappy heels.[47]

Vietnamese consumers were introduced to new materials from Europe. French wool was spun into cozy sweaters perfect for chilly Tonkin winters, although only the wealthy could afford it. New technologies enabled the arrival of synthetic fabrics such as rayon and acetate. Invented in the nineteenth century but not popularized until after World War I, rayon was an affordable alternative to silk that was touted for its durability and used to produce the revolutionary run-resistant shirt (*la chemisette indémaillable*). The Basty store in Saigon urged customers to come see the shirt for themselves and "pay tribute to [the French empire's] technological progress." Synthetic chiffon fabric—used among other things as a translucent veil over what would otherwise be a scandalously revealing dress—was another popular innovation. Initially made of silk and thus prohibitively expensive, nylon-based chiffon became accessible to all classes in the late 1930s thanks to new technology. Trench coats treated with chemicals to make them water resistant kept expensive clothing dry, and rubber slip-ons shielded men's leather shoes from Vietnam's tropical rains.[48]

In the 1930s, fashion was designed to show off female curves. Dresses cut on the bias gave fabric a slight stretch that accentuated the curvier parts of the body. Halter and strapless gowns exposed the back and upper chest. Sheer fabrics, such as voile and chiffon, hinted at what lay beneath.[49] Lingerie, a new development in Vietnam, emphasized curves—cinching waists and pushing breasts up and out—and soon became a fashion statement in its own right. After World War I, as hemlines rose, undergarments were cut smaller (figure 2.3). Bras, slips, and panties, available in silk or the less costly rayon, came in a variety of colors and prints with decorative details such as roses or lace trim sewn on.[50]

"Clothing should enhance and embellish one's natural beauty, not cover it up. Soon clothing will progress . . . [and] will no longer cover up anything at all,"[51] declared the lead designer at the Europeanization Tailor Shop in Vũ Trọng Phụng's satirical novel *Dumb Luck*. Ever the anthropologist, Vũ Trọng Phụng wittily drew attention to the relationship between fashion trends and changes in women's sexuality. Speaking to what Rolland Barthes would later term the semiotics of fashion, Vũ Trọng Phụng demonstrates

FIGURE 2.3. Advertisement for lingerie shop.
Source: La Depeche Indochinoise, January 19, 1939.

how the naming of sartorial objects provokes desire—in both the onlooker and the potential buyer.[52] The protagonist of the novel works at the Europeanization Tailor Shop, where he sells slinky outfits and lingerie sets that are given names that speak to the contradiction between the idealism of urban middle-class women's yearnings and the crassness of modern sexuality. Outfits with the demure names of "Innocence" and "Promise"—intended to "reassure her boyfriend that she promises to show up for their date that evening"—actually speak to the rise in premarital sex in the colony. "Win His Heart," designed to make "men like putty in the hands of the girls who wear this outfit," says more about the newly aggressive sexuality of its wearer than about the outfit itself. The outfit "Women's Rights," a showstopper, is reserved "for women whose husbands are afraid of them." Widows who have violated the tradition of chastity—one of the Confucian Threefold Dependencies—are outfitted in the sarcastically named "Resolute Faithfulness" or "Hesitation." Such fashions shock the public: "Young girls today dress even more provocatively than the *me tây* of the past! So modern! So slutty! My God!" exclaims a customer at the Europeanization Tailor Shop.[53] Even the Lemur Tunic, which was part of a nationalist strategy to showcase the elegance of the Vietnamese nation, found its true success in revealing the wearer's figure. Although he carefully covered the arms, nape, and legs, Nguyễn Cát Tường added darts under the bust to showcase the "gentle, lovely curves" of the female form.[54]

The concept of accessorizing an outfit delighted Vietnamese consumers, male and female alike. Displaying their newly acquired French manners, men tipped their Mossant or Fléchet hats at ladies passing on the street and adjusted their Western-style ties or French cravats before making important announcements.[55] By the mid-1930s, urbanites had replaced traditional wide-brimmed hats with tassels for the European-made wide-brimmed picture hats that they wore tipped to one side or the narrow fitting cloche hats that flattered shorter hairstyles.[56] The local parasol industry was effectively killed off when black German-made umbrellas took over the fashion landscape. Indeed, umbrellas came to function not just as shields from tropical rainstorms but as status symbols carried about in dry weather to convey a sense of Western sophistication.[57] Sunglasses also enjoyed a dual role, shielding the wearer's eyes from the hot tropical sun while imparting an unmistakable European cool.

Smaller accessories enabled consumers to individualize their outfits. Jewelry had a long tradition in Vietnam. Women wore gold earrings, gold or pearl necklaces, and bangles of jade, gold, or silver, which served as a form of portable, visible wealth for young women.[58] During the interwar years, new forms of jewelry, including earrings, necklaces, and wrist watches, signaled the wearer's class status by their quality.[59] Two- or three-strand necklaces of larger glass or jade beads adorned the neck.[60] Gemstone set jewelry such as diamonds and aquamarine (both new imports from Europe) or jade, rubies, and sapphires (from Vietnam and other areas of Asia) were now accompanied by certificates of authenticity.[61] Newlyweds pledged their commitment to one another with engagement rings, a ritual that was itself a French import. The *plaque d'identitie*, a small gold rectangle with the owner's name and date of birth engraved on it, was an upgrade of World War I era soldiers' "dog tags."[62]

By the 1930s, the animal kingdom served as a rich resource for fashion products: snake skin covered handbags and wallets, fox furs warmed the wearer, and leopard print fabric added a whiff of adventure to an outfit. Even pet dogs served as an unlikely accessory. Wealthy men and women strolled city streets with their purebred Terriers, Spaniels, Beagles, Bulldogs, and Pomeranians—whose Western heritage could be ascertained with official paperwork—or Japanese and Chinese breeds such as the Chow Chow and Pekinese. The owners often treated these pets better than they treated the human servants who worked in their homes. In Tonkin particularly, where dog meat was still a delicacy, such pets made quite a statement.[63]

As Vietnamese women began wearing more Western clothing and accessories, a new archetype emerged: Modern Girls. As mentioned in chapter 1, the Modern Girl was a global archetype that appeared in cities from New York to Shanghai. Modern Girls were easily recognizable by their Western wardrobe. With their bright colors, polka dots, ruffles, animal prints, and profusion of accessories (hats, pins, earrings, embroidered purses), they commanded the attention of onlookers.[64] Their dresses cut a slim figure with a narrow waist. Vertical darts down the bodice highlighted the curve of the breast. Hemlines skimmed just below the knee. Flowy fabrics and gored skirts gave movement to garments, creating the illusion that their wearers were floating down the street. Lace and sheer fabrics covered shoulders and necklines, per the fashion norms of the day, yet fed onlookers' imagination as to what was underneath. For more daring Modern Girls, necklines dropped low to reveal the décolletage, and Western corsets and brassieres pushed breasts up and out. Short sleeves revealed Modern Girls' upper arms; high-cut swimsuits exposed their thighs. High heels, kitten heels, and strappy sandals sexualized their feet. With shorter skirts, bare arms, low-cut blouses, belted waists, and darted bustlines, Modern Girl fashion signaled sexual lasciviousness. Modern Girl clothing came to symbolize moral failings. Modern Girls with their flirtatious Western style were a matter of grave concern to the new intelligentsia, whose members voiced their opinions—often stridently—in newspaper articles.

THE CLOTHING REFORM CAMPAIGN

By the early 1930s, the dramatic visual changes in the fashion landscape resulting from the trend of bright colors and Western styles had led to a campaign to reform women's clothing (*cuộc vận động canh cải y phục*).[65] Calls for clothing reform were part of a larger trend of politicizing clothing, particularly in areas of Asia that were grappling with colonialism and foreign interference. Proposed reforms manifested in different, even contradictory ways. One approach—more nuanced and intellectually sophisticated than it might have appeared—was to embrace the clothing of the colonizer. In Vietnam in 1907–08, the Tonkin Free School advised students to wear suits, and during the interwar years the ethnic Indian community called for a "clothing crusade," encouraging its members to dress like Westerners to increase their respectability.[66] A similar call to wear Western attire would be made in Thailand at the end of the 1930s.[67] Yet women's wear remained a more sensitive subject. In Burma and the Dutch Indies, conservatives fell into an uproar about the growing popularity of Western clothing among their women.[68] China's New Republic government, likewise concerned, issued a series of decrees policing schoolgirls and banning flashy or revealing clothing in the general female population.[69] A third sartorial response to the insults of colonialism was the creation of a new national dress, which occurred in the interwar Philippines and, as you will see, in Vietnam during the early 1930s.[70] This simple and elegant-sounding solution placed a heavy responsibility (arguably, a burden) on women to select daily outfits that would reflect well on the nation. Women's fashion during this period assumed what might be considered an inordinate level of political importance—certainly far more than in previous years.

Between 1929 and 1934, three major developments–economic, aesthetic, and political—led critics to scrutinize and critique women's fashion choices and call for reforms in women's dress.

ECONOMIC REFORMS   The initial discussions of Vietnam's clothing reform campaign developed in the context of economic nationalism. In 1929, as the world economic crisis was hitting Vietnam in the form of a collapse of rubber and rice markets, many Vietnamese grew weary of their country's dependence on the global economy. Among many other economy-centered discussions taking place at the time, the *Phụ Nữ Tân Văn* newspaper lamented the "internationalization" of the textile industry that had accompanied French colonization, thereby threatening Vietnam's financial autonomy. Early colonial economic policies effectively eliminated most of Cochinchina's weaving villages, and many in Tonkin and Annam, replacing them with French and Chinese owned industrial textile factories. After World War I, the colony began importing increasing amounts of Chinese, Indian, and American cotton due to a decrease in domestic cultivation.[71] In 1929, as economic nationalism grew in response to the financial insecurity felt on the eve of the Great Depression, the *Phụ Nữ Tân Văn* newspaper called on women to buy Vietnamese-produced silk, cotton, and satin as part of a "localization" of the textile economy, citing as a precedent the successful Indian boycott of British cloth.[72] Despite these efforts, by 1930 the local textile industry had contracted. A female journalist writing for *Hà Thành Ngọ Báo* urged readers to spend money on locally produced clothing—with the assumption they were constructed with locally grown textiles—instead of foreign fashions and criticized stores for only stocking foreign goods.[73] According to a female Vietnamese journalist, the textiles and garments arriving from Bombay and Shanghai were of low quality, with gaudy prints and an unmistakable "stench."[74]

As the Great Depression sent shockwaves through the Vietnamese economy, plunging peasants deeper into poverty, critics lambasted Modern Girls and other fashionistas for their consumerism. In the winter and spring of 1930, the *Hà Thành Ngọ Báo* newspaper published a series of articles on the topic. In January, a female journalist Phạm Thị Lan Khanh criticized women who let themselves become "slaves" to superficial trends.[75] In February and March a journalist who signed as T. T. complained that women of little means were squandering their money on new clothing and even going into debt as a result, a possible nod to the fact that sex workers went into debt bondage when paying for clothing that was necessary to attract clients.[76] "This life is too materialistic," T. T. declared. The journalist groused that women obsessed with fashion "consider clothing more important than dignity" and urged readers to shed the destructive habit of "dressing frivolously."[77] That April, a female journalist named Mỹ-Chân skewered women's obedience to the cult of fashion: "This 'fad' now, tomorrow another 'fad.' . . . In the morning you wear this kind of shirt, change at noontime, and in the afternoon change to something else."[78] The *Phụ Nữ Tân Văn*, run by New Women, also scorned the trend in Western clothing as inconvenient and untenable for women working in the fields; such clothing was useful only for wealthy urbanites indulging in a night on the town.[79] What *Phụ Nữ Tân Văn* authors failed to realize was that some of the women sporting Western attire at dance halls or on busy streets were actually impoverished peasant women who had migrated to the city to earn a living as Taxi Girls—and sometimes as unregistered sex workers. For such women, "frivolous" Western garments were a pragmatic and even necessary investment.[80]

FASHION

AESTHETIC REFORMS   Around 1932 Vietnam's urban economies began to pick up, even as its rural economy remained stalled. Middle-class women could once again afford to indulge in leisure activities and the fashion and beautification rituals that so often accompanied them. With economic privation a thing of the past for these women, the colony's clothing reform campaign underwent a radical shift of focus. No longer did the movement censure women for being too materialistic; instead, it called on women to look more elegant. Such calls—informed by Art Deco modernism, mass production of affordable accessories, and Franco-Vietnamese collaboration of the post-World War I era—encouraged women to consider clothing within the context of art and aesthetics.

During the interwar years, Western perspectives on art entered the Vietnamese public sphere. From 1918 to 1940, more than one thousand Vietnamese youth traveled to the metropole to study at French universities.[81] Some stayed abroad, but most returned with a new, European-influenced perspective not only on painting and sculpture but on aesthetics generally. In 1925, when Hanoi's École des Beaux Arts opened its doors to train students in Vietnamese and European art techniques and theory, a new Western-influenced conversation about aesthetics began in Vietnam. The school's first class graduated in 1930, and many of its alumni became public intellectuals who weighed in on discussions of aesthetics in the Vietnamese press, including the architect Nguyễn Cao Luyện, artist and writer Nhất Linh, and the painters Tô Ngọc Vân, Lê Phổ, and Nguyễn Cát Tường (see chapter 1). These latter two would play a significant role in the clothing reform campaign and go on to become very influential in the world of Vietnamese fashion and beauty.[82]

One did not need to be enrolled in a French art school to notice the significant aesthetic changes taking place in Vietnam during the interwar years. In the late 1920s, the "modern" art movement, which is best known by its later moniker "Art Deco," became a global craze, and its sleek lines and modernist aesthetic were soon transforming the Depression era urban Vietnamese landscape. Back pages of newspapers showcased highly stylized advertisements for Amilcar automobiles and Odeon records; cafés hung colorful promotions for Fred Zizi Apéritifs; and train stations displayed arresting travel posters of locomotives barreling across the Paul Doumer bridge. Colonial fairs exhibited the latest household appliances, including sculptured enamelware refrigerators in jadeite green, chrome-plated toasters with sleek lines, and Bakelite table clocks decorated with geometric motifs. Department store windows displayed hefty armoires and extravagant vanities made of exotic wood—much of which had been sourced in Vietnam before being sent off to factories in Europe—and embellished with chevron inlays. Inside, cosmetics counters proudly showed off jewel-like Coty compacts featuring abstract symmetrical designs. Boutiques hung bold Art Deco wallpaper as a backdrop for their cases of colorful Bakelite costume jewelry. Trading companies imported decorative housewares such as ashtrays, teapots, and mirrors, edged with motifs that resembled those found on the recently discovered tomb of Egypt's King Tutankhamun.

Yet one could discern the colony's Art Deco aesthetic without even setting foot in a department store, trading company, boutique, or fairground. The postwar construction boom in urban areas introduced public buildings such as the René Robin hospital, the Hanoi post office, and the Bank of Indochine with stylized wrought iron and *bas relief* ornamentation. By the mid-1930s, whole neighborhoods of single family Art Deco homes and apartment buildings had materialized near Hanoi's train station, just southwest of Hoàn Kiếm lake.[83] The Art Deco font used on mastheads of newspapers such as *Loa* or *Sài Thành*, print advertisements, and storefront signs transformed letters into geometric shapes, easily integrating the diacritic markets of the quốc ngữ lettering system into its futuristic design—and rendering them nearly unintelligible in the process, as Vũ Trọng Phụng famously mocked in his novel *Dumb Luck*.[84]

The Art Deco invasion of Vietnam's cities yielded two important perspectives that would underpin the clothing reform campaign. First, the conspicuous style and wide reach of the Art Deco campaign—from paintings to sculpture, posters to newspaper advertisements, furniture to perfume bottles—were striking even to the untrained eye. One could not help but notice the bold shapes that pointed skyward and the stylized motifs and "exotic" ornamentation in all aspects of material culture. Moreover, given that Deco-themed products were mass-produced from cheap materials and hence relatively inexpensive, they facilitated the growth of materialism and consumerism among a population that seldom indulged in trendy accessories for the home or other small luxuries.

FASHION

Second, the futuristic aesthetic of Art Deco established an undeniable link between modernity and material objects. Most Vietnamese were accustomed to a traditional Chinese-influenced aesthetic that prioritized tradition and historical precedent. With its imposing geometric shapes evoking images of machines and abundant visual references to ancient Egypt or Timbuktu, Art Deco struck a bold contrast to this familiar aesthetic, thereby introducing an entirely new way of looking at the constructed world. Not just its references to machines and modernity but its dizzying unfamiliarity must have made the viewer feel that the future had arrived. Women's clothing would henceforth be considered within the broader context of art and aesthetics introduced by Art Deco. Among other things, fashion would be assessed for its level of modernity. Women themselves, by extension, were judged by the clothing they wore. The more modern and cosmopolitan the outfit, the more progressive the wearer was presumed to be—and the more she was contributing, in her own small way, to the progress of the Vietnamese nation itself. Vũ Trọng Phụng makes this point in his satirical novel *Dumb Luck* when the clothing designer Mr. TPYN proclaims: "Every time someone buys a new modern outfit, our country will have another progressive person."[85]

These new perspectives on aesthetics would inform the clothing reform campaign. Although art theory was not invoked in debates about women's clothing until 1934, articles critiquing women's fashion began appearing in Vietnamese language newspapers as early as 1930. Most articles simply mocked women who mimicked French style in ways that were deemed uncouth. Writing for *Hà Thành Ngọ Báo* in 1930, the journalist T. T. lambasted not all women who wore Western clothing, only those who mismatched styles or otherwise betrayed their ignorance about the proper way to put together an outfit.[86] "The head is wearing a French hat, but the feet are wearing Chinese shoes,"[87] complained a journalist for *Hà Thành Ngọ Báo* in a 1933 article. The journalist Lang-Quê, whose article opened this chapter, lamented that Vietnamese people's "passion for imitation" resulted in "ridiculous ways of dressing"—what he identified as the fashion equivalent of Franco-Viet patois (*tiếng ba toa*), the mix of French and Vietnamese language that many upper-class Vietnamese associated with pretention and a lack of good breeding.[88] No matter what Vietnamese women wore, the female journalist Song Nguyệt warned, French women would never respect them. In a mordant piece of imagery, she even went so far as to suggest that French women would never see them as anything but "monkeys dressed in human clothes, with their tail sticking out."[89] These issues were far from trivial, as evidenced by the chorus of other journalists echoing these sentiments. Vietnamese women should not risk making a mockery of their nation. No less than the international image of Vietnam was at stake.

Indeed, critics of the new fashion trends began to link individual women's clothing choices to the national image, effectively making women responsible for representing the nation. That this association between fashion and the image of the nation occurred in the early 1930s is hardly surprising given the politics of the day. Penny Edwards observes that state-supported colonial ethnographers famously classified people according to their dress, and consequently "refigured clothing as a boundary marker of race and nation." In this era of racialized social sciences, many European and American anthropologists and colonial bureaucrats exoticized the people of East and Southeast Asia, whom they classified as primitive natives. Among other things, dress was invoked as a means of justifying this classification.[90] Proud Vietnamese nationalists pushed back, and rather than insisting upon their own sartorial traditions, they called for an embrace of Western fashion.[91] In a global context where suits and Oxford brogue shoes connoted not just modernity but respectability, this seemed to them to be the logical choice. Moreover, far from being an act of submission to colonial authority, fashion mimicry, as Homi Bhabha argues, was instead a powerful act of subversion. It was, in other words, an effective tool for neutralizing claims that Indigenous people were primitive and for subverting a colonial hierarchy that depended on cultural differences to maintain a distance between ruler and ruled.[92]

POLITICAL REFORMS   In the third major development of the early 1930s that influenced women's fashion, the acceptance of Western clothing that occurred in this era may also have stemmed from nationalist and anticolonial sentiment that were pushed underground by the violent colonial response to the 1930 mutiny of Vietnamese soldiers at Yên Bái and the 1930–31 uprising in Nghệ Tĩnh that was erroneously attributed to communist cells.[93] In this context of humiliating colonialism, clothing may have become, if not an outlet for nationalist ideas, at least an acceptable means of projecting an image of national respectability. This impulse dated back to World War I, when the journalist Phan Kế Bính wrote in his study of Vietnamese culture: "Let us compare ourselves with the inhabitants of other countries. . . . The men wear . . . slim pants that are practical and manly; the women wear fine, pretty clothes that are pleasing to the eye. I believe there will come a time when we will need to undertake reform [of women's clothing] to allow ourselves to align with civilized countries."[94] This idea resurfaced in the early 1930s, when *Phụ Nữ Tân Văn* admonished readers that their outfits reflected on Vietnamese civilization and counseled them to keep their choices of clothing respectable, decent, and refined.[95] The journalist Lang-Quê preached that fashion was a form of "self-respect" capable of representing a nation because "clothing is like the flag of the country."[96]

In the early 1930s, self-proclaimed clothing reformers—not an organized campaign but a smattering of very opinionated male journalists—sought to take sartorial matters into their own hands. In a move that today's fashion theorists would call editorial styling, these journalists, many of whom were men and graduates of the École des Beaux Arts, commandeered the nation on what they deemed to be a course better than the grassroots female fashion movement. Reformers pursued a middle path that was neither excessively respectful of tradition nor excessively enthusiastic about Europeanization. Their cautious approach entailed a careful management of the role of Western fashion in Vietnam—and, by extension, a management of the country's international reputation. Proponents of Vietnamese Modernism, their hope was to use everyday culture (clothing) to contest the power dynamic of the colonizer over the colonized. Fashion reformers embarked on this project in two ways: they proposed a national Vietnamese dress, and they worked hard to educate women on how to dress in a way that they believed would reflect a respectable, middle-class sensibility.

In 1934, Nguyễn Cát Tường, only recently graduated from art school, joined the calls for clothing reform. As rich works by Martina Nguyen and Phạm Thảo Nguyên have shown, Nguyễn Cát Tường and his designs sparked a fashion revolution in Vietnam. Cát Tường went a step further than most other clothing reformers to call for the designing of a "national" dress, a trend that was appearing in other colonized areas of Asia, most notably China, India, and the Philippines.[97] He opened the discussion in February 1934 with a call for Vietnamese women to develop a "unique look" that would distinguish them from women in China, France, Japan, and other countries. Vietnam, he wrote, "needs a civilized way to show off the beauty of its people."[98]

As an artist, Nguyễn Cát Tường held up beauty as key to rehabilitating the nation's international reputation. Over the next year, Nguyễn Cát Tường published dozens of articles in the *Phong Hóa* newspaper making the case that women's clothing needed to be reimagined. More specifically, he argued that Vietnamese women—and by extension Vietnam itself—had for too long suffered an image associated with downtrodden peasantry. This image, he insisted, was in desperate need of redemption. It is hardly surprising that Nguyễn Cát Tường would publish his solutions to this problem in the *Phong Hóa* and *Ngày Nay* newspapers, the mouthpieces of the Self-Reliant Literary Group (*Tự Lực Văn Đoàn*), a champion of Vietnamese Modernism that aimed to improve the lives of Vietnamese people through beautifully designed material objects, including art, architecture, furniture, and clothing.[99] Nguyễn Cát Tường explained his reasoning: "While clothing may be used to cover the body, it can be a mirror that reflects the intellectual level of a country. If you want to know which country is making progress, whether [in the realm of] fine art or not, just look at that country's clothes."[100]

In early March 1934, just a week after making the case for a national dress, Nguyễn Cát Tường unveiled sketches of just such a dress in the *Phong Hóa* newspaper (figure 2.4). Explaining that his goal was to improve the traditional Vietnamese tunic, he told readers that he hoped his designs would help convey an image of Vietnamese women—and, by extension, the nation—as modern and upper class. Nguyễn Cát Tường maintained the basic concept of the traditional tunic: a long-sleeve top that fell to the knees, with a slit up each side and a row of buttons running diagonally from the collar to the underarm. The tunic would be worn over pants—an ensemble that had enjoyed tremendous popularity in Vietnam since the days of Minh Mạng in the mid-nineteenth century. His design, however, differed from the traditional one in three key ways: the tunic was comprised of two panels, it included the addition of stylistic embellishments ("reforms"), and the fit was updated. Later that month, in the *Phong Hóa* newspaper, Nguyễn Cát Tường's updates to the traditional tunic were published—one by one, presumably to tantalize readers. Each update—to sleeves, collar, cuffs, fit, and pants—included multiple options, allowing women to arrive at a highly personalized version of the dress.

FIGURE 2.4 The Lemur Tunic.
Source: *Phong Hóa*, March 23, 1934.

The first update was to the sleeves. The artist-turned-designer made the case that the tight sleeves found on traditional four- and five-panel tunics inhibited movement and circulation and that adjustment was necessary for modern women who were more active (see chapter 4). In their place, he suggested puffy sleeves that he considered not just more comfortable but "more hygienic," echoing rhetoric about personal hygiene (see chapter 4). The design widened the upper arms, then narrowed them from the elbow to the wrist, where buttons could be fastened to seal in warmth during the winter or opened to air out the arms in the summer. He offered four styles: "the lad's tongue," "the heart shape," "the waist of a gourd," and "the shrimp tail" because those cuffs fanned out in a way that resembled the crustacean's tail.[101]

Next, Nguyễn Cát Tường proposed a new collar. Perhaps inspired in part by the anti-Chinese sentiment of the day, he dismissed the

Chinese-style standing collar, which he deemed unsuitable for a hot climate such as Vietnam's. He published three new designs for a collar, each of which folded down like those of a European-style blouse. Variations included lace and scalloped embellishments. Some of his designs presented a collar that crossed over women's necks and, like the collar of a five-panel tunic, fastened above the right shoulder with a Western-style button.[102]

The most shocking element of the Lemur design was the way it accentuated the wearer's curves. Like the Chinese qipao, which underwent a similar process of form-fitting tailoring during this period, it represented a significant departure from the traditional figure-hiding tunic.[103] Nguyễn Cát Tường tightened the front and back panels to narrow the abdomen and added darts below the bust to taper the bodice, thereby sharpening the contrast between the bust and the abdomen. He also cinched the waist, further calling attention to the shapely body underneath. The new tunic included longer front and back flaps that fell to the shins, lending a flowing effect.[104]

Nguyễn Cát Tường designed the tunic to be worn over white pants, following the trend set by the schoolgirls of the era. The artist updated the shape of the pants by making them more fitted through the buttocks and thigh, raising the crotch, and replacing the drawstring waist with a button or sash that cinched the waist. At the knee, he let the fabric out, creating a flair at the ankles.[105] The effect was to accentuate the curve of the hips. As his design spread in popularity, it helped normalize white pants, which were still considered controversial.[106]

Nguyễn Cát Tường's unveiling of the completed outfit, dubbed the Lemur Tunic (*áo dài Lemur*), in person at the 1934 Lạc Thiên fair was a pivotal moment in Vietnamese fashion history.[107] In even the most conservative provinces, women were said to don Nguyễn Cát Tường's designs, complete with white pants, colorful tunic, high heels, and hair styled short."[108] After the debut, Nguyễn Cát Tường toured Vietnam to promote his tunic in the big cities. He staged fashion shows and was even invited to the royal palace to offer Empress Nam Phương a special fitting of the coveted outfit.[109] Thereafter, the empress was seen mainly in the Lemur Tunic for the rest of the decade.

The tunic came to be known for dramatically improving the appearance of the wearer. And Nguyễn Cát Tường's ability enhance women's beauty gave him a reputation as an "expert on women" (*nhà chuyên môn về phụ nữ*).[110] A reader of the *Phong Hóa* newspaper sang the garment's praises in a letter to the editor: the Lemur Tunic "not only preserves the graceful beauty of the girl, but also makes her [all the more] beautiful." The design, the female journalist Phan Thị Nga wrote, made women's faces "more dazzlingly resplendent, adding a glow and plumpness to the face, [making] women stand up straight and adding a bounce to their gait.[111] Given this kind of reputation, the Lemur Tunic became wildly popular. Within a year of the style's debut, tailor shops were selling styles right out of Lemur's catalogue.[112] His styles could be found in shops as far away as Phnom Penh.[113] "Tailor shops immediately picked up the styles that [he] published . . . one [customer] became ten and ten became a hundred girls [who] raced to wear his style. The trend began in Hanoi, then moved to Annam, then to most of the girls in Saigon. Tailor shops in Saigon are now racing to produce the trend."[114]

Notwithstanding its runaway popularity, the Lemur Tunic met with considerable backlash. One adopter of the tunic recounted being followed by a curious crowd, only to find that a disapproving forty-five-year-old woman had slashed the back panel of her tunic with a razor.[115] As mentioned previously, the journalist and novelist Vũ Trọng Phụng mocked Nguyen Cát Tường's pretentious and hypocritical ways. In his novel *Dumb Luck*, Vũ Trọng Phụng based his famous character, the tailor Mr. TYPN, after Nguyễn Cát Tường. Mr. TYPN, an acronym for Mr. I Love Ladies (*Tôi yêu phụ nữ*), a Francophile obsessed with being modern, designs shockingly revealing outfits for Modern Women. He flaunts his success and "modernity," yet when he catches sight of his own wife dressed in one of his tunics he exclaims: "Oh my god, what a whore!"[116] Specifically, the tunic became associated with excess and superficiality. Never one to miss an opportunity to poke fun at emerging trends, the *Vịt Đực* newspaper mocked Modern Girls for wearing the Lemur Tunic, lipstick, and strappy high heels with painted toenails, for perming and bleaching their hair to a brown shade, and for toting a handbag with no cash in the wallet, a sly allusion to the way these women frittered away all of their money on clothing.[117]

So controversial was the Lemur Tunic that it sparked a fight between the *Loa Tuần Báo* newspaper and the *Phong Hóa* newspaper, which had published Nguyen Cát Tường's work in the first place. Writers at *Loa Tuần Báo* skewered Nguyen Cát Tường with a handful of articles devoted to a critique of the Lemur Tunic. Led by Thanh Lâm, a university student, the newspaper organized the critique around three main issues. Thanh Lâm's first complaint was that the Lemur Tunic "lacked simplicity, an essential element of modern art." Given that Nguyen Cát Tường was first and foremost an artist, this insult must have rankled. Thanh Lâm pontificated about the definition of art, which according to him manifested beauty in simple, elegant lines. The Lemur Tunic, he wrote, had too many gratuitous elements that rendered it ridiculous, including lace collars, puffy sleeves, and "shrimp tail" cuffs. Consequently, Thanh Lâm concluded, the tunic lacked "natural simplicity" and was unsuitable for women to wear as everyday clothing. Thanh Lâm instead defended the traditional tunic for its minimalism and discretion.[118] Embedded in his claim that the Lemur Tunic was overly ornate was a criticism of its sexuality. He contrasted the Lemur Tunic, with its darts that tightened the bodice and accentuated the curve of the breast, with the traditional tunic, which he praised for its uncomplicated tailoring that maintained the "hidden beauty" of Vietnamese women and only hinted at the shape of their body.[119] The insinuation here was that it was in poor taste to show off one's curves, as the Lemur Tunic did; far better to conceal those curves inside the shapeless traditional tunic and leave the rest to the viewer's imagination.

Loa Tuần Báo's second criticism of the Lemur Tunic was that it was poorly designed. Being an artist not a tailor, Nguyễn Cát Tường had published only sketches of his designs, not scaled patterns or measurements to guide the tailor. As the journalist Tư Húi observed, Nguyen Cát Tường's designs looked good on paper, but tailors had trouble re-creating his design to fit the average woman's body. Consequently, tailors had to invite Nguyễn Cát Tường into their shops for help with constructing the actual garment.[120] Thanh Lâm further noted that although Nguyễn Cát Tường had made the case that he was eliminating parts that were not functional, such as the high collar, he had gone on to add other parts that detracted from the tunic's function, such as a tight, stiff bodice that constricted women's bodies as they went about their daily activities.[121]

The third criticism of the áo dài Lemur was that the tunic its creator had claimed would represent Vietnam with a national dress was actually borrowed from foreign styles—and those of the colonizer to boot.[122] "If you stand up to modify the country's clothes, you must come up with a full range of Vietnamese fine arts," wrote Thanh Lâm in *Loa Tuần Báo*.[123] Instead,

Thanh Lâm charged, the Lemur Tunic was a hybrid Franco-Vietnamese design: "The things [Nguyễn Cát Tường] claimed to have invented were all borrowed from European clothes."[124] Indeed, Nguyễn Cát Tường did little to hide the French influences, giving the tunic a French translation of the last syllable of his name and going so far as to advertise his shop in French, even though the advertisements appeared in Vietnamese-language newspapers.[125] Thanh Lâm accused him of pilfering all his "new" elements from styles already published in the French *Femina* magazine: "I can't help but laugh," he wrote, because "the collar is the same as that on my [Western] pajamas, the new sleeves are the same as on my [French] chemise," and, he claimed, the pants were taken from the design of the French military uniform. "Where is that Vietnamese characteristic [of the Lemur Tunic]? Maybe it's just in the places you haven't fixed?"[126] He reasoned that those who were impressed only liked it because of the hybrid influence; the tunic itself was nothing new from an artistic point of view.[127] The editorial board of *Loa* even published an article accusing Nguyễn Cát Tường of merely appropriating the style of me tây and Modern Girls. "Strangely enough," the newspaper noted with sarcasm, "the artist's masterpiece was created at the very moment in our society when the dancing girl trend emerged." In other words, his design was merely an appropriation of an existing fad.[128]

There was truth to Thanh Lâm's critique: the "new" elements of the Lemur Tunic were borrowed from French fashion. Yet Nguyễn Cát Tường's approach was consistent with a trend of the interwar years promoting Franco-Vietnamese collaboration—and a mingling of cultural and political influences. The trend dates back to 1919, when in an effort to neutralize anticolonial threats the Minister of Colonies Albert Sarraut called for Franco-Vietnamese political collaboration. The proposal, part of a broader plan announced before World War I to transition the empire from a politics of assimilation to one of association, encouraged Indigenous participation in politics (excluding, of course, those groups calling for independence). French support of collaboration politics empowered French-educated middle-class urban Vietnamese who believed "modernization" was the key to gaining Vietnamese political and economic rights. In other words, Franco-Vietnamese collaboration was paradoxically used to further the nationalist project.[129]

The trend of Franco-Viet collaboration spread from the political world to the world of culture and aesthetics, launching a series of New

Arts movements, including fine arts, Indochinese architecture, New Theater, New Poetry, and New Music. For example, when Victor Tardieu founded the École des Beaux Arts d'Indochine, where Nguyễn Cát Tường was educated, Tardieu's goal was not to impose French artistic styles on Vietnamese students but to foster a local interpretation of modernity.[130] Vietnamese artists, even those who embraced a European aesthetic, did not necessarily consider themselves political collaborators. As Caroline Herbelin has detailed in her work on colonial architecture, the interwar years saw the rise of "Indochinese architecture," a form of syncretic design that incorporated Asian motifs within European structures, often incorporating Art Deco elements. Popularized by the French architects Ernest Hébrard and Félix Dumail, who designed the Finot Museum in Hanoi and the Banque d'Indochine in Saigon, respectively, the *métissage* style quickly caught on among the architecture students at the École des Beaux Arts d'Indochine, many of whom were Nguyễn Cát Tường's school peers.[131] In 1933, Nguyễn Cao Luyện and Hòang Như Tiếp founded an architectural firm in Hanoi that constructed single family homes and major public projects renowned for their artful mingling of Vietnamese and Western styles. Likewise, Võ Đức Diên designed the Cercle Nautique on Hòan Kiếm lake in Hanoi, a stunning monument to métissage architecture. A similar blend of French and Vietnamese styles appeared in other art movements of the era, most obviously in the new theater, new poetry, and new music movements. Nguyễn Cát Tường's use of French elements in his design should thus not be read as simple imitation, but as part of a larger trend of artistic métissage that defined the new art movements of the interwar period.

Borrowed elements aside, the Lemur Tunic seemed fresh and new to middle-class Vietnamese women who liked the look of French clothing and wanted to gently update their style as they emerged from the bleak days of the Great Depression. The Lemur Tunic was, in other words, popular in part because it was a "safe" way to incorporate Western styles in their clothing. Those who donned it would be accused neither of dressing like a me tây nor of slavishly imitating a French woman.

The Lemur Tunic was only the starting point for fashion reformers, who were undeterred by *Loa's* critiques. That summer, Nguyễn Cát Tường, along with other artist-cum-fashion reformists including Tô Ngọc Vân and Trần Quang Trân, released a series of other fashion designs, published in a pamphlet titled "Beautiful Summer of 1934" (*Đẹp mùa nực 1934*). The pamphlet introduced new fashions beyond the Lemur Tunic, most of which were Western clothing concepts with a Vietnamese flair. Among the styles introduced was a Western-style swimsuit that exposed the upper thighs and showcased the decolletage. Belted at the waist, it celebrated female curves. The designers also rolled out drawings for beach pajamas in a range of flattering colors. The design consisted of flowy pants worn with a shirt that came to the hips, criscrossed at the front and tied with a sash at the waist, much like the four-panel tunic. Nguyễn Cát Tường reprinted designs for the sleeves and collars of the Lemur Tunic and suggested styles and prints for each body type: tall, short, thin, thick. The designers introduced dresses to be worn at specific times and places: day dresses, housedresses, beach pajamas. The pamphlet also included an array of accessories—jewelry, makeup, open-toed high heels, closed-toe heels—some were original designs by the authors and others were inventory from stores advertising in the pamphlet. Fashion reformers—most notably Nhất Linh, a graduate of the École des Beaux Arts and later esteemed novelist in the New Literature movement—also offered updates for peasant clothing. Nhất Linh designed a new peasant dress that would be affordable while allowing the poor to "enjoy the beauty of clothing." The design, which came in a range of colors and had a short-sleeve option and multiple options for the collar, was intended for warm weather. Western-style underwear—an alternative to the yếm (a traditional halter-style undergarment)—and sandals updated with a strap for style and function were also recommended.[132]

FASHION PRESCRIPTIONS

For all the popularity of the Lemur Tunic, by the mid-1930s, Western fashion was there to stay in Vietnam. Along with their touting of a national dress, reformers presented new ways to teach women how to look good in Western clothing. Vietnamese trendsetters, many of whom had either lived in Paris or, like Nguyễn Cát Tường, trained as artists at École des Beaux-Arts de l'Indochine, took it upon themselves to advise women on what to wear, how to wear it, and when to wear it. Drawing on their artistic knowledge of shape, color, and composition, these artists took it upon themselves to redirect women toward an image of beauty defined by the artists themselves. No longer would Vietnam be associated with what they considered the drabness and despair of the country's peasantry; instead, the country would sparkle with the sophistication of progressive urbanites.[133] In short, they sought to use women to rehabilitate the image of Vietnam.

In embracing the new fashion guidelines, Vietnamese women also absorbed new rules of social conduct, influenced by French as well as Vietnamese social norms. In Vietnam, an overt connection between fashion prescriptions and social rules appeared in a 1936 column in the *Ngày Nay* newspaper, titled "Social Relations: Behavior and Dress" (*Xã Giao: Phép xử thế, Phục Sức*). Building on Norbert Elias's theory that with state centralization in Europe came new standards of civility imposed on the domestic populace, one could draw similar conclusions about the rise of cosmopolitan nationalism in Vietnam and calls for a new etiquette of manners and dress that would "civilize" the nation.[134]

The main emphasis in fashion prescriptions was on maintaining a presentable, well-groomed, and fundamentally bourgeois appearance.[135] In 1932, the journalist Côn Sinh declared: "The fine art of dress is [neither] in the primitive [nor] elaborate . . . but in the clean and elegant."[136] Eager fashionistas learned to keep their clothing pressed and spotless and to avoid going out in public—whether to the market or the workplace—with tangled hair.[137] "A self-respecting person never wears crumpled or ragged clothing to entertain guests, greet people on the streets, or pay a visit to someone," *Ngày Nay* reminded readers.[138] Embedded in many such discussions was subtext about the relationship between clothing and class: "When visiting a poor friend or one who lives simply, don't overdress 'like a queen'; when visiting the house of a wealthy friend, dress well enough to prevent their servants from looking at you with disdain; and when visiting powerful people, dress elegantly but modestly."[139]

A well-maintained appearance, readers learned, was essential to their love life. Self-appointed fashion experts warned readers that men would judge women by how well put-together they were, and whether their outfit was clean and pressed.[140] Wives should be sure to wear flattering clothing even at home: "Dress decently at home or your husband will get bored," exhorted one journalist, insinuating that husbands would cheat if their wives looked slovenly.[141]

As the flood of Western clothing into Vietnamese markets coincided with the popularization of Western leisure activities, newspapers issued specific instructions on what to wear and when to wear it. Sartorial know-how became a mark of civility: "A polite person . . . should know what clothes to wear when," read a *Ngày Nay* article.¹⁴² Casual dress was strictly for daywear. Formal wear, such as glamorous gowns or clothing with an exaggerated flowing silhouette, should be saved for dancing, parties, the opera, horse races, weddings, festivals, and fairs, not worn on a mere trip to the market or a day at the office. To spare readers the humiliating faux pas of wearing a tennis dress to a professional tennis match, *Ngày Nay* sternly admonished that sports attire was for playing sports, not watching them. And by all means, the *Ngày Nay* newspaper implored readers, never [ever] wear sexy or modern clothing to a funeral.¹⁴³

Even male wardrobes could not escape strict rules of time and place. For starters, men should wear a Spencer jacket, smoking jacket, or a *costume de thé* when attending a celebration. An overcoat was strictly for daytime use, and a thin gray wool coat was fitting to wear to a horse race.¹⁴⁴ Attending a Western wedding? Wear a formal coat (*jaquette*) or a dress jacket (*veston habillé*); if the party extends into the evening, change into a smoking jacket. In the summer, the shorter Spencer jacket was considered sufficient for formal events.¹⁴⁵

Always eager for an opportunity to mock pretentious social norms, the *Vịt Đực* newspaper dissected the French fashion rule: "The modern woman must be a clock. They have to make it so that you can tell whether it's two o'clock or two-thirty by looking at the shirt they're wearing." *Vịt Đực* followed up with a quip about how this "offended the watch salesman," who would undoubtedly lose business. *Vịt Đực* went on to satirize the many outfit changes that women were expected to make on a typical day: "Wake up, change for a bike ride, change for breakfast, chose the appropriate outfit for the dish served: wear navy blue for a dish with fish, red for a dish with roasted meat, green for a dish with melon. When a certain male friend comes to eat at your mother's house, wear a 'naughty' style; when you go to your boyfriend's house for dinner, wear the style 'Invite me!' Change your clothes when you drink water; change clothing for a date night; and put on a new outfit to quarrel with your husband." In an instance of wickedly dark humor, *Vịt Đực* even referenced the recent rash of suicides among lovelorn young girls drowning themselves in Hanoi's West Lake after their parents had tried to force them into arranged marriages: "I advise you [prospective] suicides not to wear very nice clothes because . . . it's a waste of money."¹⁴⁶

Western-style sleeping pajamas were especially popular, much to the horror of tastemakers. The proper use of pajamas became a litmus test of sophistication—and conversely, the improper use a mark of fatal uncouthness. With their soft, flowing fabrics, delicate prints, bows, rosettes, and rhinestones, sleeping pajamas were comfortable and pleasing to the eye, and women loved wearing them. Women "glided around the house in front of loved ones and sometimes in front of strangers," wearing their pajamas or night shirts in public.[147] It is understandable why some Vietnamese women might think sleeping pajamas could be worn outside: models on sewing patterns and advertisements for ready-to-wear pajamas appeared in pointed kitten heel mules, suggesting they would be worn outdoors.[148] Indeed, a style of pants and shirt, also called "pyjamas," was worn at European beaches. It was not uncommon to hear French colonists express their disdain for this misappropriation of pajamas, much like the exchange between a newly arrived Frenchman and the journalist Lang-Quê that opened this chapter.[149] As fashion journalists noted, such women were ignorant of the fashion edict condemning the wearing of sleeping pajamas to receive guests or in public rude and dirty. He and other fashion journalists likened these sleeping pajama-wearing bums to African "savages" who adorned themselves with whatever flashy metals they happened to find.[150]

Many fashion dos and don'ts were, not surprisingly, linked to age. As you will see in chapter 3, the concept of female aging, once associated with wisdom and respect, would be cast in a negative light during the interwar years. Social norms required that women wear certain types of clothing according to their age.[151] Publishing advice columns in newspapers, self-proclaimed fashion experts directed women in their twenties to wear bright colors and avoid heavy gold and silver or big coats. As for women in their thirties, they should dress casually and avoid the bright colors of their younger years. Colors had the power to age a woman, readers were told: younger women who wore black shirts in the traditional style were said to look like old ladies; conversely, women in their late forties who wore bright colors looked inappropriately childish—and only called more attention to their "sunset beauty."[152] Newspapers were filled with such cheap shots at aging women.

As norms governing body shape were changing during the interwar years, the concept of clothing fit gained importance. Whereas traditional Vietnamese clothing was expected to fit loosely, Western clothing conformed to the body. By the mid-1930s, women's clothing imported from France created a silhouette featuring broad shoulders, a narrow waist, and slim hips. Basque waist dresses emphasized the flat stomach/narrow waist look in contrast to the gathered material that added plump to the bust. Skirts and dresses were cut on the bias to give the fabric a slight stretch and skim a woman's curves. Collars opened onto the decolletage, with some necklines dipping scandalously low into a cleavage covered only by chiffon or lace. Ill-fitting clothing was a fashion faux pas.[153] For example, fashion authorities schooled women to avoid wearing shorts if their figure was unattractive.[154] When jade green became the hot color of 1939, it came with a warning that it was for tall slim figures only; short or bulky women were to avoid the color at all costs.[155] Of course, there was a backlash to form-fitting clothing. In 1938, the Vịt Đực newspaper published an article mocking women for wearing revealing clothing. During the hot season, women in the countryside were wearing "shorts that reveal bare thighs" and "shirts that show off their Yên Sở melons," referencing the new fashion for larger breasts.[156]

Fashion cognoscenti guided women in the selection of the most stylish and flattering colors, patterns, and fabrics. In newspaper articles, they educated women in the nuances of color theory and how to match clothing to their skin tone for "harmony and gentleness."[157] Fresh, bright-colored clothes highlighted youth, they were told; dark-colored clothing should be reserved for small women with pale skin whose skin ages easily.[158] A splash or two of color was encouraged but only within limits. Tastemakers reminded readers not to turn themselves into a "walking advertisement" with too many bright colors.[159] Readers learned to avoid wearing colorful clothing to work or to the market because such colors would "distract people in the cities," who would presumably "watch [the wearer] and forget their job."[160] Colors that were too vivid could even "damage the eyeball of the onlooker."[161]

The palate of acceptable colors was dictated by the season. In an article titled "Weather and Clothing Color," readers learned that to the senstive eyes of the fashion observer bright colors "hurt our eyes and make our brains tired" in the summer heat; soft, cool colors such as white, ivory, celery, and aqua were more appropriate in the summer months.[162] This seasonal rule trumped even considerations of weather or temperature; even if winter offered up an unseasonably balmy day, readers learned, summer colors were strictly for summer months. On summer days, pastels were advisable under the hot sun; when the cool winds arrived after 6 P.M., purple and greens became acceptable.[163] In the cooler seasons, women were counseled to wear marine shades, a jet-black top and white pants, or a café au lait colored top with dark pants and a dark colored Western-style coat.[164]

Although young women began experimenting with colorful tunics in the 1920s, colorful clothing remained limited to urban areas, and even in cities bright colors could offend onlookers.[165] When "old-fashioned conservatives" saw women in bright colors, "their eyes widened and teeth clenched, and they cackled: 'Too much!' ['ăn mặc quá lắm!']." Bright colors and white pants, they believed, aroused men and "made it easy for indecent men to lose control and give in to their desires."[166] Some elderly men were indeed titillated by the changing fashion landscape. When visiting Saigon for the first time in four years, an elderly man from Trà Vinh was shocked by the ubiquity of brightly colored clothing, which until only recently had been reserved for festivals. When a female journalist asked his opinion of the fashion changes, a smile crept onto the corners of his lips as he admitted that the new look was easy on the eyes: "What Modern Women do, I won't dare to pass judgement on, nor will I argue with their style of dress," he said. Then, in a classic bit of understatement, he added: "It makes them even more clever and pretty."[167]

Women also absorbed lessons on how to choose the most appropriate patterned fabrics. Floral prints were all the rage in 1936. Fashion doyens coached readers to stand three or four meters away from a print to gain the perspective necessary to identify the two dominant colors and the extent to which they blended together. Women learned to choose the colors of a pattern according to the color of their skin and the season. Small prints were flattering; large prints dwarfed the wearer, or so the fashion advice of the day went. Only tall women should wear prints on a horizontal line; all other women should choose a vertical line to make them appear taller.[168]

Women had an array of fabrics from which to choose: domestic silk, Indian cotton, French wool, acrylic, and rayon. Fashion experts warned against wearing light or sheer fabrics such as linen or lace that would reveal their undergarments.[169] With an air of weary disdain, the self-styled fashion mentor Nguyễn Cát Tường advised women that in Europe chiffon was strictly for private dancers; one should never wear it out in the streets. The gossamer fabric was widely considered inappropriate for public wear and a crude attempt to subvert decency standards. Some dared to wear long layers of chiffon skirts over short shorts or skirts, but in doing so they were accused of trying to attract "prying eyes for indecent attention to the body."[170]

FASHION

Even traditional style did not escape the watchful eye of Vietnam's fashion police. Articles reminded readers to wear the "national uniform" and a modified turban for customary formal occasions, such as Tết, weddings, funerals, and anniversary celebrations of a loved one's death.[171] When attending a formal occasion such as a celebration, wedding, or the Tet new year, readers were advised to wear a blouse or tunic and pants. Tunics could be blue, red, purple, yellow, "but not white, no matter how hot" because white was the color for funerals. When it was chilly, a Western overcoat worn over Vietnamese clothing was acceptable, as long as the coat was not too casual.[172]

Colonialism and the accompanying flood of Western products introduced female consumers in interwar Vietnam to new fashion ideas. Women began to reconsider the traditional five-panel tunic, with its boxy fit and dark colors. Outliers in society, including women married to Western men or women experimenting with Western leisure activities and lifestyles, quickly adopted Western fashion. But such fashion experimentation was frowned upon by some social critics who associated it with seemingly unsavory women such as me tây or Modern Girls. Even more embarrassing were those women who did not master Western fashion rules and wore sleeping pajamas on the street.

In response, fashion reformists—most of them men—called for rules governing the adoption of Western clothing and created their own hybrid styles. In the spirit of Vietnamese Modernism, the goal of these reformists was to help Vietnam shed its image as a downtrodden land of colonized peasants without resorting to slavish mimicry of the colonizer. Trained in the arts, the reformists had a keen sense of how to convey and manipulate political ideas via images. They knew that something as simple as a Lemur Tunic or a beaded handbag had the power to change the image of an entire nation. By directing readers to retain "traditional" elements of Vietnamese clothing while tapping into international fashion trends, reformists sought to create a new and sophisticated Vietnam. The reformists' approach was effectively an inversion of the Modern Girls' approach. Whereas Modern Girls took *Western* fashion and adapted it to the Vietnamese context, reformists took *Vietnamese* fashion and incorporated elements of Western style.

The obsession with women's fashion that swept the public sphere during the 1930s was in large part a reaction to the dramatic changes that had recently arisen in women's roles in family and society. Increasing numbers of women were rejecting traditional expectations and embracing individualism. As I explore in the following chapters, these women were attending colonial schools, participating in sports and leisure activities, and making decisions about their own futures independent of their parents. Many such changes, which threatened to destabilize the very nature of Vietnamese society, manifested on the street in the form of women's everyday fashion choices. As fashion reformists sought to manage the complexities of sartorial symbolism, Vietnamese fashion became politicized as never before.

Chapter Three

COSMETICS

Kếu couldn't stand it anymore. She took a risk. She hid the box of Coty face powder and modern things she had bought . . . a pair of high-heeled shoes . . . a tight-fitting blouse that reached down to the hips, lined with lace; and a colorful áo dài, dotted with intricate Chinese flowers; a leather purse with jewels embroidered on it.

She bought these things, but dared not leave them at home. She sent them to her friend Bich Ngoc's house on Hàng Trống Street. From then on, every afternoon, she put the box of face powder into the bag and she went to Miss Bich Ngoc's house. When she got there, she pulled off her hair turban and took out a comb to untangle her hair and part it on the side. She curled her hair, letting a few ringlets stick out from behind her ears. She then dusted powder all over her face, ears, and nape. She stretched out her neck to rub it evenly. She paused and stretched out her lips to apply lipstick, but her friend had taught her . . . to pucker her mouth and draw a lip line in the shape of a heart. She put on white pants, stood up . . . and added a colorful tunic, smoothing it out. That's it, her shoes, purse, and dress [were complete]. She admired herself in the mirror: she turned one way and then back again . . . she liked what she saw. After about half an hour, [the mood changed] she disrobed, requested a bowl of water, and hastily washed off her makeup. She peeled off her new outfit, donned her old dark clothes, and hurried home.[1]

Kếu is the main character in Nguyễn Công Hoan's short story "Miss Kếu, a Modern Girl," published in 1933 and still popular today. Kếu faces an internal struggle, one that many young women experienced during the interwar years. On one hand, she wants to please her parents who, earlier in the story, insisted that she behave according to traditional norms. They dismiss makeup and trendy clothing as slutty (*đĩ*) and scold her for literally letting her hair down. On the other hand, Kếu feels the pull of her own desires. She craves the excitement of "Modern Girl" life introduced via the Europeanization trend and yearns to cut her hair, whiten her teeth, wear makeup, and go dancing like her friends. Bích Ngọc pokes fun at Kếu, warning her that if she continues to dress in drab clothes and keep her face plain, she'll be reduced to marrying an old scholar—a fate that would no doubt please her parents.

Kếu's character is an archetype of the many women, young and old alike, in interwar Vietnam who delighted in the creative self-discovery that emerged through the glossy reds and pinks of lipstick and nail polish. Thanks to a variety of globalizing forces—most notably Hollywood cinema, innovations in transportation, syndicated news columns and photographs, and beauty contests—beauty culture was spreading like wildfire around the world during the interwar period. With new beauty companies emerging in Europe, the United States, and Japan, the cosmetics industry exploded in popularity, and women around the world—like Nguyễn Công Hoan's characters Kếu and her friend Bích Ngọc—quickly became its devoted customers.

In the years leading up to World War I, Vietnam would have seemed an unlikely place for the cosmetics industry to thrive. Before the war, Vietnamese women twisted their long hair up in a bun or a turban as Kếu did, lightly powdered their face only on special occasions, and concealed their black lacquered teeth behind a demure smile. Cosmetics were reserved for theater actresses and sex workers, and the line between those two groups of women was suspected to be blurry. Virtuous young women who subscribed to the *khuê các* ideal of the sequestered maiden were expected to hide their natural beauty, not flaunt it or manipulate it with makeup. As for married women, they were to reserve their beauty only for their husbands; those who had reached menopause surrendered gracefully to the aging process, which lent the benefit of social esteem.

Notwithstanding these unlikely circumstances, the cosmetics industry met with an enthusiastic, even rapturous, consumer response upon its arrival in Vietnam—even during the lowest points of the Great Depression. The industry pursued a gamut of savvy marketing strategies to woo Vietnam's traditionally modest women. Foreign companies purchased advertising space in newspapers to seduce female readers and priced their products affordably enough that even a peasant woman could treat herself to the occasional tube of lipstick. Within a mere two decades, the cosmetics industry in Vietnam had exploded with beauty institutes, hair salons, department store beauty counters, beauty shops, and even mail-order services connecting rural women with urban-based products. Women easily learned trends and obtained their beauty know-how from movies, newspaper tutorials, and advertisements.

In this chapter, I argue that the cosmetics industry thrived in Vietnam because it managed to tap into an important customer base: women who, like Nguyễn Công Hoan's fictional character Kếu, had begun to question the expectations society and family had for them. Vietnamese women of all ages, influenced by the trend of individualism sweeping interwar Vietnam, began to carve out a new role for themselves in their family and society. Not only did the newly made-up women look dramatically different, but many of them—especially in the cities and to a lesser extent in the countryside—were behaving differently as well. Women indulged their vanity, and those who were single or widowed went out with friends at night and pursued romantic relationships. Reflective of the growing trend in individualism throughout Vietnamese society during the interwar years, these women put their own desires before those of family members, whether parents, in-laws, husbands, or children. Nguyễn Công Hoan's fictional character Kếu is a window into that cultural shift.

This shift was not lost on those who came to see cosmetics as a tangible expression—and even a tool—of women's revolt against traditional norms. As the story of "Miss Kếu, a Modern Girl" reveals, a widespread social anxiety developed around the issue of women dabbling in makeup. This trend alarmed critics, who interpreted the changes women were making to their features with makeup and skin care as a rejection of Vietnamese traditions and ideals. Critics sounded the alarm on women's ability to alter their looks, lure men, and flaunt their sexuality with a mere fluttering of their eyelashes. Whereas clothing had, for the most part, been perceived as a tool with which to upgrade the nation, cosmetics was considered a threat.[2]

THE BEAUTY REVOLUTION ARRIVES IN VIETNAM

Prior to the twentieth century, cosmetics in Vietnam fell into two general categories: makeup and skin care, the latter of which was more socially acceptable. Cosmetics use was limited to stage actresses and sex workers. Only on special occasions such as the Lunar New Year or village festivals did women outside of these professions dust themselves with a light veil of powder or anoint themselves with perfume oils such as pine, rose, and jasmine. Skin care addressed problems such as acne, blemishes, rosacea, wrinkles, and freckles, which had long been treated as dermatological issues in the Sino-Vietnamese medical tradition. Traditional treatments included ointments such as plant-based oils, of which eucalyptus was considered the most effective. A secondary treatment was dietary modifications based on the Vietnamese understanding that food controlled the energy of the body, expressed as temperature, and that deviations from temperature norms manifested in medical conditions. Too much cooling in the body caused sallow skin among other health issues and was treated with hot foods, including spices, chili peppers, alcohol, and caffeine. Too much heat in the body, a more common ailment, caused blemishes and acne and was treated with cooling foods, ideally raw vegetables.[3]

The cosmetics that would become popular in Vietnam during the interwar period were a recent phenomenon in Europe as well. Although lipstick, powder, eye kohl, blush, and other forms of makeup dated as far back as the Egyptian period, makeup had gone out of fashion among middle- and lower-class women in Europe during the Middle Ages. This widespread rejection stemmed from the rather tawdry association of makeup with sex work as well as the realization that many forms of makeup were toxic.[4] In the nineteenth century, the Industrial Revolution ushered in new technologies in Western cosmetics that made for better quality, more affordability, and more consistent products. Chemists found ways to manufacture synthetic colors and scents, diminishing the need for expensive raw materials—some of which happened to be sourced in Southeast Asia and Vietnam in particular. Meanwhile, a public health campaign being waged in France was changing public attitudes toward cosmetics. Public health experts in the metropole presented care for the body in moral terms and even tacitly approved of women's use of cosmetics as part of their personal care ritual. Thus did makeup come to be considered respectable and cease to be the sole province of sex workers.[5]

COSMETICS

After World War I, a global beauty culture, based largely on Western ideals, developed in which cosmetics became wildly popular. The new culture was propagated through transportation innovations that enabled products to be sent to markets around the world and through improved communication networks, including print journalism, photography, and cinema. Women all over the world purchased cosmetics to help them reproduce the styles of beauty queens and Hollywood starlets. New trends in fashion and leisure revealed more of their skin, calling for body lotions, waxing, and shaving, and shorter hairstyles exposed more of their face, calling for makeup and other facial enhancements.[6] French women in particular relished the new beauty trends, and by the end of the decade, they were spending more time and money on makeup than women in any other part of the world.[7]

The mania for cosmetics swept Vietnam as well, even amid the privations of the Great Depression. This phenomenon can be attributed in part to the sociocultural changes occurring during the interwar years: animated by the trend of individualism, Vietnamese women began questioning their obligations to family and society at large. Breaking away from a family structure in which their own needs were secondary, they demanded more agency in choosing their destiny. As you will see, this struggle played out in debates about marital relations that applied not just to young women but to middle-aged women as well. Specifically, women wanted to choose their marital partner, end the tradition of chastity for widows, and dissolve the institution of polygamy.

During the interwar period, young women began to reconsider—and even reject—the marriages their parents had arranged for them, preferring, instead, romantic love. This trend was already popular in the West, but it remained scandalous in Vietnam.[8] The concept of individuals forging their own destiny did not exist in traditional Vietnamese culture; under the system of filial piety, children were expected to defer to their parents' decisions about their lives. Indeed, the Gia Long code that governed Vietnam before colonization made the failure to adhere to the precepts of filial piety a crime punishable by death.[9] Those entrenched notions fell into question during the interwar years when the colonial education system churned out graduates knowledgeable in French culture and Chinese Republican ideals of individualism were widely discussed in the Vietnamese press. The Vietnamese literary world abounded with stories of romantic love, and the New

Poetry movement presented the notion of love for love's sake as a mark of modernity.[10] Known as the generation of *Tố Tâm*—after the protagonist of Hoàng Ngọc Phách's novel of the same name—a spate of young women committed suicide allegedly because their parents refused to allow them to marry for romantic love. (Although widely covered by the media, the "epidemic" may have been overblown. In their analysis of suicide statistics from the interwar period, Linh Vu and Nguyen Van Ky question the suicide "epidemic" and assert that suicide rates in Vietnam were much lower than in France and were not more prevalent among young women.[11])

Women also challenged the nature of their marriages. New Women and Vietnamese modernists called for an end to the practice of polygamy.[12] Typically practiced by wealthier families, polygamy served the patrilineal social structure because it provided a means for the male line to proliferate by ensuring offspring. Among other things, the practice served as a solution to the era's problems of female infertility.[13] The new generation educated in the Franco-Annamite school system was predisposed to oppose polygamy due to the French embrace of romantic love and contempt for the polygamy practiced in the North African colonies. The controversy came to a head in 1934, when Emperor Bảo Đại angered traditionalists by insisting on a monogamous marriage—notwithstanding his notorious promiscuity.[14]

Finally, women, particularly those in Tonkin, demanded an end to the tradition of the chaste widow. The Confucian Threefold Dependencies directed women to follow the will of their father, husband, and sons. Given that the husband's will was assumed to extend past his death, widows were to remain chaste as a show of loyalty. Even when a husband met an early death—a real possibility in the early twentieth century—his widow would spend the remaining decades of her life alone and in the service of her deceased husband's family. Her status as a widow had significant implications not only for her personal happiness but also for her financial survival, particularly if she had young children. Many young widows went on to become sex workers out of sheer desperation. Inspired by the trend of individualism, New Women and their male allies called on Vietnamese society to show compassion for widows' predicament and allow them to remarry.[15]

The interwar years thus saw a reorganization of the romantic market in Vietnam. With young women insisting on choosing their spouse, couples embracing monogamy, and widows remarrying, women claimed more agency in their romantic life. In their search for romantic partners, Vietnamese women wore mascara and eyeshadow to enlarge their eyes, lipstick to brighten their smile, and perfume to leave a lingering scent. New forms of leisure also led to a greater interest in cosmetics. Young urban women enjoyed spending evenings at the local fair or at dance halls, where the dim lighting called for bolder makeup. Some young women, similar to the character Kếu at the beginning of this chapter, managed to defy their parents without the parents ever knowing it, simply by washing all traces of the Modern Girl lifestyle from their faces. As for older women, they did their best to defy nature itself—and their traditional role as dowdy but necessary members of society—by purchasing products that promised to rejuvenate skin, prevent wrinkles, and add a youthful flush to their face.

Beauty culture also thrived during the interwar years because cosmetics sold at a relatively low price point. With their dazzling colors, alluring packaging, and promise of transforming the wearer, cosmetics served as an intoxicating luxury that was affordable to almost everyone. Even during the Great Depression, women in Vietnam continued to spend money on makeup: a phenomenon economists call the Lipstick Effect. Middle-class women easily purchased makeup with their own income or money from their parents; even some lower-class women occasionally splurged on a tube of lipstick. Tosika powder, imported from Japan, cost only forty-seven cents in 1936.[16] Of course, during the Depression, the most impoverished peasant women could not afford the basic necessities of life, let alone powder or lipstick, which led some to resort to occasional sex work. The catch was that sex workers tended to rely on a sultry, heavily made-up look to attract customers. In many cases, brothel owners and pimps offered a cash advance to cover the necessary clothing and cosmetics. The loan would, of course, need to be repaid through labor, resulting in a relationship of debt bondage.[17] So it was that even Vietnam's poorest women ended up partaking of one of the colony's hottest new trends.

Vietnamese women learned about the latest beauty advances through advertising. Some foreign cosmetic companies simply reprinted advertisements designed for Western markets; other firms designed advertisements to appeal to the local market. As Vietnam's consumer economy developed, commercial art provided a sustainable income to local professional artists, many of whom had trained as illustrators at the École des Beaux Arts in Hanoi. Glamorous women graced posters in the windows of beauty shops, colorful placards at trolly stops arrested passersby, and newspaper advertisements touted beauty products' miraculous benefits. Some cosmetics companies even peppered their Vietnamese-language advertisements with French words, drawing on the prestige associated with the language of the colonizer.[18] As was typical in the 1930s, advertisements that ran in the Vietnamese press were rendered in the striking Art Deco style, with its sharp lines, highly stylized images, geometric fonts, and artful use of negative space.[19]

Though targeting Vietnamese consumers, beauty companies usually had European women as models in their advertisements.[20] In some cases it is possible that the companies simply never converted their original European advertisements for the local market, but it is likely that many deliberately used European models to capitalize on their associations with white prestige.[21] Even the Mỹ Viện Amy, a Vietnamese-owned beauty institute, featured an image of a French woman to promote its products.[22] Occasionally, however, Vietnamese consumers saw their own compatriots in advertisements, and by 1930 the French-owned Keva and Swiss-owned Tokalon began featuring Asian women and hiring local artists, recent graduates of the École des Beaux Arts.[23] One Tokalon ad, signed by the Vietnamese artist Luyên, featured a bevy of international beauties (figure 3.1): a Vietnamese woman gazing into the distance, a Japanese woman looking demure, a Chinese woman in a *qipao* dress and Marcelled curls dusting on powder, and a blonde European woman bathing nude, a nipple exposed, with an ecstatic smile.[24]

FIGURE 3.1. Advertisement for Tokalon Powder.
Source: *Phong Hóa*, October 26, 1934.

COSMETICS

FIGURE 3.2. Advertisement for Coty brand cosmetics.
Source: Phong Hóa, August 18, 1933.

Vietnamese women were inundated with powerful cosmetics advertising messages that offered a new language of beauty and a new way of understanding women's role in the world (figure 3.2). As Sumei Wang has shown, cosmetics marketing campaigns taught women not only about the products themselves but about Western values and lifestyles.[25] Advertising assumed an air of wisdom and gravitas that convinced customers that traditional Vietnamese beauty practices had become passé.[26] Kathy Peiss's observation about the United States during the interwar period was equally true for

Vietnam: "Makeup was seen (and sold) as a medium of self-expression in a consumer society where identity had become a purchasable style."[27]

Crucially, advertisements framed beauty products as key to attracting men and finding a husband. Even though this strategy was hardly unique to Vietnam, it was particularly successful among a generation caught up in forging a new romantic destiny for itself. Addressing "young women who want to get married," Tokalon assured women that men were fascinated by smooth white skin and promised that Tokalon cream would lead men to fall in love with them.[28] Forvil touted its perfume, powder, and cream as "the weapons that women must use when looking for love."[29] An article in the Đông Pháp newspaper about a woman who had received ten marriage proposals attributed her success to her radiant skin and revealed that she used Tokalon cream—likely a covert sponsor of the story.[30] Once a man had been successfully snagged, women learned that a rigorous maintenance of makeup and beauty regimes was essential to prevent him from straying. A 1929 article by a female journalist in Hà Thành Ngọ Báo, clearly aimed at middle-aged women, cited the example of a "45-year-old woman with leaky breasts, dry hair, and bad skin" to warn that if women let themselves go, their husbands would find another woman: "I don't mean to say that a woman's makeup is enough to stop the husband from cheating, but if we do not please the husband he will not stick around."[31]

Women were assured that a nicely made-up face would improve not just their marital situation but their social status. Companies boasted that their products were used by the "elegant ladies in Paris," and Cécé perfume marketed their product to "elegant people."[32] A Forvil advertisement claimed that "'upper-class, intellectual ladies' used Forvil perfume, powder, and cream to entice men."[33] Such claims resonated in an era of social mobility and conspicuous consumption. Women were further led to believe that they could attain not just beauty but the cachet of a celebrity or beauty queen. Film industries, print capitalism, and beauty contests spawned female celebrities whom cosmetics companies eagerly enlisted to promote their products. As the criteria for determining beauty arose not from the beholder but from Hollywood studios or panels of "expert" beauty contest judges, female celebrities and beauty queens became, to a degree, homogenized images of beauty ideals. Cosmetics products were, of course, the expected vehicle by which to reach those ideals. Lux soap advertisements linked soap to beauty and glamour rather than to laundry and household chores.³⁴ In Vietnam, Lux and Cadium brand soap assured customers that beautiful actresses used their products, with Lux using Marcelle Chantal and Crème Simon featuring Geneviève Félix.³⁵

Science was another powerful marketing tool. During the interwar years, European, American, and Japanese cosmetics companies marketed their products as marvels of modernity: developed through cutting-edge research, backed by evidence, and to be used with technologically advanced applicators.³⁶ "Science" communicated to consumers that beauty, or the lack or loss thereof, was no longer a matter of fate. Using the correct scientific tools, women could take matters into their own hands to maintain or even craft their own beauty.³⁷ Such an idea resonated among young women captivated by Vietnam's new trend in individualism. Tokalon boasted that its creams owed their efficacy to research by Dr. Stejskal in Vienna.³⁸ A certain Dr. Pierre touted the cutting-edge technology behind Forvil products, and the Vietnamese company Viễn Đệ likewise marketed its hair care products as being science-based.³⁹ Companies often named cosmetic products after their active chemical ingredients to highlight their supposed science-based virtues.⁴⁰ Tho Radia, an antiwrinkle cream made with thorium chlor and radium bromure—ingredients declared harmful and banned in 1937 by the French government—not only had a scientific-sounding name but had been invented by one Dr. Alfred Curie (figure 3.3). He was no relation of Pierre and Marie Curie (the famous science duo), but the company dropped his name in hopes that customers would make this association nonetheless.⁴¹

Stunning, jewel-like packaging, typically featuring the chic minimalism of Art Deco, made cosmetics products nearly irresistible. Sauzé released a compact with a sleek design of geometric figures that evoked the look of fine jewelry.⁴² Crème Siamoise, a French product, arrived in an elegant white octagonal box edged with black ribbon and partitioned day and night creams. On top of the box was a picture of a Janus-type single head with two faces, one with her eyes open (for the day cream) and the other with her eyes closed (for the night cream).⁴³ Vietnamese beauty companies followed suit. Kim Hue Oil was packaged in an elegant purple marbled box, and the label for "Jasmin perfume" was adorned with delicate flowers.⁴⁴

Thanks to technological innovations in packaging, women could enjoy products that were easier to apply and less apt to spill. Beauty creams could be squeezed from tubes; powder dispensed from loose sachets or pressed

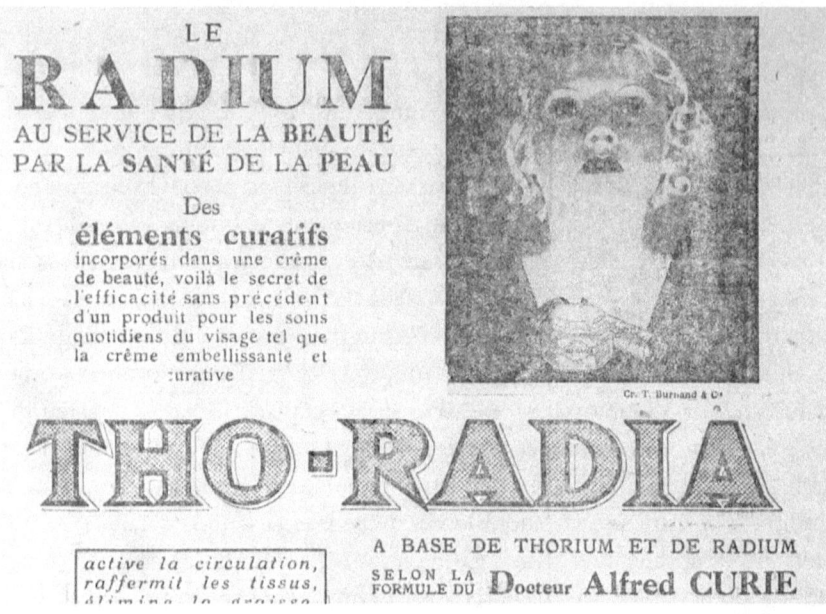

FIGURE 3.3. Advertisement for Tho Radia.
Source: *Sài Gòn*, October 4, 1933.

compacts; lipstick twisted up and down within a narrow metal cylinder; and lip gloss applied with a brush affixed to the small pot that held the gloss.[45] Complicated beauty regimes, such as the aforementioned Crème Siamoise day and night creams, were packaged together in sectioned pots.[46] Portable, compact products enabled busy women to touch up their makeup on the go—especially Modern Girls who stayed out late dancing.

Initially, Vietnamese women found cosmetics only at French-owned trading companies, which imported an array of hard to find items from the metropole. By the mid-1920s, they could waltz into department stores, where the sparkling cosmetics counter—itself resembling an enormous jewel—beckoned.[47] Vietnamese women who did not speak French or were uncomfortable in the company of European bourgeois shopped for beauty products in Vietnamese- or Chinese-owned beauty stores. Customers who could not make it to the big city flipped through mail-order catalogues from high-end distributors such as Saigon's Kéva Beauty Institute or large Vietnamese-owned beauty companies.[48]

COSMETICS

With female literacy rates soaring, women learned about the proper application of their cosmetics by reading instructional articles that regularly appeared in newspapers. In presenting daily beauty regimes as a quasi-scientific undertaking, the instructional articles appealed to women's intellect, a hitherto neglected resource.[49] Newspapers such as *Ngày Nay* and *Đàn-Bà* ran regular instructional columns outlining various application methods, including ways to hold brushes, the nuances of matching powder to skin color, and shading techniques to create the illusion of a higher nose or narrower face. *Đàn-Bà* newspaper's weekly column "Đẹp và Đẹp" (Beautiful and Beautiful) offered tips on makeup techniques and fashion advice. Vietnamese women also consumed instructional articles translated from French and American newspapers such as *Paris Soir Dimanche*, *Eve*, *Almanach d'Eve*, *Journal de la Femme*, and *American Weekly*.[50] Savvy advertisers sponsored articles that subtly promoted their products. A 1939 article in the *Đàn-Bà* newspaper presented readers with a problem: "Ladies, how do you wash off your makeup?" and then proceeded to outline a regime advising them to use Tho Radia.[51]

Wealthy French and Vietnamese women looking to be pampered made appointments at Vietnam's exclusive "beauty institutes." The most famous of these was the Kéva Institute, a branch of the luxurious Parisian spa of the same name, situated on the elegant Chasseloup Laubat Boulevard in Saigon. Beauty institutes offered spa treatments along with one-on-one consultations with experts, who developed personalized beauty regimens to address perceived flaws with skin-lightening serums, freckle removal, facials, antiaging treatments, makeup application, and makeup tattooing. Clients enjoyed specialized hair conditioning treatments as well as scalp massages and purported dandruff cures. Some even sought weight-loss treatments and electric shock treatments said to melt fat. Once the more taxing procedures were out of the way, clients could relax with manicures, pedicures, and eyebrow shaping.[52]

In 1935, a Vietnamese-owned beauty institute, the Institute de Beauté Madeleine, opened in a stunning Art Deco building on Bonnard Street in Saigon. Founded by Paris-trained Madeleine Bùi, mentioned in chapter 1, the institute brought French products—exclusively the Klytia brand—to Vietnamese women at a reasonable price. Her business philosophy was likely influenced by her father, Bùi Quang Chiêu. A member of the moderate Constitutionalist party, he called for equal rights for Vietnamese without going so far as to demand independence from the French. Just as her father called for the right to assemble, the right to vote, the right to a free press, and the right to travel within the colony, Madeleine Bùi called for the right for Vietnamese women to enjoy the same kinds of beauty indulgences as French women. She told newspapers her mission was to provide a place where Vietnamese women could feel comfortable accessing Parisian quality care without a language barrier. The institute offered an array of services such as beauty treatments, antiaging treatments, massages, and makeup application classes. A doctor was even on staff to perform rhinoplasty to heighten the bridge of one's nose; Miss Bùi assured potential customers that the operation would be pain- and scar-free.[53]

In Hanoi, women could frequent the Ma Beauté Institute, run by the French-trained Miss Yetta, who may have learned her beauty secrets as a former Valaque (sex worker from Eastern Europe). The institute offered treatments for aging, blemishes, acne, and excessive hair growth; ultraviolet treatments for rosacea and acne; and manicures and pedicures. It also touted Miss Yetta's expertise in hair dying and electric hair curling.[54] The Mỹ viện Amy (Amy Institute), located on Hàng Than Street in the 36 Streets section, appealed to a more middle-class, exclusively Vietnamese clientele. The institute, which capitalized on its chic hybrid Franco-Vietnamese name—"Amy" was a French name and "Mỹ viện" meant "beauty institute"—advertised in Vietnamese-language newspapers and offered a variety of skin treatments, including brightening procedures, mole removals, and blemish remedies. The institute touted its electric pulse machines and medicine to treat Keloid scars, melaleuca, and rough skin. The Mỹ viện Amy pampered women with massages and makeup sessions, teeth-whitening services, hair treatments, and electronic hair perms. Women could also purchase concoctions said to promote hair health or even lighten bruises.[55]

Beauty institutes were not the only authorities that women could consult in Vietnam. Celebrity beauty experts and aestheticians from institutes in France made occasional and much-anticipated appearances in the colony. In 1932, Dr. Suzanne Noël, the world-famous cosmetic surgeon who pioneered the mini-facelift, traveled to Saigon, where she collaborated with Lemanson Delalande, a doctor to the city's wealthiest and most image-conscious women. While in town, Dr. Noel delivered a well-attended public lecture in Saigon on surgical solutions to aging.[56] In 1935, newspapers celebrated the visit of a certified aesthetician from the Paris flagship of the Elizabeth Arden Institute, who appeared at the luxurious Frederic's Salon on Rue Paul Bert in Hanoi.[57]

For lower-middle-class women who could not afford a beauty institute but wanted a little pampering or an updated style, salons were a less expensive alternative. As salons became ubiquitous in France after World War I, the trend caught on in the colony as well, quickly spreading from big cities to provincial capitals. The innumerable beauty salons in Vietnam not only serviced an eager and expanding clientele but presented new entrepreneurial opportunities for Vietnamese women. Salons were owned and operated almost exclusively by women, who in turn hired other women to work there.[58] Salons in Vietnam cultivated an image of European authenticity, starting with French-language names such as "Grand Salon de Coiffure," "Salon de Coiffure Tương lai" (literally Salon for Hairstyles of the Future, a reference to its ultra-modern styles), and the Au Figaro salon on Bonnard Street in Saigon, which touted its adherence to "strict European rules of beauty treatment."[59] While most beauty products sold in Vietnam were imported from Europe, the United States, or Japan, some were manufactured in Vietnam. Similar to what Eugenia Lean identifies as a vernacular beauty industry in early twentieth-century China, a local industry in Vietnam produced and sold products, provided services, and disseminated knowledge to Vietnamese women. Whereas Lean finds evidence of factory-based manufacturing in China, the extant historical sources do not indicate that a comparable industry existed in Vietnam. I surmise that most, if not all, manufacturing of cosmetics and face creams took place in homes and pharmacies. Sources indicate that a sizeable portion of the vernacular industry was run by female entrepreneurs, most of whom sold products through mail order using new networks of transportation and communication. As for the pharmacies, they were male-dominated. While these goods were produced in Vietnam, they incorporated some foreign ingredients and foreign scientific knowledge. This chapter will discuss vernacular products in the context of the new technologies of beauty enumerated below.[60]

Some women pursued alternatives to foreign manufactured beauty products. In some cases, they continued to use traditional practices taught to them by their mothers and grandmothers; others embraced natural beauty remedies for the first time. Vietnamese newspapers of the interwar years encouraged women to solve their beauty problems with products found in their own kitchen. *Khoa Học*, a scientific journal, regularly published recipes for perfume, scented oils, face cream, face powder, and rouge–recipes used by local pharmacists and ordinary women alike.[61] Egg whites and rice powder were foundational ingredients for face masks, which might also include milk, cucumber, or tomato juice, elderflowers, olive oil, or friar's balsam.[62] Lemon juice and honey cleansed skin. Rose water, cow's milk, and mint leaves soothed blemishes. Olive oil, almond oil, and paraffin oil removed makeup, and butter, cocoa butter, and crème fraiche made for luxurious moisturizers.[63] Beets and other root vegetables stained lips and cheeks, rice powder had a secondary use as face powder, and the water left over from prerinsing rice nourished hair.

Rural women likely made their own beauty products when they could not access imported goods; other women did not trust the chemical ingredients of manufactured items. Some women undoubtedly turned to homemade products to economize, but many recipes called for pricey French imports such as almond or paraffin oil or cow's milk, which although locally sourced could be expensive. The natural approach aligned with traditional practices in the French countryside, where women had passed down beauty recipes to their daughters for generations.[64] Many such recipes, as well as those Indigenous to Vietnam, were translated and published in Vietnamese newspapers. The satirical newspaper *Vịt Đực* couldn't resist offering its own recipe for treating oily skin: "Wash off your makeup and rub *eau de rose* and egg white on your face. Then go out onto the street and into the sun and the eggs will turn into omelets or fried eggs. Pull them off your face and go ahead and eat them."[65]

NEW TECHNOLOGIES OF BEAUTY

As the global beauty craze swept the world, there was money aplenty to be made in Vietnam. Beauty companies pulled off the double goal of tapping into existing beauty trends—powder, face cream, lipstick—while offering novel products that promised customers a new *look*. New looks soon became emblematic of the new individual-minded young woman. Women not only changed the way they looked, but in doing so partook in a process of massive cultural change that was diminishing the power that a woman's family had over her life.

COSMETICS

Eyes

During the interwar years, eye makeup flew off the shelves as urban Vietnamese women strove to achieve Marlène Diétrich's legendary "passionate eyes."[66] Advances in packaging technology enabled eyes to be touched up repeatedly and on the go with delicious pallets of color. The famous stylist Nguyễn Cát Tường, who design the Lemur Tunic, also drew on his aesthetic expertise to advise women on how to use eye makeup to complement their coloring. Women with black hair and dark eyes should use a pastel gray eye shadow, he advised; those with reddish tones in their hair or skin should use brown. Women learned to apply shadow to the upper eyelid with a concentration of color in the middle that faded out to the sides and were cautioned to avoid overdoing it because excessive eye makeup made deep-set eyes appear older.[67]

Color, of course, was nothing without the definition imparted by long thick eyelashes. Women dotted almond oil on their lashes—a French trick—and used tiny scissors to carefully trim the thin ends of their lashes in hopes that they would grow back thicker.[68] Most effective, however, was mascara, which made lashes "more charming and dreamy."[69] Vietnamese women in the interwar years benefited from recent technological innovations in the mascara industry. Although mascara use dates as far back as the Egyptians, Romans, and Persians, who used a wand-like apparatus to apply kohl to the lashes, it was not until the mid-nineteenth century that the company Rimmel London developed a nontoxic mascara, a mixture of coal dust and petroleum jelly applied to eyelashes with a small brush. In the twentieth century, when silent films required much fluttering of the eyelashes, a lash mania developed in the United States, Europe, and urban areas of the colonized world.

Before long Vietnamese women were able to touch up their eyes on the go with compacts that included a cake of dry mascara and a small brush. Upscale compacts included an eye pencil or eyeshadow as well. Women moistened the mascara brush with water—though some improvised with saliva—scrubbed the wet brush across the black mascara cake, and then using the same brush applied it to their lashes. The brush helped to separate lashes that stuck together. In the early 1930s, a handheld eyelash curler hit the market, as did eyelash growth-promoting drugs. Tube-based mascara was not invented until the late 1930s.[70]

Women also highlighted their eyes by shaping their eyebrows. The look of the 1930s was a thin, arched brow that was thought to lift the eyes and brighten the face.[71] Some women applied mascara to their eyebrows to darken and manipulate the hairs that that they had chosen to keep on their arches. Women who couldn't master the art or couldn't be bothered with plucking their brows simply shaved them. Using a makeup pencil or charred matchstick, they filled in the spotty areas of what remained of their brows, and in some cases, they drew them from scratch.[72] This look had its detractors. A 1936 article in *Điễn Tín* quoted a husband complaining that "there is nothing more terrible than waking up early in the morning, looking at his wife's face and seeing an octopus without a single eyebrow!"[73]

Mouth

The changes to the mouth and teeth brought about by the Western cosmetics industry during the interwar era marked a reversal of centuries of Vietnamese tradition. The practice of dying teeth black had long been commonplace throughout Asia—in Japan, the Philippines, Java, Bali, Borneo, and among some minority groups in Laos, Thailand, India, and in southern China, as well as some Pacific islands. In Vietnam, the practice dated back to at least the third century CE. Teeth-dying was a ritual performed at puberty in Vietnam and in other parts of Asia. The complicated, four-step operation required more than two weeks, during which time the teeth were treated with acidic substances to help them absorb the color, and black lacquer was applied and allowed to set for a few days. The lacquer was believed to protect the teeth and was considered attractive. Đào Duy Anh insisted that "no matter how beautiful a person is, if her teeth do not blacken quickly, her beauty will fade." Natural white teeth, on the other hand, were considered unappealing and associated with animals, spirits, and demons.[74]

The practice of teeth-dying was abandoned in many other parts of Asia, most notably Japan, during the modernization campaigns of the late nineteenth century.[75] Although the French did not impose any bans on teeth-dying in Vietnam, the practice gradually fell out of fashion in urban areas during the colonial period, but it remained popular in rural areas through the mid-twentieth century.[76] As had been the case with Western fashion, women who cohabited with Western men, known as me tây, were the first demographic group to adopt the Western style of natural white teeth. Due to the association between me tây and white teeth, white teeth initially connoted licentiousness. In 1908, leaders of the Tonkin Free School encouraged students to modernize their look by, among other things, keeping their teeth white much as did young women in Japan. In the 1920s, as teachers and students in urban areas became increasingly familiar with French culture, they began rejecting the black teeth tradition. Those looking to reverse the existing lacquer shaved and bleached their teeth, procedures that were both expensive and painful and undoubtedly damaged their teeth. Vietnamese students studying in the metropole had their teeth whitened by French dentists, and those who remained in Vietnam went to Western-trained dentists, such as the Minh-Sinh practice in Hanoi.[77] By the mid-1930s, white teeth had become socially acceptable among most middle-class urbanites.[78] Nonetheless, even as late as 1938, some older Vietnamese continued to associate white teeth with sex work.[79]

As the white teeth trend swept urban areas, so too did the trend of an open-mouthed smile. Before the interwar years, Vietnamese society valued tight-lipped, closed-mouthed smiles and soft giggles among women.[80] Then, with the popularity of Western cinema, the Hollywood smile became the desired look among Modern Girls, whom the Ngày Nay newspaper characterized as "always happy, their mouths smiling, their teeth exposed."[81] The change to an open-mouthed smile was embraced by some: "[the] mouth has been underestimated over time. Poets rarely ever wrote about it, but even an ugly face can become beautiful with a bright, charming smile if there's a magical light shining on it. . . . A smile has a good effect on the spirit and a smiling face is a sign of a full and pure heart."[82] Likewise, a 1939 Đàn-Bà article advised that women who wanted to look young "should always keep smiling; it is a sign of your faith in a good future."[83]

With open-mouthed smiles and white teeth in vogue, Western-style dental care and oral hygiene that prioritized whiteness became a necessity. A female journalist writing for the Đàn-Bà newspaper advised readers: "The mouth is a fresh velvet flower, the flower of the face, which enhances its charm. You have to take great care of it."[84] Men and women who eschewed the black lacquering tradition scrubbed their teeth with salt to prevent browning and redden the gums, believed to be a sign of health.[85] Toothpaste companies, such as the Kolynos brand, promised products that would deliver both health benefits and a beautiful smile as well.[86] Dental brands sought creative ways to tap into new consumer markets. The makers of Bi-Oxyne, a whitening toothpaste, specifically targeted students predisposed by their colonial education to embrace Western trends. In Huế, the product was sold alongside textbooks at the AJS book and sundries store.[87] By the mid-1930s, it was not uncommon for dentists such as Dr. Lam Quang Si in Hanoi to offer cosmetic services, including teeth cleaning and dental veneers, a technique developed in the late 1920s in the United States for movie stars that became widely popular by the mid-1930s.[88]

The lipstick worn by the Modern Girls of the interwar era was a new touch. Until the late nineteenth century, lip color was rather toxic and sold in small pots and applied with a brush. Change arrived during the Industrial Revolution when Japanese cosmetics firms entered the market selling a variety of bright lip colors made with safer, less toxic ingredients.[89] Meanwhile, German scientists invented a synthetic alternative to carmine, the red pigment derived from insects that had been used for centuries and to which many women were allergic. Soon afterward, a more muted and natural-looking synthetic shade of red was introduced.[90] During World War I, the lipstick tube and push-up stick were invented, which made application easier and neater.[91] Colors quickly went in and out of fashion. The reds of the 1920s were associated with old ladies by the 1930s, when pinks and corals were the craze.[92] In the 1930s, women had the choice of two types of lip color: lip gloss (*son mỡ*) and a dry, matte lipstick (*son khô*). Dry lipstick was more durable and long-lasting; lip gloss looked dewy and sparkling and wiped off easily, without leaving a stain.[93]

Women used lipstick not just to color their lips but to manipulate the shape of them. To achieve that perfect Joan Crawford look, women all over Vietnam leaned in close to their mirror, held their lips taut, applied the lipstick onto the top and bottom, and then traced around their lips with a red lip pencil, emphasizing the cupid's bow to achieve a perfect heart shape.[94] Instructional articles taught women tricks to make wide mouths narrow or thicken thin lips, and lip exercises increased blood flow, lending plumpness and color. Women learned that less was more: those who overindulged appeared to have smeared a whole tube of lipstick all over their mouth, warned the *Hà Thành Ngọ Báo* newspaper.[95] A final dab of Vaseline, glycerin, or "Cô Ba," a locally produced petroleum jelly, made the lips appear wet and shiny.[96]

Lipstick had its critics. Some women complained that it stained their clothing and left them with dry, chapped lips.[97] The acerbic and in some cases toxic chemicals used in lipstick left many women with a literal bad taste in their mouth. As a result, some women made their own product from wax, almond oil, and honey, adding pigment from beets, radishes, or powdered orcanette (a member of the borage family).[98] In 1936, a Belgian brand addressed complaints about the unpleasant taste of lipstick by introducing lip products that purportedly tasted like champagne and burgundy wine.[99]

Skin Care

By 1914, a growing market for face creams had emerged in Europe, the United States, China, and Japan, and by the interwar years, the international cosmetics industry was selling a wide array of products designed to cleanse, nourish, and protect the skin.[100] This industry tapped a preexisting and lucrative vernacular market in Vietnam, which had a long tradition—transmitted largely by practice—of skin-care regimes.[101] Blemishes and conditions such as rosacea and eczema were typically considered dermatological problems and addressed with a traditional Sino-Vietnamese approach. As Vietnam "had a tradition of 'informed self-medication' driven by advertisements and instructional articles," a plethora of printed recipes and advertisements for products began appearing in colonial newspapers.[102]

Traditional Vietnamese medicine had long associated a clear complexion with good health and nutrition. Skin-care knowledge circulating during the interwar years similarly linked skin health to overall well-being and presented the organ as delicate and vulnerable to the slightest of health issues.[103] The complexion was believed to be highly sensitive to bodily rhythms: "erratic eating, sleepless nights, an inactive digestive system give you sallow skin and early wrinkles," according to interwar era beauty articles.[104] Rest was key to beauty, as a Đàn-Bà article reminded readers.[105]

Particularly important to skin clarity was the quality of the food consumed, women learned. Vietnamese medical knowledge linked conditions such as acne and rosacea to an imbalance of the yin and yang of the body caused in part by diet.[106] Women learned the necessity of plant-based diets for a radiant complexion and heeded warnings to avoid "hot" foods such as alcohol, tea, coffee, chili peppers, vinegar, and canned food, which increased yang.[107] Skin-care regimes even specified hours for eating certain foods to maximize skin health: meat was to be eaten only at lunch, and light, plant-based meals in the evening.[108] To keep their skin supple and youthful, women learned to stay hydrated and to consume a tablespoon of olive oil or paraffin oil every day.[109]

Proper hygiene (discussed in chapter 4) was likewise equated with beauty and considered "the best elixir" for all skin problems.[110] Beauty institutes such as Saigon's Kéva Institute offered courses in skin hygiene.[111] Women were admonished to remove their makeup nightly and to meticulously cleanse their face. Newspapers advised women to replace used towels with freshly washed white, soft, fragrant towels.[112] Cadum and Marseille brands of soap, delicate enough for facial skin, were recommended for their anti-bacterial qualities.[113] Local soap companies such as the Savonnerie Nguyên Hữu, offered a product that was both hygienic and fragrant.[114] Women learned to make their own facial soap with ingredients common in French cooking. Almond oil or paraffin oil removed makeup; a quick rinse with diluted lemon juice or cow's milk revived the skin after a long day.[115] Women were even advised to mind the temperature of the water—cold water tightened pores and softened skin—and to wash with rainwater, as the lime in tap water was deemed corrosive.[116]

Magazine articles exhorted readers to "restore" their skin after the arduous events of the day, preferably with professional (and sometimes expensive) "restoring creams."[117] Consumers had their choice of domestic creams such as Trường Xuân Milk or imported creams, such as Crème Siamoise, Elizabeth Arden, and Tokalon. The Tokalon company appealed to consumers' interest in scientific innovations with a restoration cream including "biocel," a "substance found in animals that can help restore the skin," extracted into the cream.[118]

Cosmetics advertisements incited near-panic about blemishes. "Women who would otherwise see a pretty reflection in the mirror with a sweet smile are greeted with acne and blemishes," began an advertisement for Madame Huỳnh Công Sáu's acne cream. Acne was often treated with painful procedures involving needles and harsh ointments.[119] There was no shortage of beauty practitioners competing to treat this blight on women's complexions.[120] Newspapers printed recipes for homemade acne treatments that included chevenis oil, rose water, and egg whites.[121] Women also learned to prevent acne through regular exercise, staying in well-ventilated areas, and tending to their digestion.[122]

During the interwar years, industrially produced skin-color-altering products became popular throughout the world. Women with pale skin were sold products to make it tan; women with darker skin were sold products to lighten it. Cosmetics companies made claims about "nature," science, race, social status, and refinement to encourage women to achieve their desired skin tone.[123] In Vietnam, light skin had historically been a preference even before French colonization; it connoted a life of upper-class leisure, whereas dark skin betrayed a life of toiling under the sun. Women of all classes thus did their best to avoid the sun with wide-brimmed hats and long-sleeved clothing. In the Sino-Vietnamese medical tradition, women whitened their skin by washing it with a rice powder concoction or applying a herbal Chinese formula called "qui bai fang."[124] Western cosmetics companies jumped at the opportunity to profit from the skin-lightening craze. Products such as Crème Siamoise and Butil cream promised to lighten skin.[125] Addressing "young women who want to get married," advertisements for Tokalon whitening cream appealed to their anxiety about finding a mate.[126] Women also used homemade skin lighteners consisting of a benzoin tincture and rose water.[127]

In Europe and the United States, deeply tanned skin was all the rage in the 1930s. The trend has been attributed to the fashion designer Coco Chanel, who famously brought back an accidental tan after a vacation on the Côte d'Azur in the 1920s. Tanning soon became associated with fashion, health, and the carefree lifestyle of Modern Girls. European and American tanning trends never became popular in Asia due to their association with peasantry, but tanning appears to have caught on among certain Vietnamese Modern Girls in the late 1930s. A 1939 *Đàn-Bà* newspaper article explained: "With the popularity of sports and leisure, styles for women have changed. Before you wanted your skin to be pale and white; now you are even using dark powder to make you appear tan."[128] Vietnamese women applied face powder to "look like they had rosy, healthy cheeks" and to achieve that "just-came-back-from-a-vacation" look.[129] The tanning trend, however, was likely short-lived and limited in scope; it is referenced only twice in the available Vietnamese-language press, and both references are from the summer of 1939.

Aging

During the interwar years, the cosmetics market opened to older women as perceptions of aging changed in France and Vietnam. In nineteenth-century

Europe and the United States, women over the age of thirty-five had been dismissed as elderly and unattractive; not until the early twentieth century did it become acceptable for older women to pursue beauty regimes.[130] A similarly dramatic shift in attitudes toward older women occurred in Vietnam during the interwar years, when women in their thirties and forties were encouraged to embrace their beauty and sexuality. Meanwhile, eschewing the traditional vow of chastity, Vietnamese widows of all ages were considering remarriage and embraced beautification.[131] Yet in no way did cosmetics companies' courting of older customers amount to a welcoming acceptance of them as they were. Instead, as Lois Banner argues, older women's vanity was acceptable only to the extent that it involved explicit attempts to look younger through the alteration of gray hair, wrinkles, and other features associated with age.[132]

Aging had traditionally been a source of pride for the women of Vietnam. Before World War I, elderly Vietnamese women had commanded respect from their essential role in the family, which was often multigenerational. The significance of family and family roles was reflected in the language: Vietnamese pronouns, even in conversations among strangers, were determined by one's presumed position in the family, such as big sister, little brother, young auntie, older uncle. Although Vietnam was a patriarchal society, elderly women did command considerable respect. Given their role in producing children—and by extension the grandchildren and great-grandchildren who would go on to tend to the family's ancestral rites—they commanded even more respect as they aged and advanced to the elder generation. Indeed, the pronouns used to refer to elder women—*bà* (grandmother) and *cụ* (great-grandmother)—were a source of pride insofar as they spoke to their status in a family and the wisdom acquired through age and experience.[133] Ironically, the "privilege" of being invited to partake in beautification rituals—or more precisely, antiaging interventions—had the perverse effect of eroding the considerable self-esteem these women had traditionally derived from their advancing age.[134]

The phenomenon described here signaled a shift away from Vietnam's long-standing family-centric social system and toward a new trend of individualism. The shift is evident in the literature of the period, which increasingly portrayed Vietnamese youth in a more positive light than the elderly.[135] Vũ Trọng Phụng's 1936 novel *Dumb Luck*, a satirical critique of the interwar Europeanization and modernization movements, contrasts the characters of Mrs. Deputy Customs Officer and Grandpa Hồng to highlight the colony's changing social structure. So desperately does Grandpa Hồng want to become the eldest member of his family and thus be honored with the pronoun "cụ" (great-grandfather) that he deliberately attempts to look older than he is and goes so far as to attempt to murder his own father in order to assume the coveted role of patriarch. In contrast, Mrs. Deputy Customs Officer (Bà Phó Đoan), the forty-something widow of a Frenchman, colors her gray hair and cakes her face with powder and lipstick in a desperate attempt to appear younger. She is insulted when Xuân, the protagonist, betrays her age by calling her "bà"—the deferential pronoun used for a lady of a grandmother's generation that would have commanded respect only two decades earlier.[136]

Given this rather abrupt shift in attitude about a woman's age, antiaging products and procedures were advertised aggressively in Vietnamese language newspapers during the interwar years. The Kéva Institute promised to help women "stay young and beautiful forever" through specialized creams and surgical procedures.[137] The Institute de Beauté Madeleine advertised a machine that smoothed out those wrinkles that made women "much uglier than their sisters."[138] "Time attacks you, but Coty will defend you and keep you looking young" promised one 1936 advertisement.[139] Science served as a powerful tool in such advertisements. Tokalon promised that "science has discovered a substance to restore beauty." The claims made for the company's pink and white creams were increasingly outlandish: they would take ten years off one's skin, they would make a forty-five-year-old look like a young girl.[140] Likewise, an advertisement for Tho Radia, a radium-based product, promised that the product would "make the old look young" using scientific innovations to "suppress wrinkles" (see figure 3.3)—assuming the radium-poisoned consumer lived long enough to see wrinkles appear in the first place.[141]

Instructional articles taught women how to apply makeup to hide their age. They were advised to use vibrant lipstick colors and avoid dark eye makeup after the age of thirty.[142] White powder should likewise be avoided because the face should have a pinkish—though not red—tint to connote youth. Blush the tops of cheeks, near the ears and eyes, but "avoid the bridge of the nose or the features will appear old." "Square faces age easily," so those cursed with this feature learned to soften the angles of their face with powder.[143] Meanwhile, stark images in advertisements warned

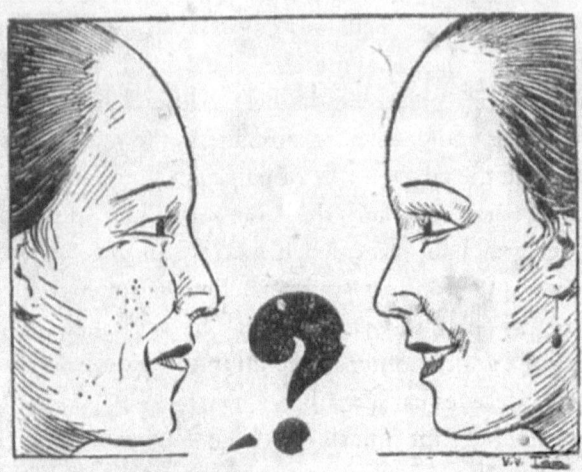

FIGURE 3.4. Advertisement for Keva Beauty Institute.
Source: *Phụ Nữ Tân Văn*, July 3, 1930.

women to fear for the future of their looks. A 1930 advertisement for the Kéva Institute features two silhouettes facing each other, on the left an old woman and on the right a young one (figure 3.4). The two women are separated by a question mark inviting the prospective customer to ask herself whether aging might be preventable after all.[144] A 1935 advertisement for Tokalon cream shows two hands clasping a fortune teller's crystal ball. Inside the ball is an image of a European woman superimposed with the years 1935, 1936, and 1937 (figure 3.5)—leading women to consider their own dire futures without the magic cream.[145]

Women even embraced specific behavioral interventions to avoid aging their skin. Cold water face rinses and egg white masks were said to smooth skin; positioning the face upward inhibited the progression of neck

COSMETICS

FIGURE 3.5. Advertisement for Tokalon cream.
Source: Phong Hóa, September 20, 1935.

wrinkles; avoiding squinting or raising eyebrows thwarted crow's feet and forehead creases. To prevent wrinkles, women avoided sun exposure or wore sunglasses, a chic new fashion accessory. Hands, so often overlooked as a telltale sign of aging, were to be massaged and properly cared for.[146] Above all, an article in the *Ngày Nay* newspaper declared, a positive attitude was key to staying young.[147] And the *Đàn-Bà* newspaper concurred: a bad mood was enough to age a woman.[148]

Powder

Traditional Vietnamese face powder was made with ground rice. Women of the Nguyễn royal court in Huế used the precious *phấn nụ* powder, said to make skin radiant and heal everything from acne and rosacea. The secret recipe was passed down from royal mother to daughter; daughters-in-law were prohibited from knowing the ingredients.[149] Commoners used ordinary powder to lighten dark skin, brighten sallow skin, even out patchy skin tones, and conceal acne, blemishes, freckles, and age spots.

Both foreign and domestic powders were advertised aggressively in Vietnam. Tokalon, a Swiss brand of powder, promised to "make the skin retain a peach-like color all day without being overly shiny," and to "make your skin as beautiful as rose petals."[150] The Japanese brand Tosika—touted as fragrant and smooth, less expensive, and nontoxic—was sold in a compact for a mere forty-seven cents.[151] As powder had been popular in Vietnam long before the interwar years, there was no dearth of domestic-made product brands, including Xuân Hương powder, Đại Quang, and Trân Châu brands of powder.[152]

Powder use required skill to match a woman's skin tone and blend flawlessly (figure 3.6). Nguyễn Cát Tường instructed women to choose a color to match their skin tone because such a color would "subtly increase your beauty." He advised women to avoid typical mistakes of a novice wearer, including caking on powder, leaving patchy colors of powder that resembled a tortoise shell, or neglecting to dust powder on the back on their necks or the tops of their hands, thereby betraying a different skin tone

FIGURE 3.6. Instructions for applying powder.
Source: Ngày Nay, July 26, 1936.

than that of their well-powdered face.[153] Women also learned to use powder to manipulate the shape of the face. Women with "flat" noses applied eye shadow to the sides of the nose to make the bridge of the nose appear taller; women with "tall" noses "flattened" them by applying a pinkish powder to the top of the bridge. A little pink powder at the center of the chin would highlight the protrusion of the chin, and a little powder where the earlobes connected to the face would bring the ears into relief.[154] With enough powder, "even a gray-haired lady could again look young like an 18-year-old," the ever-sarcastic *Vịt Đực* newspaper quipped.[155]

To brighten their face and give it a rosy, youthful glow, women applied rouge. Originally made with lead and alum—both toxic—rouges were being made of safer materials by the end of the nineteenth century.[156] During the interwar years, rouges were available in both powder and cream form.[157] Women learned to coordinate their rouge colors to their outfits and to choose those that complemented their skin tone. As with powder, women learned that rouge could be used to manipulate the structure of a woman's face: a round face could be slimmed with angular brush strokes, and a thin face could be plumped up with circular strokes and rosier blush colors.[158]

Unfortunately, blush, like powder, proved difficult to work with in Vietnam's sticky tropical heat. Perspiration and rain caused blush to melt or slide off.[159] Using a magnifying glass, women meticulously applied a glycerin-based primer to give their makeup staying power. This trick came with a caveat, however: too much glycerin caused makeup to crack or even darkened the skin permanently.[160] The satirical newspaper *Vịt Đực* suggested an alternative solution: "Take the white part of moon cake rolls and place it on the surface of your face before going out. It's very durable and doesn't hurt the skin. And if your adventures keep you out for a long time and you get hungry, you can peel it off. It's very delicious and healthy!"[161]

Hair

Historians know little about the precolonial history of hair in Vietnam. In the period leading up to the first century CE, both women and men wore their hair short and shaven, which was the practice in many Southeast Asian societies at the time.[162] When the Viet people came under Chinese rule, from the first through the tenth century, hair was considered a gift from one's ancestors and cutting it off was frowned upon.[163] Chinese imperial rulers thus mandated long hair for women and men alike; both sexes typically wore their long hair tied up in a bun or a turban. By the time of French colonization, women in Tonkin wore their hair in a turban with a lock of hair twisted and hanging out, and women in Cochinchina tied their hair in a bun covered in a square scarf (*khăn chít đầu*) atop their head to protect them from the sun.[164]

As in other parts of Asia, Vietnamese men adopted Western-style short haircuts before women did.[165] As discussed in the introduction of this book, short hairstyles first appeared among Vietnamese men in 1906. The short hair trend—and the cultural change it symbolized—became further normalized at the end of World War I, when troops returning from the war arrived with French-style short hair that, in addition to looking more Western and modern, was considered more hygienic.[166] Barber shops, such as Salon de Coiffure Michel Phu and Au Progrès Coiffeur in Saigon, popped up throughout Vietnam and, as the latter name suggests, linked short hair to modernity.[167] Yet Vietnamese men did not completely abandon Vietnamese aesthetics and continued to wear the traditional tunic and turban on formal occasions. In the 1920s, a ready-made turban-hat to top off the new shorter haircut was invented as a time-saving alternative to the labor-intensive traditional turban.[168]

The shift in Vietnamese women's hairstyles followed international trends, with one Vietnamese paper referring to European women as the "older sisters" of hair fashion.[169] Even before World War I, women in Europe and the United States had been experimenting with shorter cuts, curls, and color. After the war, young European women shocked society with short, boyish bob cuts; by the 1930s, a more feminine trend emerged although women kept their hair cut to the shoulders or above. New technologies introduced after World War I made permanent hair curling safer, enabling women to add soft waves.[170] The Western hairstyle trend spread quickly through the medium of Hollywood films. Modern Girls in Japan also bobbed and curled their hair.[171] In China, as modernists reconsidered beauty practices such as footbinding and long hair came under scrutiny. Chinese feminists framed the argument for shorter hair in terms of hygiene and liberation; Chinese New Republic authorities, for their part, interpreted it as an act of rebellion and put limits on schoolgirls sporting bobs, perms, and even side parts.[172]

In the late 1920s, New Women began to embrace the shorter hairstyles. The movement began with Mrs. Huỳnh Thị Bảo Hoà, a founder and president of the Đà Nẵng women's union. Thanks to her example, it caught on in Hanoi and then Saigon. By 1936, it was no longer scandalous for women to cut their hair shoulder-length or above and leave it loose and uncovered.[173] They shifted their part from the middle of the forehead to a more seductive side-part, "sliding down the face, like a staircase."[174] They kept their hair out of their face with barrettes, colorful ribbons, tortoise shell pins, and stylish scarfs, and curled their locks with perms or curling irons, despite the popular belief that curly-haired women were jealous and had hot tempers.[175]

Not everyone subscribed to European hair ideals. For those women who wanted to update their style but were not ready to go short, Nguyễn Cát Tường promoted a chic new look: *tóc vấn trần*. In the tóc vấn trần style, women parted their long hair to the side and pulled it back at the nape of the neck, at which point they twisted it up and around the crown of their head to form a halo. To make the hair appear thicker, local beauty shops eagerly supplied fake hair pieces or a velvet scarf over which women twisted their hair, artificially augmenting the thickness of their mane.

In the 1930s, women had their choice of an array of products with which to style their hair. Popular imported brands included Capri hair dye, Lotion Forgère conditioner, and Pétrol Hahn, a kerosene-based product for cleaning hair.[176] Domestic products included Kim Hue Oil and Viến Đệ eucalyptus oil for dandruff and hair loss.[177] Women also treated their hair with homemade recipes derived from coconut oil, garlic root, dandelion water, olive oil, amber oil, and citron essence.[178]

Criticism of attitudes about short hair fell along generational lines, with the older generation insisting that short hair "contradicted the national essence [quốc túy]"—language borrowed from broader debates about modernism versus Confucianism. The *Phụ Nữ Tân Văn* newspaper, a leading proponent of women's right to cut their hair, pointed out the hypocrisy of these arguments, especially coming from men, who had begun cutting their own hair a few decades earlier.[179] One journalist made the nationalist argument that only under Chinese rule was long hair imposed on Vietnamese women and pointed to the ancient Vietnamese "coconut" haircut that involved shaving the sides of the head.[180] Another *Phụ Nữ Tân Văn* journalist, Madame Bạch Liên, noted that, given the amount of backlash surrounding the issue, to cut one's hair short was a genuine act of bravery.[181]

The new hairstyles freed urban Vietnamese women from the many problems and inconveniences associated with long hair, including the time and effort spent washing and brushing it, the hygienic problems it posed (lice, strands of hair falling into cooking pots), and the aches and pains caused by the sheer weight of it.[182] Long hair could also be a source of embarrassment when women sat on their hair in public—a definite faux pas. Writing in defense of short hair, the *Phụ Nữ Tân Văn* journalist Madame Bạch Liên shared a personal anecdote from her long-haired days. Catching someone in the act of trying to steal one of her chickens, she rushed outside to stop him—only to catch her long hair on something, stop to untangle it, and allow the thief to escape in the process.[183]

Short hair freed Vietnamese women to lead more active lives, making it especially popular among New Women. In the hot, humid climate of Vietnam, short hair was light and cool.[184] It enabled women to exercise, ride a bicycle, and play tennis or ping-pong with ease.[185] It was also more comfortable when giving birth and in the postpartum recovery period, when women's bathing options were restricted to a month of steam baths and they could not wash their hair.[186] One *Phụ Nữ Tân Văn* journalist equated short hair with national productivity: Long hair often slowed down operations by getting tangled in a plow or the motor of a boat. "In the civilized countries of the world, women have short hair," she concluded.[187]

Hands and Nails

Hands have historically been an indicator of class in Vietnam and Asia more broadly. Thick hands with dry, cracked skin and short, dirty, frayed fingernails evidenced a life of working in the fields and signified a peasant class status. Men and women of the mandarin class highlighted their status by growing their nails up to twelve centimeters long and fastidiously grooming them.[188] Members of the aspiring urban middle class, eager to distance themselves from their peasant counterparts, eagerly embraced Western hand and nail products.

The most notable change in hand care in Vietnam came with the invention of nail polish. Liquid nail polish became popular throughout North America and Europe soon after it was introduced by the Cutex brand in the mid-1920s.[189] Nail color added a "touch of freshness" to one's hands, Nguyễn Cát Tường declared to his readers. In the early 1930s, polish colors remained within the spectrum of light pinks, matching the "natural" hues of a nicely made-up face. By mid-decade, however, new colors hit store shelves, designed to match women's clothing. They included vivid colors such as cherry red, sapphire blue, emerald green, deep purple, and bright orange.[190]

Nguyễn Cát Tường was only too happy to help women select their ideal polish color, suggesting shades to complement one's skin tone. He taught how to enhance the shape of one's fingers: crimson nail polish was said to make fingers look stubby, whereas light pink elongated them. Fashion rules dictated that women "wear sparkly nail polish in the early evening and matte nail polish at night . . . [when attending] a funeral, wear a dark nail color." Interestingly, nail polish was not used only by Modern Girls: even women who kept their teeth black used the product, though they were advised to stick to dark colors—presumably to match their teeth.[191] This seeming paradox of lacquered teeth and nail polish is but one example of how women in interwar Vietnam experimented with the "traditional" and "modern" simultaneously; the two categories were hardly exclusive.

With all of the new products for nails came a new emphasis on nail care. Women learned to buff, clean, and file nails into a rounded almond-like shape or a sharpened point. Advice columns told women to perform stretching and gripping exercises to make their hands smooth and give them delicate, doll-like fingers. With strappy shoes and sandals in fashion, toenails, like fingernails, became objects of scrutiny. Women washed, moisturized, trimmed, filed, and painted their toes to match their fingernails.[192]

Perfume

Scented oils and waters—infused with sandalwood, jasmine, rose, and neroli—had long been used by Vietnam's upper-class women. At weddings and festivals, clothing was perfumed with the smoke of incense. In general, however, perfumes were used sparingly, and strong bodily scents, even pleasant ones, were frowned upon.[193]

The French conquest brought European perfumes to Vietnam. As it turned out, this was hardly a one-way import. As Geffrey Jones notes, in the nineteenth century, as Europeans expanded their empires in the Eastern Hemisphere—including Vietnam—they acquired the raw materials necessary for perfume production. The ready access to these raw materials allowed for a lower-priced product. And the Industrial Revolution led to innovations in perfume production. New means of extracting essential oils from flowers and the ability to produce synthetic scents lowered the costs of producing perfume and allowed for a greater variety of scents.[194]

By the early twentieth century European perfume—once a luxury product—had become accessible to the world's growing middle class. After World War I, bottles designed by artists and jewelers made the vast array of perfumes all the more desirable. Department stores and trading companies in Vietnam sold famous French brands, including Coty, Cécé, Sauzé, and Gellé Frères.[195] Local markets, as well as stores in Chợ Lớn and Hanoi's 39 Streets district, sold domestic perfumes and oils such as dầu Vạn scented oil.[196] The ideal fragrance was linked to "a fresh scent blowing in the wind" and "a quiet language, a gentle silhouette, a halo that silently envelops beauty."[197] Paradoxically, fragrance was prized for its power to seduce; a recurring trope in newspapers was that perfume was a weapon with which to conquer men in the war of seduction.[198]

Critics of cosmetics frowned upon perfume usage. A 1933 article in the *Sài Gòn* newspaper made the case that Vietnamese women did not need perfume in the same way that French women did. French women, given their habit of drinking cow's and goat's milk from a young age, "sweat terribly and radiated the smell" of these animals, whereas Vietnamese women, who eschewed milk, had "no need to mask any smells."[199] Critics recoiled at the excessive use of perfume and urged women to be restrained in their application and to avoid wearing it in inappropriate circumstances, such as when visiting the infirm.[200] The aforementioned *Ngày Nay* article that called perfume a powerful weapon went on to warn that "sometimes it can also kill us if you don't know how to use it or if you use cheap perfumes."[201]

CRITIQUES OF COSMETICS

Disapproval of the influence of cosmetics on women young and old was hardly limited to Vietnam. Around the world, journalists and social critics were questioning the changes in youth culture that had become a global phenomenon during the interwar era. In some countries draconian laws were introduced to control women's behavior—a trend not lost on Vietnamese journalists who regularly reported on it. In an effort to preserve the image of German women as healthy, athletic, and wholesome, the

Nazi Party issued a series of decrees in 1933 banning, among other things, the use of makeup, which it deemed "lewd."[202] Italy's Mussolini-led government followed with similar regulations for schoolgirls. China's New Life Movement, which aimed to address poverty and imperialism by imposing Confucian values, introduced regulations for women modeled on those of Fascist Europe. In 1934 China's nationalist KMT party issued an ordinance requiring modesty in dress along with a ban on makeup among schoolgirls, aimed at "preserving their innocence." In 1935, the KMT prohibited permed hair and side parts.[203] Japan followed suit in 1935 with bans on schoolgirls cutting their hair and wearing makeup.[204]

While cosmetics were never banned in Vietnam, critics did denounce the use of makeup, Vietnam's fraught relationship with cosmetics was informed by prewar views of women's beauty generally and drew on many of the arguments put forth in the neo-Confucian trend. For one thing, a woman's beauty—whether natural or enhanced by cosmetics—was not necessarily viewed as an asset. Citing the proverb *"hồng nhan bạc phận"* ("to be beautiful is a precarious fate"), an article in a 1933 edition of *Trung Hòa Nhật Báo* notes that Vietnamese poetry is rife with stories of beautiful women struggling with a dark destiny and warns that beauty could make a woman miserable.[205] Natural beauty was, however, considered more pure and hence less dangerous than the beauty conjured through cosmetic artifice. The female journalist Nguyễn Thị Thanh Vân averred that a woman's face is as beautiful as a flower, her natural skin, without powder and foundation, is still elegant, and her lips are bright and glossy without lipstick. She insisted: "That's the type of natural beauty that's worth treasuring."[206] Madamoiselle Thanh Tâm of *Sài Gòn* newspaper agreed: "Clean clothes and well-kept shoes are enough to make a woman look good; why add makeup?"[207] Some critics observed ruefully that cosmetics enabled women to deceive men about their status, age, and appearance, an argument also made in the Japanese context. A 1930 article by a female journalist in *Phụ Nữ Tân Văn* stated flatly: "If you use make-up to accentuate [your features], that's a deceitful beauty, no matter how pleasant it is to look at."[208]

Critics warned women that excessive use of makeup would backfire and turn them ugly. Makeup, with its "chalky, flashy look," the female journalist Nguyễn Thị Thanh Vân opined for *Phụ Nữ Tân Văn*, "does not make the wearer beautiful; [on the contrary], it reduces the dignity of that person."[209] The *Hà Thành Ngọ Báo* newspaper conceded that small amounts of makeup were acceptable but that overuse would make women's skin unhealthy and unsightly.[210] Articles in French and American media were generally more accepting of cosmetics usage, but they too warned that men were repulsed by excessive makeup and that it "should be used to enhance your beauty, not give you a new face."[211]

As was typical around the world, critics in Vietnam argued that the use of cosmetics amounted to a challenge to traditional sexual mores. Their arguments were rooted in a fear that women of the interwar years were engaging in premarital sex and adultery, both of which were seen as a rebuke of the traditional family system of arranged marriages in favor of European style individualism and sexuality. Girls who broke their prearranged marital contracts brought shame on the family, often resulting in a financial penalty for her parents.

To critics, makeup represented a loss of innocence among young women and a pivot onto the road to depravity. Schoolgirls with faces plastered in makeup and lipstick looked disconcertingly like adults, according to an article in the *Đàn-Bà* newspaper. Its female author also claimed that excessive makeup caused the skin to "lose the natural beauty of childhood."[212] In his novel *To Whore* (*Làm Đĩ*), Vũ Trọng Phụng famously correlated the protagonist's journey into sex work with her early experimentation with cosmetics: "It was as if I were afraid that people could read my dirty thoughts clearly. . . . I started putting on makeup, losing my spontaneity and innocence."[213] Cosmetics were also associated with homewrecking behavior. Referencing the increasingly common predicament of a wife discovering traces of another woman's lipstick on her husbands' lips, neck, or shirt collar, the satirical newspaper *Vịt Đực* playfully reported that the lipstick industry had formulated a "non-contagious" lipstick. "Ladies, please buy this and use it to avoid the accidents that happen when lovers kiss!"[214]

Beauty institutes—where elite women disrobed for treatments, allowed spa workers to massage their body parts, and submitted to the expertise of male doctors—raised suspicions that inappropriate sexual behavior was occurring therein. In a satirical column in *Vịt Đực*, cô Ngã writes scathingly about a friend (likely fictional) who received a message at a beauty institute, after which the male practitioner sent her home with a jar of pomade to rub over the spots that he missed. The writer's friend complains that she can't reach all the spots by herself and adds cheekily: "In my opinion, the task of rubbing our bodies should be given to someone [who can] help us—for example, my husband's friend." Cô Ngã's insinuation: women who patronized beauty institutes had loose morals and might well engage in extramarital affairs.[215]

As in other areas of the world, in Vietnam cosmetics were associated not just with sexuality but with sex work. In his famous reportage *Wretched Hanoi* (*Hà Nội lầm than*), Trọng Lang associated women who wore excessive makeup and crimson lipstick with sex work.[216] In 1930, a female journalist writing for *Hà Thành Ngọ Báo* noted that women who "draw on eyebrows, wear lipstick, enhance their beauty, who are too done up, look like prostitutes."[217] The historical association between cosmetics and sex workers is reflected in common euphemisms for sex work: "the profession of lipstick and powder" (*nghề son phấn*)[218] and "the market for lipstick and powder" (*chợ bán son phấn*).[219]

The tawdry association of cosmetics with illicit sexuality cast doubt on the intellectual and professional capabilities of women generally. In a critique of feminism, journalist Hoàng Đạo sneered in the *Ngày Nay* newspaper: "Women think being equal to men means applying makeup and lounging around doing their nails like a Chinese princess."[220] The prominent nationalist Phan Bội Châu, in an interview in which he stated his support for gender equality and girls' education, insisted that cosmetics undermined these two ideals. He told the interviewer: "Women who think they are independent must have a career. If they just want to touch up their makeup, flip their hair flirtatiously . . . then all this talk of women's rights is blasphemous."[221] In 1939, the New Woman Ngọc Minh, writing in *Đàn-Bà*—a newspaper that itself published a great deal on fashion and beauty—claimed that the use of cosmetics impeded girls' academic endeavors. "When they should be spending their time on their schoolwork but instead are thinking about makeup and the like, their learning is affected," she argued. Her article went on to make the case that schools in Vietnam should follow the lead of fascist countries and prohibit students from wearing makeup.[222]

Social anxiety about cosmetics in interwar Vietnam mirrored the anxieties frequently expressed about excessive consumerism and individualism. The use of cosmetics, it was feared, would make women shallow and materialistic. In 1930, a female jounalist writing for *Hà Thành Ngọ Báo* declared rather boldly that women who regularly applied cosmetics "worshipped materialism" and that such women "rarely cultivate thought, practice good virtue, or learn to elevate their soul. True inner beauty never comes to them."²²³ A second, equally patronizing article published that year by the same female journalist reasoned that "the temperament of women is immature," leading them to be "consumed with making themselves beautiful using makeup and clothing and jewelry."²²⁴ The implication was that women needed to guard against this inherent predisposition to vanity and self-indulgence.

Critics were shocked by the money women spent on cosmetics. The *Đàn-Bà* newspaper condemned the regular use of cosmetics as money spent in vain.²²⁵ The *Sài Gòn* newspaper wondered why women would spend money to wear makeup "day in and day out? Spending money this way is ridiculous."²²⁶ *Phụ Nữ Tân Văn* warned hyperbolically that some American women actually did without food in order to pay for their precious makeup. "Bread was a second priority for them"; apparently, they would rather starve than go without makeup.²²⁷ The satirical newspaper *Vịt Đực* presented a hypothetical for those women who regularly permed their hair: "What happens if there is a war? Will the fashionable head last forever?" The author quipped that women should shave their heads and put aside the money thus saved to pay for food in the event of a future catastrophe.²²⁸

Vietnamese newspapers expressed anxiety that women in their twenties and thirties would squander family resources on cosmetics—not an unreasonable concern given that the cosmetics industry was booming despite the economic downturn. In 1930, a female journalist writing for *Phụ Nữ Tân Văn* bemoaned the amount of money women were spending on cosmetics: "It's money made from sweat and tears—your in-laws' or your own."²²⁹ (This statement alludes to the ever-combustible relationship between young Vietnamese women and their mothers-in-law, a hot-button issue during the 1930s.²³⁰) In 1934, *Hà Thành Ngọ Báo* reported that in the United States and Europe families were being plunged into poverty by wives' makeup consumption and warned that this phenomenon was occurring in urban areas of Vietnam as well.²³¹ That same year, *Trung Hòa Nhật Báo* even reported, perhaps apocryphally, that excessive consumption of cosmetics by Chinese women was spawning corruption, with politicians resorting to soliciting bribes to pay for their wives' cosmetics. The article warned married men to keep a watchful eye on the spending of these potentially "weak women."²³²

To critics, young women's use of cosmetics was not just financially irresponsible; it was part and parcel of their rejection of familial and social obligations. The sometimes considerable amounts of money that Vietnamese women spent on cosmetics was especially concerning to critics given that family money was communal. But even more worrisome for critics was that managing the family finances, one of the Four Virtues, was expected of women. Generally, the responsibility was taken on by the matriarch of multigenerational households, but daughters and daughters-in-law were expected to manage their money responsibly and, in so doing, practice for the day when they would be the ones in control of the family finances. Financial responsibility among daughters and daughters-in-law was of particular concern during the economic instability of the late 1920s, when the economy was stalled by saturated rubber and rice markets, and even more so in the early 1930s with the advent of the Great Depression.

Critics went further still and accused women who wore makeup of shirking family responsiblities beyond the strictly financial ones. A female journalist writing for the *Đông Pháp Thời Báo* newspaper reminded women not to obsess over cosmetics, as "their real duty is to the family."[233] Girls' and women's obligation, declared female journalist Nguyễn Thị Thanh Vân writing in *Phụ Nữ Tân Văn*, was to stay home with their parents and take care of them, and then, once married, to take care of their children and their husband's parents. Yet there were women who indulged in "extravagent luxuries" and "applied makeup seven times a day," leaving little time or energy to fulfill their obligations as wives and mothers. Moreover, the article continued, married women "still put on red lipstick and white powder all over their face when they go out—are they looking for outside love and ... not fulfilling their obligations as wife and mother?"[234]

Cosmetics led women to neglect not just their families but their nation as well, critics claimed. In a 1926 speech endorsing the newly formed women's union, the prominent nationalist Phan Bội Châu warned women against wasting their money on perfume, lipstick, and powder, which he considered the wrong path for reform and progress, especially at a time when the majority of Vietnamese people were going hungry.[235] In 1932, *Phụ Nữ Tân Văn*, which was consistently critical of cosmetics use, ran an article schooling its Depression era readers on this grievous problem: "In this time of economic crisis, when business is at a standstill, unemployment is soaring ... floods and other natural disasters abound ... Women buy lipstick and powder ... and squander money." The article asked incredulously: "How much do they waste on makeup and perfume each year? ... they could help the people of Nghệ Tĩnh, the unemployed, the illiterate and the homeless with that money."[236] Female journalist Thanh Tâm writing for the *Sài Gòn* newspaper echoed this sentiment:

> People in Vietnam can't even afford everyday items. They need to save their money for clothing and medical care for their children, not leave their loved ones hungry. Even if you have excess money, then you could even use the money they would have spent on makeup to raise funds for students and train young people for the future of the nation. Nonetheless, every year they spend more and more on lipstick.[237]

The *Phụ Nữ Tân Văn* and *Sài Gòn* newspapers were essentially holding women responsible for solving the nation's rampant poverty with the pocket change used to buy lipstick. In a more convincing argument, the *Hà Thành Ngọ Báo* newspaper linked cosmetics consumption to trade dependencies. Given that Vietnam did not have its own industrialized cosmetics industry, the argument went, women who purchased these products were exacerbating Vietnam's trade dependencies on European nations and the United States.[238]

Cosmetics proved to be a more vexing problem for many social critics than fashion. Clothing could potentially serve as a means of building a new image of the nation, at least as far as Vietnamese modernists were concerned. By contrast, the dominant discourse on cosmetics regarded lipstick and mascara as threatening to break the nation apart. An unlikely duo of neo-Confucian and feminist critics feared that cosmetics would promote excessive individualism, thereby undermining the family and social structures. Women of the interwar years were increasingly spending their family's money on personal beautification. Older women shrugged off the veneration they had traditionally enjoyed as matriarchs of their extended families and instead went to great lengths to hide signs of aging. Widows were now free to search for new love—and to beautify themselves to assist with this endeavor. Meanwhile, younger women were rejecting arranged marriages and taking control of their romantic destinies. The fact that they could now use cosmetics to present a more beautiful face to the world enabled them to exercise a modicum of control over their fate—not the least the possibility of securing a better husband. But critics felt this pursuit came at too high a cost—not just to families but to the nation itself.

Chapter Four

PHYSIQUE

In 1940, the *Trung Bắc Tân Văn* newspaper published a photograph of a young woman that must have shocked traditionally minded readers. The young woman is wearing a bathing suit that reveals the entirety of her arms, upper back, muscular legs, and curvaceous hips—and more (figure 4.1). The photograph was taken at Đồ Sơn Beach, a seaside resort popular among middle-class city dwellers seeking respite from the stifling summer heat. Located on a peninsula with panoramic views of the Gulf of Tonkin, Đồ Sơn was known not just for its breathtaking landscape but for the beautiful bodies that graced its sand during the interwar years. The newspaper's heading for the photograph alludes to this dual reputation: "Beautiful scenery of Đồ Sơn."[1]

This photograph highlights the dramatic change that occurred in Vietnam's concept of the ideal female physique and comportment during the interwar years. Just a generation before, the woman in this image would not have been considered attractive—nor would she have dared to strip down to a bathing suit, exposing her body in public. In 1920, the "willow leaf" figure—thin, weak, and small-breasted—predominated in media, literature, and other forms of popular culture. Slouching was considered attractive, exercise was shunned, and body parts were to be hidden from view. By the early 1930s, Vietnamese urban culture and media became enamored of a very different physique: curvy, athletic, with an ample bust and

PHYSIQUE

FIGURE 4.1. "Beautiful scenery of Đồ Sơn. A bathing suit that exposes a lot of the back and butt seems to let the sunlight seep into many places."
Source: *Trung Bắc Tân Văn*, June 23, 1940. Translation by author.

bottom, much like the woman in this photograph. Trendy clothing revealed women's curves, thighs, arms, and décolletage. Urban women rushed to department stores to purchase uplifting Western bras or rubber "falsies" to fill their dresses. At home, women diligently followed exercise routines intended to tone or round out specific parts of the body. And at seaside resorts, women happily shed their clothes, baring their arms, legs, back, and hips as they frolicked in the water.

In this chapter I investigate the complex background behind the dramatic evolution of the female body ideal in interwar Vietnam. The rapid transformation of women's bodies and comportment originated in modernist projects to improve the nation. In the 1920s, grappling with how to reverse the image of a nation weakened by colonialism, Vietnamese proponents of eugenics endorsed colonial programs that aimed to strengthen the Vietnamese race by teaching personal hygiene and physical education in schools. The resulting programs in turn normalized conversation about the female body—a topic that had long been considered a private matter in Vietnam—and celebrated the strong female bodies that were expected to produce healthy babies for the nation. In the same spirit of eugenics, New Women feminists championed sports as a means of producing stronger women who would presumably give birth to a healthier Vietnamese race. Feminists also saw sports as a way for women to liberate themselves from the expectations associated with the archetype of the sequestered maiden. This liberation manifested not just through physical strength and endurance but through participation in bicycle races, tennis matches, and long-distance walking races. By the late 1920s, modernist-minded Vietnamese of both sexes had come to value a strong and active female body. In the 1930s, the new bodily ideal was influenced less by social movements like eugenics and feminism than by the growing popularity of leisure activities like swimming, sunbathing, and dancing. Vietnamese women began allowing men to touch their scantily clad bodies on the dance floor and left their bodies exposed down to the most intimate parts at seaside resorts. By the end of the interwar years, a dramatically different, more voluptuous and visible female body had sashayed into the Vietnamese popular imagination.

"TRADITIONAL" FEMALE BODY IDEAL AND THE COLONIAL ENCOUNTER

Discussions about women's bodies during the colonial period often evoked a vision of what was called "traditional" beauty ideals as rhetorical references with which to emphasize the rapid and, for some critics, alarming rate of changing beauty ideals. Such references to "traditional" beauty drew from Chinese art. This was not surprising given the popularity of Chinese art, particularly in northern Vietnam, and the Confucian revival that arose amid debates on modernism in China as well as Vietnam during the interwar years. Images of traditional female beauty were the focus of Chinese debates about modernity, specifically the questions of footbinding and breast binding, which were regularly covered in the Vietnamese press.[2]

In this context, images of traditional beauty conveyed a new, almost nostalgic ideal of classical virtue.³

In interwar Vietnam, the rhetoric on traditional beauty focused on three related ideals (which, it should be noted, were embraced by very few real-life women): the *khuê các* woman, the willow leaf body shape, and the crane neck posture. The khuê các woman drew from the Chinese literary tradition in which virtue was associated with domestic seclusion and unmarried daughters were sequestered until marriage.⁴ During World War I, the khuê các archetype saw a resurgence in both China and Vietnam, driven mainly by the neo-Confucian trend.⁵ The khuê các ideal applied primarily to women's behaviors, but it also had implications for their appearance. According to the khuê các model, young women who remained in the khuê các with "doors closed, bolts drawn" occupied themselves with gentle indoor activities such as sewing, playing instruments, or reading in a dimly lit room, assuming they were literate.⁶ Upper-class women were encouraged to avoid the sun and strenuous activities, leaving their skin pale and their physiques weak, in contrast to their lower-class sisters whose work in the fields darkened their skin and built muscles.⁷

The second beauty ideal was a willow leaf body.⁸ The key to the willow look was a thin body, "known to inspire poetic verses,"⁹ and a narrow waist that tapered "like the back of a bee."¹⁰ A recurring theme in discussions of the willow body was weakness and "the natural beauty of the weak willow leaves."¹¹ The willow leaf image was likely derived from Chinese literature and art, in which beautiful women were often portrayed beside a willow tree, "suggesting a visual comparison between their slender frames and subtle feminine charms."¹² Similar iconography appears in discussions of the "traditional" Vietnamese women's body, which was expected to resemble willow leaves.¹³ A female journalist writing for the *Phụ Nữ Tân Văn* newspaper summed it up: "In the past, everyone loved those slender, frail-looking women."¹⁴

A third image, the "crane neck" (*hạc xương mai*), in which a woman's neck jutted forward in a scooped curve similar to the neck of a crane bird, was a beauty ideal pertaining to posture and movement. The image was considered attractive for its slender curves and evocation of art and calligraphic imagery.¹⁵ The crane-neck ideal originated in China and was a by-product of footbinding, which weakened ligaments and shifted the burden of a woman's body weight to the lower body, affecting her balance and forcing her to compensate with a forward curvature of the lumbar vertebrae. The result was a neck that extended forward and resembled that of the bird. Footbinding also greatly impeded a woman's ability to walk and limited her gait to minute steps. Although Vietnam never had a history of foot binding—something nationalists congratulated themselves for avoiding—the image of the crane neck and mincing gait were evoked nostalgically during the interwar years. Sources from interwar Vietnam evoke the Chinese imagery to describe traditional beauty: "woman with a crane on her back, [and with her] arms and legs slouched is beautiful."[16] According to the ideal, the crane-neck posture allowed the back bones to protrude.[17] With such a slouch, a woman could walk only in diminutive steps, which were considered graceful. She was not to exert herself, as any physical exercise was a sign of manual labor and lower-class status.[18]

Traditional beauty ideals of the interwar period also dictated that women have small breasts, which was considered a sign of virtue.[19] The sole purpose of breasts, in this model, was to nurse children.[20] Moralists disparaged women with larger breasts.[21] Newspaper articles from the interwar years indicate that large-breasted women in Vietnam had historically been criticized, viewed as promiscuous, and made to feel ashamed.[22] To conform to standards of beauty and modesty, women wore a *yếm* or *áo nịt*, tight garments designed to cover and compress the breasts—as well as to safeguard them from handsy men.[23]

It must have been quite a shock to the Vietnamese eye when, with the arrival of colonialism in the mid-nineteenth century, images of scantily clad—and sometimes even nude—French women embodying dramatically different figures began appearing in public spaces. Colonial buildings were adorned with statues of naked female bodies, plump and large-breasted per the *fin de siècle* style. Images of Marianne, the female representation of the French nation, exposing the tops—or even the entirety—of her breasts graced colonial monuments, statues, as well as metropolitan banknotes, coins, and stamps. In front of the governor general's palace in Hanoi stood a statue symbolizing the subservience of the colonies to *mère France*, including images of buxom Vietnamese and Cambodian women intended to symbolize the Mekong and Red Rivers and their fecundity. Nude or seminude women also appeared in advertisements for products of all kinds. French paintings of nudes at the Beaux Arts section of the 1902 French Colonial Exposition in Hanoi shocked many Vietnamese visitors, sparking a minor scandal as crowds gathered around. Some laughed nervously at A. Fourié's painting *Fille d'Eve*, in which the subject flaunts her breasts, and others mocked the unfamiliar heft and voluptuousness of her body.[24]

PERSONAL HYGIENE: A NEW FOCUS ON THE BODY TO STRENGTHEN THE RACE

The changes in attitudes about the female body that emerged in interwar Vietnam began with a new focus on health and hygiene, the colonial way. The colonial government's broad and presumably innocuous mission to improve the health and hygiene of its subjects provided the discursive space to discuss a subject—the body—that until recently had been private. The rhetoric equating personal hygiene with the strength of the nation was first invoked by the colonial administration and then appropriated by Vietnamese nationalists. The concept of public health that linked healthy state subjects and the strength of the national body was gaining traction throughout the world in the late nineteenth century. Germany, France, and England embarked on public health initiatives designed to strengthen the nation-state. Meiji Japan and port cities in China also took on public health initiatives as nationalist projects.[25] In the 1890s, the French colonial government introduced public health initiatives in Vietnam, initiatives that had developed out of a similar push in the metropole. France itself had only recently begun to embrace public sanitation and personal hygiene during the Industrial Revolution.[26] In 1871, after France's devastating casualties and ultimate defeat in the Franco-Prussian War, the Third Republic government endeavored to build a military-ready population by encouraging an increased birth rate, a decreased death rate, and healthier bodies among the French population. Informed by germ theory, the state pushed a variety of public hygiene measures, including improved public sanitation in urban areas and public education about personal hygiene habits. The aim was to reduce the transmission of infectious disease, specifically tuberculosis and syphilis, two of the biggest public health threats at the turn of the century.[27]

As was the case with Japanese initiatives in treaty port China, Dutch programs in the Netherlands Indies, and American programs in the Philippines, the French imperial government exported public health initiatives and sanitary infrastructure to facilitate the development of the colony.[28]

During the first decades of the twentieth century, the government founded the colonial health system, whose many initiatives included campaigns for vaccines and quarantine facilities to prevent outbreaks of cholera and leprosy. After World War I, the colonial state invested in public health infrastructure, building hospitals, research institutes, and dispensaries in urban and rural areas.[29] Pipes delivered running water to homes in Hanoi, Hải Phòng, and Saigon, and sewage networks eliminated waste.[30]

The state introduced public health programs based on Western medical knowledge that placed a new emphasis on the health of women's bodies. Such programs included the registration and policing of sex workers and a program to reduce neonatal death rates that emphasized hygiene and medical intervention. The state also launched initiatives to teach germ theory and hygiene habits to the local population. Fairs and exhibitions showcased innovations in hygiene and public sanitation, from innovations for the home such as bathtubs, showers, toilets, and sinks, to public works projects such as sewer systems and water treatment plants, to food safety and health measures such as pasteurization, supplemental vitamins, and antiparasitic protocols.[31] As in the metropole, schools in Vietnam taught hygiene to elementary students hoping they would convey the knowledge to their families, and a state-published newspaper, *Hygiene and Physical Education*, targeted the colony's youth.[32] These initiatives promoted information about washing the hands and body with soap, bathing in sanitized water (as opposed to the commonly used rivers and lakes), laundry techniques, and household cleaning items. Indeed, there was no shortage of soap in the colony. Brands such as Mondia, Cadium, Palmolive, and the famous Marseille soap vied for consumer attention, linking cleanliness to Hollywood actresses such as Loretta Young, or referring back in time to Cleopatra and other ancient Mediterranean beauties.[33] By the 1930s, a local soap industry had emerged in Vietnam to supply the Indigenous market, with the Savon Viêt-Nam and the Savonnerie Nguyên Hữu brands at the forefront.[34]

Health and personal hygiene education introduced new ways of understanding the body. Vietnamese people learned to equate Western ideals about hygiene with longevity and disease prevention.[35] As was common during the late nineteenth and early twentieth century, hygiene came to be discussed in eugenics terms by colonized populations or those threatened by imperialism. In Japan, Meiji reformers taught hygiene to the populace, presenting the body as a "tool" of modernization that would strengthen the nation.[36] Chinese Republicans likewise encouraged personal hygiene as a way to strengthen the race and nation, China having been dubbed "the sick man of Asia" due to political problems facing the Qing dynasty and multiple pandemics of the early Republican era.[37] A similar discourse emerged in Vietnam. The Tonkin Free School, which drew in part from Japanese models of modernization, included hygiene as part of its curriculum. In 1925, as part of the Mission Civilisatrice, the French administration made hygiene a priority in the colony. Colonial schools taught Western hygiene and stressed notions of cleanliness in Franco-Annamite schools. The Vietnamese soap company Savonnerie Nguyên Hữu deployed the same eugenicist language "Cleanliness for us is strength."[38]

The idea was picked up by Vietnamese intellectuals, who lauded modern women as good wives to the extent that they embraced hygiene as part of their child-rearing practices—and, by extension, the creation of "a healthy race."[39] The prominent Vietnamese intellectual Phạm Quỳnh encouraged women specifically to learn Western hygiene practices.[40] By the late 1930s, sanitation, hygiene, and household cleanliness were among the main goals of the League of Light (Hội Ánh Sáng), an arm of the modernist Self-Reliant Literary Group that developed housing projects in Tonkin.[41]

Hygiene also came to be equated with feminine beauty. Indeed, as Holly Grout shows, the metropolitan medical community and beauty companies began correlating hygiene and feminine self-care with beauty and thereby "legitimated respectable women's attention to women's bodies."[42] In Vietnam, where rural women were said to "drown in filth," beauty contests (see chapter 5) were introduced with the stated purpose of teaching rural woman how to beautify themselves, including how to engage in proper hygiene.[43] Beauty tutorials published in newspapers encouraged women to bathe themselves regularly, wash and comb their hair, and wear clean clothing.[44] And beauty institutes advertised services to teach women about hygiene.[45] Now that personal hygiene was being discussed in the lofty terms of medicine, education, and the strength of the nation and race, discussions about the body and bodily beauty grew more acceptable. In short, the discourse on hygiene created a space for socially acceptable discussions that highlighted bodily maintenance as a priority for a strong race and a modern nation.

SPORTS: NEW WAYS TO MOVE

Just as the colonial public health campaign to teach personal hygiene brought new attention to discussions of bodily health and national strength, the rising popularity of sports in the 1920s led to a new emphasis on strength, musculature, and athleticism. Little scholarly work has been done on the role of sports in precolonial Vietnam. Before the French arrived, Vietnamese men boxed, wrestled, practiced martial arts, and raced canoes. But the world of sports was relegated to military men or associated with manual labor; as an article from 1923 explained, Vietnamese intellectuals "considered corporal exercise . . . as a sign of inferiority . . . the image of the scholar is skinny with a gaunt face [reading] under a burning lamp."[46]

Western sports were introduced in Vietnam as a leisure activity for French colonists. The history of sports in French culture itself was linked to the rise of nationalism and eugenics. It was not until the nineteenth century that the French embraced sports with the same fervor as the English.[47] After France's stunning 1871 defeat to the Prussian Army, the French government introduced sports education to schools as part of the aforementioned broad plan to build a strong, healthy, military-ready population.[48] The colonial government brought this sporting mentality to the colony, although initially only French colonists participated in athletic pursuits. In 1902 the Cercle Sportif—an athletic club—opened in Saigon, and later in Hanoi and Huế, offering soccer and bicycling.[49] In 1912, the Cercle Hippique opened in Saigon and colonists gathered to bet on horse races and play polo. In 1925, Saigon's Cercle Sportif moved to a new location, with facilities for fencing, dancing, tennis, and, after 1933, swimming.

The sporting movement was introduced to Vietnamese youth through the French colonial educational system. In 1918, physical education was integrated into the curriculum at Franco-Annamite schools, and all new schools constructed thereafter included gymnasiums and soccer fields in their architectural plans.[50] The following year, the Vietnamese-run Physical Education School opened on the outskirts of Hanoi, offering intramural squash, volleyball, and soccer, among other sports.[51]

During the 1920s, competitive sports had grown wildly popular throughout the world, and the 1929 World Fair in Barcelona even celebrated sports as one of its main themes. In Vietnam, "the sporting movement," easily accessible to aspiring athletes, took the colony by storm, with the *Đông Pháp* newspaper declaring 1930–31 "The Year of Youth Sporting."[52] During the 1930s, the colonial government built training centers and subsidized sports clubs throughout Vietnam.[53] Fields were cleared and marked for soccer, soil was packed flat and nets set up for tennis courts, concrete was poured for squash courts, and sports clubs were organized in almost every village. Physical exercise was now practiced in public spaces with crowds cheering impressive feats of strength, speed, or skill. The sporting revolution was symbiotic with the growth of capitalism. Throughout the 1930s, sports-minded Vietnamese guzzled Ovamaltine, said to enhance athletic performance,[54] and stopped by Nguyễn Văn Trân's shop or Maison Giao Sports store to pick up tennis rackets, soccer balls, and other sports paraphernalia.[55] Sports-related stories flooded the colony's newspaper pages and radio waves,[56] and athletic teams regularly earned both money and renown through fundraiser galas, dinners, and festivals.[57]

The sporting movement sparked new discussions about the body that mirrored concurrent conversations about public health and personal hygiene. Sports enthusiasts touted the benefits of regular exercise in making the body strong and healthy.[58] They also claimed that athletic pursuits helped enable the body to resist germs and fend off diseases such as tuberculosis, one of the primary public health problems of the colonial era.[59] Proponents of the sporting movement even equated strength of body with strength of mind, promoting sports as a means of developing a healthy intellect.[60]

The sporting movement was also promoted in eugenics terms. As Agathe Larcher-Goscha writes, after more than half a century of humiliating racist and Social Darwinian rhetoric claiming that Vietnamese bodies were small and weak, many Vietnamese embraced sports as a way to regenerate the nation and race.[61] Reporting on the Hanoi School of Physical Education, *Nam Phong* magazine mentioned that the school's founder, Nguyễn Qui Toản, was inspired to pursue sports while studying in France, where he felt like the weakest student in his physical education classes. Afraid to "humiliate the whole country" in front of his French classmates, he began his own athletic training. Upon returning to Vietnam in 1918, he founded the Hanoi School of Physical Education as "a school that [contributes] to the nation, race, and hygiene of the body."[62] Another 1932 *Nam Phong* article claimed that sports would enable Vietnam, "a nation with a reputation for being as weak as we are," to grow strong "like France," where sports were popular.[63]

During the interwar years, sports were said to contribute to the "health of the race,"[64] to benefit the "race of the Hồng Lạc people"—a reference to an ancient Vietnamese civilization[65]—and to have "a good influence on the race in the future."[66] Characters in Vũ Trọng Phụng's novel *Dumb Luck* discuss sports in Darwinian terms, claiming they will "civilize" Vietnamese society and are "a harbinger of progress for Vietnam and a sign of prosperity for our race."[67] Political operatives even used sports competitions as an arena for recruiting new activists. Sports, as Judith Henchy concludes, became "an arena of physical comparison and competition which was personal, racial, and political."[68]

The sporting movement had its critics, of course. A 1929 article in *Hà Thành Ngọ Báo* reported that many parents objected to children playing sports in school because it exhausted them and distracted them from their studies.[69] In 1933, the *Phong Hóa* newspaper published a cartoon depicting an alter to which one would traditionally make offerings to their ancestors or deities. But instead of praying, women in this image were serving a tennis ball; rather than presenting offerings of food and drink to their ancestors or deities, they offered tennis balls and cocktails; and images of their ancestors and deities were replaced by short-cut, tight-fitting sports clothing (figure 4.2). The critique was clear: society was worshiping sports and consumerism. Vũ Trọng Phụng also famously mocked the sporting movement for being pretentious and delusional in assuming that stronger bodies would yield a stronger and more modern society.[70] The *Vịt Đực* newspaper even joked that an "anti-sports movement"(*phong trào phản thể thao*) existed alongside the "sporting movement" (*Phong trào thể thao*).[71]

But was the sporting movement universally popular and authentically embraced? In 1938, Nguyễn Công Hoan published the two-part fictional short story titled "The Fitness Mentality," which portrays the sporting movement as a colonial initiative forced on locals, sometimes with the threat of violence.[72] Although the stories may exaggerate the state's level of coercion, it is important to consider Nguyễn Công Hoan's message that the sporting movement felt forced onto peasants. In the first story, colonial officials require the local mandarin Mr. Huyện to perform a slew of frivolous sports-related tasks, leaving him unable to keep up with the basic duties of governing his hamlet. He must organize an event celebrating the construction of a new stadium and children's playground; learn to dance Western-style;

FIGURE 4.2. Cartoon depicting a sports themed altar. This image would have been insulting, as altars were to be dedicated to ancestors or Confucian and Buddhist figures.
Source: Phong Hóa, August 25, 1933.

and track down women who will bicycle for a race—and are willing to wear what rural folk considered scandalously revealing shorts while doing so.[73] The second part of the story opens with the villager Mịch being forced by colonial officials to attend a soccer match in Ngũ Vọng hamlet, where he will cheer on his local team as part of a fake audience showcasing the supposed popularity of sports. This absurd obligation takes a very real toll on Mịch, leaving him unable to perform some important labor required to pay off a debt bondage contract and thus at risk of imprisonment. Police proceed to hunt down all the other villagers who failed to show up at the match.[74] The message of the story is the outrageous lengths to which colonial officials would go in their zeal to promote sports among the masses. In Vietnam's postcolonial era, "the Fitness Mentality" would be interpreted by the Communist state as a statement that the sporting movement had been pushed onto Vietnamese people to distract them from the revolution. This interpretation was not entirely off the mark.

PHYSIQUE

WOMEN AND SPORTS

The colonial physical education curriculum in schools led to a "wave of women [and girls] exercising throughout our country," marveled the *Sài Thành* newspaper in 1932.[75] Vietnamese women and girls joined women all over Asia in the sports movement. Girls in the British colonies of Singapore, Malaya, and Burma, or independent states such as Siam, China, and Japan, did not shy away from hitting tennis balls or scrimmaging men on public soccer fields.[76] Throughout the 1930s, Vietnamese newspapers regularly covered women's sports and encouraged women and girls to swim, dance, play tennis, and form athletic clubs.[77] Miss Nguyễn Thị Thục Quyên, writing a letter in the *Đông Phương* newspaper, urged women not to settle for cheering on male athletes but to play the game themselves, work their muscles, get their blood circulating, and feel their cheeks flush as they danced or volleyed tennis balls with a friend.[78]

In the early 1930s, a phenomenon of female sports celebrities developed in Vietnam. Similar to the case in China, where sportswomen were national celebrities,[79] the front pages of newspapers were graced by the likes of Miss Hồ Thị Lích, a cyclist famous for riding from Saigon to Hanoi;[80] Miss Ất from Rạch Kiến, who stunned the tennis world with her backhand;[81] and Miss Hoàng Việt Nga, a student at the Chợ Lớn Girls' School, who made her name completing long-distance walking trips spanning hundreds of miles.[82] Miss Phan Thị Nga (figure 4.3), a teacher of calisthenics, traveled around the country delivering public lectures and publishing newspaper articles teaching women the health benefits of exercise and strong bodies.[83]

Female participation in sports met with an immediate backlash as physical exercise for women—especially in public settings—had long been shunned in Vietnam.[84] "The judgment of [women in sports] is very profound," reported a female journalist writing for the *Hà Thành Ngọ Báo* newspaper.[85] Reflecting on when physical education classes were first introduced, Francois Branchet, a teacher at the Girls' School in Hanoi, recalled having "almost unleashed a revolution" among parents who objected to physical education classes.[86] The female journalist who wrote for the *Hà Thành Ngọ Báo* newspaper also noted that opponents of the women's sporting trend insisted that young women should be working in the house instead of playing outside.[87] They equated women's participation in sports with vanity, foolishness, and selfish individualism.[88] Critics also warned of

FIGURE 4.3. Miss Phan Thị Nga is a teacher of calisthenics.
Source: Phan Thị Nga, Ngày Nay, undated 1935.

the effects of physical assertion on the female body. Women who played sports "like men," they cautioned, would lose their willow leaf figure and demure demeanor.[89] Indeed, as a 1929 *Hà Thành Ngọ Báo* article reported, some women were afraid to participate in sports out of fear that their muscles and body would enlarge and cause them to lose their willowy looks.[90]

Despite—or because of—all the criticism, the issue of women's participation in sports developed into a key tenet of Vietnam's women's liberation movement, with New Women and feminists championing sports education for girls.[91] The female journalist VC An declared: "Women in our country . . . need to train and practice sports to become healthier so that they can become comparable to men."[92] Responding to critics of female participation in sports, the female journalist Bích Thủy implored readers: "Please try to press for and advocate for our women to be completely liberated!"[93] The 1932 women's fair organized in part by the *Phụ Nữ Tân Văn* newspaper included sports competitions among its events, as well as a speech by Miss Phan Văn Gia, a student at the Girl's School in Saigon, who spoke about women's participation in sports as an avenue for women's liberation.[94] Although it is highly unlikely that they expected women to match men in physical strength, journalists writing for *Phụ Nữ Tân Văn* made the case that the strength women gained through playing sports would make them equal to men, presumably in more nuanced ways.

Discussions around female participation in sports introduced a new way of talking about the female body that promoted bodily health and strength.[95] Exercise was encouraged as a means of strengthening women's bodies, which were believed to be inherently weak and further enfeebled by childbirth and caring for the family. Signaling a new way of understanding time and body maintenance, articles taught women the benefits of small bouts of daily exercise for building muscle. Exercise enthusiasts also promised that fitness would reduce the occurrence of headaches, prevent tuberculosis, and enable women to develop a strong mind.[96]

Proponents of eugenics found value in women's sports insofar as strong female bodies were key to reproducing a strong race.[97] The female journalist Mỹ Chân called on women to abandon the Confucian mindset that women should not exert themselves, and instead embrace Western sports culture to "take care of their race."[98] The *Phụ Nữ Tân Văn* newspaper editor Cao Thị Khanh writing under her married name Madame Nguyễn Đức Nhuận declared: "we need to promote exercise more for girls than boys, because women are mothers of the future society" and are responsible for raising the "future of the race" (*giống nòi*) to be strong.[99]

As sports were promoted for strengthening bodies and advancing the cause of women's liberation, traditional notions about the ideal female physique and comportment were called into question. Sports enthusiasts called on women to let go of the bodily ideal associated with "the natural beauty of the weak willow branches."[100] Drawing from the language of eugenics and Social Darwinism, Miss Hoàng Việt Nga, who organized a long-distance walk from Hanoi to Hải Phòng, proclaimed that "this is a century where the strong win and the weak lose!"[101] The traditional khuê các ideal of women remaining sequestered indoors was likewise deemed incompatible with the new active lifestyle. In 1930, Madame Nguyễn Đức Nhuận urged *Phụ Nữ Tân Văn* readers to defy the expectations associated with the khuê các image and made the case that women—especially frail women—should exercise for good health. To readers who feared that an active life would degrade them into a dreaded Modern Girl, the article was emphatic that exercise could be performed in a "moral" way.[102] Miss Việt Hoa Nguyễn Thị Kế, a precocious high school student in Chợ Lớn, wrote a letter to the *Hà Thành Ngọ Báo* newspaper making the same point. Although acknowledging that being a housewife was the "sole duty of women and girls in our country," she exhorted girls to play sports nonetheless.[103]

In a rhetorical sleight of hand, some journalists managed to reconcile the new active lifestyle with the hermetic khuê các ideal, thereby neutralizing future neo-Confucian critiques. A 1929 article encouraging women to exercise pointed out that khuê các women did in fact exercise by strolling around the gardens of their house.[104] A 1932 article about an upcoming women's bike tour promised readers that "many *khuê các* girls are participating in this event"—the implication being that even strenuous public exercise would not tarnish the respectability these lady-like participants.[105] Khuê các, in other words, gradually became a more flexible term connoting respectability and class rather than a hermetic lifestyle required of young women.

The most popular sports among young women during the interwar years were tennis, long-distance walking, and bicycling, although women also swam and played soccer, volleyball, and ping-pong. Speaking to Pierre Bordieu's argument that sport choices reflected economic class, tennis in Vietnam came to be a symbol of upper- and middle-class status much as it was in the United States and France.[106] Athletic clubs, accessible only to the affluent, packed clay or laid sod for tennis courts. Some wealthy enthusiasts built courts in their own backyards or on their rooftops.[107] Even Emperor Bảo Đại joined the tennis movement, famously playing celebrity tennis stars Nguyễn Văn Chim and Huỳnh Văn Giao at the 1937 Nam Giao festival. Seeing the emperor physically exert himself in public sports—especially during the holy Nam Giao holiday, when the emperor makes offerings to the heavens—must have shocked the more conservative members of society. However, to those familiar with Bảo Đại—a Francophile playboy—it was hardly a surprise. The novelist Vũ Trọng Phụng famously mocked tennis as a symbol of social climbing and mimicking the French colonizer.[108] In urban areas across Vietnam, middle-class women played the game and even participated in tournaments, at times against male opponents. In 1930, to incentivize young women's participation in sports, the *Phụ Nữ Tân Văn* newspaper announced that a trophy would be awarded to the best female tennis player in Cochinchina. In 1932, Miss Ất from Rạch Kiến, in the Mekong Delta, won the prestigious Coupe Trịnh Đình Thảo and even went on to found her own tennis school.[109] Many other less gifted women simply delighted in bounding around the court in their crisp white tennis jumpers. As tennis know-how became a symbol of middle-class respectability, some families hired tennis teachers for their daughters as part of a broader endeavor to transform girls into desirable marriage material.[110]

Female exercise enthusiasts took up long-distance walking as a "hygienic" form of exercise that did not generate much sweat,[111] a way to improve overall fitness,[112] and in classic eugenics terms, a way to improve the "race" by contributing to the development of strong bodies.[113] Newspaper covered stories about walking celebrities such as Miss Lê Thị Thắm, the aforementioned Miss Hoàng Việt Nga, who organized multiple well-publicized tours from Hanoi-Hải Phòng-Đồ Sơn,[114] and Miss Miss Hồ Tố Quyên, whose embarked on a well-publicize trips from Saigon all the way to Hanoi, a roughly 1,600 kilometer trek.[115] These walking events not only celebrated female athletic accomplishment but fostered a sense of community among female sports enthusiasts.

Introduced by Europeans, soccer became popular throughout Asia during the colonial period and became all the rage after troops drafted from the colonies returned home from World War I, when soccer was often played on the battlefield.[116] As was the case in Japan, Malaya, Singapore, and Siam, soccer was played by women in Vietnam, particularly in Cochinchina.[117] There, southern Vietnamese women scrimmaged among themselves or even scored against men in mixed games.[118] A female journalist writing for the Hà Thành Ngọ Báo newspaper reported that critics objected to women forming teams or sporting associations, playing in public, and competing with men.[119] Middle-class parents bristled at the idea of their daughters sliding into a ball on a dirt field, legs caked in mud, like peasant women working the rice fields. Equally abhorrent was the prospect that girls dripping with sweat and fighting for the ball would lose their "feminine look" and become tomboys.[120]

The most controversial sport for women in interwar Vietnam was bicycling. The bicycle, early iterations of which had appeared in Europe in the 1820s, became wildly popular among Western men and women alike by the end of the century.[121] Vietnam was introduced to life on two wheels in the 1890s, when the colonial government began importing bicycles. Initially popular only among French colonists, bicycles were sold in the colony's trading companies and elegant department stores. Until the eve of World War I, bicycling among Vietnamese was limited to upper-class individuals who worked with or socialized among French colonists After the war, however, bicycles became affordable for the lower classes thanks to global mass production and local competition from Japanese bicycles brands smuggled into Tonkin.[122] In Vietnam, bicycles proved useful not only for transportation and sport but also for plowing fields and carrying heavy loads—thus earning them the nickname "the iron horse" (ngựa sắt).[123] In the 1920s, they became ubiquitous throughout Vietnam. Riding this popularity, the Bécé-Sport store in Chợ Lớn even claimed to produce bicycles that were designed specifically for the bodies of Vietnamese riders.[124] Newspaper pages were replete with stories of collisions with cars or pedestrians, incidents of drunken bicyclists, and bicycles wiping out on a turn during the wet season. By the 1930s, bicycles were widely used for sport and recreation. Sports sections of local newspapers chronicled well-publicized long-distance cycling tours and races,[125] and cyclists ascended to celebrity status.[126]

In the 1920s, Vietnamese New Women joined the cycling craze, and as had happened in the West during the previous century, bicycles became a tool of liberation for women. More popular among women in Hanoi and Saigon than Huế, bicycles provided women with transportation to work or the market and girls with transportation to school.[127] Bicycles even enabled those in remote areas to receive an education that they might otherwise not have had.[128] Women young and old also began using bicycles for gentle exercise. Timid women concerned with their image were assured that they could "still be graceful and beautiful" while riding and that cycling was considered quite acceptable among women in "civilized" countries.[129]

School girls and New Women opened cycling clubs all over Vietnam. Traditionalists were shocked by the spectacle of all-female long-distance cycling tours from Hà Tĩnh to Yên Sở, Phan Thiết to Saigon, and Hanoi to Saigon. In 1938, Miss Nguyễn Thị Kế, a high school student in Chợ Lớn, urged *Hà Thành Ngọ Báo* readers to join her for a cycling trip from Hanoi to Saigon. Organizers of the 1932 Phan Thiết-Saigon tour urged young women to join, reminding them that many khuê các girls were participating and implying that khuê các girls were no longer by their sequestered status, their refined lifestyle.[130]

Yet a woman on a bicycle remained a controversial issue throughout the interwar period. Female journalists reported that critics saw bicycling as vain, foolish, and unbecoming of women and insisted that any time devoted to cycling would be better spent attending to housework, one of the Confucian Four Virtues of womanhood.[131] Traditionalists claimed that the sight of women riding bicycles was inconsistent with—and hence detrimental to—the customs of the country.[132] Moralists went so far as to warn girls that they would lose their virginity in the process of straddling a bicycle seat.[133] Interestingly, a similar argument had been made in France when women began bicycling there at the turn of the century.[134] Opposition grew extreme, to the point that when the famous bicyclist Hồ Thị Lích arrived in Huế during her much-publicized long-distance tour in 1938, she was met by a jeering mob.[135] Female cyclists reported verbal assaults and even found their bikes sabotaged with sticks wedged into the spokes of their wheel.[136]

Public opposition to female bicycling had the ironic effect of turning the sport into a feminist cause. In a counterprotest to the mob previously mentioned, women formed a crowd chanting "Long Live Miss Lích" (*muôn năm cô Lích!*).[137] "We really are just bicyclists, have we committed any crimes?" wrote Miss Trần-Thị-Tý in *Hà Thành Ngọ Báo*.[138] Reacting to claims that bicycling violated Vietnamese customs, a 1932 article in the *Trung Lập Báo* newspaper presented the issue to readers in feminist terms: "If women and girls are banned from going out or riding bikes, when will Vietnamese women set foot onto the road toward liberation?"[139] Miss Nguyễn Thị Kế, the Chợ Lớn schoolgirl, implored women to defy critics by joining her on the bicycling trip from Saigon to Hanoi.[140] And after learning of an incident in Huế of sticks wedged into the wheels of female-owned bicycles, throngs of women protested by signing up for bike races.[141]

The rising popularity of sports in Vietnam led to new ways of using and seeing the body, particularly for women. Once seen as shameful evidence of lower-class life and manual labor, active and muscular bodies were now celebrated and associated with middle-class sports and leisure activities. The sporting movement, which was initially sold to women as a means of improving the Vietnamese race and civilizing the nation, was taken up by New Woman feminists as a form of liberation for young women. Women's bodies were no longer expected to be weak and sequestered at home; they were now to be used in new ways that emphasized the need for strength and endurance in new—and very public—places.

BODIES ON DISPLAY

The leisure activities popular among the urban middle class during the interwar years resulted in new ways of women's bodies being used and seen. In particular, the new leisure activities of dancing and beach-going led to a reimagining of the norms of female comportment and the ways that women displayed their bodies in public. As the Hanoi Girls' School teacher Madame Brachet reflected in 1937: "In the countryside, tradition remains; but in the cities . . . at the doors of the Albert Sarraut School, the young girls rub elbows with their male comrades. They play sports, they go to the sea, they swim; they dance. . . ." Her voice trailing off, she added: "in the arms of a man."[142]

In the early 1930s, the dancing fad that had already taken the Western world and much of Asia by storm swept into Vietnam. Middle-class urban youth tangoed and trotted in dance halls, at charity fundraisers, and at fairs and expositions. Women did the Charleston and Jitterbug in slinky dresses made of brightly colored Indian silk, cut on the bias to hug the wearer's curves. Young men pressed their palm into their partner's lower back, drawing their chests together, and thrust their hip against hip, as they twirled her around the dance floor.[143] Exchanges of partners meant, as Nguyễn Đình Lạp observed, that "any girl's plump flesh has no doubt been used as a cushion for everyone by now." Young women who allowed men to touch them were thus left "trying to navigate between 'what is pleasurable' and 'what is honorable.'"[144] Notwithstanding such moral ambiguities, the new fad of dancing made public displays of men—often multiple men—touching young women socially acceptable, at least among urban middle-class youth.

In the dance halls, out to dinner, and at the cinema, women out for a night on the town wore clothing designed to show off female curves. Evening gowns revealed backs, arms, and cleavage.[145] Delicate fabrics offered a tantalizing glimpse of the female form.[146] Bras, corsets, panties, and silk stockings shaped the body. own right. As hemlines rose after World War I, undergarments were cut smaller. Sold at boutiques such as Chez Claudine in Saigon, bras, slips, and panties, available in silk or the less costly rayon, came in a variety of colors and prints with decorative details such as roses or lace trim sewn on.[147] Even the Lemur Tunic (see chapter 2), which was part of a nationalist strategy to show off to the world the elegance of the Vietnamese nation, found its true success in revealing the wearer's figure. Although he carefully covered the arms, nape, and legs, Nguyễn Cát Tường tailored the tunic to emphasize the bust and waist.[148] He also tailored the waist and thighs of pants while flairing the ankles to make legs appear more shapely. As an artist, he knew the value of contrasting lines.

The beach resorts that popped up throughout Vietnam during the colonial period (see chapter 1) likewise played a role in transforming the way women used and displayed their bodies. Founded in the 1890s, beach resorts such as Nha Trang and Phan Thiết in Annam, and Cap Saint Jacques in Cochinchina, were famous sites of French leisure activity. Tonkin was home to Đồ Sơn and Sầm Sơn, the latter resort memorialized in a 1934 New Music (nhạc mới) song of the same name sung with Vietnamese lyrics and set to the melody of "Les Gars de la Marine."[149] At the turn of the century, beach resorts had been largely for socializing, gambling, swimming, and walking on the beach; lounging on the beach and exposing one's skin to the sun—and to onlookers—was frowned upon even among French colonists. After World War I, however, the nature of beach resorts changed. As mentioned in chapter 3, in 1926 the legendary designer Coco Chanel popularized tanning after returning from a Mediterranean vacation with sun-kissed skin. As tanned skin came to be associated with fashion and upper-class leisure, French women in the metropole and the colony began exposing their skin to the sun and lounging at the beach in hopes of achieving the same look. In the late 1920s, beach vacations would become popular among upper-middle-class Vietnamese thanks to importation of automobiles and the rise of leisure and sports activities.

Once a place for fishermen to catch food to feed their family and village, beaches became a site of luxurious seaside vacations for Vietnam's middle class. On summer weekends, wealthy urbanites flooded coastal resort areas, transforming seaside towns into sites of conspicuous consumption and exhibitionism. Seaside resorts became a study in contrasts—between urban and rural, wealth and poverty, labor and leisure, modern and traditional.

In local fishing villages, swimming, bare bodies, and tan skin had long been associated with the hard work of fishermen and women. Yet in the 1930s, middle-class urbanites came to see bodies in a new way: swimming, bare bodies, and—to a small minority—tan skin was now a symbol of leisure and luxury. This contrast is explored in the 1936 novel *Trống Mái* by Khải Hưng. The story's wealthy young protagonist Hiền travels with friends from Hanoi to spend summer vacation in Sầm Sơn, a coastal town sixteen kilometers from Thanh Hóa, where she meets Vọi, a local fisherman. A story of unrequited love as well as an indictment of materialistic middle-class urbanism, *Trống Mái* features descriptions of sporty, female voluptuous bodies in pink, red, and blue bathing suits. Interestingly, Hiền is more obsessed with Voi's body than he is with hers; the story features elaborate descriptions of his strapping, bare-chested physique. The story is thus a meditation on female sexual desire and the middle class fixation on physique.[150]

For some young women, a seaside vacation was a respite from Confucian norms governing female modesty. At the beach, young men and women cavorted in the waves and Modern Girls lounged on the sand, soaking up the rays of sun that kissed the skin of their legs, back, arms, and chest. Their bathing suits, made of knitted wool or elastic yarn, were brightly colored and tight-fitting. They were also cut high on the leg—almost to the crotch—and emphasized the curves of the bust and hips (figures 4.4 and 4.5). Women who had yet to learn to swim—or were perhaps too modest to don a swimsuit—walked up and down newly constructed paths along the shore clad in flimsy beach "pajamas" or robes.[151]

The beach became associated with bare bodies. Advertisements for bathing suits reminded readers that, along with improving health, the purpose of going to the beach was to flaunt one's figure. Beach resorts held bathing suit competitions, which *Vịt Đực* mockingly referred to as "the breast contest, thigh contest, butt contest."[152] In the 1934 short story "The Silhouettes at the Beach," the author Nhi Linh delights in creating caricatures of the different bodies one would see at the beach. Two of the characters are a study in contrast: Modern Girl Miss Thanh arrives at the resort in a skimpy bathing suit, eager to show off her ample breasts and shapely legs and allowing—and even facilitating—her beach robe to fly open with the slightest breeze. Miss Nga, a conservative girl from Hanoi with a slim figure, is so traumatized by the nakedness she feels in a borrowed bathing suit that she squats down in the whitewater until the water reaches her neck to hide her exposed body.[153]

FIGURE 4.4. A Modern Girl lounges on the sand.
Source: Trung Bắc Tân Văn, June 23, 1940.

FIGURE 4.5. Nguyễn Cát Tường's design for bathing suits.
Source: Phong Hóa, August 31, 1935.

FIGURE 4.6. A cartoon that mocks the modern education system for its frivolity, specifically accusing female teachers of being Modern Girls.
Source: *Tràng An Báo*, April 19, 1935.

Photos and cartoons of women at the beach began appearing in newspapers during the mid-1930s, likely as a way to attract readers. Such images were often presented in a way that mocked women for revealing their bodies.[154] A 1935 issue of *Tràng An Báo* newspaper shows a cartoon of five young women facing an elderly male dressed in a traditional tunic (figure 4.6). They are at a beach resort with sailboats behind them. The cartoon's caption reads "Some female teachers stand before the village education mandarin, including [teachers of] swim instruction." The women say to him: "High-ranking official, you let the male students [take] the swimming test. You have to let the female students also [take] the swimming test."[155]

The cartoon mocks the modern education system for its frivolity. Whereas the traditional Vietnamese Confucian education system offered rigorous academics, the new education system focused on sports (swimming) and excursions (trips to the beach). The reader is likely aware that scholars—exclusively male and once the most respected social class—had lost their social standing when the colonial government replaced village officials with colonial administrators, cancelled the mandarin exams, and instituted a French curriculum in schools. To add insult to injury, the colonial government had gone on to train women as well as men to be teachers. Despite—or perhaps because of—his downgraded social status, the mandarin in the cartoon conveys an attitude of unmistakable superiority vis-à-vis the bevy of women. With one arm behind his back and the other extended as though in explanation, the old scholar asserts his innate superiority over the female teachers, all but one of whom keep their arms tucked demurely behind their backs. Although the young women have replaced the likes of this elderly mandarin in the role of instructor, they remain both deferential and disrespected.

Its social meaning aside, the cartoon is noteworthy for its depictions of women's bodies. The reader is struck by the contrast between the women's roundness and detail and the semiabstract, geometric features of the man. The images of the women are clearly designed to titillate male readers and, at least in the case of the bashful young woman at the center of the image who averts eye contact, even encourage a predatory gaze. The young women are wearing one-piece bathing suits cut low to showcase their cleavage and high to show off their legs and the curves of their hips. The young women appear to be posing with their breasts jutting out and their knees slightly angled to the side to highlight the difference between their tiny waists and shapely hips. To top off the look, the young women are sporting high heels, surely an inconvenience at a sandy beach. One of the women looks directly at the old mandarin and gestures as she addresses him, her hand drawn conspicuously to call attention to her breast. These women bear more resemblance to Modern Girls than to any real-life teachers of the era—and that is precisely the point.

A 1940 edition of *Trung Bắc Tân Văn* offers readers two punishingly voyeuristic photographs of bathing suit-clad young women at the beach. The picture that opened this chapter, was taken from behind and showed a curvaceous woman in a bathing suit cut low on her back (see figure 4.1). As noted in the introduction, the picture was arresting in that the woman exposed her arms, back, and muscular legs. But the real subject of the photograph is not the young woman herself; it is her buttocks, whose round

FIGURE 4.7. A young girl happily climbing at Sầm Sơn beach resort.
Source: *Trung Bắc Tân Văn*, June 23, 1940.

cheeks have been exposed by a wayward bathing suit. The caption reveals the intent of the photographer and the editor who chose to print the photograph: "A bathing suit that exposes a lot of the back and butt seems to let the sunlight seep into many places." Using words like "expose" and "let the sunlight seep into" underscore the fact that such secret parts of the body did not usually see the light of day, the newspaper editor is aware he is pushing societal limits for decency and likely violating the woman's sense of decency.

The second picture, taken at Sầm Sơn beach resort, initially appears innocent and even approving of the stronger female form that was coming into fashion (figure 4.7). "Smiling and healthy. The sky was full of white clouds," the caption reads. "On the black peak of a mountain a young girl was happily climbing. We see in that healthy and strong body all the beauty of Sầm Sơn is full of light."[156] Yet the innocence of the girl's smile is betrayed by the angle of the camera. The photo, captured from below and behind, looks up at her legs, buttocks, and back. She is wearing a one-piece bathing suit with a halter that ties around her neck, exposing her arms and back. The suit is cut high on her leg, which is bent as she climbs a rock. Herein lies the excitement of the photograph: The reader catches a glimpse of the fabric that gathers between her buttocks and covers—just barely—her crotch.

A NEW PHYSIQUE

As the popularization of sports and leisure activities in the late 1920s changed the ways Vietnamese women used and exposed their bodies, a new bodily ideal began to enter the picture, dramatically different from the ideal of the frail "willow leaf." Reflecting on the change in style since World War I, a 1939 article in the *Đàn-Bà* newspaper mused: "It used to be popular to have a thin figure to show that you were khuê các," but "with sports more popular these days, the way women look has changed."[157] One beauty contest even offered a secondary award in the category of most athletic figure.[158] In the early 1930s, a new ideal of the female silhouette entered the Vietnamese imagination. In addition to lean muscles and straight posture, it had a "slender body and blooming breasts.[159]

These changes in Vietnam's female bodily ideal were related to global trends in body culture. Since the mid-nineteenth century, the Muscular Christianity movement—popular in Anglophone countries—promoted physical strength, and toward the end of the century the German bodybuilder Eugen Sandow convinced the world that muscular bodies were beautiful.[160] It would not be until the end of World War I that the trend in muscular male bodies became popular in France, where the "new man" began pursuing a physique that resembled that of a Greek god.[161] The trend, undoubtedly influenced by the current sports craze, caught on in Vietnam. Advertisements for the malt-based beverage Ovamaltine featured an impossibly muscular man holding an ox over his head or the chiseled muscles of a man riding a bicycle; those for another healthful beverage called Fortonic showcased a cyclist's muscles, presumably carved by the drink itself.[162] *Ngày Nay* and *Phong Hóa* newspapers published cartoons featuring humorous juxtapositions of skinny scholars, fat mandarins, and muscle-bound sportsmen. In the aforementioned novel *Trống Mái* by Khải

Hưng, the character Vọi—the object of the protagonist Hiền's lust—is described as having a muscular body like that of a Greek god. The steamy descriptions of Hiền's lustful thoughts about Vọi speak to a cultural shift that was underway during this period. Just a decade earlier, a working-class fisherman like Vọi would have been dismissed by cosmpolitan young women; it was slim-built scholars with social capital, not fishermen with muscles, who captured their imaginations—or at least that of the parents arranging their marriage. Now, with the social order upended, a woman like Hiền becomes obsessed with a humble man's gorgeous physique, even as she knows their relationship is doomed.[163] The new trend in body culture, which was particularly popular among men in fascist countries including Germany, Italy, and Spain, would only grow more pronounced through World War II.

New global trends emerged vis-à-vis the female physique as well. During the 1920s, much of the Western world favored the "flapper" figure: a rectangular-shaped body with flat breasts and a straight waist. In the 1930s, when the privations of the Great Depression left many women gaunt, the privileged ideal in much of Europe as well as in the United States became the Belle Poitrine figure—curvy with ample breasts, a tiny waist, and rounded hips.[164] France departed from that norm, and according to Mary Lynn Stewart, Metropolitan French fashion of the 1930s showcased slimmer figures with a flat belly and smaller breasts and hips, famously exemplified in the art of Erté.[165] It is unclear, however, to what degree this slim figure caught on among the general public or if it remained relegated to the realm of haute couture.

The devotees of Metropolitan haute couture favored the slim, Erté-eque figure, but the Vietnamese discourse on women's bodies showed a preference for curvier, more athletic bodies. This preference was in line with trends in other areas of Asia: in the 1930s, women in Japan and Shanghai also abandoned the weak, hunched willow-leaf look in favor of a straight posture and rounder breasts and buttocks.[166] The Vietnamese ideal figure was likely an amalgam of influences, including the slim Erté-esque women who appeared in imported metropolitan magazines, French films, or the fashion section of the widely read *La Dépêche Indochine* newspaper; international beauty queens whose pictures regularly made the front page of Vietnamese newspapers; and Hollywood's voluptuous sirens, such as Mae West, who graced cinema screens, posters, and Vietnamese newspaper gossip pages. The rhetoric around women's figures seemed to favor a shape that was neither as slim as those featured in Metropolitan haute couture nor as voluptuous as Mae West's.

Drawing from the rhetoric of both the personal hygiene movement and the sporting movement, Vietnamese proponents of the new bodily ideal touted it as the epitome of radiant health. Not surprisingly, this new ideal struck a sharp contrast with the gaunt physique common among rural women during the Great Depression. It was strong, not sickly like the willow figure; well-nourished yet not fat; and had curves in all the right places.[167] "A woman today must be a very healthy person, with strong breasts, regular muscles," proclaimed Nguyễn Cát Tường in the Ngày Nay newspaper.[168] A 1935 book Want to Be Beautiful by Mlle Mộng Khanh also described the ideal female form as "neither too thin nor too fat."[169] A sense of visual balance and proportion dominated the discourse about the new ideal figure; its rightness was assumed to be a matter of objective truth. The journalist Ngọc Lang, writing for Khoa Học Tạp Chí, declared that a woman's body should be neither thin nor fat, with balanced shoulders and full breasts.[170]

This new female figure was also associated with modernity. "Today, we live in another century . . . full of machines, science, and art with the luxuries of material life. Every year a new fad in architecture, automobiles and clothing appears and replaces the old. Perhaps our eyes, which naturally follow these changes, see the beauty in women also changing," wrote the designer Nguyễn Cát Tường. He cited French medical research and medical doctors' claims to identify the precise proportions of the body—not just the bust-waist-hip but five other zones as well—to lend an air of scientific importance and objectivity to the new bodily ideal.[171]

With the paradox of a "balanced" curvy-yet-skinny figure nearly impossible to attain, women absorbed myriad messages—some explicit, some implicit—about their weight. The Ngày Nay newspaper cautioned women not to let themselves accumulate too much body fat, and readers joined the novelist Vũ Trọng Phụng in chuckling at his character Mrs. Deputy Customs Officer, who was estimated to weigh a rotund seventy kilos.[172] Set up for an impossible ideal, women were also warned against becoming too skinny. "A skinny person," Ngày Nay warned, "loses their beauty, their joints protrude, the soft features of the body fade away, and one sees only the rough, hard lines [of their bones] that seem to form sharp corners."[173] Having dedicated himself to the mission of outfitting the nation, the clothing designer Nguyễn Cát Tường complained that Vietnamese women were either "fat and short or too skinny."[174] Acknowledging the difficulty of maintaining the not-too-fat-not-too-thin figure, beauty institutes gladly accepted money in return for services purported to make a thin woman plump and a fat woman slim.[175]

Whereas in the 1920s women embraced exercise to achieve strength and liberation, in the 1930s they did so to look good. Women learned a variety of techniques to manipulate the shape of their body. They followed the techniques made popular by the Danish international fitness sensation J. P. Müller, who preached short, targeted exercises.[176] Newspapers encouraged women to do calisthenics to keep their themselves in shape, signaling a new understanding of exercise that emphasized appearance over achievement. Far from the previous decade's eugenics-inspired calls for racial strength or New Woman feminist discourse on liberation through sports, newspapers of the 1930s cautioned women to avoid strenuous activities. Light calisthenics were promoted for the purpose of developing "poetic curves," maintaining the "treasures of our youth," and "enhancing the beauty of women."[177] Women were warned against overexerting themselves or engaging in strenuous sports that would result in an overly muscular figure.[178] Calisthenics prescriptions were light: a mere fifteen minutes per day of stretching, practicing deep breathing exercises, light dancing, or lifting objects of no more than five kilos at a time.[179]

As dawn broke each morning, women throughout Vietnam woke and quietly stole ten to fifteen minutes for themselves to exercise. They began with deep breathing exercises, said to invigorate the blood and expel toxins. They raised their hands behind their neck, pushed their elbows back, and squeezed out air on the exhale. They moved on to stretches for the back, groin, and hamstring and then did light calisthenics, including arm raises and deep knee bends. As the day progressed, they incorporated bends and stretches into their daily routines of tidying, sweeping, and other household chores.[180]

When exercise failed to achieve a "balanced" body, women resorted to dieting. Given that Depression era privations taught women to selflessly limit their food intake to ensure that their children or elderly parents had a meal, the concept of food restriction was not entirely unfamiliar.[181] Diverse narratives from abroad appeared in newspapers—of French women's rigorous diets,[182] communist youth's hunger strikes, and Gandhi's Indian

PHYSIQUE

FIGURE 4.8. Advertisement for diet pills.
Source: *Phong Hóa*, February 11, 1934.

Resistance fasts—further familiarizing urban middle-class women with the idea of food restriction. Newspaper beauty columns reminded women to eat only when hungry, to substitute meat with vegetables, and to fill up on water to quell hunger pains at night.[183] Melia cigarette advertisements hocked their products as a way to slim down. The self-proclaimed beauty expert and entrepreneur Lệ Chi delivered to readers what she believed was the hard truth: "If you want to be slim, you must fast."[184]

When fasting failed, women could choose from a variety of fringe options. Breathing exercises trained women to break the habit of breathing from the belly and instead practice shallow breathing, which was said to flatten the stomach.[185] Diet drugs made of dubious and undisclosed ingredients promised to help women lose weight and maintain their energy (figure 4.8).[186] In Saigon, the Studio Marianne, run by a French woman who touted her degree from the École Normale de Culture Physique in

FIGURE 4.9. Advertisement for Studio Marianne.
Source: La Depeche Indochinoise, February 13, 1934.

Paris, offered exercise classes and claimed to treat obesity through massages and hydrotherapy (figure 4.9).[187] And beauty institutes offered clients paraffin wax baths and electric shock treatments for targeted weight loss.[188] Mocking the absurd measures to which women resorted to get thin, the *Vịt Đực* newspaper sarcastically advised women to merely cinch a rope tightly around their stomach to curb their hunger pains—never mind the resulting pain.[189]

The new bodily ideal was not merely about weight but also gait and posture. Vietnam's beauty conscious crowd tapped into a broader Western trend promoting upright posture, which was linked to health and beauty.[190] The traditional hunched-over crane neck and the mincing gait that accompanied it were no longer considered beautiful by "modern" Vietnamese women in the 1930s.[191] Erect posture and height generally was the new ideal for both women and men.[192] The clothing designer Nguyễn Cát Tường disparaged Vietnamese women of shorter stature, encouraged them to stand tall, and advised them on how to choose clothing that would make them appear taller.[193] High heels were wildly popular. A flurry of newspaper articles taught female readers to raise their head, square their shoulders, and maintain a straight spine as they strode forward with a "strong and agile gait." Women learned a variety of techniques to improve their posture. Morning and night, they practiced deep breathing, preferably while looking up to the ceiling to open their chest.[194] They also practiced exercises to train their muscles to adopt an erect stance. They swung their arms from front to back. They walked around on tip toes with hands raised to the sky, keeping their neck and head straight. They juggled objects while looking up to the ceiling. And they hammered nails or thumbtacks into the wall as a target for stretching their arms up, placing them incrementally higher as their stretching ability improved. Women were also encouraged to engage in Western sports such as swimming, which was believed to elongate the spine.[195] Even rest was key to good posture. Women learned to loosen their muscles before bedtime, sleep in complete darkness, and choose sleep positions that fostered good posture.[196]

Poor posture, women learned, had unexpected consequences for their looks. Hunching the back and tightening the chest impeded breathing, leaving women with a sallow complexion. Desperate to avoid this fate, some women resorted to nonphysical means to improve their posture. Alcoholic beverages, believed to reduce stature, were eschewed. An attitude adjustment—"think only happy thoughts"—was understood to adjust the spine as well.[197] The resulting upright posture purportedly improved women's breathing and hence their complexion. It also gave women an enlarged bust (or so it was said) and agile, healthy bodies overall.[198] Beauty institutes offered to teach women proper posture and gait—sometimes using electrical pulses to stimulate the nerves.[199]

The most controversial aspect of Vietnam's new bodily ideal was the size of a woman's breasts. Vietnam's "old pseudo morality," as a 1936 article in Ngày Nay termed it,[200] understood breasts strictly as tools for nursing children.[201] Any connotations having to do with vanity or sexuality were frowned upon. Even the word breast (vú) was considered too vulgar for polite conversation.[202] Cho Kyo found similar attitudes in pre–World War I China and Japan, where even erotic literature and artwork idolized emaciated figures and shunned breasts.[203] This is consistent with Marilyn Yalom's

FIGURE 4.10. Image to teach women exercises to improve posture and breast perk. *Source: Phong Hóa,* April 6, 1934.

finding that, historically in the West, breasts have tended to be "coded with 'good' or 'bad' connotations," with small breasts associated with virtue and large breasts with promiscuity.[204] In Vietnam, young girls who developed larger breasts at puberty were mocked and criticized, and buxom women were made to feel self-conscious and foolish. Most women bound their breasts with a garment called the nịt vú, rumored to have originated with Buddhist nuns. The nịt vú was made of silk or other thin fabric tied tightly around the chest and neck to compress the breasts so that they were not visible under clothing.[205] Also flattening the breasts—although not as tightly as the nịt vú—was the yếm, a trapezoid or diamond-shaped garment that tied around the neck like a halter top and also around the waist. Unlike the nịt vú, the yếm did not bind the breasts tightly—although it did have a flattening effect on the curve of the breast—and seems to have been worn largely to cover the upper chest and to add a layer of warmth in colder weather.[206]

The late 1920s and 1930s saw a shift in the way breasts were viewed not just in Vietnam but around the world. With flapper fashion going out of style in the West, so too did the flat-chested look. Western women began to embrace a more voluptuous look, and bras were redesigned to push breasts aggressively upward and outward. By the end of the 1920s, women around the world were "liberating" their breasts from corsets and other binding contraptions. Women in France stopped wearing corsets and women in Korea put an end to the painful ritual of binding their breasts.[207] Vietnamese women read riveting stories about spirited women in London who made elaborate public displays of ditching their corsets and celebrating their natural breasts,[208] and about women in China who were fighting to abolish breast binding along with footbinding.[209]

As was the case with the interwar era beauty trends of white teeth and Western fashion, the fetishizing of breasts began with the mê tây, Vietnamese women who married or cohabited with Western men. Me tây were known to have larger than average breasts and muscular bodies. Marginalized not just for their impoverished backgrounds but for their round and sturdy figures, many lower-class me tây had difficulty finding a "suitable" Vietnamese husband and thus found themselves partaking of what Vũ Trọng Phụng famously called "The Industry of Marrying Westerners."[210] As they tended to be from a peasant background, me tây would have likely developed larger muscles from having worked long days in the field when they were younger. As for the size of their breasts, part of their perceived buxomness may simply have resulted from the fact that they were faced with a contingent of prospective romantic partners (French men) who were attracted to large breasts, so they did not minimize their breasts by binding them.

In the late 1920s, Vietnamese society began to reconsider the traditional practice of breast biding. A medical practitioner known simply as "Đ.T." urged women not to bind their breasts. In a eugenics-inspired argument, he made the case that binding the breasts with the nịt vú was not only painful for large-busted women but also "harmful to a woman and harmful to the race." The nịt vú, he argued, made women weak, constricted blood flow, damaged the lungs and other organs, and prevented women from nursing babies by restricting the flow of milk. D.T. also taught that women who bound their breasts faced difficulty recovering from childbirth, and that children born to weak women tended to be weak themselves and made for poor workers.[211]

In the 1930s, prominent breasts came to be mainstreamed in Vietnamese fashion and beauty culture.[212] Breasts were deemed an essential component of women's beauty in Mademoiselle Mộng Khanh's beauty manual "Want to Be Beautiful" (*Muốn Đẹp*).[213] Similarly, the female journalist Hoàng Thị Nhã, writing for the *Đông Pháp* newspaper, celebrated breasts as "an important part of a girl's beauty" that "has been overlooked in the past."[214] The female journalist cô Duyên at the *Ngày Nay* newspaper wrote: "If our natural beauty bothers the eyes of moralists, too bad for them."[215] The Lemur Tunic was deliberately cut to highlight the curve of the breast, the designer Nguyễn Cát Tường admitted.[216] He even worked with Cự Chung, the owner of a ready-to-wear clothing shop, to start production of a Vietnamese bra (*áo lót*) that would uplift the breasts. Within a year or two, the bra was sold in shops throughout the 36 Streets section of Hanoi.[217] Of course, discussions of breasts could only go so far. Hoàng Thị Nhã's article about women's breasts in *Đông Pháp*, mentioned previously, had a gaping hole in the text where twenty lines had been deleted by colonial censors.[218]

So dramatic was the change in social norms that certain male journalists felt entitled to make flippant, gratuitous, and sometimes lecherous references to women's breasts across the pages of newspapers. Exaggerated breasts were a favorite subject of mockery in newspaper cartoons (figure 4.11). Commentary about women's breasts found their way into movie reviews; in a review of the film *Le Chançon*, staring Jeanne Kiépura, the article noted her buxom figure.[219] In what was supposed to be a review of the talented musician Ái Liên's piano performance at the 1935 fundraiser for Annam's flood victims, the journalist writing for *Hà Thành Ngọ Báo* quipped that more people were paying attention to Miss H's breasts than to the music itself, referring to Ái Liên's French name, Hélène.[220]

Now that breasts were being highlighted rather than hidden, women wanted theirs to be "round and neat like an eighteen-year-old's," and beauty columns spilled over with advice on how to maintain that youthful perk.[221] Articles about breast care drew from the language of hygiene.[222] Breasts, women learned, lost their shape, volume, and bounce from bodily changes caused by aging, disease, weight loss, and nursing.[223] Certain activities

FIGURE 4.11. Teacher: "Name some of the largest mammals." Student: "The person with the biggest breasts."
Source: *Phong Hóa*, August 18, 1934. Translation by author.

purportedly damaged breasts and were to be avoided: poor posture, bathing in hot water, running, dancing, or other strenuous physical exercise.[224] The stakes were high: a *Hà Thành Ngọ Báo* article written by a female journalist warned that ugly breasts that leaked milk would cause one's husband to stray.[225] Morning after morning determined women did deep breathing exercises, arm lifts, and wall pushups in hopes of making their breasts larger, firmer, and perkier. They rubbed homemade ointments of glycerin and witch hazel in circular motions around breasts to plump them up.[226] A few desperate women who had the means even resorted to painful electric shock treatments offered by beauty institutes that claimed they could enlarge and firm the breasts.[227]

If or when breasts failed to respond to such methods, women augmented their curves with padding, known as "falsies" (*vú giả*). Popular in Europe and in the United States since the mid-nineteenth century, falsies were rubber, cotton, or other forms of stuffing worn inside a woman's bra.[228] Recognizing falsies as a foreign product—and, for that matter, big breasts as a foreign concept—the novelist Vũ Trọng Phụng sarcastically described them as a "beautification instrument" that "had been sent from France as a contribution to the Europeanization movement of the great kingdom of Vietnam." He skewers the pretentious Europeanization Tailor Shop, where "women who are progressive, civilized, and Europeanized" go to purchase their falsies.[229]

Falsies were roundly ridiculed in the mainstream press. The satirical newspaper *Vịt Đực* advised a young girl attending a military parade that the best way to avoid being groped by men in the crowd—what Dinh Trong Hieu sardonically refers to as a "public sport" of the era[230]—was to wear falsies so that perpetrators "can only squeeze fake breasts and the true breast need not be afraid," failing to address the real problem of unwanted touches.[231] Another article shared the story of a woman walking down a street in Nam Định, "her bouncing breasts attracting many pairs of lustful eyes." Then suddenly, some men rushed toward her from behind, shouting "Hey look!" The girl blushed a deep red and hurried away. It turned out that the girl's pair of rubber falsies had accidentally fallen out of her bra and dropped on the road.[232] Yet another falsie story appeared in Trọng Lang's celebrated book, *Wretched Hanoi (Hà Nội Lầm Than)*. The author recalls his surprise when, just as he was about to take a Taxi Girl for a spin on the dance floor, one of her friends whispered a suggestion to hug her tightly when dancing. He gave her a confused look. "Then you will feel her breasts!" she clarified. Being a gentleman he refused, at which point the friend revealed her wicked motivation: to get him to discover for himself that the Taxi Girl's voluptuous figure was nothing more than padding.[233]

During the interwar years, Vietnam witnessed a dramatic change in the archetypal female physique. The thin, weak, hunched-over body shrouded in loose clothing fell out of favor over the course of the interwar years. Vietnamese modernist projects of eugenics and feminism, both aiming to improve the Vietnamese nation in their own way, normalized public discussion about the female body and championed a stronger female physique and active participation in public life. With the rise of middle-class leisure activities in the 1930s, urban middle-class women became comfortable revealing their body in new ways, creating an aesthetic that emphasized the more intimate parts of the body, especially the breasts. Notwithstanding the nationalist- and feminist-tinged origins of these developments, the resulting female bodily ideal—curvy, lightly muscular, perfectly erect, with a confident gait—was consistant with the Europeanization trend. Indeed, the revolution in the image of the female body that began in part as a serious project of eugenics and feminism soon became a thoroughly bourgeois and, in many cases, rather frivolous endeavor. By the early 1930s the rhetoric about strengthening the Vietnamese nation through the body had largely been abandoned. Women were encouraged to cultivate healthy strong bodies not necessarily to strengthen the nation or claim liberation but to enhance and celebrate their own individual sexuality and identity. As we shall see in the following chapter, women were also growing more comfortable with the public gaze directed at their bodies.

Chapter Five

BEAUTY CONTESTS

"Who at *Công Luận Báo* [newspaper] has no conscience?" demanded the headline of a 1925 article published in *Công Luận Báo*'s rival paper *Đông Pháp Thời Báo*.[1] The irate letter was just one of a flurry of letters written after *Công Luận Báo* announced that it would publish the photographs of what would likely be the first beauty contest in Vietnam—or at least the first well-publicized contest. The contest was to be held among the women of Saigon, but it met with an uproar among readers from all over Cochinchina. The maelstrom focused primarily on claims that the beauty contest would violate traditional Confucian norms governing women's modesty. Pageant organizers were accused of being captured by the cult of Europeanization and were taking advantage of women or even pimping them. The featured letter was signed "Trang-Tử," the Vietnamese translation of Zhuang Zhou, a fourth century BCE Chinese philosopher. This choice of name was likely an allusion to Zhuang Zhou's premise that beauty was relative, thus calling into question the authority of the judges at *Công Luận Báo*.[2] Trang-Tử's fuming letter accused *Công Luận Báo* of being a newspaper that "serves as an agency for prostitutes." The beauty pageant, he predicted, would transform "*khuê các* girls into prostitutes." He continued: "Girls of the Four Virtues and Three Dependencies will change into girls who trim their eyelashes and blacken their eyes to compete for awards; is that civilized civilization?"[3] Drawing again on Chinese literary figures, he asserted that "the Four Great Beauties are worth thousands of gold coins, but that's only found in the inner-chambers of a noble house [khuê các]." So enraged about the flagrant violation the Four Virtues and the khuê các ideal, a boycott of *Công Luận Báo* was announced.[4]

Yet by the Great Depression Vietnamese public opinion about beauty contests had changed. Once dismissed as tawdry, the contests were soon wildly popular and associated with glamour and middle-class modernity. They drew large rambunctious audiences who cheered and threw confetti. In the event that a favorite contestant wasn't crowned, crowds sometimes descended into mayhem.

Some of the reasons for this change in attitude were obvious. By this time, the Vietnamese population had grown accustomed to media images of women wearing brightly colored tunics or Western attire, their hair cut short, their facial features highlighted by rouge, mascara, and lipstick, and their arms and legs on full display as they engaged in all manner of athletic activities. Newspapers dutifully reported results of international beauty contests, and companies advertised products using photographs of foreign beauty queens. Beauty contests can be considered an amalgamation and culmination of all the trends discussed in previous chapters.

However, beyond the obvious explanations for the shift in attitude toward beauty contests was another, more complex one. During the Great Depression, a shift in the Vietnamese social order occurred in which the middle class finally became respectable. As discussed in previous chapters, the 1920s had seen the rapid expansion of the middle class, which was comprised of business owners, merchants, low-level colonial bureaucrats, doctors, pharmacists, lawyers, teachers, and journalists, among others. For the most part, these professions were looked down upon in the Confucian social order for their associations with commerce, collaboration, or quack medicine. But during the Great Depression, as the rural poor suffered harrowing privations that the colonial state failed to alleviate, it was the middle class that organized philanthropic fund-raising activities to raise money for poverty relief. These charity events—that, not incidentally, almost always included beauty contests—sparked a newfound public respect for the middle class. Within a few years, as the middle class acquired greater social capital, the image of the beauty contests that were so intimately associated with middle-class endeavors was rehabilitated. Meanwhile, beauty contests also gained respectability through their association with fairs, which showcased all that was modern, new, and exciting. By being held at fairs and philanthropic events, beauty contests assumed an image of modern, middle-class prestige.

The rise of these special events showcasing the most beautiful women in Vietnam had a remarkable impact on the colony's female population and signaled a major cultural shift. More than any other beauty-related developments in interwar Vietnam, the rise of beauty contests marked a radical departure from the Confucian Four Virtues and khuê các model, which together had governed female conduct in the early twentieth century. In early twentieth-century Vietnam, one of the Four Virtues, *dung* (appearance) was understood to mean that women should keep their appearance neat and clean but refrain from showing off their beauty to anyone other than their husband. The khuê các model, discussed in previous chapters, was based on an archetypical character in Chinese literature—the daughter of a noble family who was sequestered at home until marriage. Young Vietnamese women of the early twentieth century were not actually sequestered, but they were expected to remain true to the khuê các ideal: modest, chaste, retiring. Beauty contests swiftly upended this ideal. Within a decade, women were—like the beauty queens themselves—sporting the latest fashions, using makeup to artificially highlight their features, and flaunting their curves in front of large and sometimes boisterous crowds. In short, the extraordinary popularity of beauty contests in interwar Vietnam ushered in a radical transformation in women's relationship with their own bodies and, more broadly, their ideas about themselves.

BEAUTY CONTESTS AND CONTESTED NORMS

During the interwar years, beauty contests exploded in popularity in the United States, Europe, and the colonized world. The contests arrived in Vietnam by way of media from the colonizing world. Although early iterations of French beauty pageants date back to the late nineteenth century Festival of the Crowning of the Muse, it was not until the interwar period that beauty pageants became a national obsession.[5] In 1920, Maurice de Waleffe, editor of the *Paris Soir* and secretary general of the newspaper conglomerate Press Latine d'Europe et d'Amerique, organized the first "La Plus Belle Femme de France" pageant in Paris to boost his publications' readership.[6] The following year the first Miss America pageant took place in Atlantic City. The International Pageant of Pulchritude, later known as the Miss Universe Pageant, debuted in 1926 in Galveston, Texas. Contestants arrived from all over the world, and competition among nations grew so fierce that a rival Miss Universe contest was introduced in Brazil to compete with the American pageant of the same name.[7]

Beauty contests, in short, became a global phenomenon. In 1929 de Waleffe introduced the "Miss Europe" contest and would go on to organize a "Miss France d'Outre Mer" pageant at the 1937 Exposition Universelle.[8] De Waleffe also founded pageants in Lebanon, Algeria, and Tunisia. Aro Velmet credits him with "having turned beauty contests into an industry in a mere two decades."[9] By the 1930s, the beauty contest trend had caught on in urban areas of Asia, with contests in Shanghai, the Dutch Netherlands Indies, Korea, Cambodia, Penang, Thailand, and the Philippines.[10]

In 1925, Saigon's popular *Công Luận Báo* newspaper staged what was likely the first beauty contest in Vietnam, and it caused quite a controversy. That it took place in Saigon is not surprising. Saigon's residents were exposed to, if not directly influenced by, French culture in significant ways. The city had the largest concentration of French colonists and the highest population of interracial families in Indochina. Furthermore, Saigon was the capital of Cochinchina, the only *pays* in Indochina under direct French rule. Since the turn of the century, French residents and mixed-race families had enjoyed café-lined boulevards, theaters, an athletics club, a zoo, and a botanical garden. As discussed in chapter 1, by the mid-1920s, when *Công Luận Báo* announced its beauty contest, Western leisure culture was beginning to gain traction and was drawing middle-class Vietnamese women as well as men into Saigon's public sphere.

It is likewise unsurprising that Vietnam's first beauty contest was organized by a newspaper. As Shawn McHale and Philippe Peycam have shown, newspapers, especially in Cochinchina, held an important place in the public sphere as a nexus of liberal political debate over modernization.[11] *Công Luận Báo* was no exception—especially under the editorship of Huỳnh Văn Chính (writing under the nom de plume Tự Do [Freedom])—and during this time it grew to become what Philippe Peycam deemed "one of the greatest success stories in the early history of the Vietnamese press."[12] Given their exploding readership in the 1920s, *Công Luận Báo* and other newspapers provided a significant advertising market and became a central conduit for the dissemination of beauty culture. Indeed, the newspaper beauty contest business model was already entrenched in metropolitan French print culture. After all, Maurice de Wallef's beauty pageants were designed as profit-generating enterprises for his metropolitan newspapers. Newspapers flew off the shelves, and de Wallef benefited greatly from readers' voracious appetite for images of pretty women.

Perhaps most significant to the story, the *Công Luận Báo* contest was staged before any major controversies or crises had erupted over the new modes of beauty and fashion that had recently arrived in Vietnam. This first beauty contest was all the more shocking to residents of Saigon. Most women in Cochinchina's cities, including the participants in the beauty contest, were still donning the traditional four- or five-panel tunics or *áo bà ba* with dark wide-legged pants, although some fashionable young women had begun experimenting with white pants and bright tunics (see chapter 2).[13] Ready-to-wear women's clothing imported from the metropole was gradually introduced, but this phenomenon was limited to urban women and rural mẹ tay living near the military bases that housed European soldiers. By 1925, when the beauty contest took place, urban women had begun wearing a little makeup—mostly face powder and lipstick to frame their white smile (urban women in Cochinchina had largely abandoned teeth-blackening a by 1920). Even in the large metropolis of Saigon, women kept their hair long and parted in the middle until the end of the decade. It was not until approximately 1930, when women had become comfortable playing a variety of sports, that female bodies became more visible in public spaces. The Modern Girl phenomenon and accompanying nationalist backlash would likewise not occur until the early 1930s.

The colony's first beauty contest, open to all the women of Saigon, spanned three months, from June 15 to September 15, 1925. Women were to submit their entries by mail in the form of photographs. Three winners would be announced by September 15, 1925, with their image published in the newspaper. Photographic beauty contests were introduced in the late nineteenth century by P. T. Barnum and soon became commonplace in the United States and, to a lesser extent, in France. Typically staged in women's periodicals, American and French photographic beauty contests were a sound business model. They taught women how to "look" and, in doing so, encouraged them to achieve that look by investing heavily in the cosmetics and fashions advertised in those same periodicals.[14] Although *Công Luận Báo* was not geared uniquely for women, editors did try to capitalize on the explosive growth in the number of literate women graduating from colonial schools and aging into newspaper readership.[15] *Công Luận Báo* also likely profited from the photos because the rules of the contest required contestants to have their portraits taken by Le Văn Bến at the Phú Toàn photography studio on Amiral Courbet Road in Saigon. Later the newspaper was accused of receiving some sort of kickback. The Phú Toàn photography studio would submit the photographs to *Công Luận Báo*, along with the contestant's name, address, and signature or personal stamp, as was a common form of identification at the time.[16]

According to contest announcements, *Công Luận Báo* would select the three most beautiful women in Saigon and award them prizes in the form of jewelry valued at fifty piasters for first prize, thirty piasters for second prize, and twenty piasters for third prize. *Công Luận Báo* promised to publish pictures of the first three winners. Newspaper editors would also choose seven more women, rank their beauty from fourth through tenth, and "indulge the ladies of the beauty contest" with prizes of luxury items, including embroidered towels, incense, and cosmetics.[17]

Although the beauty contest never made the front page of the *Công Luận Báo* newspaper—information about it was typically published on the third or fourth page of an issue—it did become the talk of the town. One female reader noted that women all over Cochinchina were excited about the contest and wanted to send in pictures to show off their beauty—all "except, of course Chung Vô Diệm," the famously homely but loyal wife of a third-century BCE Chinese war general and the main character in a popular cải lương play at the time "who is now embarrassed to show her face," insinuating that only ugly women would oppose the contest.[18]

The *Công Luận Báo* contest stirred quite a controversy in Cochinchina. The controversy, part of a broader neo-Confucian pushback against the trend in Europeanization, hinged on women's modesty and whether or not women should display their beauty in public. To Confucian-minded readers, women's preoccupation with their looks and willingness to publicly display themselves was a harbinger of the degradation of communal morality, as Judith Henchy has noted.[19] For its part, *Công Luận Báo*'s editorial board insisted that the motivation behind the beauty contest was fundamentally altruistic. In publicizing pictures of beautiful women, the contest would introduce concepts of personal hygiene to peasant women and teach them how to improve their appearance.[20] This justification, of course, smacked of classism; the patronizing rhetoric of teaching peasant women how to beautify themselves—by urban Saigon's standards, of course—echoed turn of the century metropolitan initiatives to civilize the French peasantry.[21] Moreover, as discussed in chapter 4, the rhetoric of personal hygiene and beauty drew from eugenics discourse.

The controversy fed interwar Vietnam's fierce newspaper rivalries, with journalists and readers alike publishing critiques in competing newspapers. The bulk of the criticism came from *Đông Pháp Thời Báo*. Animosity between *Công Luận Báo* and *Đông Pháp Thời Báo* dated back to 1923, when the journalist Nguyễn Kim Đính left the former to establish the latter; thereafter the two papers engaged in a heated competition for readers. In 1925, Nguyễn Kim Đính was replaced by Trần Huy Liệu, a nationalist intellectual and the future Minister of Propaganda under the Democratic Republic of Vietnam (DRV). Whereas *Công Luận Báo* favored social and economic "development," *Đông Pháp Thời Báo*, under the leadership of Trần Huy Liệu, took a strong moralistic neo-Confucian posture to criticize Europeanization trends—and the paper was not afraid to publish critiques of its rival.[22]

Đông Pháp Thời Báo had a strong female readership and employed a network of local correspondents in the countryside, some of whom were female journalists.[23] Over the course of the beauty contest, *Đông Pháp Thời Báo* printed angry letters from more than a dozen journalists and readers, all women—or at least claiming to be women—hailing from all over Cochinchina, including Saigon, Cà Mau,[24] Bạc Liêu,[25] Rạch-đào,[26] and Bến Tre.[27] The women who criticized the beauty contest were eloquent and intelligent. They cited Chinese philosophy, literature, and history as well as European philosophers. Their letters were witty and acerbic critiques, not just of the beauty contest but of the *Công Luận Báo* newspaper itself. A letter from Lê Thị H., a precocious thirteen-year-old student in Saigon, opened with a typical Vietnamese insult: a disarming and obviously false claim that she "may not be too bright or very talented," followed by a lacerating critique of the editors and their beauty contest.[28] After insisting that Vietnamese women who were raised properly would never participate, one reader said dismissively that "there's no need to even object" to the contest, insinuating that Vietnamese women know better than to even submit their photos.[29] Another reader closed a rather critical letter with an obviously sarcastic "We wish your contest quite well."[30] And one particularly witty letter writer signed off as "Lão-kỹ-nữ tự Tú-Bà," the name of a brothel madam who tricked Kiều into prostitution in the epic *Tale of Kiều* by Nguyễn Du—a winking allusion to the pimping being done by *Công Luận Báo*.[31]

Anger over the beauty contest itself erupted into personal attacks on the editors at *Công Luận Báo*. Readers demanded that the editor Tự-Do apologize.[32] Reader Trang-Tử, whose letter is discussed in the introduction, called the *Công Luận Báo* writing staff "really stupid in the extreme," and asked in disbelief: "Have I ever seen anyone as stupid as this?"[33] More colorfully, Madamoiselle Đỗ Ngọc Kim from Bến Tre called Tự-Do "a chicken infected with stink bugs, like a lizard eating a medicine . . . [spitting] vulgar words that give listeners a headache."[34] For his part, Tự-Do launched counter invectives against "those idiots." "Do you understand their stupidity? It turns out that those idiots didn't even understand it themselves—and they also thought they were right, and thus became more arrogant."[35]

Personal attacks aside, the main complaint about the contest was that "beauty contests were harmful to the customs of the country."[36] This critique stemmed from the broader discussion about Confucianism that was playing out in the Vietnamese public sphere. Female critics of *Công Luận Báo* invoked "the ancient teaching of Eastern morals" and proudly proclaimed that "women in our country have followed the Three Dependencies and the Four Virtues for over a thousand years."[37] As a very public display of women's appearance, beauty contests clearly violated the virtue of modest manner and appearance. Madamoiselle Đ.O. of *Đông Pháp Thời Báo* scoffed: "Vietnamese women who were raised properly will not join this contest."[38] Beauty contests also violated the virtue of morality, as critics understood it. A common theme in the readers' letters was the question of whether or not a beautiful woman could also be virtuous—a question that would likewise be raised about cosmetics use in the 1930s. Lieu Nhụ, a female reader from Ruelle Testari in Saigon, explained that just as flowers are rarely both beautiful and fragrant, few women are both beautiful and virtuous—and that beauty, moreover, has the potential for evil.[39] Lê Thị H., the precocious thirteen-year-old female reader from Saigon, asked if a woman could be truly virtuous if she were willing to publish her picture in the newspaper.[40] As the readers writing in to *Đông Pháp Thời Báo* interpreted "tradition," women were expected to remain at home to serve their fathers and husbands, not flaunt their looks to the outside world. Trang-Tử cited the khuê các model in which unwed upper-class young women were sequestered at home until marriage as an ideal to which to aspire.⁴¹

Readers further objected to what they believed was a Europeanization agenda on the pages of *Công Luận Báo*. Nguyễn Thị Kiêm, who would be known a leader of the the New Poetry movement under the name Nguyễn Thị Manh Manh, deplored what she characterized as an attempt by the editorial board of *Công Luận Báo* to improve Vietnam by resorting to Western culture. "Even Frédéric Nietzche praises Eastern culture and disparages Western culture," she wrote, referring to Nietzche's *Beyond Good and Evil*. "Why should we think and act otherwise?"⁴² Dismissing the French women's rights movement, reader Trang Tử wrote: "we do not care who has freedom, equality. The ancient teaching of Eastern morals will always be kept. If [*Công Luận Báo*] wants to follow 'freedom' then that is their choice, but they will not pursuade us [Vietnamese] women."⁴³

Công Luận Báo defended itself against attacks that its sponsorship of the beauty contest amounted to a violation of Confucian traditions. The editorial board acknowledged the importance of virtue but urged readers to dissociate beauty from virtue (or lack thereof) because "in this beauty contest, it's a contest of beauty only."⁴⁴ In another article defending the beauty contest, *Công Luận Báo* editors declared: "If you confuse the beauty contest with morality, you are stupid. . . . A beauty contest is a beauty contest, customs are customs, journalists are journalists. . . . Only stupid idiots can't tell the difference."⁴⁵ The editors insisted that women in all "civilized" countries sought to improve their looks, that Vietnamese women would do the same even without a beauty contest, and that the Four Virtues still prevailed.⁴⁶ The editor went on the offense, claiming that those who objected to this contest were "effectively condemning peasant women to 'a sea of filth' in an effort to rescue a thousand-year-old civilization."⁴⁷

In the debates over beauty contests, opponents and champions alike turned to the issue of nationalism to bolster their case. This is not surprising considering that the beauty contest took place in the summer of 1925, and Philippe Peycam observed that it was a "turning point in national politics, transforming Saigon into a foyer of public opposition to the colonial regime."⁴⁸ The *Công Luận Báo* editors declared that the goal of the beauty contests was "to show [the locals] as well as foreigners that the beauty of women in Vietnam is a great treasure."⁴⁹ In a letter to *Công*

Luận Báo, female reader Lieu Như from Ruelle Testari, Saigon, corrected them: "*Công Luận Báo* organized this contest to show other countries that they may have some 'precious' beautiful women, but we [know we have] have a 'continent' of beautiful women, and none of [our women] are *not* beautiful."[50] Two women writing for *Đông Pháp Thời Báo* insisted that beauty contests set a bad example for the women of Vietnam: "as [women] are not learning the duty to the nation or nationalism; [beauty contest organizers] claim to civilize people. . . . This is a sign that the morals of a country are about to fall."[51] Another female *Đông Pháp Thời Báo* reader exhorted fellow readers to fight back: "Women in our country have followed the Three Dependencies and the Four Virtues for over a thousand years, and they have weathered many storms without being shaken or moved. Then we are invaded by the French and our national defense collapses; we must join together to repair it." She asked incredulously: "You imitate Western people because you think that is the way to repair it?"[52]

Some readers recoiled at the thought that the beauty contest would encourage Vietnamese women to adopt French beauty standards.[53] A *Đông Pháp Thời Báo* reader from Cà Mau expressed disgust for contestants who "wear a pound of face powder and a ton of diamonds."[54] Hinting at fears of the trends in individualism and consumerism taking over Vietnam, *Đông Pháp Thời Báo* accused beauty contest organizers of "leading women to care so much about their body shape that they give up their female duties, and encouraging women to be frivolous and to spend excessive amounts of money on clothes and lipstick in order to look good in photos."[55]

Công Luận Báo editors even faced accusations of lechery. One angry reader wrote that the *Công Luận Báo* editors held the contest so they could spend time with pretty young women.[56] An article in *Đông Pháp Thời Báo* accused beauty contest organizers of creating opportunities for men "who are addicted to lust and destroying the home."[57] The letter writer who sardonically called herself Tú Bà after the brothel madam in *The Tale of Kieu* declared: "What [*Công Luận Báo*] is doing is selling beauty to thirsty men and profiting from it." The letter writer continued: "[The newspaper] is no different from Tú Bà."[58] In a bid to call out *Công Luận Báo* editors for hypocrisy, a reader asked: "Why don't you enter your own granddaughter's photo into the contest, as she will surely win the title of the contest?"[59]

This reader was simultaneously casting shame on both the editors and their hypothetical granddaughter.

Some readers likened the contest's link between beauty and profit to prostitution. One reader sniffed that most women would prefer to stick to tradition than participate in a contest showing off their looks for money.[60] The editorial board of *Đông Pháp Thời Báo* declared: "Our sisters treasure 'virginity' that's worth a ton of gold, not fifty coins from *Công Luận Báo*."[61] Yet another insisted that a woman with dignity and a desire to preserve her culture would never show her face and let others profit from it.[62] Taking this claim a step further, a reader described the beauty contest as "*Khuê các* [young women] turning to prostitution and bringing their made-up faces to the newspaper to present to the public."[63] Trang-Tử even went as far as to declare *Cộng Luận Báo* a newspaper for prostitutes.[64]

One female reader pointed out that the beauty contest brought no benefit to the nation; it simply enabled the newspaper to sell more copies and satisfy playboys.[65] Another female reader noted that everyone but the beauty contestants themselves—the companies selling expensive makeup, the newspaper holding the contest to attract more readers, and the voyeuristic audience—were profiting one way or another and were out of touch with the rest of a country that was struggling economically.[66] Lê Thị H., the precocious thirteen-year-old letter writer, questioned why contestants could only submit their photos through the photography studio designated by *Công Luận Báo*, insinuating that the newspaper was receiving a cut of the profits from the studio.[67] Although the *Công Luận Báo* editor claimed quite plausibly that the use of a designated photographer prevented fraud, it was unclear how real the threat of fraudulent submissions actually was.[68]

Indeed, the motivation underlying the beauty contest—and the controversy surrounding it—fundamentally came down to profit. The contest required little overhead because the paper solicited donations from merchants seeking free publicity when their products were awarded as prizes. The paper may have also profited in kickbacks from sending contestants to a single photography studio. *Công Luận Báo* ran advertisements and articles to stir up suspense and increase readership. The combination of *Công Luận Báo*'s shrewd promotional methods and the controversy stirred up by the contest itself more than doubled *Công Luận Báo*'s subscriptions in a matter of months, despite calls for a boycott.

Ironically, after all of the hoopla the contest itself appears to have been a flop. The contest was disorganized from the start, having promised prizes that it had yet to secure. A few weeks into the launch of the contest, *Công Luận Báo* was still soliciting donations from merchants, "especially shops that sell gems, jewelry, and cosmetics," to be given away as prizes, assuring the merchants that they would benefit from the exposure.[69] The contest officially ended on September 15, 1925. A few months earlier, on July 4, 1925, the newspaper had announced that Thu-Hương from Dakao was the first-prize winner, and on September 3, 1925, the paper made reference to an unnamed second-place winner.[70] But contest organizers never mentioned the other eight runners-up that they had promised to select when they originally publicized the contest, nor is it clear that any of the winners actually received their prizes. Moreover, the paper never even published photographs of the winner. In an article fittingly titled "??," a *Đông Pháp Thời Báo* reader called out the beauty contest for announcing only one winner and never publishing any photographs. The reader went on to suggest that the contest failed because women had refused to degrade themselves by participating.[71] This theory may have had merit; after all, there should have been plenty of applicants given all the press devoted to the contest. Ultimately, it seems that women just didn't feel comfortable submitting a photo of themselves for all the world to see—and judge.

THE REDEMPTION OF BEAUTY CONTESTS

Given that the Three Dependencies and the Four Virtues had been governing the comportment of Vietnamese women for over a thousand years, it is remarkable how dramatically the image of beauty contests in Vietnam changed within just a few years. By the late 1920s, the contests had become a global sensation outside of Vietnam. New forms of media, including photographs, radio broadcasts, and advertisements, spread images and detailed descriptions of fresh-faced women in beautiful dresses, sashaying across a stage for enthusiastic in-person audiences as well as readers and listeners from around the world. During the Great Depression, the lineups of dazzling young ladies provided a welcome distraction from the hardships of the economic crisis at home. As early as 1929, the Vietnamese press began covering international beauty pageants, thus familiarizing their audiences with the idea of women competing in front of large crowds to be seen as the most beautiful. Multiple Vietnamese language newspapers followed the 1931 Miss Europe pageant and published stories on the winner, Jeanne Guilla, a twenty-year-old French woman.[72] Vietnamese newspapers even covered winners from regional French contests, such as Mireille Ligit, the eighteen-year-old who won the 1938 Miss Côte d'Azur contest.[73] A Vietnamese journalist with the pen name WanCaln, a self-styled authority on the subject, published impressively detailed accounts of American beauty pageants in the *Hà Thành Ngọ Báo* newspaper.[74] The paper also published the latest results—with pictures, of course—of beauty contests such as Miss France, Miss Europe, Miss America, and Miss Universe.[75] By the mid-1930s, *Hà Thành Ngọ Báo* was printing pictures of multiple contestants from a single contest, staggered over days or weeks, a technique that generated suspense and encouraged readers to come back for more.[76]

Cosmetics companies looking to capitalize on the gendered consumerism burgeoning all over the world further promoted beauty pageants by using them to advertise their products, many of which had found their way to Vietnamese markets. Lune-Fat Felouty Dixor hired Laura Wild, the first national beauty queen of England, as its spokesperson.[77] Crème Simon's antiaging cream used images of Pauline Po, who was Miss France in 1920, and Genevieve Felix, the winner of the Montmartre pageant and later a silent film actress. Advertisements for Cadum soap promised customers that the product would make their skin as beautiful as a beauty queen's.[78] Lux soap, meanwhile, was touted as the soap used by beauty queens all over the world.[79] Local Vietnamese brands also capitalized on the popularity of beauty contests. The Quận Chúa clothing and shoes shop advertised their goods with claims that the beauty queen Cai Đông regularly wore their dresses.[80] An advertisement for Dr. Lăm Quang Sĩ's dental practice in Hanoi features a girl sharing with her father her desire to enter the Pháp-Việt night faire beauty contest and expressing concern about her imperfect teeth. Her father urges her to get porcelain veneers, assuring her that this will help her win the contest.[81]

The deluge of global media coverage and advertising campaigns certainly normalized beauty pageants around the world during the late 1920s and early 1930s, but these contests only gained traction in Vietnam as a result of significant local cultural developments, some of which have been discussed extensively in previous chapters. The changes in the gender order that swept Vietnam during this period undoubtedly made audiences more receptive to the idea of beauty pageants. Women became increasingly active in public society and less constrained by traditional roles. By 1930, girls' education was well established, and a generation of New Women trained as teachers took their place in front of classrooms or as journalists boldly expressing their opinions and questioning society. The influential newspaper *Phụ Nữ Tân Văn* denounced Confucian constraints on women and argued to its readers—male and female alike—that women should enjoy more rights. It was not uncommon to see girls on the soccer field or women bicycling, even in the countryside. And, particularly in French-influenced areas, Vietnamese women rode the tram, chatted with friends in cafes, and attended the movies with their boyfriends. In this context, a woman sashaying across the stage of a beauty pageant was no longer scandalous.

Another factor that contributed to the rehabilitation of beauty contests was the rise of beauty culture. By 1930, it was no longer shocking for young women to call attention to themselves with colorful tunics and white pants, and Western clothing was no longer considered evidence of loose morals—at least in urban areas. Women felt comfortable flashing a white smile framed by red lipstick, and they enjoyed the lightness and ease afforded by shoulder-length hair. The daily practice of calisthenics at school promoted erect posture among young ladies, and the sports matches they played encouraged an athletic build and the kind of bodily self-assurance that was on full display at beauty contests.

A third sociocultural development in interwar Vietnam that contributed significantly to the rise of beauty contests had to do with a concomitant rise in the prestige of Vietnam's middle class. As previously discussed, this rapidly expanding middle class had not initially been viewed as respectable. It was comprised of clerks and interpreters for the colonial government, merchants and business owners, journalists, doctors, pharmacists, lawyers, and teachers in colonial schools, among others—all professions associated with money or the colonial administration and hence frowned upon under the Confucian social order.[82] Moreover, with its extravagant displays of newfound wealth, its consumer mindset, and its affinity for French culture, the middle-class culture of the 1920s was considered vulgar. The social standing of the middle class would improve during the early 1930s, and with its upgraded reputation would come a new openness to beauty contests.

The rise in status enjoyed by the middle class—and the attendant rise in status of beauty contests—transpired thanks to a series of developments linked to the Great Depression. In the late 1920s, the colonial economy collapsed when the international rubber and rice markets reached the point of saturation, causing prices to plummet. Vietnam began feeling the effects of poverty almost instantly.[83] The US stock market crashed in October 1929, plunging the world into the Great Depression. The economic crisis was further exacerbated by crop failures in Nghệ An and Hà Tĩnh in the early 1930s and flooding in northern Annam in the mid-1930s. The result was mass poverty, homelessness, famine, and orphaning or abandonment of children. Urban areas recovered from the Great Depression within a few years, but peasants in the countryside suffered privations well into the mid-1930s. Notwithstanding its "civilizing mission" and claims to protect its subjects, the colonial government showed itself to be impotent in the face of such economic disaster. Instead, it was the Vietnamese middle class that stepped in to help with poverty relief.

To raise money for those afflicted by economic and environmental hardships, members of the Vietnamese middle class established philanthropic societies with roots in the village mutual aid groups.[84] These new philanthropic associations, influenced by Western culture, drew on two fundraising strategies that were new to Vietnam: they organized fairs to raise awareness among the general public while generating funds through the sale of tickets, and they staged elegant philanthropic evening dinners for a small coterie of well-heeled members of the middle class who were wealthy enough to donate to the cause.

The fairs attracted audiences with various bourgeois leisure activities—some from the Vietnamese tradition, such as cockfighting,[85] bonsai competitions,[86] and lantern lighting,[87] and some from the West, such as circus acts,[88] human chess tournaments,[89] and dancing. Almost without exception, the charity fairs and philanthropic evening dinners of the 1930s featured beauty contests as the main attraction of the evening. A 1931 fundraiser at Hoàn Kiếm Lake included a beauty contest to raise funds for victims of a tropical cyclone that had devastated central Annam in October.[90] In 1935 a group of charities staged a pageant to raise money for victims of the floods in Annam and southern Tonkin.[91] The 1937 fair in Bến Tre lined up beauty queens to raise funds for poverty relief, and only a few months later a fundraiser for flood victims in Nam Định listed a beauty contest as one of its main attractions.[92] In 1938, the Cantonese Assembly in Hanoi likewise hosted a pageant, this one for victims of the Japanese invasion in

China.[93] A 1939 fair organized by the Société d'encouragement aux études occidentales de l'Annam raised funds for students by selling tickets for a beauty contest.[94] In February 1940 philanthropic organizations l'AFINA and Oeuvres de Guerre de la Lạc Thiện held a joint event complete with a beauty pageant fundraiser.[95]

A significant portion of the fund-raising also occurred at evening gala dinners. Organized by these new philanthropic organizations and attended by middle-class members of the colony's Vietnamese, French, and Chinese communities, philanthropic dinner events were held at elegant restaurants and ballrooms located inside luxurious hotels or department stores. The events served multicourse gourmet dinners, provided a live band for musical entertainment, and offered a wooden dance floor for waltzing and foxtrotting. But the most exciting and anticipated event at the vast majority of these philanthropic fundraisers were beauty contests.

That philanthropic societies became the avenue by which beauty contests reemerged in Vietnam during the 1930s is not surprising given that the colony's early pageants had been staged by high-society mixed Franco-Vietnamese philanthropic organizations heavily influenced by Western culture. The beauty contest strategy followed the French philanthropic business model in which beauty contests proved to be a lucrative attraction for charity fund-raising events. For middle-class reformers, the lineup of beautiful women dressed in the latest fashion trends also conveyed an image of Vietnamese bourgeois modernity that would presumably impress audience members—specifically Westerners. As the business model of using a pageant of pretty young women to raise charity donations proved successful, Vietnamese and ethnic Chinese philanthropic organizations followed suit. By setting beauty contests in the noble context of middle-class philanthropy, the once tawdry—or at least controversial—image of beauty contests was rehabilitated.

It goes without saying that the glamour of the charity fundraisers and beauty contests stood in stark contrast to the circumstances of the victims they were helping—and that, in part, was the point. However altruistic their intent, these fundraisers functioned as a means of affirming the bourgeois identity of the individuals who staged them. After all, to gain admittance to a philanthropic event one had to be able to afford a ticket whose price was steep enough to cover not only the overhead but also a contribution for the target charity. The case of colonial Vietnam was not unusual. As Lauren Goodlad has shown in the example of Victorian England, middle-class identity was tied to the idea of performing charity work for the working class.[96] Van Nguyen-Marshall found a similar model of class identity in her work on philanthropic organizations in South Vietnam during the 1960s.[97] In a separate study on the charity organizations of the 1930s, Van Nguyen-Marshall shows that in the absence of French leadership, the charity work performed by the Vietnamese middle class during the Great Depression enabled this new class to assume the role of moral authorities for the nation.[98] Meanwhile, the distasteful display of middle-class vanity and indulgence in the name of philanthropy was not lost on the author Vũ Trọng Phụng. In his 1936 novel *Vỡ Đê*, he blasted the decadent fundraisers who "gave some alms for thousands of drowning compatriots," a reference to the victims of the floods in Annam.[99] "Some" in this context means not nearly enough—a mere token of generosity inadequate given the magnitude of the suffering. In alluding to the Buddhist practice of giving alms—which was believed to result in better karma for the giver—Vũ Trọng Phụng insinuates that the do-gooders may have been motivated by more than a little self-interest. Considering the paltry sums donated to so many in need, and the dubious motivations at work, optics had clearly eclipsed altruism.

The venue in which a beauty contest was held played a vital role in setting the tenor of public opinion. Just as beauty contests achieved middle-class respectability through philanthropic events, the contests became linked with middle-class modernity through their ubiquitous presence at Vietnam's fairs. Just as fairs showcased the latest technology and consumer products, the beauty pageants that took place on the fairground celebrated the literal embodiments of the modern Vietnamese woman. In a symbiotic relationship, the cutting-edge products at the fair enhanced the atmosphere of modernity at the contests, and the contests themselves promoted a desire for all things modern and beautiful.

It is not surprising that beauty contests quickly became one of the most anticipated attractions at fairs. Fairgoers had to pay an entrance fee, but typically they had to purchase a second ticket to attend the fair's beauty contest. The 1938 Huế Fair charged a relatively hefty price for contest tickets, typically the same amount as the price of admission to the entire fair. Such pricing effectively ensured that the pageant audience was predominantly, if not exclusively, middle class.[100] In some cases, women were crowned with

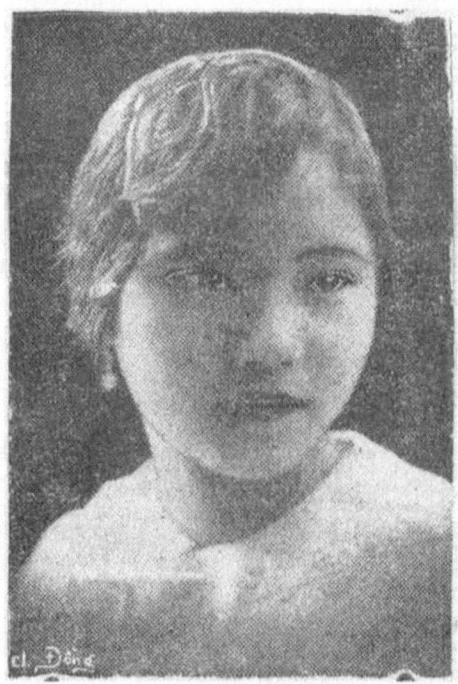

FIGURE 5.1. Beauty contestants for a Hanoi beauty contest.
Source: *Hà Thành Ngọ Báo*, February 12, 1935.

a hybrid English-French title, "Miss Foire," that spoke to the American and French cultural origins of the event.[101] The press eagerly covered the beauty contests. Young women such as the high school student Phùng Thị Phát, winner of the contest at the 1936 Faifoo Fair in Annam (figure 5.1), found their photos gracing the pages of newspapers published as far away as Saigon.[102]

Visitors came to fairs to see the latest cutting-edge inventions and sample the most modern consumer products. As discussed at length in chapter 1, fairs showcased a vision of a particular form of modernity: a consumerist modernity that could be bought and sold. Purchases made at a fair (or inspired by a visit) shaped one's identity; a person became *modern* by owning the most cutting-edge products and wearing the most up to the minute fashions. As the most important event at fairs, beauty contests became inextricably linked with this consumerist modernity. Department stores set up booths to showcase cosmetics so fairgoers could achieve that beauty queen *look*. An advertisement for a Hanoi clothing shop, which also operated a booth at the 1938 Hanoi Fair, proudly announced that it would be providing outfits for contestants at the fair's beauty contest.[103] Vendors often requested that beauty queens make an appearance at their bar or restaurant stand. When sales were lackluster among food and drink vendors at the Chợ Lớn fundraiser Hội chợ bán đồ hạ giá, fair organizers sent Miss Chợ Lớn to sip lemonade at the vendors' booths, thereby attracting more customers, particularly men who were stereotyped to be irresponsible with money.[104]

Fairs in Vietnam came to be synonymous with fashion and beauty consumer trends. Female fairgoers dressed up, and it was not uncommon to see an audience full of brightly colored tunics, white pants, high heels, and made-up faces. As discussed in chapter 2, the fashion designer Nguyễn Cát Tường drew inspiration from crowds at the 1934 Lạc Thiên fair and debuted his Lemur Tunic at the same fair the following year.[105]

By the mid-1930s, the popularity of beauty contests in Vietnam extended beyond the middle class, with contests being staged in local markets. In 1933, a market in Hanoi celebrated its opening with a pageant of a few dozen contestants.[106] (Indeed, it was in the newspaper photograph of a beauty contest held in a Saigon market that Huyền, the jealous protagonist of Vũ Trọng Phụng's 1936 novel *Làm Đĩ*, spotted her lover ogling contestants from the front row.[107]) As contests held in markets were designed to attract customers and increase earnings for vendors, they were open to all and required at most a nominal entry fee. Audiences were generally Vietnamese or other ethnic minorities; French colonists rarely attended, nor did wealthier Vietnamese and Chinese whose maids did the shopping. Attesting to the popularity of beauty contests, spin-off pageants appeared with contests for "Miss Beautiful Peasant."[108] As testament to their ubiquity—and acceptance among even conservative crowds—a pageant was even held at the inaugural ceremony of the Thái-phú pagoda in Thái Bình.[109]

By the end of the 1930s, newspapers were proudly publishing stories about women from Indochina competing in international contests. This was a relatively recent phenomenon. In 1931, Miss LV from Cần Thơ had sent her photograph to the *Đuốc Nhà Nam* newspaper along with a pleading query: "Can a beauty like me compete with women in Europe and America?" After carefully evaluating her letter and picture, the editor advised that she refrain from competing against Europeans and Americans because she would be judged by Western standards.[110] In only a few short years, attitudes changed. A Franco-Lao Eurasian woman competed in the 1935 Miss Universe pageant in Brussels.[111] In 1937, four Eurasian women represented Tonkin, Annam, Cochinchina, and Laos in the empire wide beauty contest called Miss France d'Outre Mer at the 1937 Exposition Colonial in Paris. Ten Vietnamese women were chosen to participate in a Pageant of the Pacific, a beauty contest that showcased women from nations around the Pacific Rim at the 1939 Golden Gate Exposition in San Francisco.[112]

The racial politics of that 1937 Miss France d'Outre Mer contest sparked controversy at home in Vietnam. In early 1937, the contest's founder, Maurice de Waleffe, had traveled to Vietnam during his empire wide search for women to his pageant held at the World Fair in France. Originally called "La Meilleur Marriage Française," the pageant was designed to showcase the potential for mixed-race marriages and "engineer the best colonial marriage" as a solution to France's perceived depopulation problem.[113] De Waleffe arrived in Saigon in January 1937, then traveled throughout Indochina for twenty days in search of comely unmarried Eurasian women seventeen to twenty-two years old to participate in the Miss France d'Outre Mer contest. Along with a woman to represent Laos, De Waleffe chose three *métisse* women to represent Vietnam, all from prominent families. While touring Paris, the Franco-Vietnamese Eurasian women dressed exclusively in Vietnamese clothing, likely in a disingenuous effort to exoticize themselves. Photography and newsreel images from the Paris exposition show Miss Annam wearing a pastel Lemur Tunic with a ready-made turban, and Miss Tonkin and Miss Cochinchine sported darker-colored *áo thun* over white pants.[114]

The Miss France d'Outre Mer contest was wildly popular in the metropole, but it received little attention in the local press. Even before the exposition opened, the *Sài Gòn* newspaper ran an article criticizing de Waleffe for choosing Eurasian women to represent Vietnam. Notwithstanding the fact that the contest had been designed for mixed-race contestants, the article argued that de Waleffe should have drawn from both Eurasian and Vietnamese women to showcase the full beauty of Indochina. The *Công Luận Báo* newspaper also published a scathing article calling out Miss Tonkin for an allegedly inauthentic expression of ethnic identity—specifically her dubious claim of always wearing Vietnamese clothing despite her culturally French upbringing. The author insinuates that her attire likely had little to do with ethnic pride and—alluding to the new trend in curvier figures covered in chapter 4—wonders sardonically whether Miss Tonkin was just too thin to look attractive in Western dress.[115]

The widespread media coverage of beauty trends, consumerism, and dramatically changing gender roles that characterized the interwar period certainly primed the Vietnamese public for a new outlook on beauty contests. However, it was the middle-class respectability derived from charity fundraisers and associations with the consumerist modernity promoted by fairs that were responsible for the dramatic rise in the contests' popularity during the early 1930s. So vast was the enthusiasm for these events that they would soon occur on an international scale, with Vietnamese women competing abroad. The widespread popularity of beauty contests, in short, showed that the Vietnamese public had laid to rest its long-standing devotion to Confucian norms of modesty.

BEAUTY PAGEANT OPERATIONS

Widely celebrated by the 1930s, beauty pageants typically called for contestants in newspapers or on fliers posted in public areas of cities and villages. These calls urged prospective contestants to submit photos of themselves or, in the case of a 1938 contest held by *Ngày Nay* newspaper, to nominate five women by sending photos of them to the newspaper.[116] As had been the case with the 1925 *Công Luận Báo* beauty contest, the beauty contests of the 1930s benefited newspapers in multiple ways. Newspapers collected income by capturing readers' attention—and spare change—when they published articles and photos on the contests themselves. Shop owners looking to benefit from the exposure purchased advertising space. As mentioned earlier, *Hà Thành Ngọ Báo* staggered its coverage of the Miss Europe and Miss Universe contests, publishing a picture or two a day over the course of a few weeks—or even months—to keep readers hooked. Indeed, this was the formula that the French newspaper magnate and founder of La Plus Belle de France contest used to sell papers.

In the matter of beauty contests, Vietnam represents a noteworthy exception to a global trend. Historically, beauty pageants throughout the world had been organized around race or ethnicity and had been useful in building national identities and fostering nationalism generally. This was no surprise given the global trends in nationalism and its more extreme cousin, fascism, during the interwar years. Pageant contestants initially represented localities—a hometown, province, or state—and if they won the local competitions, they went on to represent the nation and contribute to the building of a national consciousness. As representatives of the nation, pageant contestants, such as those in the case of the Philippines, "embod[ied] nationalism" by wearing makeup and clothing with recognizable elements from their culture.[117] Pageants were also an effective tool for rehabilitating the image of a nation.[118] This is best shown in the case of the interwar Republic of Turkey, which attempted to distance itself from its Ottoman past and assert a modern Western image through beauty contests.[119]

In stark contrast to other nations around the world, beauty contests in colonial Vietnam, for the most part, were not organized by ethnicity. The available historical sources suggest that there was never a Miss Vietnam contest to represent the nation, and the surviving documents offer no evidence that beauty contests were used to construct a Vietnamese national identity. Due to colonial censorship, one would expect that journalists would have shied away from speaking of the contests in explicitly racial or national terms, but such references are absent even in the most allusive or coded form. The majority of contestants in local contests may have been Kinh, the dominant ethnic group in Vietnam, but that was due to circumstances and was not any deliberate strategy. Examples of multiethnic contests include a 1935 contest in Hải Phòng that integrated Kinh with ethnic Thổ contestants from Yên Báy foothills;[120] a 1936 contest, also held in Hải Phòng, that included ethnic Chinese along with Kinh women;[121] and a 1937 contest that showcased a mixed-race Persian-Viet woman.[122] There were, of course, exceptional cases in which ethnicity did play a role. The 1937 Huế Fair was scheduled to have two separate beauty contests, one for Vietnamese women and the other for Eurasian women. The delineation of the two contests by ethnicity may have had something to do with de Waleffe's search for Eurasian beauty contestants, although it is unclear exactly when he was in Huế. If he was still in town during the fair, the separate Eurasian contest may have been staged to help him find Eurasian contestants for the Miss France d'Outre Mer in the metropole; if he had already left, the Eurasian contest may have been inspired by him. Pageants held in Chợ Lớn, Vietnam's largest Chinatown, were reserved for ethnic Chinese women,[123] and a contest in Saigon was reserved for ethnic Vietnamese participants.[124] The decision to segregate by ethnicity may have been a business decision:

the ethnic Chinese owned companies that sponsored the contest in Chợ Lớn, for instance, would have done so to appeal to an ethnic Chinese consumer market.

A possible explanation for the absence of a nationalistic Miss Vietnam contest is that the colonial government, along with companies and organizations that benefited from colonial rule, had no interest in promoting a Vietnamese national identity or, more to the point, the anticolonialist sentiment that so often accompanied it. Rather than allowing for an identity that mapped onto existing national identities, the French colonial state promoted an Indochina identity that encompassed Tonkin, Annam, Cochinchina, Cambodia, and Laos. The intent was to neutralize the power of nationalist movements and local rulers. Despite attempts on the part of the colonial government to promote an Indochina-wide identity, there were no known Miss Indochine contests or even contests for a Miss Tonkin, Miss Annam, or Miss Cochinchine.[125] (While Maurice de Waleff searched for women to represent Tonkin, Annam, and Cochinchine at the Miss France d'Outre Mer contest, his vision was statedly only for métisse women to show how the colony integrated into the empire.) As for the absence of a Miss Vietnam, another possible reason for such a lack was the French crackdown on radical nationalist activities that began in 1926 and gained momentum in the early 1930s. Airforce bombings on peasant strikes would have had an understandable cooling effect on the population, dissuading them from engaging in activities that carried more than a whiff of nationalist sentiment. In particular, middle-class Francophiles and collaborators would not have wanted to risk the appearance of sympathizing with peasant rebels or communists.

Most of the beauty contests took place in the evening, often beginning as late as 9 or 10 P.M. Audience members gathered early, excited even to catch a glimpse of the empty stage. At elite events, the audience was comprised of a mix of middle- and upper-class French, Vietnamese, and Chinese. Meanwhile, at fairs and expositions the audience consisted primarily of Vietnamese or ethnic Chinese, French men and women rarely mingled in large crowds of the colonized. On those balmy nights, light refracted from the moisture in the air, lending a warm glow to the stage. Audience members, male and female alike, their faces flushed from excitement or alcohol, waited eagerly. Children, their hands sticky with candy, fidgeted and slurped cups of *chè đậu đỏ*, a refreshing sweet red bean drink, or *chè hạt sen*, sweet lotus seed in coconut milk.

BEAUTY CONTESTS

FIGURE 5.2. Winner of 1936 Faifoo Fair beauty contest.
Source: *Sài Gòn*, May 28, 1936.

Beauty contestants, typically unmarried women in their late teens and early twenties, paced nervously backstage, smoothing out their dresses, running their fingers along the sides of their mouth to prevent their lipstick from migrating, and rubbing a knuckle under the outside corner of their eye to wipe away the inevitable smudges of mascara (figure 5.2). Most pageants had a dozen or two contestants, although one 1933 market pageant in Hanoi had as many as forty.[126] The young women, shifting their weight from heel to heel, waited to be called out and introduced.

Around 9 P.M. the pageant host took the stage and asked for the audience's attention, to cheers and rapturous applause. He proceeded to call out the contestants one by one, each woman escorted across the stage by a young Vietnamese man. In some instances, such as a 1936 pageant in Hải Phòng, audiences were shocked to see the escort take the liberty of touching contestants after he ushered them onstage—placing his hand on the small of a woman's back or around her waist, or patting her on the hip.[127] Such gestures, performed in a professional and ceremonial context, indicated that behavior once considered scandalous was now fully sanctioned by fair organizers. One contest even auctioned off kisses with the beauty contestants, with bids starting at five *đồng* and reaching as much as twenty *đồng*—likewise surprising considering that public displays of affection were taboo in this era.[128]

Contestants wore elegant clothing. Many wore trendy styles, such as brightly colored tunics and white pants or Western dresses. After Nguyễn Cát Tường debuted the Lemur Tunic at the 1934 Lạc Thiện fair, the famous outfit became the uniform at beauty contests for the rest of the decade. Some pageants had separate contests, one for women wearing "modern" attire and another for those wearing "traditional" clothes.[129] As makeup had become more accepted during the mid-1930s, pageant contestants painted their nails and appeared with skin dewy from the face cream that radiated through their powder. They flashed white smiles accentuated by cherry red lips.[130]

Once they had made their debut to the audience, pageant contestants were judged. Judging occurred in multiple ways. At informal contests staged in markets, the audience members themselves decided the winner simply by clapping the loudest. More elite pageants included an intermission, during which time a council convened in a separate room to decide who would receive the crown. The judging council at the 1935 charity fair to benefit the poor of northern Annam consisted of a range of notable officials, some of them familiar even to contemporary historians and art historians. These included the public intellectual Nguyễn Thiến Lãng, the physician Trần Văn Lai (to lend his expertise on the human body),[131] and important trend setters, such as the artists Lê Phổ and Tô Ngọc Vân, who were graduates of the prestigious École des Beaux Arts and presumably possessed a knowledge of all things beautiful.[132] Once the winner had been determined, the pageant host would ring a bell to signal to the audience that a decision had been reached, call out the winner, present her with a bouquet of flowers, and formally introduce her to the audience.[133]

It is not clear from the primary sources available what criteria the judges used to evaluate women's beauty; this absence could suggest that beauty contests had not yet formed a homogenized ideal of women's looks. Yet by piecing together anecdotes from multiple contests certain patterns emerge. The winners were typically women who held to "modern" beauty norms. They were praised for their light skin and dark hair, classically beautiful facial features, and their slim but curvy figure, which was becoming the new feminine ideal (see chapter 4). For the most part, beauty contestants dressed in the latest fashion trends and wore makeup. Eschewing the tooth-blackening traditions of their mothers, they kept their teeth pearly white. The winner of the 1935 fair held by the Hội Khai Trí Tiến Đức was described as "a beautiful girl with extremely white skin and a beautiful face; when she smiles, she reveals her golden teeth."[134] "Golden teeth" referred to unlaquered (white) teeth; people in interwar Vietnam did not share our current obsession with immaculate and often artificially whitened smiles.

Pageant winners were awarded only meager prizes. In the United States, where beauty pageants were a serious business, beauty queens typically won a few thousand dollars—an extraordinary sum in the 1930s—as well as a tour of Europe to promote the contest, advertising and modeling contracts, and a chance to star in Hollywood films.[135] In Vietnam, where pageants were a much smaller business, winners rarely made much money. The 1925 *Công Luận Báo* beauty contest offered a prize of jewelry supposedly valued at fifty francs.[136] The winner of a 1935 beauty pageant organized by the Hội Khai Trí Tiến Đức charity was awarded a marble statue in lieu of a cash prize.[137] It is possible that some beauty queens enjoyed auxiliary perks, such as paid modeling gigs for tailor shops or free merchandise in exchange for a pledge to wear clothing and accessories from a certain shop.[138] Some pageants, such as a 1935 contest in Chợ Lớn, offered second and third prizes.[139] Others awarded prizes in different categories, including kindness, poetic style, and athleticism.[140]

Beauty contests become so popular in the 1930s that audiences felt invested in the outcome. They clapped, cheered, and occasionally jeered at the contest winners. In the case of one 1933 contest held at a Hanoi market, the event did not finish until after midnight and it took another hour to break up the crowd.[141] Audiences were known to become enraged if a contest was delayed or the organizers changed the plans. Such was the case at the 1938 Huế exposition. One April evening, a crowd began to form around the stage in hopes of landing the best seat from which to admire what promised to be an extraordinary lineup of beautiful young women. By 9:15 P.M., the pageant still had yet to begin, and the audience was growing understandably restless. The wait felt intolerable in the steamy weather. "At half past nine, ten o'clock, there wasn't a single beauty," reported the *Tràng An Báo* newspaper. Crowded shoulder to shoulder, the audience grew hot and agitated. Finally, at 10:30 P.M., a spotlight hit the stage and the boisterous audience quieted down. Shockingly, the person to step onstage was not the first of a lineup of beautiful women but the male musician Nguyễn Văn Tuyên. As it happened, Nguyễn Văn Tuyên was not just any musician but one of the renowned founders of the wildly popular Vietnamese "new music" (*tân nhạc*) trend, who was there to perform his latest hit.[142] But audience members were not impressed. They were, in fact, livid. They booed the musician off stage and demanded a full refund before retiring for the evening, many of them presumably devastated. They never saw the beauty queens nor received an explanation from fair organizers. So excited were many audiences that they lingered after the contest results had been announced.[143]

Pageant audiences were easily infuriated when the winner the judges presented to them was not their idea of a beautiful woman—a phenomenon that was, of course, not unique to Vietnam.[144] At a 1935 fundraiser for flood victims in Hà Đông, the audience disagreed with the judges' choice of beauty queen. The audience weaponized confetti, intended to be tossed into the air in celebration, to pelt her in the face, forcing her to lower her head and, as one journalist wrote sarcastically, "hide her 'gorgeous' beauty."[145] In some cases the disputed results hinted at potentially shady dealings. In April 1937, the audience at a beauty contest in Huế fell smitten with Miss Germaine Saraghi, a mixed-race brunette dressed in Vietnamese clothing, but the jury awarded first prize to a Vietnamese woman sponsored by a Hanoi fashion house. The audience jeered in an attempt to force the judges to reconsider, but they refused.[146] A June 1937 pageant, also held in Huế, likewise caused quite a stir when the judges chose a woman whom both the audience and a writer for the *Sông Hương* newspaper felt was not particularly attractive. According to the article, she had a flat nose, thick lips, and a flat head. Only several days later did the truth emerge: the homely winner just happened to be a Taxi Girl employed at Mr. Lê Thanh Cảnh's dance hall, and he had rigged the contest to lure customers to his venue with the prospect of dancing with a crowned beauty queen.[147]

By the second half of the decade, beauty contests had grown so ubiquitous that the image of a beauty queen had become a common motif in Vietnamese popular culture. Readers of a 1936 edition of *Ngày Nay* were advised that a polite way to introduce a young woman was to say that she was so beautiful she could be "Miss (Province, City, Neighborhood)."[148] Beauty contests were also starting to feature prominently in popular literature.

"Future: Miss Vietnam," a short piece of fiction published in 1936, tells the story of a Miss Vietnam who wins a Miss Universe contest and returns to Vietnam to answer questions about her ideal man.[149] As mentioned previously, Vũ Trọng Phụng used the setting of a beauty contest in his novel *Làm Đĩ* to arouse jealousy from the protagonist.[150]

Most journalists wrote favorably about beauty contests during the 1930s, but there were detractors as well. As Confucian scholars had lost their social and political clout by 1930, the Three Dependencies, Four Virtues, and the khuê các way of life no longer served as an effective critique of beauty contests. Instead, the woman's magazine *Phụ Nữ Tân Văn*, published in the early 1930s, played the role of chief critic. Fiercely feminist and staffed by New Women, the magazine argued for equal rights for men and women, girls' education, and scholarships for girls to study abroad, among other things.[151] Its editors also opposed Confucian constraints on women and promoted women's participation in social and leisure activities, sports in particular. Although *Phụ Nữ Tân Văn* championed the new short haircut for its ease and practicality, it rejected other elements of modern beauty culture and rarely ran any of the fashion or makeup columns so prevalent in other newspapers. It is not surprising that *Phụ Nữ Tân Văn* vehemently opposed the introduction of beauty contests to Vietnam. A 1931 article encouraged readers to emulate Western women's academic and career ambitions, but implored them to reject the Western practice of displaying women in pageants, noting that Europeans actually laughed at their own beauty queens.[152] In a 1933 article on an infamous Turkish beauty pageant that was mired in corruption and culminated in rioting, the female journalist Trần Thị Bích asked, "Should we imitate the new European beauty pageant?" She went on to answer her own rhetorical question: "No! This custom should not be brought to our land!"[153]

Phụ Nữ Tân Văn also opposed beauty contests for their intemperance, particularly in the context of the Great Depression. The newspaper frequently cited poverty as one of the greatest problems facing the nation and opposed crude displays of excess as the people of Vietnam were suffering. *Phụ Nữ Tân Văn* frowned upon Modern Girls and all things seen as "xa xỉ," meaning excessively lavish or frivolous, on the grounds that women should not be spending money on trivialities like lipstick or powder while their compatriots were suffering.[154] The newspaper also accused beauty pageants of exploiting and profiteering off contestants. "Vietnam is a poor country," a female *Phụ Nữ Tân Văn* journalist wrote persuasively in 1933, "and rich people get up on stage and judge who the most beautiful woman is among contestants who are impoverished."[155]

In 1935 the journalist Phan Trần Chúc, who would go on to become a prolific historian, warned of the harmful psychological effects of beauty pageants on the contestants themselves. For one thing, he predicted that the contests would have a lasting detrimental impact on the many contestants who were not chosen: "The woman declared winner will grow conceited and those who did not place in the contests are left not only with a broken heart, but with a tarnished reputation for having participated in this vulgar display of their bodies."[156] Even winners, he observed, went on to have regrets. He cited the case of Raymonde Alain, the winner of the 1928 Miss France contest, who famously shocked the beauty world when she very publicly denounced pageants as disgraceful and exploitative.[157] Phan Trần Chúc even went so far as to liken pageants to human trafficking: "The girls participating are no different from the items displayed for buyers, or a bunch of highlanders in the markets who sold people to China." Cautioning readers not to blindly follow Western culture, he advised: "The beauty contest is a European import. . . . We cannot help but get a reputation for being foolish when we blindly follow a practice that [Europeans themselves] consider inhumane."[158]

Another fierce opponent of beauty contests was the *Vịt Đực* newspaper, which used humor and satire to critique the modernization movement, Europeanization, and consumerism. Two articles published in the same issue skewered the contests. The first noted that given the ubiquity of beauty contests women of no particular distinction were being declared beauty queens. The journalist lamented: "[Beauty contests] have become a plague; it is impossible to dial it back."[159] The second was a fictional letter declaring that the "talented" winner of a local beauty contest, as a high status woman of beauty, would no longer to be required to adhere to social norms, in particular flirting and borrowing money. She was now at liberty, the letter continued, to move freely from one cheap hotel to the next. The allusion was clear: these cheap hotels were notorious for clandestine sex work.[160]

Notwithstanding the critiques coming from *Phụ Nữ Tân Văn*, Phan Trần Chúc, and *Vịt Đực*, beauty contests had taken Vietnam by storm by the end of the 1930s. No longer did the events elicit the kind of outrage sparked by the *Công Luận Báo* contest in 1925 for its violation of Confucian norms.

Instead, elegantly dressed middle-class patrons of charity organizations savored fine meals along with lineups of exquisite young women. Among the less highbrow audiences at Vietnam's fairs, the enthusiasm over beauty queens sometimes lapsed into pandemonium.

The mania that developed over beauty contests in interwar Vietnam helped usher in a more open attitude in women toward their own beauty—and, by extension, their role in society. The average middle-class urban Vietnamese woman of the 1930s was a far cry from the demure, retiring khuê các woman of just a decade earlier. She rode her bicycle across town to her job teaching at a school; she caught a trolley downtown where she met friends to go shopping on Rue Catinat; she snuggled up with her boyfriend during scary scenes in the cinema; and she readily weighed in on politics in letters or editorials in the local press. Beauty pageants may have aroused envy, frustration, or resignation over what must have seemed like impossible standards of beauty, but their most salient effect was to encourage ordinary Vietnamese women to cultivate and celebrate their own humbler beauty in day-to-day life, if not necessarily to flaunt it onstage.

The contests did not just change the way women saw themselves; they also changed the way women were seen by the public. The public had developed an insatiable appetite for women's looks; at a beauty contest seemingly everyone had something to gain. The contestants, naturally, sought praise and approval, if not outright adulation. Female audience members studied the beauties for qualities to emulate and faux pas to avoid; male audience members simply leered. Fair organizers profited from ticket sales, and philanthropic organizations raised funds for their charities. Vendors hired contestants to attract customers, and newspapers published their photos to sell more papers. A more discreet and perhaps insidious form of consumption occurred in the judging process, when panels of "experts" saw fit to evaluate the contestants according to their own conventional and privileged standards. In this era of colonial capitalism, it was now acceptable not only for women to show off their beauty but for the public to openly consume it in manifold ways.

CONCLUSION

From fashion to hairstyles, lipstick shades to body shapes, beauty trends emerge in response to the social, political, economic, technological, and artistic circumstances of their time. In other words, women channel their reactions to historical events and trends in part through what they wear and how they present themselves. Interwar Vietnam was no exception. Confronted with new trends of consumerism, individualism, and modernism, among others, women navigated their way through a variety of conflicting messages about their role in society. In embracing new fashion and beauty trends, they aspired to new roles in society. In the face of public criticism, they forged their new identities through a dynamic process of rebellion and conformity.

It is no surprise that dramatic changes in Vietnam's beauty and fashion landscape occurred during the tumultuous interwar period. Over the course of only twenty years after the end of World War I, Vietnamese women witnessed profound changes in their society. The colonial economy saw a postwar boom, followed by the Great Depression, and then an economic upswing in urban areas in the late 1930s. With the consumer economy maturing after World War I, mass-produced industrialized products, including cosmetics and fashion accessories, were shipped in from France and other Western countries and eagerly bought by the emerging middle class.

CONCLUSION

The construction boom of the interwar years jolted the men and women of Vietnam into an unprecedented experience of "modernity." The world around them looked and sounded different than it had before. Vietnam's major cities developed a decidedly cosmopolitan look that drew from European as well as "Indochinese" architectural styles, and these cities reverberated with the honking of newly imported automobiles and busses. Time and space felt compressed in this modern world. Transportation innovations enabled Vietnamese men and women to quickly traverse town on bicycles and trollies or embark on beach getaways via trains or automobiles. New forms of media such as newspapers, cinema, radio, and gramophones connected the far corners of Vietnam, generating new opportunities for community interaction and enabling the rapid dissemination of trends.

Meanwhile, an array of new cultural influences rapidly transformed the Vietnamese social order, affecting the way women participated in their family and society. The implementation of the French educational system and the declining influence of Confucianism reoriented this post–World War I generation away from Confucian classics, Confucian gender dictums, and even classical Chinese artistic expression. Instead, the educated class that came of age after World War I studied French literature translated into *quốc ngữ* and learned about European cultural and social values. Some, particularly the middle class, embraced the Europeanization trend that swept Vietnamese society. Others, distraught by the rapid pace of change in society—especially as it pertained to young women—demanded a return to the traditional values and gender roles promoted by an emerging Neo-Confucian movement. Modernists offered a third alternative, one that tapped into global trends to construct a new national identity that would supersede Vietnam's image as an impoverished colony.

As I have argued in this book, Vietnam's beauty culture of the interwar years was shaped by a complex negotiation among the competing trends of Europeanization, neo-Confucianism, and Vietnamese modernism. These socio-cultural dynamics gave visible expression the clothes women wore, the way they painted their faces, the parts of their body they revealed, their posture and gait, and the nuances of their demeanor. The everyday decisions ordinary women made about their appearance was a way—conscious, unconscious, or somewhere in between—for them

CONCLUSION

to strike a claim to the role they wanted to play in the new society that lay ahead of them.

A similar transformation was playing out simultaneously in Vietnam's arts world. From theater to literature, fine art to music, poetry to architecture, the arts took a decided turn against Sino-Vietnamese artistic tradition. Yet the artists of these genres never simply copied European art. Instead, in line with the Vietnamese modernist trend, they drew on influences from Europe, East Asia, and within Vietnam itself to make sense of the world that was changing so rapidly around them. With movements dubbed Reform Theater (*cải lương*), New Poetry (*thơ mới*), and New Music (*tân nhạc*), the novelty of these artistic expressions was manifest. Architecture and fine arts were influenced by the *École des Beaux Arts de l'Indochine*, the colonial fine arts school that taught European technique while celebrating Vietnamese style, and stories were published as Western-style novels or short fiction written in the new Romanized script and awash in French syntax. As complex and diverse as these interwar arts movements may have been, collectively they represented a decisive break with tradition and a new means of self-expression.

I would like to conclude this book with the proposition that beauty culture of the interwar years can be considered yet another new arts movement. Unlike most of the aforementioned "high art" movements of the interwar years, this was a popular, grass roots, mass culture phenomenon. Vietnamese women representing a wide range of demographics—from teenage girls to grandmothers, urbanites to peasants, the fabulously wealthy to the desperately poor—expressed themselves through fashion and beauty trends. Trends spread quickly thanks to new forms of media and an upsurge of consumerism. Although the new beauty movement was embraced by only a minority of women, at times it must have struck interwar-era onlookers as omnipresent. The new styles appeared on city streets, in schools, near rural military bases, and at crowded colonial fairs. As beauty products washed off or were changed at the end of the day, it was an ephemeral art. Women could easily try new styles, update to the latest trends, or simply match their look to their situation or emotions. Whereas traditional arts could be costly and time-consuming, beauty products allowed for experimentation and risk-taking. Although no single style defined the beauty culture of the interwar years, the common denominators of the movement were a rejection of traditional notions of

CONCLUSION

beauty, an embrace of individualism and consumerism, and an insouciance verging on the rebellious.

Like many of Vietnam's new arts movements of the interwar years, beauty culture represented a break with past aesthetics. While the *looks* that appeared among Vietnamese women were not entirely new in a global context, they were radical in the Vietnamese context. Women who partook in the new beauty culture rejected the model of a sequestered, makeup-free maiden with blackened teeth and straight long hair and instead embraced a vivid pallet of colors on the face and body and a colorful lifestyle to match. The Industrial Revolution introduced synthetic textiles such as rayon, chiffon, and water permeable fabric, and new fashions such as the Spenser jacket and gored skirt must have seemed as foreign as the French colonists themselves. Even the preferred shape and posture of women's bodies was new.

The ways in which Vietnamese women used cosmetics and fashion to express themselves were often quite artistic. Their faces and bodies were the canvas; the tools with which they expressed themselves were richly pigmented cosmetics and clothing that cut striking and innovative silhouettes. These tools—easily accessible in this era of late colonial capitalism, when European consumer goods flooded the market in Vietnam and the middle class had the disposable income to purchase them—enabled women to freely try on a variety of *looks*. They experimented with European trends; they considered how their fashion choices reflected on the national image, per Vietnamese modernists; and, in the face of Neo-Confucian critiques, they tweaked their look to appear more modest. As for beauty contestants, they delighted audiences with performances of modernity through their meticulously painted faces, curated outfits, and perfect posture. By embracing beauty trends, women expressed their artistry through an attention to nuance and a playful exploration of possibilities.

It is not surprising that the major players in the New Arts movement greatly influenced the beauty culture of the era, as you have seen in the chapters of this book. Graduates of the newly opened *École des Beaux Arts d'Indochine*, for example, approached the beauty movement with such fervor that they all but commandeered it. The artist Nguyễn Cát Tường designed the Lemur Tunic as both an alternative to tacky Western clothing and a modern take on the Vietnamese tunic. Nguyễn Cát Tường, sometimes in collaboration with a fellow artist Lê Phổ and Nhất Linh, designed

CONCLUSION

numerous other outfits, published makeup tutorials, fashion advice columns, and directions for shaping the body with calisthenics, all with the goal of helping Vietnamese women "improve" their looks. Fellow artists and graduates of the *École des Beaux Arts d'Indochine* Lê Phổ and Tô Ngọc Vân served as judges for beauty contests. Art school students waxed philosophically about the artistic merits of women's fashion and beauty in newspaper columns and articles, and many of them found employment illustrating advertisements for cosmetics firms. Nguyễn Văn Tuyên, the founder of the New Music movement, entertained beauty contest audiences, and the darling of both the New Music and Reformed Theater movements, Ái Liên, was a fashion icon and a beauty pageant winner. The New Poetry leader Nguyễn Thị Kiêm (also known as Nguyễn Thị Manh Manh) denounced beauty contests, yet publicly defended the right for women to cut their hair and encouraged them to play sports, even if it meant abandoning the ideal of a weak, "willow leaf" figure. And authors in the new literature movement made frequent use of fashion and cosmetics as a literary tool with which to dramatize the myriad changes occurring in society.[1] As for the Neo-Confucian critics of the new beauty trends, their critiques often included metaphors alluding to the Chinese or Vietnamese art of previous generations, such as "a body like a willow leaf" or "a neck like a crane." In making reference to Sino-Vietnamese cultural figures like Tú-Bà (the brothel owner in the Tale of Keu), Zhuang Zhou (philosopher who insisted that beauty is relative), and Chung Vô Diệm (the ugly wife of king Tề Tuyên), these critics evoked the gravitas of literature, philosophy, and history.

In pushing boundaries and disrupting the status quo, art movements often pose certain risks, and the beauty movement of the interwar era was no exception. As discussed in the introduction, this movement was risky for some of the women who embraced it and faced damage to their reputations, marital prospects, and family relationships as a result. But it was also risky for Vietnam itself. The new beauty culture brought about social discord and galloping cultural change. Critics argued that it also put Vietnam's international reputation on the line. As women were tasked with the burden of representing the nation (per the Vietnamese modernists) and the morality of society (per the Neo-Confucianists), the way they presented themselves could reflect poorly on the nation. Whether it was tennis jumpers donned by spectators at a tournament or cherry red nail polish worn to a funeral, the colony's Vietnamese fashion cognoscenti were aghast at the lack of fashion know-how among some women. The wearing of French-style sleeping pajamas in public was likewise considered naïve and uncouth, and Vietnam's reputation suffered accordingly (at least so the cognoscenti believed). In hindsight, these purportedly "bad" choices can be considered bold and innovative. Wearing sleeping pajamas in public was, for instance, a creative choice: the thin fabric felt light and comfortable in the tropical heat; the dainty flower prints made women feel feminine; and the short sleeves, low-cut neckline, and empire waist flattered their figures.

The fashion trends that dominated Vietnamese media during the interwar years waned during the early 1940s. The war made beauty culture seem suddenly frivolous and anachronistic. In July 1940, the Vichy government took power in the metropole, and over the next few years the state centralized the French economy, seized private factories, and redirected manufacturing toward the war effort. European commodities ceased to be exported to Vietnam, a development that would have not just economic but cultural repercussions for the colony.[2] Within a few months of the Vichy takeover the war arrived in Indochina, and in September 1940 Japanese troops invaded Vietnam. The bourgeois lifestyle of travel and leisure was no longer possible given the Japanese occupation and increasing Allied bombings.[3] Sports and calisthenics, previously sources of fun and fitness enjoyed by the bourgeoisie, were now quasi-military endeavors undertaken largely by fascist paramilitary youth groups.[4] Residents of vulnerable areas were evacuated to the countryside. Nightlife, vacationing, and other leisure activities dried up. Cap Saint Jacques, a beachside town once bustling with carefree vacationers, was now occupied by the Japanese military.[5] Morin movie theaters in Huế sold few tickets; Hải Phòng's grand metropolitan opera had a plethora of empty seats; and dance halls on the infamous Khâm Thiên street just outside Hanoi were patronized less by free-spirited young people than by soldiers seeking a night in the arms of a Taxi Girl. Those hotels not taken over by the Japanese Navy sat vacant in seaside resort towns such as Đồ Sơn or Nha Trang and Phan Rang, which were in close proximity to the bombings that had occurred near Hải Phòng and Cam Ranh Bay, respectively.

Maritime trade, including boats bringing goods from France to Vietnam, came to a standstill when Japan invaded the rest of Southeast Asia in December 1941. Land trade—of legal goods and contraband alike—ceased in January 1942 when Japan seized the port of Rangoon. Few commodities

CONCLUSION

could be imported into the region, and certainly not luxury items such as clothing, shoes, fabric, or cosmetics.

Vietnam's textiles were repurposed for the wartime effort and became scarce. The occupying Japanese military seized control of cotton production in Hà Đông and silk production in Bình Định and forced textile factories in Nam Định and Chợ Lớn to redirect production toward the Japanese war effort. Rayon was claimed by the military; silk production was reserved for making parachutes. A few shrewd local tailors managed to procure fabric, only to find that the demand for new clothing had all but dried up. With fewer and fewer customers patronizing Nguyễn Cát Tường's tailor shop, he downsized and moved away from the elegant Hoàn Kiếm lakeside shop to Hàng Da in the 36 Streets section.[6] In early 1944, Allies intensified the bombings, targeting industrial production, including textile mills in Hải Phòng and Nam Định.

As the war made commodities scarce, the trends of materialism and modernity that had flourished in interwar Vietnam not only waned but became positively dangerous. The Lipstick Effect that had prevailed throughout the Great Depression faded during World War II, when privations were compounded by political unrest and the constant threat of violence. Women were apprehensive about being seen in Western-style clothing, fearing that Japanese troops would mistakenly identify them as sympathetic to the French—or, worse, as me tây, women in romantic relationships with Europeans. By the end of the war, French police and the Việt Minh rebels, acting separately, arrested many members of the Self-Strengthening Literary Movement, which had propagated the idea that the way to uplift and modernize Vietnamese society was through beautiful material things, including women's clothing.[7] As often happens during wartime, consumerism ground to a halt, and the premium once placed on glamour was replaced by a new emphasis on austerity.

On the evening of March 8 and into the morning of March 9, 1945, the Japanese staged a coup d'etat, removing the colony's French administration and imprisoning many of its officials. The Japanese went on to establish a nominally independent Empire of Vietnam headed by Bảo Đại, the erstwhile playboy king whose dapper fashion choices and Francophilia had once made him seem like a French puppet, although by this point he had become more of a nationalist. The coup d'etat changed the nature of the war, plunging Vietnam into chaos. As Japanese forces were exceptionally brutal with civilians, it became even more dangerous for Vietnamese women to be seen wearing Western clothing or makeup.

On September 2, 1945, Japan signed the Instrument of Surrender, officially ending the war. That same day, Hồ Chí Minh declared the independence of Vietnam, and within a few months he launched the Vietnamese Revolution known as the First Indochina War. Led by the Việt Minh, which claimed to be a united front but was stacked mainly by communists, the conflict was directed as much against the materialistic excess of the period as it was against French colonial rule. In other words, during the First Indochina War, the Việt Minh fought the Vietnamese middle and upper classes as much as they fought the French.

Communist Party grievances with their own countrymen were strikingly similar to the grievances of Confucianists two decades earlier. Despite obvious political differences regarding social hierarchies and the government, both the Confucianists of the interwar era and the Việt Minh demanded adherence to ascetic principles. Both groups denounced materialism, consumerism, individualism, and the bourgeois lifestyle in which class-based posturing was expressed through conspicuous consumption and leisure activities. Communists, like the Confucianists before them, called for women to embrace an austere look in the name of the greater good of society. In some sense things had come full circle—the attitude toward beauty culture from the Confucianists to the Communists was not all that different.

Three wars and more than half a century later, Nguyễn Cát Tường's vision of the Lemur Tunic as a powerful symbol of the Vietnamese nation would finally be realized.[8] The dress—or at least an iteration of it—would become identified with the postwar unified nation in 1995, when it was highlighted at the Miss World Pageant in Tokyo. The modern áo dài, based on Nguyễn Cát Tường's Lemur Tunic, was subsequently used to promote tourism.[9] In 2012, Vietnam's vice minister of culture proposed to recognize the áo dài as Vietnam's official national dress. The Ho Chi Minh City Women's Museum staged a permanent exhibit devoted to the áo dài, and in 2014 the designer Lê Sĩ Hoàng opened a privately owned áo dài museum, also in Ho Chi Minh City. In 2016 the Hanoi Municipal People's Committee even organized an áo dài festival.[10]

The rise of the internet and social media has sparked a revival of interest in the fashion and beauty history of Vietnam. In June 2020, *Harper's Bazaar*

CONCLUSION

Vietnam published a history of the áo dài.[11] A whole industry has developed around a revival of the recipe for the face powder of elite Huế ladies (see chapter 3).[12] Beauty connoisseurs regularly post family photographs on websites and social media, and YouTube is replete with Vietnamese-language tutorials for achieving the look of any decade.

Art, by its very nature, challenges the status quo. Lively debates about the way women dressed, the color of their lipstick, their posture and the shape of their body, and how they appeared in public settings reflected the subversive power of the women's beauty movement in interwar Vietnam. Beauty critics, largely male, sought to manage this movement through elaborate and sometimes doctrinaire rules on how to dress, how (and whether) to apply cosmetics, what women's bodies should look like, and how to appear in polite society. Embracing the disparate visions of cultural nationalism represented by the Europeanization movement, the Vietnamese modernist movement, and the Neo-Confucian movement, such critics worked tirelessly to persuade women embody their own ideal image of the nation. Yet their instructional articles, novel fashion prescriptions, beauty columns, misogynistic satire, and snarky remarks were only partially successful. Trends such as sleeping pajamas in public, "mismatched" clothing, and heavy makeup made manifest ordinary women's insistence on doing things their own way. The choices women made each morning as they stood before the mirror—as minute and mundane as they might have seemed—would have, in the aggregate, a strong and enduring impact on Vietnam's understanding of itself.

NOTES

INTRODUCTION

1. Tuyết Vân, "Mốt," *Vịt Đực*, September 14, 1938, 4.
2. Tuyết Vân, "Mốt," *Vịt Đực*, September 14, 1938, 4.
3. "At home obey the father; married obey the husband; widowed obey the son" (Tại gia tòng phụ; xuất giá tòng phu; phu tử tòng tử). The doctrine "Tam Tòng" is often translated as the "Three Submissions," "Three Obediences," "Three Followings," or "Three Dependencies." I will follow Li-Hsiang Lisa Rosenlee's translation, "Three Dependencies." Li-Hsiang Lisa Rosenlee, *Confucianism and Women: A Philosophical Interpretation* (State University of New York Press, 2006), 89–91.
4. Such women were saddled with debt bondage agreements that, as a result of unscrupulous labor practices, could take years to pay off. Christina Firpo, *Black Market Business* (Cornell University Press, 2020).
5. Kathy Peiss, *Hope in a Jar: The Making of America's Beauty Culture* (University of Pennsylvania Press, 1998).
6. Tạ Thị Thúy, *Việc nhượng đất, khẩn hoang ở bắc kỳ từ 1919 đến 1945* (NXB Thế Giới, 2001); and Gwendolyn Wright, *The Politics of Design in French Colonial Urbanism* (University of Chicago Press, 1991), 171.
7. "To call Vietnamese society "Confucian," therefore, is to use the term in a loose sense to refer to a cluster of practices and ideas that appear to have some recognizable coherence." Shawn McHale, *Print and Power: Confucianism, Communism, and Buddhism in the Making of Modern Vietnam* (University of Hawaii Press, 2004), 76.
8. Historians have shown that Vietnamese women certainly had more rights than Neo-Confucianists portrayed of the past. Nhung Tuyet Tran, *Familial Properties: Gender, State, and Society in Early Modern Vietnam, 1463–1778* (University of Hawaii Press, 2019).

INTRODUCTION

9. Quang Anh Richard Tran, "From Red Lights to Red Flags: A History of Gender in Colonial and Contemporary Vietnam" (PhD diss., University of California at Berkeley, 2011).
10. Martina Thucnhi Nguyen, "Wearing Modernity: Lemur Nguyễn Cát Tường, Fashion, and the Origins of the Vietnamese National Costume," *Journal of Vietnamese Studies* 11, no. 1 (Winter 2016): 76–128.
11. Christopher Goscha, *Vietnam: A New History* (Basic Books, 2016), 73–82.
12. Women who engaged in relationships with foreign soldiers were likely already outcasts in Vietnamese society. Some came from poor families; some were widows, who were required to remain chaste per Confucian tradition; others had been abandoned by their husbands; many had run away from abusive in-laws; and some, sadly, had been raped by colonial troops and, having thus lost their virginity, were considered unfit to be brides. Such women, seemingly destined for a solitary life, took the bold step of taking Western lovers. It is not surprising that the trends of white teeth and unbound breasts that they embraced became associated with a rejection of the norms governing sexuality and marriage.
13. The exceptions were Hanoi, Hai Phong, and military bases, all of which were established as French concessions where French law prevailed.
14. Goscha, *Vietnam: A New History*, 82–84.
15. *Lịch sử Việt Nam, 1858–1896* (NXB Khoa Học Xã Hội, 2003), 608–754; Goscha, *Vietnam: A New History*, 90–93; and Alexander Woodside, *Community and Revolution in Modern Vietnam* (Harvard University Press, 1976), 28–31.
16. The emperor reportedly abused his staff; his concubines had bruises and bite marks; royal maids were found strangled. The colonial state tolerated Emperor Thành Thái's indiscretions—to a point. It is interesting that it was not the dead maids nor bite marks that led the state to depose him; it was his unwillingness to cooperate with French officials. French officials, enraged by his insubordination, spread rumors that the emperor had gone insane. With a crisis on their hands, colonial officials considered abolishing the Vietnamese monarchy outright. In 1907, colonial officials forced Emperor Thành Thái to abdicate the throne. "Un Roi Fou," *Le Journal*, October 7, 1907.
17. Prince Cường Để was of the Nguyễn Cảnh line of royal succession. For an earlier example of Vietnamese modernism, see Nguyễn Trường Tộ, a mid-nineteenth century Catholic who had initially collaborated with the French and attempted to convince Emperor Tự Đức to modernize Vietnam by replacing the Confucian education system with European-style education. Vinh Sinh, "Nguyen-Truong-To and the Quest for Modernization in Vietnam," *Japan Review*, no. 11 (1999): 55–74.
18. Liza Dalby, *Kimono: Fashioning Culture* (Vintage, 1993), 83–84.
19. Phan Khôi had worked with Phan Châu Trinh on the Duy Tân movement to modernize Vietnam through education, economic expansion, and political reform. Nguyễn Q. Thắng, *Phong trào Duy Tân: Các khuôn mặt tiêu biểu* (NXB Văn Hóa Thông Tin, 2006).
20. Monks were the exception to this dictum.
21. Côn Sinh, "Lối phục—sức của người mình: Hay các 'mốt' tân thời," *Hà Thành Ngọ Báo*, July 24, 1932; Hoàng-Đạo "Phụ nữ ra ngoài xã hội," *Ngày Nay*, November 1, 1936; Phan khôi, "Lịch sử tóc ngắn: Annam kể từ 1906" *Ngày Nay*, February 15, 1939;

INTRODUCTION

Nguyễn Văn Ký, *La Société Vietnamienne face à la modernité: Le Tonkin de la fin du XIXe siècle à la seconde guerre mondiale* (L'Harmattan, 1995), 240; Maurice M. Durand and Nguyen Tran Huan, *An Introduction to Vietnamese Literature*, trans. D. M. Hawke (Columbia University Press, 1985), 111–13; and Phan khôi, "Lịch sử tóc ngắn: Annam kể từ 1906," *Ngày Nay*, February 15, 1939.

22. The Kimono remained popular for Japanese women through the 1920s. Dalby, *Kimono: Fashioning Culture*, 72–80.
23. Nguyễn Văn Ký, *La Société Vietnamienne face à la modernité: Le Tonkin de la fin du XIXe siècle à la seconde guerre mondiale* (L'Harmattan, 1995), 240; and Maurice M. Durand and Nguyen Tran Huan, *An Introduction to Vietnamese Literature*, trans. D. M. Hawke (Columbia University Press, 1985), 111–13.
24. Christopher Goscha identified a similar message in Nguyen Van Vinh's fashion and political choices. Christopher Goscha, "The Modern Barbarian: Nguyen Van Vinh and the Complexity of Colonial Modernity in Vietnam," *European Journal of East Asian Studies* 3, no. 1 (2004): 155.
25. Homi Bhabha, "Of Mimicry and Man: The Ambivalence of Colonial Discourse," *Discipleship: A Special Issue on Psychoanalysis* 28 (Spring 1984): 125–33.
26. Inspired by the Japanese model of modernization, Vietnamese reformers Phan Bội Châu and Prince Cường Để established the Việt Nam Duy Tân Hội (1904) movement to restore Vietnamese independence and founded the Đông Du movement (1906–1907), encouraging Vietnamese students to travel to Japan to study the Japanese modernization model.
27. Lê Thị Kinh, *Phan Châu Trinh qua những tài liệu mới* (NXB Đà Nẵng, 2001), 14–16; Vũ Đức Bằng, "The Đông Kinh Free School, 1907–1908," in *Aspects of Vietnamese History*, ed. Walter F. Vella (University of Hawaii Press, 1973), 59–67; Pierre Brocheux and Daniel Hémery, *Indochina: An Ambiguous Colonization, 1858–1954* (University of California Press, 2009), 233; and Marta Lopatkova, "Vần quốc ngữ: Teaching Modernity Through Classics," in *Southeast Asian Education in Modern History: Schools, Manipulation, and Contest*, ed. Pia Jolliffe and Thomas Bruce (Routledge, 2018), 107.
28. David Marr, *Vietnamese Tradition on Trial, 1920–1945* (University of California Press, 1981), 200.
29. As Kimloan Vu-Hill points out, wage labor existed before French colonization in the form of itinerant temporary migrant workers helping with harvest. Kimloan Vu-Hill, *Coolies Into Rebels: Impact of World War I on French Indochina* (Les Indes Savantes, 2011), 22.
30. The Vietnamese middle class had precolonial origins, but a full-fledged middle-class identity only began to develop in the context of the economic and social conditions brought about by colonial politics and economic practices.
31. Martin Murray, *The Development of Capitalism in Colonial Indochina (1870–1940)* (University of California Press, 1980); and Brocheux and Hémery, *Indochina: An Ambiguous Colonization*, 116–80.
32. Trần Thanh Hương, "Tìm hiểu quá trình hình thành giai cấp tư sản Việt Nam," *Nghiên cứu Lịch sử* 11+12 (2003): 93–97; Murray, *The Development of Capitalism in Colonial Indochina*, 171–210; and Philippe M. Peycam, *The Birth of Vietnamese Political Journalism: Saigon, 1916–1930* (Columbia University Press, 2012), 114.
33. A nascent middle class began to form at the beginning of the century.

INTRODUCTION

34. Colonial professional school dated back to 1886. Trinh Van Thao, *L'école Française en Indochine* (Karthala, 1995).
35. Thorstein Veblen, *The Theory of the Leisure Class* (1899; repr. Sage, 1970), 80–82.
36. Philippe Peycam, "From the Social to the Political: 1920s Colonial Saigon as a 'Space of Possibilities' in the Vietnamese Consciousness," *Positions: Asia Critique* 21, no. 3 (2013): 496–546; and Greg Lockhart, "Introduction: First Person Narratives from the 1930s," in *The Light of the Capital: Three Vietnamese Classics*, ed. Greg Lockhart and Monique Lockhart (Oxford University Press, 1996), 9.
37. Kim Ninh, *A World Transformed: The Politics of Culture in Revolutionary Vietnam 1945–1965* (University of Michigan Press, 2002), 22; Claude Eugène Maître, "L'enseignement indigène dans l'Indo-Chine Annamite," in *La revue pédagogique*, 52 (Janvier–Juin 1908): 144–60; Trinh Van Thao, *Vietnam: Du Confucianisme au Communisme* (L'Harmattan, 1990), 14; and Goscha, *Vietnam: A New History*, 82–84.
38. Peycam, "From the Social to the Political," 509–10.
39. Cải Lương was influenced by Western comedy patterns, storylines, and music. Jason Gibbs, "Spoken Theatre, La Scène Tonkinoise, and the First Modern Vietnamese Songs," *Journal for the Society of Asian Music* 31, no. 2 (Spring/Summer 2000): 1–33.
40. The École des Beaux Arts de l'Indochine, opened in 1924 under the leadership of Victor Tardieu and Nguyễn Nam Sơn, taught Western classical art instruction and trained craftsmen to be artists. Rather than imposing Western artistic ideals, research by Nora Taylor shows that Tardieu was known to embrace local aesthetics and techniques. Nora Annesley Taylor, *Painters in Hanoi: An Ethnography of Vietnamese Art* (University of Hawaii Press, 2009), 27.
41. Realism journalism (*phong sự*) explored the darker side of Vietnamese society, including extreme poverty, sex work, and human trafficking among others. Literature followed suit, sparking a 1935 debate about the merits of "art for art's sake" (realistic depictions of life, including the darker sides) or "art for humanity" (idealism and romantic arts). See Judith A. N. Henchy, "Performing Modernity in the Writings of Nguyễn An Ninh and Phạm Văn Hum" (PhD diss., University of Washington, 1995), 196–200.
42. Nguyễn Thanh Thảo, "Công Luận Báo và phong trào Thơ Mới," *Nghiên Cứu Khoa Học* 4 (2014): 79–83.
43. Marr, *Vietnamese Tradition on Trial*, 200; Henchy, "Performing Modernity in the Writings of Nguyễn An Ninh and Phạm Văn Hum"; and Goscha, *Vietnam: A New History*, 82–84.
44. Henchy, "Performing Modernity in the Writings of Nguyễn An Ninh and Phạm Văn Hum," 124–25.
45. Anecdotal evidence reveals stories of Vietnamese women buying clothing and perfume for their French girlfriends. Vu-Hill, *Coolies Into Rebels*, 93–112; and André Dumarest, "La formation de classes sociales en Pays Annamites" (PhD diss., University of Lyon, 1935), 64.
46. Xu Xiaoqun, *Cosmopolitanism, Nationalism, and Individualism in Modern China: The Chenbao Fukan and the New Culture Era, 1918–1928* (Lexington, 2014); and Yang Nianqun, "The Rise and Fall of 'Individualism' Before and After the May Fourth Movement," *Chinese Studies in History* 52, no. 3–4 (2019): 209–22.

INTRODUCTION

47. Samuel Popkin, *The Rational Peasant: The Political Economy of Rural Society in Vietnam* (University of California Press, 1979), 170–82; David G. Marr, "Concept of 'Individual' and 'Self' in Twentieth-Century Vietnam," *Modern Asian Studies* 34, no. 4 (2000): 769–96; and Lockhart, "Introduction: First Person Narratives from the 1930s," 9–10.
48. Peycam, "From the Social to the Political," 496–546; Marr, "Concept of 'Individual' and 'Self' in Twentieth-Century Vietnam," 769–96; Ben Tran, *Post-Mandarin: Masculinity and Aesthetic Modernity in Colonial Vietnam* (Fordham University Press, 2017), 85–104; Lockhart, "Introduction: First Person Narratives from the 1930s," 9–10; Alexander Woodside, "The Development of Social Organizations in Vietnamese Cities in the Late Colonial Period," *Pacific Affairs* 44, no. 1 (Spring 1971): 39–64; Mark Philip Bradley, "Becoming 'Van Minh': Civilizational Discourse and Visions of the Self in Twentieth-Century Vietnam," *Journal of World History* 15, no. 1 (March 2004): 65–83; Martina Thucnhi Nguyen, *On Our Own Strength: The Self-Reliant Literary Group and Cosmopolitan Nationalism in Late Colonial Vietnam* (University of Hawaii Press, 2021), 25; Dương Như Đức, "Education in Vietnam Under French Domination, 1862–1945," (PhD diss., Southern Illinois University at Carbondale, 1978); and Henchy, "Performing Modernity in the Writings of Nguyễn An Ninh and Pham Văn Hum."
49. In Vietnam, the movement to chose one's own spouse was called the Free Love movement. Romantic love tapped into a global trend. The choice of marriage was a key issue of the May Fourth Movement in China, and in the United States the movement was called "Compassionate Marriage." Nancy F. Cott, "The Modern Woman of the 1920s, American Style," in *A History of Women in the West*, ed. Françoise Thébaud (Harvard University Press, 1994), 80–81; Đặng Thị Vân Chi, *Vấn đề phụ nữ trên báo chí tiếng Việt trước năm 1945* (NXB Khoa Học Xã Hội, 2007), 108–9; and Neil Jamieson, *Understanding Vietnam* (University of California Press, 1993), 165.
50. In Korea, Neo-Confucianists resisted Japanese colonialism by promoting the Korean Confucian identity. See Hyun Jeong Min, "New Women and Modern Girls: Consuming Foreign Goods in Colonial Seoul," *Journal of Historical Research in Marketing* 5, no. 4 (2013): 512. In China, much of the Neo-Confucian trend was promoted by the New Life movement. See Haiyan Lee, "The Cult of Qing," in *Revolution of the Heart a Genealogy of Love in China, 1900–1950* (Stanford University Press, 2007), 34–35.
51. McHale, *Print and Power*, 74.
52. Lopatkova, "Vấn quốc ngữ: Teaching Modernity Through Classics," 103–21.
53. Trần Trọng Kim, *Nho Giáo* (NXB Văn Hóa Thông Tin, 2001/1932); Trinh Van Thao, *Vietnam: Du Confucianisme au Communisme*, 268–69; McHale, *Print and Power*, 48, 77; Tran Thi Phong Hoa, "Franco-Vietnamese Schools for Girls in Tonkin at the Beginning of the Twentieth Century," *Harvard-Yenching Institute Working Paper Series*, 2010; Lopatkova, "Vấn quốc ngữ: Teaching Modernity Through Classics," 103–21; and Hue Tam Ho Tai, *Radicalism and the Origins of the Vietnamese Revolution* (Harvard University Press, 1992), 91.
54. As early as the 1860s, girls were educated in the colony's French schools, established to teach children of French colonists and open to the children of wealthy Indigenous families. The Franco-Annamite school system were the first schools open to Indigenous children of all social classes.

INTRODUCTION

55. Scholars were expected to work for donation. Đặng Thị Vân Chi estimates that female teachers earned five to ten times that of a laborer. Đặng Thị Vân Chi, *Vấn đề phụ nữ trên báo chí tiếng Việt trước năm 1945*, 51.
56. On quốc túy and the search for a "national essence," see McHale, *Print and Power*, 66–95; and Brocheux and Hémery, *Indochina: An Ambiguous Colonization* 238.
57. Henchy, "Performing Modernity in the Writings of Nguyễn An Ninh and Phạm Văn Hum," 208.
58. Shawn McHale argues that since there were no longer Confucian exams or academies in the interwar years, Confucian debates played out in the newspapers. McHale, *Print and Power*, 76.
59. Marr, *Vietnamese Tradition on Trial, 1920–1945*, 193.
60. Xia Shi, *At Home in the World: Women and Charity in Late Qing and Early Republican China* (Columbia University Press, 2018).
61. Hue Tam Ho Tai, *Radicalism and the Origins of the Vietnamese Revolution*, 94–95.
62. The fall of the mandarin system reduced the influence of Confucian philosophy on the public. With no guaranteed future in the state bureaucracy—nor the prestige that once accompanied it—fewer students studied the Confucian classics, thus reducing general public knowledge of Confucianism. Finally, Vietnamese intellectuals began to question Confucian philosophy, particularly Confucian gender roles and morality; by World War I, the cynicism had spread to Vietnam's youth and urban populations. Vũ Huy Phúc, *Lịch sử Việt Nam, 1858–1896* (NXB Khoa Học Xã Hội, 2003), 608–754; Goscha, *Vietnam: A New History*, 90–93; and Woodside, *Community and Revolution in Modern Vietnam*, 28–31.
63. Goscha, *Vietnam: A New History*, 107.
64. Liz Connor, *The Spectacular Modern Woman: Feminine Visibility in the 1920s* (Indianna University Press, 1994), xiii.
65. Roger Levy, "Indo-China in 1931–1932," *Pacific Affairs* 5, no. 3 (1932): 205–17.
66. Nancy F. Koehn, "Estee Lauder and the Market for Cosmetics," *Harvard Business School Cases* 801-362 (February 2001): 1–44.
67. Christina Firpo, *Black Market Business: Selling Sex in Northern Vietnam, 1920–1945* (Cornell University Press, 2020).
68. Anne Booth, "Crisis and Response: A Study of Foreign Trade and Exchange Rate Policies in Three Southeast Asian Colonies in the 1930s," in *Weathering the Storm*, ed. Pierre Brocheux (Brill, 2000), 295–320; and Martin Thomas, *The French Empire Between the Wars* (Manchester University Press, 2017), 93–124.
69. See Martina Thucnhi Nguyen, *On Our Own Strength*.
70. On such reforms, see Patric Jory, *A History of Manners and Civility in Thailand* (Cambridge University Press, 2021); and Jenny B. White, "State Feminism, Modernization, and the Turkish Republican Woman," *NWSA Journal* 15, no. 3 (2003): 145–59.
71. Pierre Bourdieu, *Distinction: A Social Critique of the Judgement of Taste*, trans. Richard Nice (Harvard University Press, 1984).
72. Lois W. Banner, *American Beauty: A Social History . . . Through Two Centuries of the American Ideal* (Knopf, 1983).
73. Kathy Peiss, *Hope in a Jar: The Making of America's Beauty Culture* (University of Pennsylvania Press, 1998); and Kathy Peiss, "On Beauty . . . and the History of Business," *Enterprise and Society* 1, no. 3 (September 2000): 485–506.

INTRODUCTION

74. Geoffrey Jones, *Beauty Imagined: A History of the Global Beauty Industry* (Oxford University Press, 2010).
75. Chō Kyō and Kyoko Iriye Selden, *The Search for the Beautiful Woman: A Cultural History of Japanese and Chinese Beauty* (Rowman and Littlefield, 2012).
76. Antonia Finnane, *Changing Clothes in China: Fashion, History, Nation* (Columbia University Press, 2008); and Toby Slade, *Japanese Fashion: A Cultural History* (Berg, 2009).
77. Barbara Sato, *The New Japanese Woman: Modernity, Media, and Women in Interwar Japan* (Duke University Press, 2003).
78. Hyaeweol Choi, *Gender and Mission Encounters in Korea: New Women, Old Ways: Seoul-California Series in Korean Studies*, vol. 1 (University of California Press, 2009); and Hyaeweol Choi, *New Women in Colonial Korea: A Sourcebook* (Routledge, 2013).
79. Chiara Formichi, *Healthy Progress: Muslim Women as Modernizers in Twentieth Century Indonesia* (Stanford University Press, forthcoming).
80. Holly Grout, *The Force of Beauty: Transforming French Ideas of Femininity in the Third Republic* (Louisiana State University Press, 2015).
81. Mary Lynn Stewart, *For Health and Beauty: Physical Culture for Frenchwomen, 1880s-1930s* (Johns Hopkins University Press, 2001).
82. Mary Lynn Stewart, *Dressing Modern Frenchwomen: Marketing Haute Couture, 1919-1939* (Johns Hopkins University Press, 2008).
83. David Pomfret, "'A Use for the Masses': Gender, Age, and Nation in France, Fin de Siècle," *American Historical Review* 109, no. 5 (December 2004): 1439-74; Elizabeth Ezra, "Colonialism Exposed: Miss France d'Outre-mer, 1937," in *Identity Papers: Contested Nationhood in Twentieth Century France*, ed. Steven Ungar and Tom Conley (University of Minnesota Press, 1996), 51-65; and Aro Velmet, "Beauty and Big Business: Gender, Race and Civilizational Decline in French Beauty Pageants, 1920-1937," *French History* 28, no. 1 (2014): 72.
84. Henri Joseph Oger, *Introduction Générale à l'étude de la technique du peuples annamitess: Essai sur la vie matérielle, les arts et industries du peuple d'Annam* (Geuthner, 1908).
85. Eugène Langlet, *Le Peuple Annamite: Ses moeurs, croyances et traditions* (Berger-Levrault, 1913).
86. Pierre Huard, "Le noirissement des dents en Asie oriental et en Indochine," *France-Asie* 3 (July 1948): 808-12.
87. Phan Kế Bính, *Việt Nam phong tục (Moeurs et coutumes du Vietnam)*, vol. 2, trans. Nicole Louis-Hénard (École Française d'Extrême-Orient, 1980).
88. Nhất Thanh, *Đất lề quê thói: Phong tục Việt Nam* (1970; repr. NXB Hồng Đức, 2016).
89. Nguyễn Ngạc and Nguyễn Văn Luận, *Un Siècle d'Histoire de la Robe des Vietnamiennes* (Ministère de la Culture et de l'Éducation et de la Jeunesse, n.d.).
90. Đoàn Thị Tình, *Trang phục Việt Nam* (NXB Mỹ Thuật, 2006).
91. Trần Quang Đức, *Ngàn năm áo mũ: Lịch sử trang phục Việt Nam giai đoạn 1009-1945* (NXB Thế Giới, 2013).
92. Ngô Đức Thịnh, *Trang phục cổ truyền các dân tộc Việt Nam* (NXB Tri Thức, 2018).
93. Ann Marie Leshkowich, "Fashioning the Field in Vietnam: An Intersectional Tale of Clothing, Femininities, and the Pedagogy of Appropriateness," in *Fashion and Beauty in the Time of Asia*, ed. S. Heijin Lee, Christina H. Moon, and Thuy Linh

Nguyen Tu (New York University Press, 2019), 127–53; Martina Thucnhi Nguyen, "Wearing Modernity," 76–128; Martina Thucnhi Nguyen, *On Our Own Strength*; and Trần Thị Phương Hoa, "Making the Vietnamese Áo Dài Tunic National Heritage: Fashion Travel Through Tradition, Colonialism, Modernity," *International Journal of Heritage Studies* 27, no. 8 (2021): 806–18.

94. Phạm Thảo Nguyên, *Áo dài Lemur và bối cảnh Phong Hoá và Ngày Nay* (NXB Hồng Đức, 2019).
95. Nguyễn Văn Ký, *La Société Vietnamienne face à la modernité: Le Tonkin de la fin du XIXe siècle à la seconde guerre mondiale* (L'Harmattan, 1995); Phan Kế Bính, *Việt Nam phong tục (Moeurs et coutumes du Vietnam)*, vol. 2, trans. Nicole Louis-Hénard (École Française d'Extrême-Orient, 1980).
96. Dinh Trong Hieu, "Le face, le ventre et autres symboliques du corps chez les Viets," in *La Colonisation des Corps: de l'Indochine au Viet Nam*, ed. François Guillemot and Agathe Larcher-Goscha (Vendémiaire, 2014).
97. Hong-Kong T. Nguyen, "Beauty Culture in Post-Reform Vietnam: Glocalization or Homogenization?," *SocArXiv* (January 30, 2020), https://doi.org/10.31235/osf.io/pkny6; Lisa Drummond, "The Modern 'Vietnamese Woman': Socialization and Women's Magazines," in *Gender Practices in Contemporary Vietnam*, ed. L. Drummond and H. Rydstrøm (Singapore University Press, 2004) 158–78; Nina Hien, "Ho Chi Minh City's Beauty Regime: Haptic Technologies of the Self in the New Millennium," *Positions: Asia Critique* 20 (2012): 473–93; and Ann Marie Leshkowich, "Fashioning the Field in Vietnam: An Intersectional Tale of Clothing, Femininities, and the Pedagogy of Appropriateness," in *Fashion and Beauty in the Time of Asia*, ed. S. Heijin Lee et al, (New York University Press, 2019).
98. Thuy Linh Nguyen Tu, *Experiments in Skin: Race and Beauty in the Shadows of Vietnam* (Duke University Press, 2021).
99. Founded in Ho Chi Minh City in 2016, Style-Republik has now opened a business school. Accessed November 18, 2022, style-republik.com.

1. THE DISSEMINATION OF BEAUTY TRENDS

1. "Exposition de Bruxelles Section Française: Compagnie de commerce et de navigation d'Extrême-Orient," *La Dépêche colonial illustrée*, August 31, 1910, 201; and Dieter Brötel, "French Economic Imperialism in China, 1885–1904/1906," *Itinerario* 23, no. 1 (1999): 52–61.
2. The first rail lines were built in Vietnam at the end of the nineteenth century, but it would not be until 1936 that the Transindochinois rail line finally connected Saigon to Hanoi and across the border to Yunnan.
3. For an outstanding historical study of the migration of French women to Vietnam, see Mary-Paule Ha, *French Women and the Empire: The Case of Indochina* (Oxford University Press, 2014).
4. "Établissement de MM. Rochat et Beaumont," *Le Tonkin en 1900* (Société Française d'Éditions d'Art), 216; and Archives of Les Entreprises Colonial Françaises: Comptoires Français de l'Inde, Indochine, Indes Néelandaises, Malaisie, Saim, accessed July 5, 2022, https://www.entreprises-coloniales.fr/inde-et-indochine.html#groupesindochinois.

1. THE DISSEMINATION OF BEAUTY TRENDS

5. "Wassiamull Assomul et Cie.," *Phụ Nữ Tân Văn*, May 21, 1931; Thạch Phương and Lê Trung Hoa, eds., *Từ Điển Thành phố Sàigòn-Hồ Chí Minh* (NXB Bản Trẻ, 1999), 418–19; and François Tainturier, "Architectures et urbanisme sous l'administration française," in *Saigon 1698–1998 Kiến Trúc/Architectures, Quy hoạch/Urbanisme*, ed. Le Quang Ninh and Stéphane Dovert (NXB Thành phố Hồ Chí Minh, 1998), 185–87.
6. Nguyễn Vinh Phúc, *Phố và Đường Hà Nội* (NXB Giao Thông Vận Tải, 2010), 590–92; Trần Huy Liệu, ed., *Lịch sử thủ đô Hà Nội* (NXB Sử Học, 1960), 164–70; Hoàng Đạo Thúy, *Phố phường Hà Nội xưa* (NXB Văn Hoa-Thông Tin, 2000); Lê Thước, Vũ Tuân Sán, Vũ Văn Tỉn, Trần Huy Bá, and Nguyễn Văn Minh, *Lược Sử Hà Nội* (NXB Văn Hoá Thông Tin, 1964).
7. Hội Đồng Lịch Thành Phố, ed., *Địa Chí Hải Phòng*, vol. 1 (NXB Hải Phòng, 1990), 9; and Hội Đồng Lịch Thành Phố, ed., *Lược Khảo Đường Phố Hải Phòng* (NXB Hải Phòng, 1993), 398–99.
8. Jean L. Druesedow "Ready-to-Wear," in *Encyclopedia of Clothing and Fashion*, vol. 3, ed. Valerie Steele (Charles Scribner's Sons, 2005), 87; Michael B. Miller, *The Bon Marche: Bourgeois Culture and the Department Store, 1869–1920* (Princeton University Press, 1981), 3–16; Bill Lancaster, *The Department Store: A Social History* (Leicester University Press, 1995); and Heinz-Gerhard Haupt, "Small Shops and Department Stores," in *The Oxford Handbook of the History of Consumption*, ed. Frank Trentmann (Oxford University Press, 2012), 284.
9. Kerrie L. MacPherson, ed., *Asian Department Stores* (University of Hawaii Press, 1998); and Sylvia Li Wen Chan, "Department Stores in Singapore: The History of the Mass Consumption in Business Institution" (Master's thesis, Nanyang Technological University, 2002).
10. Tomoko Tamari, "Rise of the Department Store and the Aestheticization of Everyday Life in Early 20th Century Japan," *International Journal of Japanese Sociology* 15, no. 1 (2006): 99–118.
11. Han Cheung, "An 'Uplifting' Shopping Experience," *Taipei Times*, November 29, 2015.
12. Jeesoon Hong, "Transcultural Politics of Department Stores: Colonialism and Mass Culture in East Asia, 1900–1945," *International Journal of Asian Studies* 13, no. 2 (2016): 123–50; Jin-Seok Oh and Howard Kahm, "Colonial Consumerism: Capitalist Development and the Internal Management of Department Stores in Late Colonial Korea," accessed July 9, 2022, http://www.worldbhc.org/files/full%20program/A8_B8_OhKahmColonialConsumerism.pdf; and Hyun Jeong Min, "New Women and Modern Girls: Consuming Foreign Goods in Colonial Seoul," *Journal of Historical Research in Marketing* 5, no. 4 (2013): 494–520.
13. "Sébastient Godard, puis Godard, Fischer&Cie, Hanoi," Archives of Les Entreprises Colonial Françaises, accessed July 5, 2022, https://www.entreprises-coloniales.fr/inde-indochine/Godard+Fischer-Hanoi.pdf.
14. By 1937, Les Établissements Boy Landry had stores in Saigon, Hải Phòng, Hà Nội, Đà Lạt, Tourane, Cần Thơ, Phnom Penh, Thakhet, and Shanghai. Archives Entreprises Coloniales Française, files on Les étabissements Boy Landry, accessed December 1, 2022, https://www.entreprises-coloniales.fr/inde-indochine/Boy_Landry-Saigon.pdf; Files on the "Société Coloniale des Grands Magasins," accessed July 11, 2022, www.entreprises-coloniales.fr; "Grand Magasin Charner,"

1. THE DISSEMINATION OF BEAUTY TRENDS

L'Echo Annamite, November 27, 1924; and "Inauguration des grands magasins Morin Frères," *L'Avenir du Tonkin*, November 8, 1929.
15. Geoffrey Crossick and Serve Jaumain, eds., *Cathedrals of Consumption: The European Department Store, 1850–1939* (Ashgate, 1999).
16. Untitled article, *Đông Pháp*, September 26, 1937.
17. "L'Êternelle féérie des GMR," *L'Avenir du Tonkin*, December 12, 1928.
18. Nguyễn Văn-Tao, "Đi rạo Gô – Đa," *Loa*, November 2, 1936.
19. "Việc Bắc-kỳ: Sở Gô-đa mới đặt thêm một chức quản lý," *Hà Thành ngọ báo*, January 18, 1928; and "Hanoi: Ver le Têt," *L'Avenir du Tonkin*, February 6, 1934.
20. *L'Echo Annamite*, September 28, 1925.
21. Thorstein Veblen, *The Theory of the Leisure Class* (1899; repr. Sage, 1970).
22. "L'Êternelle féérie des GMR," *L'Avenir du Tonkin*, December 12, 1928.
23. Geoffrey Crossick and Serge Jaumain, "The World of the Department Store: Distribution, Culture, and Social Change," in *Cathedrals of Consumption: The European Department Store, 1850–1939*, ed. Geoffrey Crossick and Serve Jaumain (Routledge, 2020), 1–45; Lancaster, *The Department Store*; and Rosalind Williams, *Dream Worlds: Mass Consumption in Late 19th Century France* (University of California Press, 1991).
24. Holly Grout, *The Force of Beauty: Transforming French Ideas of Femininity in the Third Republic* (LSU Press, 2015), 34.
25. "Foire-exposition de Hanoi: Le salon de couture des GMR," *L'Avenir du Tonkin*, December 12, 1929; Advertisement, "Grands Magasins Charner Saigon," *Trung Lập Báo*, February 14, 1925; and "Grands Magasins Charner," *L'Echo Annamite*, November 27, 1924.
26. Those found guilty were sentenced to three years in prison. "Hoàng Mễ bị 3 năm tù," *Hà Thành ngọ báo*, May 31, 1933; "Vì sao mà khám phá được cái trộm ở hiệu Gô – đa," *Hà Thành ngọ báo*, August 9, 1930; "Tin trong nước Bắc kỳ: Việc ăn cắp 7700 thước vải của hiệu Gô-đa," January 9, 1935; and "Việc Hà Nội: Đi đầu trần để vào Gô-đa xoáy mũ, một chàng công tử 'càn-long' bị bắt," *Đông Pháp*, September 15, 1933.
27. Advertisement, "Grands Magasins Charner Saigon: Tuần lễ bán dầu thơm," *Trung Lập Báo*, June 16, 1927.
28. Holly Grout, *The Force of Beauty: Transforming French Ideas of Femininity in the Third Republic* (Louisiana State University Press, 2015), 34.
29. Christina Firpo, *Black Market Business: Selling Sex in Northern Vietnam, 1920–1945* (Cornell University Press, 2020), 128–29.
30. Firpo, *Black Market Business*.
31. Advertisement, "Au Figaro," *Phụ Nữ Tân Văn*, September 25, 1930; and Advertisement, "Salon de coiffure Moderne," *Sài Gòn*, April 13, 1933.
32. Advertisement, "Phúc Thịnh," *Hà Thành Ngọ Báo*, December 21, 1935.
33. Advertisement, "Quảng Hưng Long," *Trung Hòa Nhật Báo*, June 7, 1924.
34. Advertisement, "dầu Vạn," *Sài Gòn*, October 30, 1932.
35. Advertisement, "Nhà thuốc tây Khương-bình Tịnh," *Sài Gòn*, October 13, 1932.
36. L'Agence Générale des colonies, ed., *Bulletin de l'Agence Générale des colonies*, vol. 14, part 1, (January 1921): 523; and Clodion, "Les Recettes de chemins de fer," *L'Eveil économique de l'Indochine*, October 4, 1931.

1. THE DISSEMINATION OF BEAUTY TRENDS

37. Leisure was also one of the drivers of late-nineteenth-century Parisian city planning. See Laurent Turcot, *Sports et Loisirs: Une histoire des origins à nos jours* (Folio, 2016). Of course, although leisure was one of the aims for designing such cities in Indochina, *La Mission Civilisatrice* drove the fantasy of "civilizing" the native in the image of Frenchmen. Cityscapes were one such target in this larger plan.
38. Alexander Woodside, "The Development of Social Organizations in Vietnamese Cities in the Late Colonial Period," *Pacific Affairs* 44, no. 1 (Spring 1971): 39–64.
39. Phyllis M. Martin, *Leisure and Society in Colonial Brazzaville* (Cambridge University Press, 1995), 3–4.
40. Veblen, *The Theory of the Leisure Class*, 80–82.
41. "Phong trào 'theo mới,'" *Phụ Nữ Tân Văn*, March 22, 1934.
42. Toby Slade, *Japanese Fashion: A Cultural History* (Berg, 2009), 4.
43. Cát Tường, "Vài điều nên tránh," *Ngày Nay*, November 15, 1936.
44. Christine Bard, *Les femmes dans la société française au 20e siècle* (Armand Colin, 2004), 115–16.
45. Vera Mackie, "Sweat, Perfume, and Tobacco: The Ambivalent Labor of the Dancehall Girl," in *Modern Girl on the Go: Gender, Mobility, and Labor in Japan*, ed. Alisa Freedman, Laura Miller, and Christine R. Yano (Stanford University Press, 2013); Andrew David Field, *Shanghai's Dancing World: Cabaret Culture and Urban Politics, 1919–1954* (Chinese University Press, 2010); Su Lin Lewis, *Cities in Motion: Urban Life and Cosmopolitanism in Southeast Asia, 1920–1940* (Cambridge University Press, 2016); Taylor E. Atkins, *Blue Nippon: Authenticating Jazz in Japan* (Duke University Press, 2001), 59; David Ambaras, *Bad Youth: Juvenile Delinquency and the Politics of Everyday Life in Modern Japan* (University of California Press, 2006), 160; and Frederic Wakeman, *Policing Shanghai, 1927–1937* (University of California Press, 1996), 108.
46. Minh Châu, "Thư Hà Thành," *Tràng An Báo*, November 25, 1938; "'Hôtel La Pagode' tối thứ bây 13 Avril," *Hà Thành ngọ báo*, April 16, 1935; and Erica Peters, *Appetites and Aspirations in Vietnam: Food and Drink in the Long 19th Century* (Rowman and Littlefield, 2012), 182–214.
47. Dana S. Hale, *Races on Display: French Representations of Colonized Peoples, 1886–1940* (Indiana University Press, 2008), 13.
48. James Herbert, *Paris 1937: Worlds on Exhibition* (Cornell University Press, 1998); and Paul Greenhalgh, *Ephemeral Vistas: The Expositons Universelles, Great Exhibitions and World's Fairs 1851–1939* (Manchester University Press, 1998).
49. Shanny Peer, *France on Display: Peasants, Provincials, and Folklore in the 1937 Paris World's Fair* (State University of New York Press, 1998), 5.
50. Hale, *Races on Display*, 13; and Panivong Norindr, *Phantasmatic Indochina: French Colonial Ideology in Architecture, Film, and Literature* (Duke University Press, 1996), 15.
51. For colonial fairs and expositions in the Dutch Netherlands Indies, see Arnout van der Meer, *Performing Power: Cultural Hegemony, Identity, and Resistance in Colonial Indonesia* (Cornell University Press, 2021), 17; and Chiara Formichi, *Healthy Progress: Muslim Women as Modernizers in Twentieth Century Indonesia* (Stanford University Press, forthcoming).

1. THE DISSEMINATION OF BEAUTY TRENDS

52. "Hội chợ Faifoo đã khai mạc," *Sài Gòn*, May 29, 1936; "Mây thua nước tóc tuyết nhường màu da," *Sài Gòn*, May 28, 1936; "Hội chợ Huế," *Sông Hương*, March 20, 1937; "Đi quanh hội chợ Huế," *Tràng An Báo*, April 19, 1938; *Hội chợ Huế: Chương Trình* (Imp. Tiếng Dân, 1936); "Hội chợ Huế kỳ thứ ba đã khai mạc rất long trọng," *Tràng An Báo*, April 19, 1938; and *Catalogue official: 3eme Foire de Hué: Fêtes de Paques du 15 au 24 avril 1938, program official* (1938), 3.
53. van der Meer, *Performing Power*, 17.
54. "Hội chợ Lạc Thiện," *Ngày Nay*, December 24, 1938; "Cuộc chợ phiên ở hội khai trí lấy tiền giúp dân bị nạn bão lụt, trung kỳ," *Hà Thành ngọ báo*, February 12, 1935; and "Cuộc chợ phiên ở Hội Khai Trí lấy tiền giúp dân bị nạn bão lụt, trung kỳ," *Hà Thành ngọ báo*, February 12, 1935.
55. Opening ceremonies of fairs were narrated on the radio "La Kermess 1937," *Les Nouvelliste d'Indochine*, January 16, 1937; "3ème Foire de Hué du 15 au 24 Avril 1938, Programme Officiel," 1938; "La Foire de Hanoi," *L'Annam Nouveau*, December 4, 1932; "Le Succés de l'exposition du vieux Hanoi," *L'Annam Nouveau*, December 8, 1932; "Une Kermesse en l'honneur du roi," *L'Annam Nouveau*, December 29, 1932; "Quan Toàn Quyền Robin đã về khánh thành cuộc đấu xảo tơ lụa tỉnh Hadong," *Hà Thành Ngọ Báo*, October 23, 1935; "Đi quanh hội chợ Huế," *Tràng An Báo*, April 19, 1938; "Hội chợ Lạc Thiện," *Ngày Nay*, December 24, 1938; and "Đức Hoàng-thượng và đức Hoàng-hậu ngự giá ra vinh xem cuộc triển-lãm các đồ thủ-công của dân Mường phủ Quì," *Tràng An Báo*, February 25, 1938.
56. "Hội chợ Huế," *Sông Hương*, March 20, 1937; and "Hội chợ Faifoo đã khai mạc," *Sài Gòn*, May 29, 1936.
57. "Catalogue official; 3eme Foire de Hué: Fetes de Paques du 15 au 24 avril 1938, program official" (1938); "Hội chợ Huế," *Sông Hương*, March 20, 1937; "Đức Hoàng-thượng và đức Hoàng-hậu ngự giá ra vinh xem cuộc triển-lãm các đồ thủ-công của dân Mường phủ Quì," *Tràng An Báo*, February 25, 1938; "La Grande Kermesse," *La Dépêche d'Indochine*, December 21, 1921; "Hội chợ Huế năm 1939," *Tràng An Báo*, April 7, 1939; and "Hội chợ Faifoo đã khai mạc," *Sài Gòn*, May 29, 1936.
58. "Đi quanh hội chợ Huế," *Tràng An Báo*, April 19, 1938; "Hội chợ Lạc Thiện," *Ngày Nay*, December 24, 1938; and "Đức Hoàng-thượng và đức Hoàng-hậu ngự giá ra vinh xem cuộc triển-lãm các đồ thủ-công của dân Mường phủ Quì," *Tràng An Báo*, February 25, 1938.
59. Nhị Linh, "Hội Chợ Hanoi 1938," *Ngày Nay*, November 19, 1938.
60. In his novel, *Vỡ Đê*, Vũ Trọng Phụng described the typical fair going women as slathered with lip gloss and caked-on face powder. Vũ Trọng Phụng, *Vỡ Đê* (NXB Văn Học, 2017/1936), 174.
61. Phan Thị Nga, "Chị em Hội An với y phục Cát Tường," *Ngày Nay*, March 10, 1935; and "Hội chợ Lạc thiện ở Huế," *Tràng An báo*, November 15, 1935.
62. "Đi quanh hội chợ Huế," *Tràng An Báo*, April 19, 1938; and "Hội chợ Huế kỳ thứ ba đã khai mạc rất long trọng," *Tràng An Báo*, April 19 1938.
63. "Tiếng dội trong hội chợ," *Sài Gòn*, April 17, 1935.
64. Vũ Trọng Phụng, *Vỡ Đê*, 174.
65. "Mười điều tâm niệm," *Vịt Đực*, November 16, 1938.
66. "Mười điều tâm niệm," *Vịt Đực*.
67. As multiple European countries enacted legislation guaranteeing paid vacations, French calls for guaranteed vacation time erupted in response to the mandated

1. THE DISSEMINATION OF BEAUTY TRENDS

eight-hour instituted in 1919. In 1936, the Popular Front government finally codified a mandatory two-week vacation per annum into law, and vacationing had become a political statement of workers' rights in France. Garry Cross, "Vacations for All: The Leisure Question in the Era of the Popular Front," *Journal of Contemporary History* 24, no. 4 (1989): 599–621; Ellen Furlough, "Making Mass Vacations: Tourism and Consumer Culture in France, 1930s to 1970s," *Comparative Studies in Society and History*, 40, no. 2 (1998): 248; Patrice Boussel, *Histoire des Vacances* (Berger-Levrault, 1961), 27–161; and Stephen G. Jones, *Workers at Play: A Social and Economic History of Leisure, 1918–1939* (Routledge & Kegan Paul, 1986).

68. Jason Gibbs, "The West's Songs, Our Songs: The Introduction and Adaption of Western Popular Music in Vietnam before 1940," *Asian Music* 35, no. 1 (2003): 57–84; "Grand Hotel de Doson," *L'Avenir du Tonkin*, March 28–29, 1934; "Les Sports Fédération Française de Lawn-Tennis: Le Championnat de Doson," *L'Avenir du Tonkin*, August 11, 1934; "Chronique de Haiphong: L'été s'approche!," *L'Avenir du Tonkin*, April 27, 1932; "Doson: Beaucoup d'animation," *L'Avenir du Tonkin*, June 24, 1929; "Le Grand Hôtel de Doson," *L'Éveil économique de l'Indochine*, March 24, 1929; "PingPong," *Hà Thành Ngọ Báo*, May 27, 1935; Vũ Bằng, "Lịch sử Đồ Sơn," *Trung Bắc chủ nhật*, June 28, 1942 (reprinted https://trithucvn.org/van-hoa/lich-su-do-son-vu-bang.html, accessed May 5, 2022); and Advertisement, "Đồ-Sơn – Hôtel An-Hưng," *Hà Thành Ngọ Báo*, May 19, 1933.

69. France saw car use explode during interwar years. Gwendolyn Wright, *The Politics of Design in French Colonial Urbanism* (University of Chicago Press, 1991), 186; David Del Testa, "Automobiles and Anomie in French Indochina," in *France and Indochina Cultural Representations*, ed. Kathryn Robinson and Jennifer Yee (Lexington, 2005), 65; Nancy A. Nicols, *Women Behind the Wheel: An Unexpected and Personal History of the Car* (Pegasus, 2024); and Adam Stanley, "Hearth, Home, and Steering Wheel," *The Historian* 66, no. 2 (Summer 2004): 249.

70. Aline Demay, *Tourism and Colonization in Indochina (1898–1939)* (Cambridge Scholars, 2014), 79.

71. "Người Mỹ thăm Đông-dương: Các nhà du-lịch tới Cap Saint Jacques," *Hà Thành Ngọ Báo*, March 14, 1930.

72. Tùng-Hiệp, "Sầm-Sơn đầy ánh sáng," *Trung Bắc Tân Văn*, June 23, 1940.

73. Sumei Wang, ed., introduction to *The East Asian Modern Girl: Women, Media, and Colonial Modernity During the Interwar Years* (Brill, 2021), 1–9.

74. Christopher Goscha, "Bao Dai and Sihanouk: La fabrique Indochinoise des rois coloniaux," in *La colonization des corps: De l'Indochine au Vietnam*, ed. François Guillemot and Agathe Larcher-Goscha (Vendémiaire, 2014), 132; and Judith A. N. Henchy, "Performing Modernity in the Writings of Nguyễn An Ninh and Phạm Văn Hùm" (PhD diss., University of Washington, 2005), 3.

75. Ben Tran, *Post-Mandarin: Masculinity and Aesthetic Modernity in Vietnam* (Fordham University Press, 2017), 1–20.

76. Many of the articles run on this page were syndicated from French newspapers. It is not surprising that the paper encouraged women to follow French fashion because the director was Henry Chavigny de Lachevrotière, a pro-colonial Martinique-Vietnamese *métis* who pushed his readers to adopt French culture.

77. Song Nguyệt, "Lời chúng em: Phụ nữ với thời trang," *Hà Thành Ngọ Báo*, March 7, 1930; Phạm Thị Lan Khanh, "Lời chúng em: Mốt của chị em," *Hà Thành Ngọ Báo*,

1. THE DISSEMINATION OF BEAUTY TRENDS

January 9, 1930; and Mỹ-Chân, "Lời chúng em: Trang sức," *Hà Thành Ngọ Báo*, April 28, 1930.
78. Cô Ngã, "Mốt," *Vịt Đực*, August 17, 1938; and Cô Ngã, "Mốt," *Vịt Đực*, October 12, 1938.
79. Tiêu-liêu, "Mốt," *Vịt Dúc*, June 29, 1938; and Cô Ngã (Ngữa), "Mốt," *Vịt Dúc*, July 20, 1938.
80. Cô Ngã, "Mốt," *Vịt Dúc*, July 13, 1938.
81. Lệ Chi, "Có ai đi học giùm môn thuốc nầy," *Điển Tín*, February 20, 1937; and Advertisement, "Institut de beauté Venus," *Đông Pháp*, December 6, 1935.
82. Nadine André-Pallois, "École Supérieure des Beaux-Arts de l'Indochine," in *The Routledge Encyclopedia of Modernism* (Taylor and Francis, 2016), rem.routledge.com/articles/ecole-superieure-des-beaux-arts-de-lindochine, https://doi.org/10.4324/9781135000356-REM1401-1; Nadine André-Pallois, *L'Indochine: un lieu d'échange culturel. Les peintres français et indochinois (fin XIX-XXe siècle)* (EFEO, 1997); Pierre Paliard, *Un art vietnamien: Penser d'autres modernités. Le Projet de Victor Tardieu pour l'École des Beaux Arts de l'Indochine à Hanoi en 1924* (L'Harmattan, 2014); Phạm Thảo Nguyên, *Áo dài Lemur và bối cảnh Phong Hoá và Ngày Nay* (NXB Hồng Đức, 2019), 11–12; and Martina Thucnhi Nguyen, *On Our Own Strength: The Self-Reliant Literary Group and Cosmopolitan Nationalism in Late Colonial Vietnam* (University of Hawaii Press, 2021), 81–84.
83. Nguyen, *On Our Own Strength*, 82–83; and Phạm Thảo Nguyên, *Áo dài Lemur và bối cảnh Phong Hoá và Ngày Nay*, 11.
84. Phạm Thảo Nguyên, *Áo dài Lemur và bối cảnh Phong Hoá và Ngày Nay*, 31.
85. Geoffrey Jones, *Beauty Imagined: A History of the Global Beauty Industry* (Oxford University Press, 2010), 129.
86. Pierre Brocheux and Daniel Hémery, *Indochina: An Ambiguous Colonization, 1858–1954* (University of California Press, 2009).
87. *L'Avenir du Tonkin*, August 19, 1911. Donald Dean Wilson found the first reference to a movie theater in Nam Dinh in 1913. Donald Dean Wilson Jr., "Colonial Việt Nam on Film: 1896 to 1926," (PhD diss., City University of New York, 2007), 83; and Brocheux and Hémery, *Indochina: An Ambiguous Colonization*, 232–33; In 1934, an executive from the MGM film corporation even came to Vietnam to promote Hollywood pictures in the colony. "Rồi làm thành ngôi sao," *Hà Thành Ngọ Báo*, July 6, 1934.
88. Nancy F. Cott, "The Modern Woman of the 1920s, American Style," in *A History of Women in the West*, ed. Françoise Thébaud (Harvard University Press, 1994), 80.
89. See, for example, "Nghe Đâu," *Hà Thành Ngọ Báo*, March 17, 1934.
90. Doctor Dekobra was probably Maurice Dekobra, one of the most famous authors of the era who himself would visit Saigon in 1933. Việt Quang, "Ở xứ các "ngôi sao" chiếu bóng," *Hà Thành Ngọ Báo*, June 28, 1931; and "Nhà tiểu thuyết Maurice Dekobra sẽ đến Sài Gòn," *Hà Thành Ngọ Báo*, November 13, 1933.
91. Wancaln, " . . . Rồi làm thành ngôi sao," *Hà Thành Ngọ Báo*, July 6, 1934.
92. Vũ Trọng Phụng, *Làm đĩ* (NXB Văn Học, 2015), 135.
93. Phan Thị Nga, "Một diều dang chu y trong phong trào phu nư," *Tràng An Báo*, March 20, 1936; and Thuy Tinh, "Đội Tiên Phong," *Hà Thành Ngọ Báo*, September 13, 1933.

1. THE DISSEMINATION OF BEAUTY TRENDS

94. See the memoire of Michel Đức Chaigneau, a Franco-Vietnamese man born in 1803. Michel Đức Chaigneau, *Souvenirs de Hué (Cochinchine)* (L'Imprimerie Impériale, 1857). Because Vietnamese lineage is traced through the father, children of French men and Vietnamese women were regarded as uprooted. Of course, compounding the ancestral issue was the political reality that the French father represented the colonial government that invaded Vietnam. See Christina Firpo, *The Uprooted: Race, Children, and Imperialism in French Indochina, 1890–1980* (University of Hawaii Press, 2016).
95. Firpo, *The Uprooted*, 53–54; and Vũ Trọng Phụng, "Kỹ nghệ lấy tây," in *Kỹ nghệ lấy tây & cơm thấy cơm cô* (NXB Văn Học, 2006), 9–101.
96. Alain Ruscio, "Nous avons débarqué au milieu du people le plus étrange," in *La Colonisation des Corps: de l'Indochine au Viet Nam*, ed. François Guillemot and Agathe Larcher-Goscha (Vendémiaire, 2014), 72.
97. Barbara Sato, *The New Japanese Woman: Modernity, Media and Women in Interwar Japan* (Duke University Press, 2003); Sarah E. Stevens. "Figuring Modernity: The New Woman and the Modern Girl in Republican China," *NWSA Journal* 15, no. 3 (2003): 82–103; Jiyoung Suh, "The 'New Woman' and the Topography of Modernity in Colonial Korea," *Korean Studies* 37 (2013): 11–43; Richard Reitan, "Claiming Personality: Reassessing the Dangers of the 'New Woman' in Early Taishō Japan," *Positions: East Asia Cultures and Critique* 19, no. 1 (Spring 2011): 83–107; Hu Ying, *Tales of Translation: Composing the New Woman in China, 1899–1918* (Stanford University Press, 2000); Katrina Gulliver, *Modern Women in China and Japan: Gender, Feminism and Global Modernity Between the Wars* (IB Tauris, 2012); and Hyaewoel Choi, *New Woman in Colonial Korea: A Sourcebook* (Routledge, 2013): 1–15.
98. Until 1925, most teachers were French men and women; it would not be until the late 1920s that Vietnamese women were earning degrees in high enough numbers to enter the teaching workforce in larger numbers.
99. In 1927, French feminists Edith Pye and Camille Drevet toured Indochina, causing a stir among the colonial police and Vietnamese journalists. Mona L. Siegel, "The Dangers of Feminism in Colonial Indochina," *French Historical Studies* 38, no. 4 (October 2015): 661–90; and Henchy, "Performing Modernity in the Writings of Nguyễn An Ninh and Phạm Văn Hùm."
100. Huỳnh Thị Bảo Hòa, "Vì sao tôi cúp tóc," *Phụ Nữ Tân Văn*, August 31, 1933; Đoàn tâm Đan, "Bà Trịnh Thục Oanh nói về thời trang," *Ngày Nay*, January 30, 1935; and Mme Bạch Liên, "Ý kiến của tôi đối với việc cúp tóc," *Phụ Nữ Tân Văn*, June 21, 1934.
101. "Phụ nữ với thể dục," *Hà Thành Ngọ Báo*, March 14, 1930.
102. Việt Bằng, "Dân thể thao Hà Thành đón cô Hồ Thị Lích," *Vịt Đức*, September 14, 1938; and "Chuyện Đó, Đây," *Tràng An Báo*, June 3, 1938. Nguyễn Thị Kế, "Cô Việt Hoang Thị Kế nữ học sinh trường Cholon định xướng lên một cuộc đi xe đạp từ nam ra bắc," *Hà Thành Ngọ Báo*, April 2, 1931. "Phụ nữ với thể thao: bà dốc nghĩa đã giựt chức vô địch ping pong," *Sài Gòn*, May 11, 1932. "Cô Hoàng Việt Nga nói về cuộc đi bộ Hanoi-Haiphong," *Hà Thành Ngọ Báo*, October 12, 1930; and Nguyễn Thị Kế, "Cô Việt Hoang Thị Kế nữ học sinh trường Cholon định xướng lên một cuộc đi xe đạp từ nam ra bắc," *Hà Thành Ngọ Báo*, April 2, 1931.

1. THE DISSEMINATION OF BEAUTY TRENDS

103. At its peak of publishing, *Phụ Nữ Tân Văn* sold eight thousand five hundred copies a week. This sales rate held for two years. David Marr, *Vietnamese Tradition on Trial, 1920–1945* (University of California Press, 1981), 220.
104. Mme Bạch Liên, "Ý kiến của tôi đối với việc cúp tóc," *Phụ Nữ Tân Văn*, June 21, 1934; and *Chantecler: littéraire, satirique, humoristique*, October 15, 1933.
105. Male authors also included Đào Trinh Nhất, Trịnh Đình Thảo, Tản Đà, Trần Trọng Kim, Bùi Thế Mỹ, Diệp Văn Kỳ, and Huỳnh Thúc Kháng. Pictures published in Thiện Mộc Lan, *Phụ nữ Tân-văn: Phấn son tô điểm sơn hà* (NXB Văn hóa Sài Gòn, 2010), 83, 170, 176.
106. Nguyễn Đức Nhuận used the pages of his newspaper to advertise his fabric shop, located on Rue Catinat, on the ground floor of the building that housed his press room. "Nhung hai da, Ô hai Lòng, và Lưới Mùng có Bông," *Phụ Nữ Tan Văn*, August 1, 1929. Bùi Thị Thanh Hương, "Báo Phụ nữ Tân văn: Những việc làm và tư tưởng mới," *Tạp chí Khoa Học ĐHSP TPHCM* 46 (2013): 160–67; Vân Hương, "Gái đời nay: Lời một vị phu nhân có nền nếp mắng răn con gái là bậc tân học," *Phụ Nữ Tân Văn*, September 12, 1929; Nguyen, *On Our Own Strength*, 100–107; Đặng Thị Vân Chi, *Vấn đề phụ nữ trên báo chí tiếng Việt trước năm 1945* (NXB Khoa Học Xã Hội, 2008), 136–37; Thiện Mộc Lan, *Phụ nữ Tân-văn: Phấn son tô điểm sơn hà* (NXB Văn hóa Sài Gòn, 2010), 31–33; Madeleine E. Aitchison, "Who Holds the Mirror? The Creation of an Ideal Vietnamese Woman, 1918–1934" (master's thesis, University of Hawaii, 2018); and Shawn McHale, "Printing and Power: Vietnamese Debates Over Women's Place in Society, 1918–1934," in *Essays Into Vietnamese Pasts*, ed. Keith W. Taylor and John K. Whitmore (Cornell University Press, 1995), 192.
107. Hồ Biểu Chánh, *Tân phong nữ sĩ*, 1937.
108. Hồ Biểu Chánh, *Tân phong nữ sĩ*, 1937.
109. She refuses, however, to marry him. Hồ Biểu Chánh, *Tân phong nữ sĩ*, 1937.
110. Alys Eve Weinbaum, Lynn M. Thomas, Priti Ramamurthy, and Uta G. Poiger, eds., *The Modern Girl Around the World: Consumption, Modernity, and Globalization* (Duke University Press, 2008); Lewis, *Cities in Motion*, 246–52; Lucy Healey, "Modernity, Identity, and Constructions of Malay Womanhood," in *Modernity and Identity: Asian Illustrations* (1994); Chie Ikeya, *Refiguring Women, Colonialism and Modernity in Burma* (University of Hawaii Press, 2011), 96–119; Mary Lynn Stewart, *Dressing Modern Frenchwomen: Marketing Haute Couture, 1919–1939* (Johns Hopkins University Press, 2008), 200–23; and Choi, *New Woman in Colonial Korea*, 1–15.
111. Sato, *The New Japanese Woman*, 48.
112. Weinbaum, Thomas, Ramamurthy, and Poiger, eds., *The Modern Girl Around the World*; and Wang, introduction to *The East Asian Modern Girl*, 1.
113. Wang, introduction to *The East Asian Modern Girl*, 1.
114. Jun'ichiro Tanizaki, *Naomi* (1924; repr. Vintage, 2001); Freedman, Miller, and Yano, *Modern Girl on the Go*; and Miriam Silverberg, "The Modern Girl as Militant," in *Recreating Japanese Women, 1600–1945*, ed. Gail Lee Bernstein (University of California Press, 1991).
115. Suh, "The 'New Woman' and the Topography of Modernity in Colonial Korea"; Jiyoung Suh, "The Flâneuse and the Landscape of Colonial Soeul in the 1920s–1930s," *Sociétés: Revue des sciences humaines et sociales* 135 (2017): 63–72;

1. THE DISSEMINATION OF BEAUTY TRENDS

Anne Sokolsky, "Reading the Bodies and Voices of 'Naichi' Women in Japanese-Ruled Taiwan," *US-Japan Women's Journal* 46 (2014): 51–78; Wang, *The East Asian Modern Girl*; Stevens, "Figuring Modernity," 84; Chua Ai Lin, "Singapore's 'Cinema-Age' of the 1930s: Hollywood and the Shaping of Singapore Modernity," *Inter-Asia Cultural Studies* 13, no. 4 (December 2012): 592–604; Rachel Leow, "Age as a Category of Gender Analysis: Servant Girls, Modern Girls, and Gender in Southeast Asia," *Journal of Asian Studies* 71, no. 4 (2012): 980; and Choi, *New Woman in Colonial Korea*, 1–15.

116. Firpo, *Black Market Business*, 162–86.
117. Henchy, "Performing Modernity in the Writings of Nguyễn An Ninh and Phạm Văn Hùm," 237–41.
118. Phan Thị Nga, "Một diêu dang chu y trong phong trào phu nư," *Tràng An Báo*, March 20, 1936.
119. Thuy Tinh, "Đội Tiên Phong," *Hà Thành Ngọ Báo*, September 13, 1933.
120. As Nora Taylor pointed out, Modern Girls never appeared in art, where women were the subject of choice and represented in a five-panel tunic. Email correspondence with Nora Taylor, May 22, 2023.
121. "Phong Trào 'Theo Mới,'" *Phụ Nữ Tân Văn*, March 22, 1934, 1–2.
122. Nguyễn Công Hoan, "Cô Kếu, gái tân thời," 1933.
123. Nguyễn Đình Lạp, "Thanh niên trụy lạc," in *Phóng Sự Việt Nam*, ed. Phan Trọng Thưởng, Nguyễn Cừ, and Nguyễn Hữu Sơn, vol. 2 (NXB Văn Học, 2000).
124. Khái Hưng, *Trống Mái*, 1936.
125. B., "Hội chợ Faifoo đã khai mạc," *Sài Gòn*, May 29, 1936.
126. Christopher Goscha, "Bao Dai and Sihanouk: La fabrique Indochinoise des rois coloniaux," in *La colonization des corps: De l'Indochine au Viet Nam*, ed. François Guillemot and Agathe Larcher-Goscha (Vendémiaire, 2014); and Christopher E. Goscha, "Monarchies colonials et décolonisations compares dans l'Empire Français: Bao Dai, Norodom Sihanouk et Mohammed V," *Monde(s)* 2, no. 12 (2017): 41–69.
127. "Vua Bảo Đại sắp về nước," *Phụ Nữ Tân Văn*, June 11, 1931; "Le jeune empereur d'Annam, Bao-Daï, va prochainement retourner dans son pays qu'il s'efforcera de modernizer," *Le Petit Parisien*, August 3, 1932; "L'empereur d'Annam Bao Dai quittera la France demain par le paquebot 'd'Artagnan,'" *Le Petit Parisien*, August 11, 1932; Phan Thứ Lang, *Bảo Đại: Vua cuối cùng Triều Nguyễn* (NXB Văn Nghệ, 2009), 34–41, 53–58; and Sa Magesté Bao Dai, *Le dragon d'Annam* (Plon, 1979).
128. The colonial government also used Bảo Đại's return to give credence to reforms of local government that would otherwise appear unilateral. Goscha, "Bao Dai and Sihanouk: La fabrique Indochinoise des rois coloniaux," 148–49; and Bruce McFarland Lockhart, *The End of the Vietnamese Monarchy* (Council on Southeast Asian Studies, Yale University, 1993), 49–51.
129. Nguyên Duy Ninh, "Le Roi et la jeunesse," *L'Annam Nouveau*, November 6, 1932; and "Le jeune empereur d'Annam, Bao-Daï, va prochainement retourner dans son pays qu'il s'efforcera de modernizer," *Le Petit Parisien*, August 3, 1932.
130. "Le jeune empereur d'Annam, Bao-Daï, va prochainement retourner dans son pays qu'il s'efforcera de modernizer," *Le Petit Parisien*, August 3, 1932; and Phan Thứ Lang, *Bảo Đại*, 34–41, 53–58.

1. THE DISSEMINATION OF BEAUTY TRENDS

131. "Chung quanh lễ sách phong cô Mariette Jean Nguyễn Hữu Hào làm Hoàng hậu nước Nam," *Phụ Nữ Tân Văn*, March 29, 1934; "Hoàng Thượng gặp cô Mariette Jeanne Nguyễn Hữu Hào ở đâu?," *Đông Pháp*, March 18, 1934. Multiple rumors circulated about how the two met, mostly focusing on the idea that the French government arranged the marriage for political reasons. Phan Thứ Lang, *Bảo Đại*, 83; and Sa Magesté Bao Dai, *Le dragon d'Annam*, 78–81.
132. "Annam Dissatisfied with Young Emperor's Fiancee: Girl, Reared in Paris Convent, Is Catholic; Emperor Is Buddhist," *Lewston Daily Sun*, March 20, 1934. A 1937 article about the empress notes that her reading was limited to French language, she spoke to her children in French, and she struggled to understand the Huế dialect of Vietnamese. "Yết Kiến Nam Phương Hoàng Hậu," *Tràng An Báo*, April 4, 1937; and Lockhart, *The End of the Vietnamese Monarchy*, 88–89.
133. Phan Thứ Lang, *Bảo Đại: Vua cuối cùng Triều Nguyễn* (NXB Văn Nghệ, 2009), 83; and Sa Magesté Bao Dai, *Le dragon d'Annam*.
134. "Ai tình và tôn giáo: Chung quanh chuyện cô Mariette Jean Nguyễn Hữu Hào làm Hoàng Hậu," *Phụ Nữ Tân Văn*, March 15, 1934.
135. "Ai tình và tôn giáo: Chung quanh chuyện cô Mariette Jean Nguyễn Hữu Hào làm Hoàng Hậu," *Phụ Nữ Tân Văn*, March 15, 1934.
136. "Một đại lễ của Nam triều," *Đông Pháp*, March 12, 1934; "Hoàng Thượng làm lễ gáo yết tại điện Phụng tiên," *Hà Thành Ngọ Báo*, March 18, 1934; "Tại chốn thân kinh: Trưa thuứ bảy, hoàng hậu đã tới Huế," *Đông Pháp*, March 19, 1934; Ngọc Tran, "Cô Nguyễn Thị Lan đã được các quan đại thần Nam Triều tiế đón tại lau công quán," *Hà Thành ngọ báo*, March 20, 1934; "Trước khi cô Mariette Jeanne Nguyễn Hữu Hào từ giã Nam kỳ," *Hà Thành Ngọ Báo*, March 23, 1934; and "Các bà phủ thiếp, mệnh phụ Nam triều đến lầu công quán rước Hoàng hậu vào Đại nội," *Hà Thành Ngọ Báo*, March 23, 1934.
137. The technique was mastered by Nguyễn Phan Chánh. See Nora Annesley Taylor, "The Artist and the State: The Politics of Painting and National Identity in Hanoi, Vietnam, 1925–1995" (PhD diss., Cornell University, 1997) 61, 90.
138. The emperor famously had vacation homes in Nha Trang, Đà Lạt, Buôn Ma Thuột, Cap Saint Jacques, and Hà Nội.
139. "Le jeune empereur d'Annam, Bao-Daï, va prochainement retourner dans son pays qu'il s'efforcera de moderniser," *Le Petit Parisien*, August 3, 1932; and Phan Thứ Lang, *Bảo Đại*, 34–41, 53–58.
140. Paul Munier, "L'Evolution de la société Annamite," *La Tribune Indochinoise*, March 5, 1937; and Phạm Thảo Nguyên, *Áo dài Lemur và bối cảnh Phong Hoá và Ngày Nay* (NXB Hồng Đức, 2019), 33.
141. Huỳnh Thị Bảo Hòa, "Vì sao tôi cúp tóc," *Phụ Nữ Tân Văn*, August 31, 1933; and Mme Bạch Liên, "Ý kiến của tôi đối với việc cúp tóc," *Phụ Nữ Tân Văn*, June 21, 1934.
142. Đoàn tâm Đan, "Bà Trịnh Thục Oanh nói về thới trang," *Ngày Nay*, January 30, 1935.
143. "Phụ nữ nam ky đối với cô Henriette Bùi: Bữa tiệc trà long trọng trên trăm người dự," *Sài Gòn*, June 21, 1935; Ha, *French Women and the Empire*, 201–02; "A l'école de musique," *La Tribune Indochinoise*, July 13, 1927; "Ceux qui nous reviennent," *La Tribune Indochinoise*, January 21, 1934; Vân-Hoàn, "Mỹ-nhơn viện" của cô Madeleine Bùi, lênh-ái ông Bùi Quang Chiêu," *Hà Thành Ngọ Báo*, April 20, 1935;

2. FASHION

Advertisement, "Institute de Beauté Madeleine," *La Tribune Indochinoise*, May 15, 1936; "Une visite à l'Institute de Beauté de Mlle Madeleine Bui," *La Tribune Indochinoise*, April 12, 1935; Henchy, "Performing Modernity in the Writings of Nguyễn An Ninh and Phạm Văn Hùm," 224; "En quelques mots," *La Tribune Indochinoise*, September 21, 1936; and "Mỹ nhơn viện Madeleine," *Công Luận báo*, April 15, 1935.

144. After 1954, Ái Liên remained in communist northern Vietnam, where she was perhaps the most popular entertainer, although she was forgotten in southern Vietnam. "Thì sắc đẹp," *Hà Thành Ngọ Báo*, February 12, 1935; Võ Đức Diên, "Về cuộc thi quần áo phụ nữ ở Hội chợ tơ lụa Hà Đông," *Hà Thành Ngọ Báo*, October 25, 1935; Chướng tai nghịch mắt," *Đông Pháp*, January 31, 1935; "Hanoi," *Hà Thành Ngọ Báo*, February 10, 1935; "Chương trình về tuần lễ từ thiện," *Hà Thành Ngọ Báo*, May 2, 1936; "Hội kịch Bả kỳ," *Đông Pháp*, February 14, 1935; Jason Gibbs, "Spoken Theatre, La Scene Tonkinoise, and the First Modern Vietnamese Songs," *Journal for the Society of Asian Music* 31, no. 2 (Spring/Summer 2000): 1–33; and Ngành Mai, "Đoàn cải lương Ái Liên lưu diễn khắp Đông Dương," *Radio Free Asia*, November 14, 2015, accessed December 1, 2022, https://www.rfa.org/vietnamese/news/programs/TraditionalMusic/traditional-music-1114-nm-11132015151203.html.

2. FASHION

1. Lang-Quê, "Ý kiến độc giả: Vấn đề ăn mặc của người Việt-Nam," *Trung Lập Báo*, June 16, 1932.
2. Lang-Quê, "Ý kiến độc giả: Vấn đề ăn mặc của người Việt-Nam," *Trung Lập Báo*, June 16, 1932.
3. For an excellent analysis of the intellectual battle for the image of Vietnam, see Judith A. N. Henchy, "Performing Modernity in the Writings of Nguyễn An Ninh and Phan Văn Hùm" (PhD diss., University of Washington, 2005).
4. The most thorough study of Vietnamese sartorial history is Trần Quang Đức, *Ngàn năm áo mũ: Lịch sử trang phục Việt Nam giai đoạn 1009–1945* (NXB Thế Giới, 2013).
5. The looms of the period could weave fabrics no wider than thirty to forty centimeters, so tailors had no choice but to construct garments from half-panels to cover the body. Martina Thucnhi Nguyen, *On Our Own Strength: The Self-Reliant Literary Group and Cosmopolitan Nationalism in Late Colonial Vietnam* (University of Hawaii Press, 2021), 82.
6. Phan Kế Bính, *Việt Nam phong tục (Moeurs et coutumes du Vietnam)*, vol. 2, trans. Nicole Louis-Hénard (École Française d'Extrême-Orient, 1980), 179; Nhất Thanh, *Đất lề quê thói: Phong tục Việt Nam* (1970; repr. NXB Hồng Đức, 2016), 156; N. Cát Tường, "Nhân dịp hội tơ lụa Hà Đông đổi mới y phục phụ nữ: Tính ưa đẹp và hay trang điểm," *Ngày Nay*, November 13, 1935; Đào Duy Anh, *Việt Nam văn hóa sử cương* (1938; repr. NXB Văn hóa-Thông tin, 2000), 209; E. Langlet, *Le Peuple Annamite: Ses moeurs, croyances et traditions* (Berger-Levrault, 1913), 82; Trần Quang Đức, *Ngàn năm áo mũ*, 237–38; Nguyễn-Ngạc and Nguyễn Văn Luận, *Un Siècle d'Histoire de la Robe des Vietnamiennes* (Ministère de la Culture

de l'Éducation et de la Jeunesse, n.d.), 22; Martina Thucnhi Nguyen, "Wearing Modernity: Lemur Nguyễn Cát Tường, Fashion, and the Origins of the Vietnamese National Costume," *Journal of Vietnamese Studies* 11, no. 1 (Winter 2016): 83; and Henri Joseph Oger, *Introduction Générale à l'étude de la technique du people annamites: Essai sur la vie matérielle, les arts et industries du peuple d'Annam* (Geuthner, 1908), 54–55.

7. Since the sixteenth century, the Đại Việt kingdom was ruled by the Trịnh lords in the north (Đàng Ngoài) and the Nguyễn lords in the territories south of the Linh River (modern day Gianh River) (Đàng Trong).
8. Hidden under the five-panel tunic, women held their breasts in place with a nịt vú, a garment that bound the breasts. Y-sĩ Đ. T., "Nịt vú," *Hà Thành Ngọ Báo*, March 8, 1929.
9. Trần Quang Đức, *Ngàn năm áo mũ*, 237–38; L. Cadière, "Le changement de costume sous Vo-Vuong, ou une crise religieuse à Hue au XVIIIe siècle," *Bulletin des amis de vieux Hue* 4 (1915): 417–24; Thanh Lâm, "Ông Nguyễn Cát Tường cùng y-phục phụ nữ," *Loa Tuần Báo*, April 26, 1934; Nguyễn Gia Miêu, "Trông màu trời, chọn sắc áo," *Lao động cuối tuần*, June 13, 2004; Martina Thucnhi Nguyen, "Wearing Modernity," 85; and Philip Huard and Maurice Durand, *Connaissance du Viet-Nam* (EFEO, 1954), 178.
10. Alexander Woodside, *Vietnam and the Chinese Model: A Comparative Study of Vietnamese and Chinese Government in the First Half of the Nineteenth Century* (Harvard University Press, 1988), 134; Nguyễn Văn Ký, *La société Vietnamienne face à la modernité: Le Tonkin de la fin du XIXe siècle à la seconde guerre mondiale* (L'Harmattan, 1995); Martina Thucnhi Nguyen, *On Our Own Strength*, 83; Nhất Thanh, *Đất lề quê thói: Phong tục Việt Nam*, 152, 156; Nguyễn Gia Miêu, "Trông màu trời, chọn sắc áo," *Lao động cuối tuần*, June 13, 2004; Ann Marie Leshkowich, "Áo dài," in the *Encyclopedia of Clothing and Fashion*, vol 1, ed. Valerie Steele (Scribner, 2005), 60–62.
11. "Áo dài Cát Tường," *https://vandoanviet.blogspot.com/2017/05/ao-dai-cat-tuong.html*, accessed November 22, 2021.
12. Phan Kế Bính, *Việt Nam phong tục (Moeurs et coutumes du Vietnam)*; and Trần Quang Đức, *Ngàn năm áo mũ*.
13. Martina Thucnhi Nguyen, *On Our Own Strength*.
14. Phan Thị Nga, "Chị em Hội An với y phục Cát Tường," *Ngày Nay*, March 10, 1935.
15. Henri Oger, *Technique du peuple annamite* (EFEO, 2009/1909), 152; Langlet, *Le Peuple Annamite*, 81; and Christiane Fournier, "La femme coolie sous le soleil de feu du Tonkin," *Le Petit Écho de la mode*, October 31, 1937.
16. Nhất Thanh, *Đất lề quê thói*, 168–69.
17. Langlet, *Le Peuple Annamite*, 87.
18. Mikiko Ashikari, "The Memory of the Women's White Faces: Japaneseness and the Ideal Image of Women," *Japan Forum* 15, no. 1 (2003): 55–79; Mina Roces, "Gender, Nation, and the Politics of Dress in 20th Century Philippines," *Gender and History* 17, no. 2 (August 2005): 354–77; Chie Ikeya, "The Modern Burmese Woman and the Politics of Fashion in Colonial Burma," *Journal of Asian Studies*, 67, no. 4 (November 2008): 1282; Patrick Jory, *A History of Manners and Civility in Thailand* (Cambridge University Press, 2020), 129; and Nguyen Van Vinh, "Question de costume," *Annam Nouveau*, November 3, 1932.

2. FASHION

19. Nguyen Van Vinh, "Question de costume."
20. Hoang Ngoc Thanh, *Vietnam's Social Development as Seen Through the Modern Novel* (Peter Lang, 1991), 68–70.
21. Tha Sơn, "Tại sao thiếu niên ta thích bận âu phục?," *Hà Thành Ngọ Báo*, October 29, 1932; Nguyễn Cát Tường, "Y phục của phụ nữ," *Phong Hóa*, February 23, 1934; Hoàng-Đạo, "Phụ nữ ra ngoài xã hội," *Ngày Nay*, November 1, 1936; Martina Thucnhi Nguyen, "Wearing Modernity," 88; and Nguyen Van Vinh, "Question de costume," *Annam Nouveau*, November 3, 1932.
22. At that point, the population of *me tây* was still very small, limited to a few daughters of wealthy families in the city, and a handful of women gathered by military bases in the countryside.
23. Phạm Thảo Nguyên uses the term "Phong trào cạo răng trắng, mặc quần trắng." Phạm Thảo Nguyên, *Áo dài Lemur và bối cảnh Phong Hoá và Ngày Nay*.
24. N. Cát Tường, "Nhân dịp hội tơ lụa Hà Đông đổi mới y phục phụ nữ: Tính ưa đẹp và hay trang điểm," *Ngày Nay*, November 13, 1935.
25. Phan Kế Bính, *Việt Nam phong tục*, 179.
26. Reflecting on this trend in a 1935 interview, Trịnh Thục Oanh, an author and headmistress at a girls' school in Hanoi, pinpointed 1920 as the first time she saw schoolgirls in white pants and colorful tunics. See Đoàn tâm Đan, "Bà Trịnh Thục Oanh nói về thời trang," *Ngày Nay*, January 30, 1935. Multiple newspaper articles in 1924 reference the white pants trend in the rather morbid context of dead female bodies needing identification or young women reported missing and what they were last seen wearing, suggesting the trend was widespread. The real discussions about this trend, however, would not take place in print until 1929, when intellectuals began considering fashion reform. That the trend in colorful tunics and white pants was not discussed at length until the end of the decade suggests that it emerged gradually and hence did not trigger any major controversy.
27. Cát Tường, "Thời tiết với màu sắc y phục," *Ngày Nay*, September 20, 1936.
28. French women were instructed to bring white and light-colored linen clothing to the colony "to show colonial embodiment, purity, and visibility from afar." Jennifer Boittin, *Undesirable: Passionate Mobility and Women's Defiance of French Colonial Policing 1919–1952* (University of Chicago Press, 2022), 96.
29. T. Th., "Đàn bà mặc quần trắng," *Hà Thành Ngọ Báo*, September 2, 1929.
30. T. Th., "Đàn bà mặc quần trắng," *Hà Thành Ngọ Báo*, September 2, 1929.
31. Kimberly Christman-Campell, *Skirts: Fashioning Modern Femininity in the Twentieth Century* (St. Martin's Press, 2022).
32. H. N., "Y phục phụ nữ," *Khoa học*, June 15, 1934.
33. Dinh Trong Hieu, "Le face, le ventre et autres symboliques du corps chez les Viets," in *La Colonisation des Corps: de l'Indochine au Viet Nam*, ed. François Guillemot and Agathe Larcher-Goscha (Vendémiaire, 2014), 37.
34. Chiêu Anh Kế, "Trong Nam kỳ: Cô Hồng Vân với quần áo mới," *Ngày nay*, March 10, 1935; and "Xã Giao: Phép xử thế, Phục Sức," *Ngày nay*, November 15, 1936.
35. "Quan Toàn Quyền Robin đã về khánh thành cuộc đấu xảo tơ lụa tỉnh Hadong," *Hà Thành Ngọ Báo*, October 23, 1935.
36. "Phong tục tiếng nói Nam-kỳ khác Bắc kỳ thế nào?," *Hà Thành Ngọ Báo*, May 24, 1933; and Nguyễn An Toàn, "Chị em cứ đi xe đạp!," *Công Luận Báo*, May 24, 1938.
37. T. Th., "Đàn bà mặc quần trắng," *Hà Thành Ngọ Báo*, September 2, 1929.

2. FASHION

38. Nguyễn Cát Tường, "Y phục của phụ nữ," *Phong Hóa*, February 23, 1934.
39. Hoàng-Đạo, "Phụ nữ ra ngoài xã hội," *Ngày Nay*, November 1, 1936.
40. Nguyễn Ngạc and Nguyễn Văn Luận, *Un Siècle d'Histoire de la Robe des Vietnamiennes*, 52.
41. Vũ Trọng Phụng, *Làm đĩ* (1935; repr. NXB Văn Học, 2015), 67–68.
42. "Phong tục tiếng nói Nam-kỳ khác Bắc kỳ thế nào?," *Hà Thành Ngọ Báo*, May 24, 1933; "Mười điều tâm niệm," *Vịt Đực*, November 16, 1938; Trọng Lang, *Hà Nội lầm than* (1938; repr. NXB Hội Nhà Văn, 2015), 16; Claudia Brush Kidwell and Valerie Steele, *Men and Women: Dressing the Part* (Smithsonian Institution, 1989), 15, 133; and Mary Louise Roberts, *Civilization without Sexes: Reconstructing Gender in Postwar France, 1917–1927* (University of Chicago Press, 1994).
43. "Xã Giao: Phục Sức," *Ngày Nay*, November 1, 1936; and C. Willet Cunnington and Phillis Cunnington, *The History of Underclothes* (Michael Joseph, 1951), 253–56.
44. Adveriesment, "Maison Giao Sports," *Công Luận Báo*, August 17, 1937; and CL Jeunesse, "Đời tinh thần vật-chất và tình cảm của phụ-nữ Việt-Nam: Ăn mặc làm đỏm," *Đàn-Bà*, June 2, 1939.
45. CL Jeunesse, "Đời tinh thần vật-chất và tình cảm của phụ-nữ Việt-Nam: Ăn mặc làm đỏm," *Đàn-Bà*, June 2, 1939; and Karen, L. Labat, "Swimsuits," in *Encyclopedia of Clothing and Fashion*, vol. 1, ed. Valerie Steele (Scribner, 2005), 154–55.
46. Advertisement, "Cu Chung shop," *Phong Hóa*, September 20, 1935. In the late nineteenth century, after the technique for vulcanizing rubber was discovered, rubber-soled shoes could be worn in wet environments without breaking down. The early twentieth century saw the mass production of athletic shoes. Angel Chang, "Sports Shoes," *Encyclopedia of Clothing and Fashion*, vol. 3, ed. Valerie Steele (Scribner, 2005), 214–15.
47. Advertisement, "Chấn Long," *Phong Hóa*, May 11, 1934; and Advertisement, "Paris Chaussures," *Ngày Nay*, October 11, 1936.
48. Advertisement, "Basty," *Ngày Nay*, October 11, 1936; "Hàng mới lạ Dùng trong mùa mưa," *Phụ Nữ Tân Văn*, August 1, 1929; Advertisement, "Morin Frères Dancing," "3eme Foire de Hué du 15 au 24 Avril 1938, program official"; Carol J. Salusso, "Rayon," *Encyclopedia of Clothing and Fashion*, vol. 3, ed. Valerie Steele (Scribner, 2005), 81–83; Tom Greatrex, "Raincoat," *Encyclopedia of Clothing and Fashion*, vol. 3, ed. Valerie Steele (Scribner, 2005), 79; and Advertisement, "The Dragon" Raincoat, *Phụ Nữ Tân Văn*, June 22, 1932.
49. Mitchel Gray, *The Lingerie Book* (St. Martin's Press, 1980), 29.
50. Cunnington and Cunnington, *The History of Underclothes*, 217; Jill Fields, "Fighting the Corsetless Evil: Shaping Corsets and Culture, 1900–1930," in *Beauty and Business*, ed. Philip Scranton (Routledge, 2001), 109; and Jane Farrell-Beck and Colleen Gau, *Uplift: The Bra in America* (University of Pennsylvania Press, 2002), 188–92.
51. Vũ Trọng Phụng, *Dumb Luck: A Novel*, trans. Nguyễn Nguyệt Cầm, ed. Peter Zinoman (University of Michigan Press, 2003), 62.
52. Rolland Barthes, *The Fashion System*, trans. Matthew Ward and Richard Howard (University of California Press, 1990).
53. Vũ Trọng Phụng, *Dumb Luck*, 61–62.
54. "Một kiểu áo," *Ngày Nay*, November 13, 1935; and Việt Sinh, "Quần áo mới," *Ngày Nay*, January 30, 1935.

2. FASHION

55. "Mua hàng của Vạn-Lợi," *Đông Phương*, October 21, 1929; and "Phong tục tiếng nói Nam-kỳ khác Bắc kỳ thế nào?," *Hà Thành Ngọ Báo*, May 24, 1933.
56. Advertisement, "5 ngàn cái ngữa," *Sài Gòn*, December 22, 1937.
57. Thanh Lâm, "Ông Nguyễn Cát Tường cùng y-phục phụ nữ," *Loa Tuần Báo*, April 26, 1934; Oger, *Introduction Générale à l'étude de la technique du people annamites*, 38; Đoàn Tâm Đan, "Bà Trịnh Thục Oanh nói về thời trang," *Ngày Nay*, January 30, 1935; and Phan Thị Nga, "Chị em Hội An với y phục Cát Tường," *Ngày Nay*, March 10, 1935.
58. Đào Duy Anh, *Việt Nam văn hóa sử cương* (1938; repr. NXB Văn hóa-Thông tin, 2000), 214; and "Theo tục ngữ phong dao: xét về sự sanh hoạt của phụ nữ nược ta," *Phụ Nữ Tân Văn*, August 8, 1929.
59. Mỹ-Chân, "Lời chúng em: Trang sức," *Hà Thành Ngọ Báo*, April 28, 1930.
60. "Trang Nhã," *Đàn-Bà*, September 22, 1939.
61. Advertisement, "Ngọc Thạch," *Đàn-Bà*, June 30 1939.
62. Côn Sinh, "Lối phục—sức của người mình: Hay các 'mốt' tân thời," *Hà Thành Ngọ Báo*, July 24, 1932.
63. Vũ Trọng Phụng, *Kỹ nghệ lấy tây, Cơm thầy cơm cô* (NXB Văn Học, 2004); and "Mốt Mới: Giống vật là một thứ trang sức," *Ngày Nay*, August 2, 1936.
64. Côn Sinh, "Lối phục—sức của người mình . . . Hay các 'mốt' tân thời," *Hà Thành Ngọ Báo*, July 20, 1932; and "Xã Giao: Phục Sức," *Ngày Nay*, November 29, 1936.
65. "Y phục của phụ nữ Annam," *Phụ Nữ Tân Văn*, May 17, 1934; and Trần Quang Đức, *Ngàn năm áo mũ*, 350–51.
66. Natasha Pairaudeau, *Mobile Citizens: French Indians in Indochina, 1858–1954* (Nordic Institute of Asian Studies, 2016), 265.
67. The cultural mandates of the Phibun administration, issued between 1939 and 1942, encouraged Westernized dress. See Jory, *A History of Manners and Civility in Thailand*, 129.
68. Chie Ikeya, *Refiguring Women, Colonialism and Modernity in Burma* (University of Hawaii Press, 2011); and Charles Sullivan, "Years of Dressing Dangerously: Modern Women, National Identity and Moral Crisis in Sukarno's Indonesia, 1945–1966," (PhD diss., University of Michigan, 2020).
69. Kee-Sun Lung, "The Politics of Hair and the Issue of the Bob in Modern China," *Fashion Theory: The Journal of Dress, Body, and Culture* 1, no. 4 (1997): 353–66; "Các cô thiếu nữ Tàu không được tự do?," *Sài Gòn*, August 22, 1934; "Bao nhiêu gái tân thời phải đuổi hết ra khỏi rạp hát," *Hà Thành Ngọ Báo*, August 25, 1935; and "Muốn làm 'bà lớn' không được theo mốt tóc ngắn," *Hà Thành Ngọ Báo*, June 9, 1935.
70. Geneve Clutario, *Beauty Regimes: A History of Power and Modern Empire in the Philippines, 1898–1941* (Duke University Press, 2023), 183–221.
71. Martin J. Murray, *The Development of Capitalism in Colonial Indochina 1870–1940* (University of California Press, 1980), 248–51, 350; and Oger, *Introduction Générale à l'étude de la technique du people annamites*, 58.
72. Hồng Hạnh, "Nói chuyện may mặc," *Phụ Nữ Tân Văn*, July 18, 1929. The author was probably referencing the Swadeshi Movement, 1905–1910, and later boycotts of British textiles. See Christopher Bayly, "The Origins of Swadeshi (Home Industry): Cloth and Indian Society (1700–1930)," in *The Social Life of Things: Commodities in Cultural Perspective*, ed. A. Appadurai (Cambridge University Press, 1986).

2. FASHION

For information on Indian boycotts of British textiles, see Lisa Trivedi, *Clothing Ghandi's Nation: Homespun and Modern India* (Indiana University Press, 2007). A similar boycott was taking place in China. See Karl Gerth, "Consumption and Nationalism: China," in the *Oxford Handbook of the History of Consumption*, ed. Frank Trentmann (Oxford University Press, 2012), 422.

73. T. T., "Cùng ai chưa hiểu rõ: Vấn đề phục sức," *Hà Thành Ngọ Báo*, March 8, 1930. A similar buy-local textile movement occurred in Burma, a colony also grappling with colonial manipulation of the local textile industry and a flood of inexpensive Indian and Chinese imports. See Ikeya, "The Modern Burmese Woman and the Politics of Fashion in Colonial Burma," 1288.
74. Phạm thị Lan Khanh, "Lời chúng em: Mốt của chị em," *Hà Thành Ngọ Báo*, January 9, 1930.
75. Phạm thị Lan Khanh, "Lời chúng em: Mốt của chị em," *Hà Thành Ngọ Báo*, January 9, 1930.
76. Christina Firpo, *Black Market Business: Selling Sex in Northern Vietnam, 1920–1945* (Cornell University Press, 2020), 95.
77. T. T., "Một điều nên cải cách: Lối ăn mặc của người mình," *Hà Thành Ngọ Báo*, February 18, 1930; and T. T., "Cùng ai chưa hiểu rõ: Vấn đề phục sức," *Hà Thành Ngọ Báo*, March 8, 1930.
78. Mỹ-Chân, "Lời chúng em: Trang sức," *Hà Thành Ngọ Báo*, April 28, 1930.
79. "Chị em nữ học sanh nên mặc áo dài là phải," *Phụ Nữ Tân Văn*, October 27, 1932.
80. Firpo, *Black Market Business*, 162–63.
81. Kimloan Vu-Hill, *Coolies Into Rebels: Impact of World War I on French Indochina* (Les Indes Savantes, 2011).
82. Pierre Paliard, *Un Art Vietnamien: Penser d'autres modernité: Le Projet de Victor Tardieu pour l'École des Beaux Arts de l'Indochine à Hanoi en 1924* (L'Harmattan, 2014); Nora Annesley Taylor, "The Artist and the State: The Politics of Painting and National Identity in Hanoi, Vietnam 1925–1995" (PhD diss., Cornell University, 1997), 60; and Gwendolyn Wright, *The Politics of Design in French Colonial Urbanism* (University of Chicago Press, 1991), 25–116.
83. Nicola Cooper, "Urban Planning and Architecture in Colonial Indochina," *French Cultural Studies* 11, no. 1 (2000): 75–99; Ulrike von Hirschhausen, "International Architecture as a Tool of National Emancipation," *Hungarian Historical Review* 7, no. 2 (2018): 331–47; Paliard, *Un Art Vietnamien*; and Caroline Herbelin, *Architectures du Vietnam Colonial: Repenser le métissage* (Institute National d'histoire d'art, 2016).
84. Vũ Trọng Phụng, *Dumb Luck: A Novel*, trans. Nguyệt Cầm Nguyễn, ed. Peter Zinoman (University of Michigan Press, 2002). For a magnificent example of *quốc ngữ* Art Deco lettering, see the masthead of 1938 editions of *Sài Thành* newspaper and print advertisements for Nguyen Chi Hoa's clothing boutique "Nguyen Chi Hoa," *Phụ Nữ Tân Văn*, July 24, 1930.
85. Vũ Trọng Phụng, *Dumb Luck*, 66.
86. T. T., "Một điều nên cải cách: Lối ăn mặc của người mình," *Hà Thành Ngọ Báo*, February 18, 1930; and T. T., "Cùng ai chưa hiểu rõ: Vấn đề phục sức," *Hà Thành Ngọ Báo*, March 8, 1930.
87. "Phong tục tiếng nói Nam-kỳ khác Bắc kỳ thế nào?" *Hà Thành Ngọ Báo*, May 24, 1933.

2. FASHION

88. Lang-Quê, "Ý kiến độc giả: Vấn đề ăn mặc của người Việt-Nam," *Trung Lập Báo*, June 16, 1932.
89. Song Nguyệt, "Lời chúng em: Phụ nữ với thời trang," *Hà Thành Ngọ Báo*, March 7, 1930.
90. Penny Edwards, "Restyling Colonial Cambodia (1860–1954): French Dressing, Indigenous Custom and National Costume," *Fashion Theory* 5, no. 4 (November 2021): 391.
91. In a brilliant study of the philosophical paradigms of Nguyễn An Ninh and Phan Văn Hùm, Judith Henchy argues that the intellectuals actively resisted the image of a primitive native. See Henchy, "Performing Modernity in the Writings of Nguyễn An Ninh and Phan Văn Hùm."
92. Homi Bhabha, "Of Mimicry and Man: The Ambivalence of Colonial Discourse," *Discipleship: A Special Issue on Psychoanalysis* 28 (Spring 1984): 125–33.
93. David Del Testa, "Workers, Culture, and the Railroads in French Colonial Indochina, 1905–1936," *French Colonial History* 2, no. 1 (2002): 181–98.
94. Phan Kế Bính, *Việt Nam phong tục (Moeurs et coutumes du Vietnam)*, 181.
95. "Chị em nữ học sanh nên mặc áo dài là phải," *Phụ Nữ Tân Văn*, October 27, 1932.
96. Lang-Quê, "Ý kiến độc giả: Vấn đề ăn mặc của người Việt-Nam," *Trung Lập Báo*, June 16, 1932.
97. In 1926, the Republican Government in China declared the *qipao* the national dress. See Wessie Ling, "Chinese Clothes for Chinese Women: Fashioning the Qipao in 1930s China," in *Fashion Forward*, ed. Alissa de Witt-Paul and Mira Crouch (Inter-Disciplinary Press, 2011), 353–65. In India, the Khadi was used to construct a common visual vocabulary for a nationalist movement in a country separated by language, religion, caste, class, and region to communicate their political dissent and their visions of community. See Trivedi, *Clothing Ghandi's Nation*. In her study of the American colonial period and the postcolonial period, Mina Roces found that "the label 'carer of national tradition' shifted between men and women in 20th century Philippines, but the status associated with it privileged men over women." See Roces "Gender, Nation, and the Politics of Dress in 20th Century Philippines."
98. Nguyễn Cát Tường, "Y phục của phụ nữ," *Phong Hóa*, February 23, 1934.
99. Martina Thucnhi Nguyen, *On Our Own Strength*.
100. Nguyễn Cát Tường, "Nhân dịp hội tơ lụa Hà Đông đổi mới y phục phụ nữ: Tính ưa đẹp và hay trang điểm," *Ngày Nay*, November 13, 1935.
101. Nguyễn Cát Tường, "Y phục của phụ nữ," *Phong Hóa*, February 23, 1934; Nguyễn Cát Tường, "Y phục của phụ nữ," *Phong Hóa*, March 2, 1934; and "Bà Trịnh Thục Oanh nói về thời trang," *Ngày Nay*, January 30, 1935.
102. Nguyễn Cát Tường, "Y phục của phụ nữ," *Phong Hóa*, February 23, 1934; Nguyễn Cát Tường, "Y phục của phụ nữ," *Phong Hóa*, March 9, 1934; Nguyễn Cát Tường, "Y phục của phụ nữ," *Phong Hóa*, March 16, 1934; and Nguyễn Cát Tường, "Tây hay Tàu," *Ngày Nay*, November 13, 1935.
103. Ling, "Chinese Clothes for Chinese Women."
104. "Một kiểu áo," *Ngày Nay*, November 13, 1935; and Việt Sinh, "Quần áo mới," *Ngày Nay*, January 30, 1935.
105. Nguyễn Cát Tường, "Y phục của phụ nữ," *Phong Hóa*, March 16, 1934; Nguyễn Cát Tường, "Mấy mẫu quần mới," *Phong Hóa*, May 4, 1934; and "Quần phụ nữ," *Ngày Nay*, November 13, 1935.

2. FASHION

106. Chiêu Anh Kế, "Trong Nam kỳ: Cô Hồng Vân với quần áo mới," *Ngày Nay*, March 10, 1935.
107. Nguyễn Văn Ký, *La Société Vietnamienne face à là modernité*, 252. A 1936 source claims that Nguyễn Thị Hậu, a student at the teacher's school, was the first to wear the tunic in Hanoi. Phan Thị Nga, "Một điều đáng chú ý trong phong trào phụ nữ," *Tràng An Báo*, March 20, 1936.
108. Phan Thị Nga, "Chị em Hội An với y phục Cát Tường," *Ngày Nay*, March 10, 1935.
109. Phạm Thảo Nguyên, *Áo dài Lemur và bối cảnh Phong Hoá và Ngày Nay*, 33.
110. Advertisement, "Quận Chúa," *Ngày Nay*, November 5, 1938.
111. Phan Thị Nga, "Chị em Hội An với y phục Cát Tường," *Ngày Nay*, March 10, 1935.
112. Advertisement, "Maison Mode," *Sài Gòn*, April 17, 1935.
113. Phạm Thảo Nguyên, *Áo dài Lemur và bối cảnh Phong Hoá và Ngày Nay*, 37.
114. "Y phục của phụ nữ có cần cải cách không?," *Công Luận Báo*, November 17, 1936.
115. Chiêu Anh Kế, "Cô Hồng Vân Quần Áo Mới," *Ngày Nay*, March 10, 1935.
116. Vũ Trọng Phụng, *Dumb Luck*, 69–70.
117. "Duy Tân," *Vịt Đực*, June 22, 1938.
118. Thanh Lâm, "Ông Nguyễn Cát Tường cùng y-phục phụ nữ," *Loa Tuần Báo*, April 26, 1934; and Thanh Lâm, "Y phục phụ nữ 'mo đéc' hay là kiểu 'Lemur' của ông Nguyễn Cát Tường," *Loa Tuần Báo*, May 17, 1934.
119. Thanh Lâm, "Y phục phụ nữ 'mo đéc' hay là kiểu 'Lemur' của ông Nguyễn Cát Tường," *Loa Tuần Báo*, May 17, 1934.
120. Tư Húi, "Công ty," *Loa Tuần Báo*, May 17, 1934.
121. Thanh Lâm, "Y phục phụ nữ 'mo đéc' hay là kiểu 'Lemur' của ông Nguyễn Cát Tường," *Loa Tuần Báo*, May 17, 1934.
122. Tư-Húi, "Mép thợ ngồi," *Loa*, July 5, 1934.
123. Thanh Lâm, "Họa sĩ Lemur và khoa mỹ thuật của ông ấy," *Loa Tuần Báo*, June 21, 1934.
124. Thanh Lâm, "Ông Nguyễn Cát Tường cùng y phục phụ nữ," *Loa Tuần Báo*, April 26, 1935.
125. Advertisement, "Lemur," *Ngày Nay*, November 18, 1939.
126. Thanh Lâm, "Y phục phụ nữ 'mo đéc' hay là kiểu 'Lemur' của ông Nguyễn Cát Tường," *Loa Tuần Báo*, May 17, 1934.
127. Thanh Lâm, "Ông Nguyễn Cát Tường cùng y phục phụ nữ," *Loa Tuần Báo*, April 26, 1935.
128. "Bộ cánh tân thời," *Loa*, July 18, 1935.
129. Far from being lackies for the colonial administration, many such collaboration-minded Indigenous politicians, particularly those in the Constitutionalist Party, argued for more economic and political rights for Vietnamese within the framework of the French colonial empire. See Ralph B. Smith, "Bui Quang Chieu and the Constitutionalist Party in French Cochinchina, 1917–1930," *Modern Asian Studies* 3, no. 2 (1969): 131–50; and Megan Cook, *The Constitutionalist Party in Cochinchina: The Years of Decline, 1930–1942* (Monash University Center of Southeast Asian Studies, 1977).
130. Taylor, "The Artist and the State," 60.
131. Herbelin, *Architectures du vietnam colonial*, 122–23.
132. "Một kiểu y phục nhà quê," *Phong Hóa*, June 1, 1934.
133. Martina Thucnhi Nguyen, *On Our Own Strength*, 79–81.

2. FASHION

134. Patrick Jory makes a similar argument in the case of the Phibun-era Thailand. See Jory, *A History of Manners and Civility in Thailand*, 123; and Norbert Elias, *The Civilizing Process: Sociogenetic and Psychogenetic Investigations* (Blackwell, 2000), 148.
135. "Xã Giao: Phục Sức," *Ngày Nay*, November 1, 1936; and Lang-Quê, "Ý kiến độc giả: Vấn đề ăn mặc của người Việt-Nam," *Trung Lập Báo*, June 16, 1932.
136. Côn Sinh, "Lối phục—sức của người mình: Hay các 'mốt' tân thời," *Hà Thành Ngọ Báo*, July 24, 1932.
137. "Xã Giao: Phép xử thế, Phục Sức," *Ngày Nay*, November 15, 1936; and "Xã Giao: Phục Sức," *Ngày Nay*, November 29, 1936.
138. "Xã Giao: Phục Sức," *Ngày Nay*, October 25, 1936.
139. "Xã Giao: Phép xử thế, Phục Sức," *Ngày Nay*, December 6, 1936.
140. "Bài học về xã giao và làm dáng của giáo sư Joan Harlow," *Đàn Bà Mới*, October 5, 1936; and "Xã Giao: Phép xử thế, Phục Sức," *Ngày Nay*, December 6, 1936.
141. "Xã Giao: Phép xử thế, Phục Sức," *Ngày Nay*, December 6, 1936.
142. "Xã Giao: Phục Sức," *Ngày Nay*, November 1, 1936.
143. "Xã Giao: Phục Sức," *Ngày Nay*, November 1, 1936; "Xã Giao: Phép xử thế, Phục Sức," *Ngày Nay*, November 15, 1936; and "Xã Giao: Phục Sức," *Ngày Nay*, November 29, 1936.
144. "Xã Giao: Phục Sức," *Ngày Nay*, November 1, 1936.
145. "Xã Giao: Phục Sức," *Ngày Nay*, November 22, 1936.
146. "Mốt," *Vịt Đực*, June 22, 1938.
147. "Xã Giao: Phục sức," *Ngày Nay*, November 1, 1936; "Phong tục tiếng nói Nam-kỳ khác Bắc kỳ thế nào?," *Hà Thành Ngọ Báo*, May 24, 1933; and "Chị em nữ học sinh nên mặc áo dài thì phải," *Phụ Nữ Tân Văn*, October 27, 1932.
148. Shoes were not to be worn inside the house in Vietnam, with the exception of house slippers. Considering that the uncomfortable and impractical kitten heels were new to Vietnam, it is understandable that one would automatically assume they were outside shoes.
149. Lang-Quê, "Ý kiến độc giả: Vấn đề ăn mặc của người Việt-Nam," *Trung Lập Báo*, June 16, 1932.
150. "Xã Giao: Phục Sức," *Ngày Nay*, November 1, 1936; and Lang-Quê, "Ý kiến độc giả: Vấn đề ăn mặc của người Việt-Nam," *Trung Lập Báo*, June 16, 1932.
151. Phi Khanh, "Đẹp và đẹp," *Đàn-Bà*, June 23, 1939.
152. "Trang nhã: trang sức cho hợp tuổi," *Đàn-Bà*, December 1, 1939.
153. Đoàn tâm Đan, "Bà Trịnh Thục Oanh nói về thời trang," *Ngày Nay*, January 30, 1935.
154. Phi Khanh, "Đẹp và đẹp," *Đàn-Bà*, June 23, 1939.
155. "Đẹp và đẹp," *Đàn-Bà*, April 21, 1939.
156. Cô Ngã, "Mốt," *Vịt Đực*, July 27, 1938.
157. Việt Sinh, "Quần áo mới," *Ngày Nay*, January 30, 1935.
158. Côn Sinh, "Lối phục—sức của người mình: Hay các "mốt" tân thời," *Hà Thành Ngọ Báo*, July 20, 1932; and Việt Sinh, "Quần áo mới," *Ngày Nay*, January 30, 1935.
159. Cát Tường, "Vài điều nên tránh," *Ngày Nay*, November 15, 1936.
160. "Xã Giao: Phục Sức," *Ngày Nay*, November 29, 1936.
161. Cát Tường, "Thời tiết với màu sắc y phục," *Ngày Nay*, September 20, 1936.
162. Cát Tường, "Thời tiết với màu sắc y phục," *Ngày Nay*, September 20, 1936.

163. M. H., "Đẹp và đẹp," *Đàn-Bà*, June 30, 1939.
164. Côn Sinh, "Lối phục—sức của người mình . . . Hay các 'mốt' tân thời," *Hà Thành Ngọ Báo*, July 20, 1932; and "Xã Giao: Phục sức," *Ngày Nay*, November 1, 1936.
165. Tố Quyên, "Y phục nữ Nam kỳ: chị em tân thời vẫn muốn mặc đẹp, nhưng lại không biết làm sao may mặc cho đúng theo ý muốn của mình!," *Công Luận Báo*, February 1, 1937.
166. Nhất Chi Mai, "Quần trắng áo lam," *Phong Hóa*, July 7, 1932.
167. Tố Quyên, "Y phục nữ Nam kỳ: chị em tân thời vẫn muốn mặc đẹp, nhưng lại không biết làm sao may mặc cho đúng theo ý muốn của mình!," *Công Luận Báo*, February 1, 1937.
168. "Xã Giao: Phục Sức," *Ngày Nay*, November 1, 1936.
169. Côn Sinh, "Lối phục—sức của người mình . . . Hay các 'mốt' tân thời," *Hà Thành Ngọ Báo*, July 20, 1932; and "Y Phục," *Đàn Bà Mới*, February 24, 1936.
170. Cát Tường, "Vài điều nên tránh," *Ngày Nay*, November 15, 1936.
171. "Xã Giao: Phục Sức," *Ngày Nay*, November 1, 1936; and Nguyễn Văn Ký, *La société Vietnamienne face à la modernité*, 243–44.
172. "Xã Giao: Phục Sức," *Ngày Nay*, November 1, 1936.

3. COSMETICS

1. This account of Kếu's internal conflict over cosmetics is a paraphrased summary of the story. Nguyễn Công Hoan, *Cô Kếu, gái tân thời*, 86–87. In *Truyện Ngắn Hay Chọn Lọc*. NXB Văn học, 2018.
2. This speaks to Kathy Peiss's argument that the businesses of cosmetics and fashion developed on different tracks. Kathy Peiss, "On Beauty . . . and the History of Business," *Enterprise & Society* 1, no. 3 (September 2000): 485–506.
3. Phan Thị Nga, "Chị em Hội An với y phục Cát Tường," *Ngày Nay*, March 10, 1935; "Ý kiến tự do—sự đẹp," *Phụ Nữ Tân Văn*, May 2, 1929; Dự Khuyết, "Nước hoa," *Ngày Nay*, September 27, 1936; and Phan Kế Bính, *Việt Nam phong tục (Moeurs et coutumes du Vietnam)*, vol. 2, trans. Nicole Louis-Hénard (École Française d'extrême-orient, 1980), 90–91.
4. Geoffrey Jones, *Beauty Imagined: A History of the Global Beauty Industry* (Oxford University Press, 2010), 62.
5. Holly Grout, *The Force of Beauty: Transforming French Ideas of Femininity in the Third Republic* (Louisiana State University Press, 2015), 25–29, 160–61; and Toby Slade, *Japanese Fashion: A Cultural History* (Berg, 2009), 118.
6. Grout, *The Force of Beauty*, 10; Jones, *Beauty Imagined*, 102–3, 125, 150; and C. Willet Cunnington and Phillis Cunnington, *The History of Underclothes* (Michael Joseph, 1951), 234.
7. "Người Huê Kỳ mỗi ngày xài hết bao nhiêu tiền son phấn?," *Phụ Nữ Tân Văn*, May 16, 1929.
8. The movement was known as "compassionate marriage" in the United States. Nancy F. Cott, "The Modern Woman of the 1920s, American Style," in *A History of Women in the West*, ed. Françoise Thébaud (Harvard University Press, 1994), 80–81.
9. Nguyễn Thanh Trừng, *Vision de la femme dans la littérature du Sud-Vietnam (de 1858 à 1945)* (L'Harmattan, 2012), 35.

3. COSMETICS

10. Harriet M. Phinney, "Objects of Affection: Vietnamese Discourses on Love and Emancipation," *Positions: East Asia Cultures Critique* 16, no. 2 (2008): 332–35; Đặng Thị Vân Chi, *Vấn đề phụ nữ trên báo chí tiếng Việt trước năm 1945* (NXB Khoa Học Xã Hội, 2008), 108–9; and Neil Jamieson, *Understanding Vietnam* (University of California Press, 1995), 125–26.
11. Hoàng Ngọc Phác, *Tố Tâm: Tâm-lý tiêu thuyết* (1925; repr. NXB Van Nghệ, 1988). The suicide epidemic was probably driven by the privations of the Great Depression. See Linh Vu, "Drowned in Romance, Tears, and Rivers: Young Women's Suicide in Early Twentieth Century Vietnam," *Explorations* 9 (Spring 2009): 36–37. Judith Henchy suggests that discussions of suicide among young women were a way of discussing "bourgeois ennui in a gendered way." Judith A. N. Henchy, "Performing Modernity in the Writings of Nguyễn An Ninh and Pham Văn Hùm," (PhD diss, University of Washington, 2005); and Nguyễn Van Ký, "Rethinking the Status of Vietnamese Women in Folklore and Oral History," in *Viêt-Nam Exposé: French Scholarship on Twentieth-Century Vietnamese Society* (University of Michigan Press, 2002), 102.
12. Nguyễn Thị Bạch Minh, "Chế độ da thê," *Phụ Nữ Tân Văn*, August 20, 1931.
13. Taking second, third, or subsequent wives was a solution for female infertility or low fertility, which in the early twentieth century was quite common due to an inability to conceive, prior injuries giving birth, or menopause.
14. Jennifer Boittin, *Colonial Metropolis: The Urban Grounds of Anti-Imperialism and Feminism in Interwar France* (University of Nebraska Press, 2010); Bruce McFarland Lockhart, *The End of the Vietnamese Monarchy* (Council on Southeast Asian Studies, Yale University, 1993), 88.
15. Phan Khôi, "Chữ trinh: Cái nết với cát tiết," *Phụ Nữ Tân Văn*, September 19, 1929.
16. Advertisement, "Tosika Powder," *Ngày Nay*, September 20, 1936; and Henchy, "Performing Modernity in the Writings of Nguyễn An Ninh and Pham Văn Hùm," 247–48.
17. Christina Firpo, *Black Market Business: Selling Sex in Northern Vietnam, 1920–1945* (Cornell University Press, 2020), 95.
18. John Michael Swinbank, "Girl with Lotus and M-16: the Equivocal Legacy of the École des Beaux-arts de l'Indochine 1924–1945," *World History Connected* 17, no. 3 (2020); Advertisement, "Crème Siamoise," *Phụ Nữ Tân Văn*, May 16, 1929; Advertisement, "Elizabeth Arden," *Ngày Nay*, December 27, 1935; Advertisement, "Pétrol Hanh," *Phụ Nữ Tân Văn*, November 19, 1931; and Advertisement, "Tho Radia," *Sài Gòn*, October 4, 1933.
19. Cosmetics advertisements were typically positioned on the third or fourth page of the newspaper, alongside advertisements for cigarettes, baby formula, diet pills, venereal disease remedies, furniture, and trading companies. Cosmetics advertisements targeted young and middle-aged literate women.
20. Advertisement, "Tokalon," *Phong Hóa*, September 20, 1935; Advertisement, "La velouty de dixor," *Hà Thành Ngọ Báo*, July 24, 1932; Advertisement, "Coty," *Ngày Nay*, October 18, 1936; and Advertisement, "Crème Siamoise," *Phụ Nữ Tân Văn*, May 16, 1929.
21. Anne McClintock, *Imperial Leather: Race, Gender and Sexuality in the Colonial Contest* (Routledge, 1995), 209.
22. Advertisement, "Mỹ Viện Amy," *Ngày Nay*, September 7, 1940.

3. COSMETICS

23. Geoffrey Jones, *Beauty Imagined*, 129–30; Advertisement, "Kéva," *Phụ Nữ Tân Văn*, May 9, 1929; and Advertisement, "Tokalon," *Hà Thành Ngọ Báo*, June 29, 1934.
24. Advertisement, "Tokalon," *Phong Hoá*, October 26, 1934.
25. Sumei Wang, ed., conclusion to *The East Asian Modern Girl: Women, Media, and Colonial Modernity During the Intewar Years* (Brill, 2021), 198.
26. Peter Zinoman, ed., introduction to *Dumb Luck: A Novel*, by Vũ Trọng Phụng, trans. Nguyệt Cầm Nguyễn (University of Michigan Press, 2002), 14–15.
27. Kathy Peiss, *Hope in a Jar: The Making of America's Beauty Culture* (University of Pennsylvania Press, 1998), 4.
28. Advertisement, "Tokalon," *Ngày Nay*, October 5, 1936.
29. Advertisement, "Forvil," *Hà Thành Ngọ Báo*, December 18, 1935.
30. Advertisement, "10 người hỏi xin cưới trong 1 tháng: Tại sao các đàn ông chết mệt về cô thiếu nữ này?," *Đông Pháp*, April 16, 1936.
31. Bà Đốc Kỳ, "Lại về vấn đề làm dáng," *Hà Thành Ngọ Báo*, March 22, 1929.
32. Advertisement, "Cécé Perfume," *Ngày Nay*, September 7, 1940; and Advertisement, "Tokalon," *Ngày Nay*, October 4, 1936.
33. Advertisement, "Forvil," *Hà Thành Ngọ Báo*, December 18, 1935.
34. Peiss, "On Beauty . . . and the History of Business," 496.
35. Advertisement, "Lux soap," *Hà Thành Ngọ Báo*, July 13, 1934; Advertisement, "Lux soap," *Công Luận Báo*, May 3, 1933; and Advertisement, "Cadum soap," *Hà Thành Ngọ Báo*, May 12, 1936. Advertisement, "Crème Simon," *Lục Tỉnh Tân Văn*, November 9, 1929.
36. Indeed, during World War I the rapid development of the Japanese chemical industry allowed for advancements in cosmetics and skin care. Yongmei Wu, "Colonial Modernity, Beauty, Health, and Hygiene: Centering on Japanese Cosmetics, Cleaning Supplies, and Medicine Advertisements in Shengjing Times (Shengjing Shibao)," in *The East Asian Modern Girl: Women, Media, and Colonial Modernity During the Intewar Years*, ed. Sumei Wang (Brill, 2021), 126.
37. Grout, *The Force of Beauty*, 159–60, 189–90; and Cott, "The Modern Woman of the 1920s, American Style," 88–90.
38. Advertisement, "Tokalon," *Ngày Nay*, October 4, 1936; and Advertisement, " Điều bí mật của người đàn bà không bao giờ già," *Đông Pháp*, May 22, 1938.
39. Advertisement, "Forvil," *Phụ Nữ Tân Văn*, April 26, 1934; and Advertisement, "Viễn Đệ products," *Hà Thành Ngọ Báo*, April 29, 1933.
40. Grout, *The Force of Beauty*, 173.
41. Dr. Alfred Curie was neither a radium scientist nor a member of the famous Curie family, and Marie Curie even took legal action against the company. Lucy Jane Santos, *Half Lives: The Unlikely History of Radium* (Pegasus, 2021); and Advertisement, "Tho Radia," *Sài Gòn*, October 4, 1933.
42. Grout, *The Force of Beauty*, 167–68.
43. Advertisement, "Crème Siamoise," *Phụ Nữ Tân Văn*, May 16, 1929.
44. Advertisement, "Dầu Kim Huệ," *Phụ Nữ Tân Văn*, September 25, 1930; and Advertisement, "Nước hoa 'Jasmin,'" *Phong Hoá*, June 2, 1933.
45. Advertisement, "Gibbs," *Đàn-Bà*, December 8, 1939; and Grout, *The Force of Beauty*, 166–67.
46. Advertisement, "Crème Siamoise," *Phụ Nữ Tân Văn*, May 16, 1929.

3. COSMETICS

47. "Grands Magasins Charner," *L'Echo Annamite*, November 27, 1924.
48. Advertisement, "Kéva," *Phụ Nữ Tân Văn*, May 16, 1929.
49. Grout, *The Force of Beauty*, 159–60.
50. "Tự nhiên trong vẻ đẹp," *Ngày Nay*, September 20, 1936; "Em muốn trẻ mãi: những phép tô điểm không cần son phấn," *Ngày Nay*, October 25, 1936; "Nước Da," *Ngày Nay*, July 19, 1936; "Trang điểm mùa hạ hai con," *Ngày Nay*, August 2, 1936; and "Một ngày kia em ngắm lại dung nhan," *Ngày Nay*, September 20, 1936.
51. Advertisement, Tho Radia, *Đàn-Bà*, April 7, 1939.
52. Advertisement, "Kéva," *Phụ Nữ Tân Văn*, May 16, 1929; Advertisement, "Kéva," *Phụ Nữ Tân Văn*, August 8, 1929; Advertisement, "Kéva," *Phụ Nữ Tân Văn*, July 3, 1930; Vân-Hoàn, "Mỹ-nhơn viện" của cô Madeleine Bùi, lênh-ái ông Bùi Quang Chiêu," *Hà Thành Ngọ Báo*, April 20, 1935; "Những điều đàn bà nào cũng nên biết—Phép giữ gìn cho còn thanh xuân và xinh đẹp," *Phụ Nữ Tân Văn*, August 8, 1929; Steven Zdatny, *Fashion, Work, and Politics in Modern France* (Springer Nature, 2006), 120; and Ngọc Lang, "Phép sửa sắc đẹp," *Khoa Học Tập Chí*, January 15, 1933.
53. Vân-Hoàn, "Mỹ-nhơn viện" của cô Madeleine Bùi, lênh-ái ông Bùi Quang Chiêu," *Hà Thành Ngọ Báo*, April 20, 1935; "Mỹ nhơn viện Madeleine," *Cộng Luận Báo*, April 15, 1935.
54. Advertisment, "Mỹ viện 'Ma Beauté,'" *Ngày Nay*, November 25, 1939.
55. Advertisement, "Mỹ viện Amy," *Đàn-Bà*, April 14, 1939; Advertisement, "Mỹ viện Amy," *Ngày Nay*, September 7, 1940; and Advertisement, "Mỹ viện Amy," *Đàn-Bà*, September 8, 1939.
56. "Cô nào xấu mà muốn hóa ra đẹp . . . thì đi nghe nữ bác sĩ A. Noel Diễn Thuyết," *Hà Thành Ngọ Báo*, April 17, 1932; "Nữ bác sĩ A. Noel tới Saigon," *Hà Thành Ngọ Báo*, April 28, 1932; Kathy Davis, "Cosmetic Surgery in a Different Voice: The Case of Madame Noel," *Women's Studies International Forum* 2, no. 5 (September-October 1999): 473–88; and Paula Martin, *Suzanne Noël: Cosmetic Surgery, Feminism and Beauty in Early Twentieth-Century France* (Taylor and Francis, 2014).
57. Advertisement, "Elizabeth Arden," *Ngày Nay*, December 27, 1935.
58. Mlle Lý Liên, "Một nghề mới cho chị em," *Nhật Tân*, October 17, 1934.
59. Advertisement, "Grand Salon de Coiffure," *Thời Vụ*, May 20, 1938; Advertisement, "Salon de coiffure Tương Lai," *Công Luận Báo*, April 26, 1932; and Advertisement, "Au Figaro," *Phụ Nữ Tân Văn*, September 25, 1930.
60. Eugenia Lean, *Vernacular Industrialism in China: Local Innovation and Translated Technologies in the Making of a Cosmetics Empire, 1900–1940* (Columbia University Press, 2020), 103–14.
61. Lean, *Vernacular Industrialism in China*, 79–119.
62. "Bôi lòng trắng trứng," *Ngày Nay*, September 13, 1936; "Nước Da," *Ngày Nay*, July 19, 1936; "Trang Điểm," *Ngày Nay*, November 25, 1936; and Phi Khanh, "Đẹp và đẹp," *Đàn-Bà*, June 9, 1939.
63. "Cách làm mặt nạ để bôi bổ da mặt," *Đàn-Bà*, September 22, 1939; and "Bôi lòng trắng trứng," *Ngày Nay*, September 13, 1936.
64. Grout, *The Force of Beauty*.
65. Cô Ngã, "Mốt," *Vịt Đực*, July 13, 1938.
66. "Tự nhiên trong vẻ đẹp," *Ngày Nay*, September 20, 1936.
67. Cát Tường, "Cách đánh phấn và sáp," *Ngày Nay*, August 16, 1936.

3. COSMETICS

68. M. H. "Một vài phương pháp đẹp," *Đàn-Bà*, May 19, 1939. In the 1920s, trimming the eyelashes was believed to help the lashes grow back fuller.
69. T. L. Hoàng, "Đẹp và đẹp," *Đàn-Bà*, November 17, 1939.
70. A 1939 *Đàn-Bà* newspaper article mentioned—and warned against—eyelash growth-enhancing drugs. Although it is not clear to which eyelash growth drug *Đàn-Bà* was referring, in 1938 the United States government passed the Food, Drug, and Cosmetics Act to regulate cosmetics in response to damage caused by eyelash products made with Paraphenylenediamine, which triggered allergic reactions that resulted in skin ulcerations around the eyes or even death. T. L. Hoàng, "Đẹp và đẹp," *Đàn-Bà*, November 17, 1939; Alice T. Gasch, "Lash Lure and Paraphenylenediamine: Toxic Beauty Past and Present," *American Academy of Ophthalmology*, November 2, 2017, https://www.aao.org/senior-ophthalmologists/scope/article/lash-lure-paraphenylenediamine-toxic-beauty; and Jones, *Beauty Imagined*, 102–3.
71. Mộng-Hoa, "Đẹp và đẹp," *Đàn-Bà*, July 14, 1939; and "Phụ Nữ: Đôi lông Mày," *Ngày Nay*, July 19, 1936.
72. Côn Sinh, "Lối phục—sức của người mình: Hay các 'mốt' tân thời," *Hà Thành Ngọ Báo*, July 20, 1932.
73. "Lông mày, nút ruồi, cặp vú," *Điễn Tín*, March 27, 1936.
74. Mikiko Ashikari, "The Memory of the Women's White Faces: Japaneseness and the Ideal Image of Women," *Japan Forum* 15, no. 1 (2003): 55–79; Slade, *Japanese Fashion*, 116; P. Huard, "Le noircissement des dents en Asie oriental et en Indochine," *France-Asie* 3 (July 1948): 808–12; "Mấy lời phân trần về bài 'Tục nhuộm răng của người mình' ở Phụ nữ tân văn số 54," *Phụ Nữ Tân Văn*, August 21, 1930; Đào Duy Anh, *Việt Nam văn hóa sử cương* (1938; repr. NXB Văn hóa-Thông tin, 2000), 214–14; Nguyễn Xuân Hiển, "Betel-Chewing in Vietnam: Its Past and Current Importance," *Anthropos* 101 (2006): 504–7; Mark W. McLeod and Nguyen Thi Dieu, *Culture and Customs of Vietnam* (Greenwood Press, 2001), 129; Nguyễn Văn Ký, *La Société Vietnamienne face à la modernité: Le Tonkin de la fin du XIXe siècle à la seconde guerre mondiale* (L'Harmattan, 1995), 233–34; E. Langlet, *Le Peuple Annamite: Ses moeurs, croyances et traditions* (Berger-Levrault, 1913), 89; Nhất Thanh, *Đất lề quê thói: Phong tục Việt Nam* (1970; repr. NXB Hồng Đức, 2016), 43; and Phan Kế Bính, *Việt Nam phong tục (Moeurs et coutumes du Vietnam)*, 187.
75. Ashikari, "The Memory of the Women's White Faces," 55–79; and Slade, *Japanese Fashion*, 116.
76. Huard, "Le noircissement des dents en Asie oriental et en Indochine," 808.
77. "Vài lời khuyên về sự săn sóc nơi miệng," *Phụ Nữ Tân Văn*, August 21, 1930; Nguyễn Văn Ký, *La Société Vietnamienne face à la modernité*, 233–34; and Advertisement, "Minh Sinh," *Phụ Nữ Tân Văn*, August 14, 1940.
78. "Xã Giao: Phép xử thế, Phục Sức" *Ngày Nay*, November 15, 1936; "Xã Giao: Phục Sức," *Ngày Nay*, November 29, 1936; and Nguyễn Văn Ký, *La Société Vietnamienne face à la modernité*, 233–34.
79. Cô Ngã, "Mốt," *Vịt Đực*, August 17, 1938.
80. Cô Duyên, "Miệng Cười," *Ngày Nay*, July 19, 1936; and Hue Tam Ho Tai, *Radicalism and the Origins of Vietnamese Revolution* (Harvard University Press, 1992), 93.
81. Huyền Cẩn, "Bước chân theo dịp dàn," *Ngày Nay*, March 10, 1935.
82. Cô Duyên, "Miệng Cười," *Ngày Nay*, July 19, 1936.

3. COSMETICS

83. "Trang nhã: trang sức cho hợp tuổi," *Đàn-Bà*, December 1, 1939.
84. Mailan, "Đẹp và đẹp," *Đàn-Bà*, December 1, 1939.
85. Kiều Vân, "Đẹp và đẹp," *Đàn-Bà*, April 28, 1939; and "Đàn bà mặc quần trắng," *Hà Thành Ngọ Báo*, September 2, 1929.
86. Advertisement, "Kolynos," *Công Luân Báo*, August 17, 1939.
87. "Rất lợi cho các bạn học sanh," *Cười*, October 1, 1937.
88. Advertisement, "Minh Sinh," *Phụ Nữ*, August 14, 1940; and Advertisement, "Tôi sẽ dự cuộc đấu sắc tại hội chợ Pháp Việt tới đây," *Công Luận Báo*, June 14, 1933.
89. Slade, *Japanese Fashion*, 118.
90. Sarah Schaffer, "Reading Our Lips: The History of Lipstick Regulation in Western Seats of Power," *Food and Drug Law Journal* 62, no. 1 (2007): 165–225.
91. Jessica Pallingston, *Lipstick: A Celebration of the World's Favorite Cosmetic* (Macmillan, 1999).
92. Cát Tường, "Cách đánh phấn phấn và sáp," *Ngày Nay*, August 23, 1936; and Cô Duyên, "Tô môi," *Ngày Nay*, August 2, 1936.
93. Cô Duyên, "Tô môi," *Ngày Nay*, August 2, 1936.
94. "Tự nhiên trong vẻ đẹp," *Ngày Nay*, September 20, 1936; and Cô Duyên, "Tô môi," *Ngày Nay*, August 2, 1936.
95. Cô Duyên, "Tô môi," *Ngày Nay*, August 2, 1936; Cát Tường, "Cách đánh phấn phấn và sáp," *Ngày Nay*, August 23, 1936; Mộng-Hoa, "Đẹp và đẹp," *Đàn-Bà*, July 14, 1939; Kiều Vân, "Đẹp và đẹp," *Đàn-Bà*, April 28, 1939; and Côn Sinh, "Lối phục—sức của người mình: Hay các 'mốt' tân thời," *Hà Thành Ngọ Báo*, July 20, 1932.
96. Cát Tường, "Cách đánh phấn và sáp," *Ngày Nay*, August 23, 1936; and Advertisement, "Sáp Mỡ Cô Ba," *Lục Tỉnh Tân Văn*, December 10, 1929.
97. Cô Duyên, "Tô môi," *Ngày Nay*, August 2, 1936; and Tiêu-liêu, "Mốt," *Vịt Đực*, June 29, 1938.
98. Phan Thị Bạch Vân, "Vài điều có ích cho chị em bạn gái," *Hà Thành Ngọ Báo*, January 20, 1928; and "Bạn Gái Điểm Trang," *Tin Mới*, August 14, 1940.
99. "Cái hôn mùi sâm," *Ngày Nay*, September 27, 1936.
100. Jones, *Beauty Imagined*, 62.
101. Eugenia Lean found a similar mode of disseminating skin-care knowledge in China. Lean, *Vernacular Industrialism in China*, 79–119.
102. Laurence Monnais and Noémi Tousignant, "The Colonial Life of Pharmaceuticals: Accessibility to Healthcare, Consumption of Medicines, and Medical Pluralism in French Vietnam, 1905–1945," *Journal of Vietnamese Studies* 1, no. 1–2 (February/August 2006): 141.
103. Cô Duyên, "Phụ nữ: Cách đánh phấn," *Ngày Nay*, July 26, 1936; and "Giữ dìn nhan sắc," *Ngày Nay*, November 8, 1936.
104. "Giữ dìn nhan sắc," *Ngày Nay*, November 8, 1936; Kiều Vân, "Đẹp và đẹp," *Đàn-Bà*, April 28, 1939; and Phi Khanh, "Đẹp và đẹp," *Đàn-Bà*, June 9, 1939.
105. "Các bà nên biết cách nằm ngủ," *Đàn-Bà*, November 27, 1936.
106. Yin was associated with bodily cooling and yang was associated with bodily heat; the yin and yang of the body could be controlled through the consumption of "hot" and "cold" foods. "Hot" foods, included spices such as chilis, garlic, and ginger, certain fruits such as mango, meats such as beef, chicken, and ham, and fried foods, among others. "Cool" foods included duck meat, seafood, sour foods,

certain vegetables, and most fruits. Over consumption of one led to a deficit of the other and thus an imbalance in the body's yin and yang energy. The result was a variety of health afflictions, most commonly seen in the skin. In the Vietnamese medical system, "hot" foods exacerbate skin conditions by upsetting the balance of yin and yang within the body, causing acne and other complexion problems.

107. Mộng Hoa, "Đẹp và đẹp," *Đàn-Bà*, July 28, 1939; and Phi Khanh, "Đẹp và đẹp," *Đàn-Bà*, June 9, 1939.
108. Kiều Vân, "Đẹp và đẹp," *Đàn-Bà*, April 28, 1939.
109. Phi Khanh, "Đẹp và đẹp," *Đàn-Bà*, June 9, 1939.
110. "Giữ dìn nhan sắc," *Ngày Nay*, November 8, 1936; "Ý kiến tự do—sự đẹp," *Phụ Nữ Tân Văn*, May 2, 1929; Mary Lynn Stewart, *For Health and Beauty: Physical Culture for Frenchwomen, 1880–1930s* (Johns Hopkins University Press, 2001), 60; and Grout, *The Force of Beauty*, 164.
111. Advertisement, "Keva," *Phụ nữ Tân Văn*, August 8, 1929.
112. Kiều Vân, "Đẹp và đẹp," *Đàn-Bà*, April 28, 1939; and Vân Đài, "Cái khăn mặt," *Ngày Nay*, December 6, 1936.
113. Advertisement, "Cadum soap," *Đàn Bà Mới*, February 17, 1936; and C. Đ., "Giữ vẻ đẹp," *Ngày Nay*, December 6, 1936.
114. Advertisment, "Savonnerie Nguyên Hữu," *Phụ Nữ Tân Văn*, August 20, 1931.
115. Mộng-Hoa, "Đẹp và đẹp," *Đàn-Bà*, July 14, 1939; Cô Bạch Vân, "Trang điểm," *Ngày Nay*, October 18, 1936; and Phan Thị Bạch Vân, "Vài điều có ích cho chị em bạn gái," *Hà Thành Ngọ Báo*, January 20, 1928.
116. C. Đ., "Giữ vẻ đẹp," *Ngày Nay*, December 6, 1936; Kiều Vân, "Đẹp và đẹp," *Đàn-Bà*, April 28, 1939; Cô Duyên, "Phụ nữ: Cách đánh phấn," *Ngày Nay*, July 26, 1936; and Cô Bạch Vân, "Trang điểm," *Ngày Nay*, October 18, 1936.
117. Advertisement, "Sữa Trường Xuân," *Phụ Nữ Tân Văn*, May 10, 1934; and Advertisement, "Crème Siamoise," *Phụ Nữ Tân Văn*, May 16, 1929.
118. Advertisement, "Tokalon," *Phong Hóa*, September 20, 1935; and Advertisement, "Điều bí mật của người đàn bà không bao giờ già," *Đông Pháp*, May 22, 1938.
119. Advertisement, "Madame Huỳnh Công Sáu," *Phụ Nữ Tân Văn*, June 22, 1932.
120. Advertisement, "Kéva," *Phụ Nữ Tân Văn*, August 8, 1929; Advertisement "Tokalon," *Nhật Tân*, November 7, 1934; and Advertisement, "Thuốc xứt mụn Vân Đài," *Phụ Nữ Tân Văn*, May 5, 1932.
121. "Bạn Gái Điểm Trang," *Tin Mới*, August 14, 1940.
122. "Trang nhã: Trang sức cho hợp tuổi," *Đàn-Bà*, December 1, 1939.
123. Alys Eve Weinbaum, Lynn Thomas, Priti Ramamurthy, and Uta G. Poiger, eds., *The Modern Girl Around the World* (Duke University Press, 2008), 38–39.
124. Huiliang Li found evidence dating back to the Eastern Jin Dynasty (317–420 CE) in which skin lighteners were developed from *Angelicae dahurica*, *Atractylodes macrocephala* Koidz, *Dictamnus dasycarpus* Turcz, *Ampelopsis japonica* (Thunb), Makino, *Aconitum coreanum* (Levl.), Raipaics, *Poria cocos* (Schw.), Wolf, *Vigna cylindrica* Skeels, *Beauveria bassiana* (Bals.), Vaillant, *Santalum album* L., *Gallus domesticus* Brisson, and *Benincasa hispida* (Thunb). See Cong Huiliang Li, "TMC in Skin Whitening and Lightening: The Eternal Pursuit in East Asia," *Global Cosmetics Industry*, April 4, 2013, https://www.gcimagazine.com/marketstrends/regions/bric/TCM-in-Skin-Whitening-and-Lightening-The-Eternal-Pursuit-in-East-Asia-201466981.html.

3. COSMETICS

125. Advertisement, "Crème Siamoise," *Phụ Nữ Tân Văn*, May 16, 1929; Advertisement, "Crème Siamoise," *Phụ Nữ Tân Văn*, May 16, 1929; Advertisement, "Butil," *Hà Thành Ngọ Báo*, June 6, 1934; and Advertisement, "Butil," *Hà Thành Ngọ Báo*, September 16, 1934.
126. Advertisement, "Tokalon," *Ngày Nay*, October 5, 1936; and Advertisement "Tokalon," *Nhật Tân*, November 7, 1934.
127. "Bạn Gái Điểm Trang," *Tin Mới*, August 14, 1940.
128. C. L. Jeunesse, "Đời tinh thần vật-chất và tình cảm của phụ-nữ Việt-Nam: Ăn mặc làm đỏm," *Đàn-Bà*, June 2, 1939.
129. M. H., "Đẹp và đẹp," *Đàn-Bà*, June 30, 1939.
130. Lois W. Banner, *American Beauty: A Social History . . . Through Two Centuries of the American Ideal* (Knopf, 1983), 225.
131. Đào Duy Anh, *Việt Nam văn hóa sử cương*, 244; and Jamieson, *Understanding Vietnam*, 105.
132. Banner, *American Beauty*, 225.
133. Đào Duy Anh, *Việt Nam văn hóa sử cương*, 244; and Jamieson, *Understanding Vietnam*, 105.
134. Banner, *American Beauty*, 225.
135. Jamieson, *Understanding Vietnam*, 105.
136. Vũ Trọng Phụng, *Dumb Luck*, 12.
137. Advertisement, "Kéva," *Phụ Nữ Tân Văn*, August 8, 1929.
138. Vân-Hoàn, "Mỹ-nhơn viện" của cô Madeleine Bùi, lệnh-ái ông Bùi Quang Chiêu," *Hà Thành Ngọ Báo*, April 20, 1935.
139. Advertisement, "Coty," *Ngày Nay*, October 18, 1936.
140. Advertisement "Tokalon," *Nhật Tân*, November 7, 1934; Advertisement, "Tokalon," *Tiểu Thuyết Thứ Bảy*, September 16, 1939; and Advertisement, " Điều bí mật của người đàn bà không bao giờ già," *Đông Pháp*, May 22, 1938.
141. Advertisement, "Tho Radia," *Sài Gòn*, October 4, 1933.
142. "Trang nhã: Trang sức cho hợp tuổi," *Đàn-Bà*, December 1, 1939.
143. Phi Khanh, "Đẹp và đẹp," *Đàn-Bà*, June 23, 1939.
144. Advertisement, "Kéva," *Phụ Nữ Tân Văn*, July 3, 1930.
145. Advertisement, "Tokalon," *Phong Hóa*, September 20, 1935.
146. C. Đ., "Giữ vẻ đẹp," *Ngày Nay*, December 6, 1936; M. H. "Một vài phương pháp đẹp," *Đàn-Bà*, May 19, 1939; and Phi Khanh, "Đẹp và đẹp," *Đàn-Bà*, June 23, 1939.
147. "Em muốn trẻ mãi: những phép tô điểm không cần son phấn," *Ngày Nay*, October 25, 1936.
148. Mộng Hoa, "Đẹp và đẹp," *Đàn-Bà*, July 28, 1939.
149. "Đi tìm phấn nụ Hoàng cung," *Sức Khoẻ Gia Đình*, April 3, 2016, https://suckhoegiadinh.com.vn/lam-dep/di-tim-phan-nu-hoang-cung-21458. Special thanks to Dịu Hương Nguyễn for pointing this out.
150. Advertisement, "Tokalon," *Ngày Nay*, October 4, 1936.
151. Advertisement, "Tosiko Powder," *Ngày Nay*, September 20, 1936.
152. Advertisement, "Phấn Xuân Hương," *Sài Gòn*, January 5, 1934; Advertisement, "Đại Quang Dược Phòng," *Phụ Nữ Tân Văn*, September 25, 1930. Trân châu phấn sold for $0.30 a box in 1939. See "Trân châu phấn," *Công Luận Báo*, August 17, 1939.
153. Cát Tường, "Cách đánh phấn và sáp," *Ngày Nay*, August 16, 1936; and Cát Tường, "Cách đánh phấn phấn và sáp," *Ngày Nay*, August 23, 1936.

3. COSMETICS

154. Cát Tường, "Cách đánh phấn phấn và sáp," *Ngày Nay*, August 23, 1936; Mộng-Hoa, "Đẹp và đẹp," *Đàn-Bà*, July 14, 1939; and T. L. Hoàng, "Đẹp và đẹp," *Đàn-Bà*, November 17, 1939.
155. Déel, "Mốt," *Vịt Đực*, September 28, 1938.
156. Grout, *The Force of Beauty*, 29.
157. Mộng-Hoa, "Đẹp và đẹp," *Đàn-Bà*, July 14, 1939.
158. Bích Dương, "Cách đánh phấn cho hợp màu áo," *Ngày Nay*, October 25, 1936; and Cát Tường, "Cách đánh phấn và sáp," *Ngày Nay*, August 16, 1936.
159. For humorous critiques of this problem, see "Mốt," *Vịt Đực*, August 21, 1938; "Mốt," *Vịt Đực*, September 21, 1938; and Cô Duyên, "Phụ nữ: Các đánh phấn," *Ngày Nay*, July 26, 1936.
160. Côn Sinh, "Lối phục—sức của người mình . . . Hay các 'mốt' tân thời," *Hà Thành Ngọ Báo*, July 20, 1932; Phan Thị Bạch Vân, "Vài điều có ích cho chị em bạn gái," *Hà Thành Ngọ Báo*, January 20, 1928; Mộng-Hoa, "Đẹp và đẹp," *Đàn-Bà*, July 14, 1939; Advertisement, "Butil," *Hà Thành Ngọ Báo*, June 6, 1934; and Advertisement, "Tokalon," *Ngày Nay*, October 4, 1936.
161. "Mốt," *Vịt Đực*, September 21, 1938.
162. The practice of shorn hair continued in Cambodia, Laos, and Siam through the nineteenth century. See Penny Edwards, "Restyling Colonial Cambodia (1860–1954): French Dressing, Indigenous Custom and National Costume," *Fashion Theory*, 5, no. 4 (2001): 389–416.
163. Jaimeson, *Understanding Vietnam*, 60.
164. Tam Hữu, "Mái tóc của phụ nữ tương lai," *Phụ Nữ Tân Văn*, June 28, 1934; Henri Joseph Oger, *Introduction Générale à l'étude de la technique du people annamites: Essai sur la vie matérielle, les arts et industries du peuple d'Annam* (Geuthner, 1908), 44–45; Trần Quang Đức, *Ngàn năm áo mũ: Lịch sử trang phục Việt Nam giai đoạn 1009–1945* (NXB Thế Giới, 2013), 351–52; "Muốn xinh hơn đàn bà Bắc-kỳ nên bỏ cái mốt cũ vấn khăn," *Hà Thành Ngọ Báo*, September 11, 1929; Nhất Thanh, *Đất lề quê thói: Phong tục Việt Nam*, 164–65; and Đào Duy Anh, *Việt Nam văn hóa sử cương*.
165. Men in Burma also went through a similar cultural discussion about hair. See Chie Ikeya, *Refiguring Women, Colonialism, and Modernity in Burma* (University of Hawaii Press, 2011), 100; and Bạch Ba, "Đức tính của phụ nữ đối với xã hội có ảnh hưởng gì chăng," *Trung Hòa Nhật Báo*, August 7, 1934.
166. Nguyễn Văn Ký, *La Société Vietnamienne face à la modernité*, 242; Phan Kế Bính, *Việt Nam phong tục*, 185; and Bạch Ba, "Đức tính của phụ nữ đối với xã hội có ảnh hưởng gì chăng," *Trung Hòa Nhật Báo*, August 7, 1934.
167. Advertisement, "Salon de coiffure Michel Phu," *Đông Pháp Nhật Báo*, February 5, 1926; and Advertisement, "Au Progrès Coiffeur," *Trung Lập Báo*, June 16, 1932.
168. Nguyễn Văn Ký, *La société Vietnamienne face à la modernité*, 243–44.
169. "Âu Châu bao giờ cũng là chị cả trong khu vũ 'mốt' của đàn bà." "Mốt di đen dâu," *Đàn-Bà*, August 25, 1939.
170. The bob appeared in both China and France before the war. Kee-Sun Lung, "The Politics of Hair and the Issue of the Bob in Modern China," *Fashion Theory: The Journal of Dress, Body, and Culture* 4, no. 1 (1997): 356; and Zdatny, *Fashion, Work, and Politics in Modern France*, 61–62, 73, 122–23.
171. Slade, *Japanese Fashion*, 124–25.

3. COSMETICS

172. Kee-Sun Lung, "The Politics of Hair," 356; and "Muốn làm 'bà lớn' không được theo mốt tóc ngắn," *Hà Thành Ngọ Báo*, June 9, 1935.
173. Huỳnh Thị Bảo Hòa, "Vì sao tôi cúp tóc," *Phụ Nữ Tân Văn*, August 31, 1933; Tố Quyên, "Y phục nữ Nam kỳ: chị em tân thời vẫn muốn mặc đẹp, nhưng lại không biết làm sao may mặc cho đúng theo ý muốn của mình!," *Công Luận Báo*, February 1, 1937; and "Xã Giao: Phục Sức," *Ngày Nay*, November 29, 1936.
174. Côn Sinh, "Lối phục—sức của người mình: Hay các 'mốt' tân thời," *Hà Thành Ngọ Báo*, July 20, 1932.
175. Nguyễn Cát Tường, "Một kiểu áo pyjama," *Phong Hóa*, August 3, 1934; and Nhất Thanh, *Đất lề quê thói: Phong tục Việt Nam*, 45.
176. Advertisement, "Pétrole Hahn," *Phụ Nữ Tân Văn*, November 19, 1930; and Advertisement, "Capri," *Ngày Nay*, September 7, 1940.
177. Advertisement, "Dầu Kim Huệ," *Phụ Nữ Tân Văn*, September 25, 1930; Advertisement, "Ba Cô," *Phụ Nữ Tân Văn*, April 13, 1933; Advertisement, "Viễn Đệ," *Hà Thành Ngọ Báo*, April 29, 1933; and Advertisement, "Ba Cô," *Khoa Học*, May 15, 1933.
178. Nguyễn Ngạc and Nguyễn Văn Luận, *Un Siècle d'Histoire de la Robe des Vietnamiennes* (Ministère de la Culture et de l'Éducation et de la Jeunesse, n.d.), 22; and Cô Thúy, "Đẹp và đẹp," *Đàn-Bà*, December 8, 1939.
179. Tam Hữu, "Mái tóc của phụ nữ tương lai," *Phụ Nữ Tân Văn*, June 28, 1934.
180. Huỳnh Thị Bảo Hòa, "Vì sao tôi cúp tóc," *Phụ Nữ Tân Văn*, August 31, 1933.
181. Mme Bạch Liên, "Ý kiến của tôi đối với việc cúp tóc," *Phụ Nữ Tân Văn*, June 21, 1934.
182. Tam Hữu, "Mái tóc của phụ nữ tương lai," *Phụ Nữ Tân Văn*, June 28, 1934.
183. Huỳnh Thị Bảo Hòa, "Vì sao tôi cúp tóc," *Phụ Nữ Tân Văn*, August 31, 1933; and Mme Bạch Liên, "Ý kiến của tôi đối với việc cúp tóc," *Phụ Nữ Tân Văn*, June 21, 1934.
184. Tam Hữu, "Mái tóc của phụ nữ tương lai," *Phụ Nữ Tân Văn*, June 28, 1934.
185. C. L. Jeunesse, "Đời tinh thần vật-chất và tình cảm của phụ-nữ Việt-Nam: Ăn mặc làm đỏm," *Đàn-Bà*, June 2, 1939; and Huỳnh Thị Bảo Hòa, "Vì sao tôi cúp tóc," *Phụ Nữ Tân Văn*, August 31, 1933.
186. Huỳnh Thị Bảo Hòa, "Vì sao tôi cúp tóc," *Phụ Nữ Tân Văn*, August 31, 1933. The author is referencing the nằm lửa, a mother roasting tradition from the early twentieth century when postpartum women were confined to bed over a burning stove, and women were secluded in a room and isolated after childbirth for one month, during which they could not bathe with water—but only a herbal steam bath. See Thuy Linh Nguyen, *Childbirth, Maternity, and Medical Pluralism in French Colonial Vietnam, 1880–1945* (University of Rochester Press, 2016), 39–40.
187. Huỳnh Thị Bảo Hòa, "Vì sao tôi cúp tóc," *Phụ Nữ Tân Văn*, August 31, 1933.
188. Nhất Thanh, *Đất lề quê thói: Phong tục Việt Nam*, 43–44; and Langlet, *Le Peuple Annamite*, 90.
189. Jones, *Beauty Imagined*, 102–3.
190. Nguyễn Cát Tường, "Cách trang điểm móng tay và móng chân," *Ngày Nay*, August 30, 1936.
191. Nguyễn Cát Tường, "Cách trang điểm móng tay và móng chân," *Ngày Nay*, August 30, 1936.

3. COSMETICS

192. Nguyễn Cát Tường, "Cách trang điểm móng tay và móng chân," *Ngày Nay*, August 30, 1936; Nguyễn Cát Tường, "Cách trang điểm móng tay và móng chân," *Ngày Nay*, September 6, 1936; M. H., "Một vài phương pháp đẹp," *Đàn-Bà*, May 19, 1939; and Cô Thị, "Đẹp và đẹp," *Đàn-Bà*, December 15, 1939.
193. "Ý kiến tự do—sự đẹp," *Phụ Nữ Tân Văn*, May 2, 1929.
194. The Industrial Revolution allowed for synthetic fragrances to be made from the extraction of essential oils from plants—often sourced in the colonies—which allowed the perfume industry to move away from the expensive practice of using whale fat. Moreover, in the 1890s, advancements in organic chemistry that isolated olfactory molecules made for a product composition that could be sold at an even more affordable price point. Jones, *Beauty Imagined*, 20–22.
195. Advertisement, *Phụ Nữ Tân Văn*, May 16, 1929; and Advertisement, "Sauzé," *Sài Gòn*, December 6, 1934.
196. Advertisement, "dầu Vạn," *Sài Gòn*, October 30, 1932.
197. Dự Khuyết, "Nước hoa," *Ngày Nay*, September 27, 1936.
198. "Xã Giao: Phép xử thế, Phục Sức," *Ngày Nay*, November 15, 1936; and "Xã Giao: Phục Sức," *Ngày Nay*, November 29, 1936.
199. Mlle Thanh Tâm, "Phấn son với đàn bà Đức," *Sài Gòn*, September 28, 1933.
200. Dự Khuyết, "Nước hoa," *Ngày Nay*, September 27, 1936; and Xã Giao: Phục Sức," *Ngày Nay*, November 29, 1936.
201. "Xã Giao: Phép xử thế, Phục Sức," *Ngày Nay*, November 15, 1936.
202. Mlle Thanh Tâm, "Phấn son với đàn bà Đức," *Sài Gòn*, September 28, 1933; Yvonne Barbara Houy, "Of Course the German Woman Should Be Modern: The Modernization of Women's Appearance During National Socialism," (PhD diss., Cornell University, 2002), 189–93; Irine Guenther, *Nazi Chic? Fashioning Women in the Third Reich* (Berg, 2004), 99–106; and Jones, *Beauty Imagined*, 124.
203. "Các cô thiếu nữ Tàu không được tự do?," *Sài Gòn*, August 22, 1934; "Muốn làm 'bà lớn' không được theo mốt tóc ngắn," *Hà Thành Ngọ Báo*, June 9, 1935; and Madeleine Y. Dong, "Who Is Afraid of the Chinese Modern Girl?," in *The Modern Girl Around the World: Consumption, Modernity, and Globalization*, ed. Alys Eve Weinbaum, Lynn M. Thomas, Priti Ramamurthy, and Uta G. Poiger (Duke University Press, 2008), 215–16.
204. "Ông Tùng Điền, thượng thư Bộ giáo dục Nhật Bản cấm nữ học sinh cắt tóc," *Hà Thành Ngọ Báo*, September 25, 1935.
205. Đông Bích, "Mấy điều mê tín," *Trung Hòa Nhật Báo*, December 2, 1933.
206. Nguyễn Thị Thanh Vân, "Quốc Dân Diễn Đàn," *Phụ Nữ Tân Văn*, July 24, 1930.
207. Mlle Thanh Tâm, "Phấn son với đàn bà đức," *Sài Gòn*, September 28, 1933.
208. Slade, *Japanese Fashion*, 118; Nguyễn Thị Thanh Vân, "Quốc Dân Diễn Đàn," *Phụ Nữ Tân Văn*, July 24, 1930.
209. Nguyễn Thị Thanh Vân, "Quốc Dân Diễn Đàn," *Phụ Nữ Tân Văn*, July 24, 1930.
210. "Dân Mỹ mở ra rất nhiều trường dạy làm duyên," *Hà Thành Ngọ Báo*, September 14, 1934.
211. Joan Harlow, "Bài học về xã giao và làm dáng của giáo sư Joan Harlow," *Đàn Bà Mới*, October 5, 1936.
212. Cô Ngọc Minh, "Hãy để ý đến: Cách ăn mặc của nữ học-sinh," *Đàn-Bà*, June 2, 1939.
213. Vũ Trọng Phụng, *Làm Đĩ* (1936; repr. NXB Văn hoa, 2010).

214. Tiêu-Liêu, "Mốt," *Vịt Đực*, June 29, 1938.
215. Cô Ngã, "Mốt," *Vịt Đúc*, July 20, 1938.
216. Trọng Lang, *Hà Nội lầm than* (1938; repr. NXB Hội Nhà Văn, 2015), 16.
217. Mỹ-Chân, "Lời chúng em: Trang sức," *Hà Thành Ngọ Báo*, April 28, 1930.
218. "Rổ rành đàn bà vào nghề son phấn," *Hà Thành Ngọ Báo*, September 18, 1929.
219. "Ý kiến của chị Hoàng Liên Bích, Ngã Tư sở," *Thông Tin*, April 25, 1943.
220. Hoàng-Đạo, "Phụ nữ ra ngoài xã hội," *Ngày Nay*, November 1, 1936.
221. Phan Săm Được, "Ý kiến của ông Phan Bội Châu đối với vấn đề phụ nữ," *Phụ Nữ Tân Văn*, July 4, 1929.
222. Cô Ngọc Minh, "Hãy để ý đến: Cách ăn mặc của nữ học-sinh," *Đàn-Bà*, June 2, 1939.
223. Mỹ-Chân, "Lời chúng em: cái nết đánh chết cái đẹp," *Hà Thành Ngọ Báo*, April 2, 1930.
224. Mỹ-Chân, "Lời chúng em: Trang sức," *Hà Thành Ngọ Báo*, April 28, 1930.
225. Cô Ngọc Minh, "Hãy để ý đến: Cách ăn mặc của nữ học-sinh," *Đàn-Bà*, June 2, 1939.
226. Mlle Thanh Tâm, "Phấn son với đàn bà Đức," *Sài Gòn*, September 28, 1933.
227. "Người Huê Kỳ mỗi ngày xài hết bao nhiêu tiền son phấn?," *Phụ Nữ Tân Văn*, May 16, 1929.
228. Cô Ngã, "Mốt," *Vịt Đực*, October 12, 1938.
229. Nguyễn Thị Thanh Vân, "Quốc Dân Diễn Đàn," *Phụ Nữ Tân Văn*, July 24, 1930.
230. That same year, Nhất Linh published Đoạn Tuyệt, a scathing rebuke of the relationship between young wives and their mother-in-law. Nhất Linh, *Đoạn Tuyệt* (1934; repr. NXB Hội Nhà Văn, 2016).
231. "Dân Mỹ mở ra rất nhiều trường dạy làm duyên," *Hà Thành Ngọ Báo*, September 14, 1934.
232. Đông-Bích, "Lỗi tại đàn bà," *Trung Hòa Nhật Báo*, August 18, 1934.
233. Phan Thị Bạch Vân, "Đông phương mỹ nhơn," *Đông Pháp Thời Báo*, October 20, 1927.
234. Nguyễn Thị Thanh Vân, "Quốc Dân Diễn Đàn," *Phụ Nữ Tân Văn*, July 24, 1930.
235. Phan Bội Châu, *Nữ quốc dân tu tri* (NXB KNXB, 1926), 23.
236. "Phụ nữ ta nên bớt xa xỉ," *Phụ Nữ Tân Văn*, February 25, 1932.
237. Mlle Thanh Tâm, "Phấn son với đàn bà Đức," *Sài Gòn*, September 28, 1933.
238. "Dân Mỹ mở ra rất nhiều trường dạy làm duyên," *Hà Thành Ngọ Báo*, September 14, 1934.

4. PHYSIQUE

1. *Trung Bắc Tân Văn*, June 23, 1940.
2. See Wang Ping, *Aching for Beauty: Footbinding in China* (Knopf Doubleday, 2002); Beverley Jackson, *Splendid Slipper: A Thousand Years of Erotic Tradition* (Ten Speed Press, 1997); and Fan Hong, *Footbinding, Feminism and Freedom: The Liberation of Women's Bodies in Modern China* (Frank Cass, 1997).
3. Email discussions with Kristen Brennan, May 5, 2022.
4. The khuê các woman is discussed in the Introduction. Also see Xiaorong Li, *Women's Poetry of Late Imperial China: Transforming the Inner Chambers* (University of Washington Press, 2012), 147.

5. Eugenia Lean, *Vernacular Industrialism in China: Local Innovation and Translated Technologies in the Making of a Cosmetics Empire, 1900–1940* (Columbia University Press, 2020), 96–97.
6. Mlle D. Luông, "Phụ nữ với chiếc xe đạp," *Công Luận Báo*, September 1, 1938.
7. "Phụ nữ và Thể thao," *Đông Pháp*, December 6, 1936; and "Chị em Nam Việt với quả bóng tròn," *Hà Thành Ngọ Báo*, June 6, 1933.
8. Thanh Lâm, "Y phục phụ nữ 'mo đéc' hay là kiểu 'Lemur' của ông Nguyễn Cát Tường," *Loa Tuần Báo*, May 17, 1934. See also "Phụ nữ với thể dục," *Hà Thành Ngọ Báo*, March 14, 1930; and "Chị em nam việt với quả bóng tròn," *Hà Thành Ngọ Báo*, June 9, 1933.
9. "Cô Hoàng Việt Nga nói về cuộc đi bộ Hanoi-Haiphong," *Hà Thành Ngọ Báo*, October 12, 1930. For sources referencing traditional ideal of thin bodies, see Cô Duyên, "Phái yếu," *Ngày Nay*, August 2, 1936; "Phụ nữ và thể thao," *Đông Pháp*, December 6, 1936; and C L Jeunesse, "Đời tinh thần vật-chất và tình cảm của phụ-nữ Việt-Nam: Ăn mặc làm đỏm," *Đàn-Bà*, June 2, 1939.
10. Nhất Thanh, *Đất lề quê thói: Phong tục Việt Nam* (1970; repr. NXB Hồng Đức, 2016), 45.
11. Thanh Lâm, "Y phục phụ nữ 'mo đéc' hay là kiểu 'Lemur' của ông Nguyễn Cát Tường," *Loa Tuần Báo*, May 17, 1934; Mỹ Chân, "Phụ nữ với thể dục," *Hà Thành Ngọ Báo*, March 14, 1930; and "Chị em nam việt với quả bóng tròn," *Hà Thành Ngọ Báo*, June 9, 1933.
12. Kristen L. Chiem, "Beauty Under the Willow Tree: Picturing Virtuous Women in 19th Century China," in *Modernity in the Arts of East Asia, 16th–20th Centuries*, ed. Kristen L. Chiem and Lara C. W. Blanchard (Brill, 2017), 90.
13. Trương Quí Bình, "Phụ nữ nước ta có nên tập thể thao không?," *Hà Thành Ngọ Báo*, September 9, 1929; "Chị em nam việt với quả bóng tròn," *Hà Thành Ngọ Báo*, June 9, 1933; Mỹ Chân, "Phụ nữ với thể dục," *Hà Thành Ngọ Báo*, March 14, 1930; Y-sĩ Đ.T., "Nịt vú," *Hà Thành Ngọ Báo*, March 8, 1929; and Trân Vân K., "Cùng các chị em bạn gái," *Hà Thành Ngọ Báo*, October 22, 1930.
14. Kiều Oanh, "Phụ nữ với thể dục," *Phụ Nữ Tân Văn*, April 21, 1932. See also Cô Duyên, "Phái yếu," *Ngày Nay*, August 2, 1936; and "Cô Hoàng Việt Nga noí về cuộc đi bộ Hanoi-Haiphong," *Hà Thành Ngọ Báo*, October 12, 1930.
15. Conversations with Kristen Brennan, May 5, 2022.
16. Thông Reo, "Làm cho rỏ mặt đàn bà nước Nam," *Trung Lập Báo*, March 21, 1931.
17. C L Jeunesse, "Đời tinh thần vật-chất và tình cảm của phụ-nữ Việt-Nam: Ăn mặc làm đỏm," *Đàn-Bà*, June 2, 1939.
18. "Cô Hoàng Việt Nga nói về cuộc đi bộ Hanoi-Haiphong," *Hà Thành Ngọ Báo*, October 12, 1930; and Cô Duyên, "Phái yếu," *Ngày Nay*, August 2, 1936.
19. "Bộ Ngực Đàn Bà," *Ngày Nay*, November 29, 1936; and Y-sĩ Đ.T., "Nịt vú," *Hà Thành Ngọ Báo*, March 8, 1929.
20. See the proverb "Đàn bà không vú lấy gì nuôi con"; and Y-sĩ Đ.T., "Nịt vú," *Hà Thành Ngọ Báo*, March 8, 1929.
21. Cô Duyên, "Bộ Ngực Đàn Bà," *Ngày Nay*, November 29, 1936.
22. Bà Triệu, of course, was the exception. As famous for her large breasts as she was for fighting off the Chinese in the third century, Bà Triệu was never shamed but also never portrayed as sexy until the twenty-first century. Y-sĩ Đ.T., "Nịt vú,"

4. PHYSIQUE

Hà Thành Ngọ Báo, March 8, 1929; Nguyễn Cát Tường "Y phục của phụ nữ," *Phong Hóa*, March 23, 1934; Cát Tường, "Một môn thể thao 'cách luyện bộ ngực,'" *Phong Hóa*, June 15, 1934; and Cô Duyên, "Bộ Ngực Đàn Bà," *Ngày Nay*, November 29, 1936.

23. Y-sĩ Đ.T., "Nịt vú," *Hà Thành Ngọ Báo*, March 8, 1929; Nguyễn-Ngạc and Nguyễn Văn Luận, *Un Siècle d'Histoire de la Robe des Vietnamiennes* (Ministère de la Culture de l'Éducation et de la Jeunesse, n.d.), 18; and Nguyễn Văn Ký, *La Société Vietnamienne face à là modernité: Le Tonkin de la fin du XIXe siècle à la seconde guerre mondiale* (L'Harmattan,1995), 252.
24. Catherine Méneux, "'Initier nos colonies d'Indo-Chine à l'art Français': La section Beaux-Arts à l'exposition international de Hanoi (1902–1903)," in *Sociétés, expositions et revues dans l'empire français, 1851–1940*, ed. Dominique Jarrassé and Laurent Houssais (Editions Esthétiques du Divers, 2015), 59–72; Penny Edwards, "'Propagender': Marianne, Joan of Arc and the Export of French Gender Ideology to Colonial Cambodia (1863–1954)," in *Promoting the Colonial Idea: Propaganda and Visions of Empire in France*, ed. Tony Chafuer and Amanda Sackur (Palgrave Macmillan, 2002), 116–30; Nicola J. Cooper, "Gendering the Colonial Enterprise: La Mère-Patrie and Maternalism in France and French Indochina," in *Empires and Boundaries: Rethinking Race, Class, and Gender in Colonial Settings*, ed. Harald Fischer-Tiné and Susanne Gehrmann (Routledge, 2008); and Marilyn Yalom, *A History of the Breast* (Knopf, 1998), 128, 139, 184.
25. See Ruth Rogaski, *Hygienic Modernity: Meanings of Health and Disease in Treaty-Port China* (University of California Press, 2004).
26. France, of course, manufactured the famous Marseille soap for centuries, but it was not until the late nineteenth century that the French embraced personal hygiene. With the Industrial Revolution, soap production was easier and prices fell, enabling it to be sold throughout the world. The concurrent Haussmann renovations of Paris brought running water into individual homes and apartments, facilitating good hygiene practices. Geoffrey Jones, *Beauty Imagined: A History of the Global Beauty Industry* (Oxford University Press, 2010), 70–73.
27. Mary Lynn Stewart, *For Health and Beauty: Physical Culture for Frenchwomen, 1880s–1930s* (Johns Hopkins University Press, 2001), 2.
28. See Chiara Formichi, *Healthy Progress: Muslim Women as Modernizers in Twentieth Century Indonesia* (Stanford University Press, 2025); William Johnston, *A History of Tuberculosis in Japan* (Harvard University Press, 1995); Rogaski, *Hygienic Modernity*; and Warwick Anderson, *Colonial Pathologies: American Tropical Medicine, Race, and Hygiene in the Philippines* (Duke University Press, 2006).
29. Laurence Monnais, *Médecine et colonization: L'aventure indochinois* (CNRS Editions, 1999); Vũ Trọng Phụng, *Luc Xi: Prostitution and Venereal Disease in Colonial Hanoi*, trans. Shaun Kingsley Malarney (University of Hawaii Press, 2011); Christina Firpo, *Black Market Business: Selling Sex in Northern Vietnam 1920–1945* (Cornell University Press, 2020), 59–89; and Annick Guénel, "The Creation of the First Overseas Pasteur Institute, or the Beginning of Albert Calmette's Pastorian Career," *Medical History* 43, no. 1 (1999): 1–25.
30. Gwendolyn Wright, *The Politics of Design in French Colonial Urbanism* (University of Chicago Press, 1991), 183.

4. PHYSIQUE

31. "XIIe Foire de Hanoi, 25 Novembre au 9 décembre 1934, Catalogue official; 3eme Foire de Hué: Fetes de paques du 15 au 24 avril 1938, program official," 1938; and B. "Hội chợ Faifoo đã khai mạc" *Sài Gòn*, May 29, 1936.
32. For the metropole, see Stewart, *For Health and Beauty*, 56–74. In Vietnamese schools, see "Les Âu Trĩ Viên et la diffusion de l'hygiène élémentaire dans les villages," *Nam Phong*, September 1922, and for the state newspaper, see "Vệ sanh thể dục tạp chí," *Công Luận Báo*, September 18, 1925.
33. Advertisement, "Savon Lux," *L'Avenir du Tonkin*, March 18, 1937; Advertisement, "Cadum," *Đàn Bà Mới*, February 17, 1936; and "Savon Palmolive," *Đàn Bà Mới*, February 24, 1936.
34. Advertisement, "Savon Viêt-Nam," *La Tribune Indochinoise*, April 12, 1935; Advertisement, "Savonnerie Nguyên Hữu," *Phụ Nữ Tân Văn*, August 20, 1931; and Martin Murray, *The Development of Capitalism in Colonial Indochina (1870–1940)* (University of California Press, 1980), 348.
35. "Mấy lời tóm tắt về phép vệ sinh," *Nam Phong*, issue 19, n.d., 42–44.
36. Jong-Chan Lee, "Hygienic Governance and Military Hygiene in the Making of Imperial Japan, 1868–1912," *Historia Scientiarum: International Journal of the History of Science Society of Japan* 18, no. 1 (2008): 1–23.
37. Yongmei Wu, "Colonial Modernity, Beauty, Health, and Hygiene: Centering on Japanese Cosmetics, Cleaning Supplies, and Medicine Advertisements in Shengjing Times (Shengjing Shibao)," in *The East Asian Modern Girl: Women, Media, and Colonial Modernity During the Interwar Years*, ed. Sumei Wang (Brill, 2021), 101–2; Lean, *Vernacular Industrialism in China*, 97.
38. Advertisment, "Savonnerie Nguyên Hữu," *Phụ Nữ Tân Văn*, August 20, 1931; Marta Lopatkova, "Văn quốc ngữ: Teaching Modernity Through Classics," in *Southeast Asian Education in Modern History: Schools, Manipulation, and Contest*, ed. Pia Jolliffe and Thomas Bruce (Routledge, 2018), 103–21.
39. Cô Duyên, "Đàn bà ngày nay," *Ngày Nay*, August 16, 1936.
40. Hue Tam Ho Tai, *Radicalism and the Origins of Vietnamese Revolution* (Harvard University Press, 1992), 100.
41. Martina Thucnhi Nguyen, *On Our Own Strength: The Self-Reliant Literary Group and Cosmopolitan Nationalism in Late Colonial Vietnam* (University of Hawaii Press, 2021), 187.
42. Holly Grout, *The Force of Beauty: Transforming French Ideas of Femininity in the Third Republic* (Louisiana State University Press, 2015), 25, 40; and Stewart, *For Health and Beauty*, 59–62.
43. Trang-Tử, "Ai bảo Công-Luận Báo không có tri âm?," *Đông Pháp Thời Báo*, September 2, 1925.
44. For the best example, see "Ý kiến tự do—sự đẹp," *Phụ Nữ Tân Văn*, May 2, 1929.
45. Advertisement, "Keva," *Phụ Nữ Tân* Văn, August 8, 1929.
46. "Le sport signe des temps," *La Tribune Indochinoise*, January 25, 1923; Agathe Larcher-Goscha, "Sports, colonialism et identiés nationales: première approches du 'corps à corps colonial' en Indochine (1918–1945)," in *De l'Indochine à l'Algerie: la jeunesse en movement des deux côtés du miroir colonial, 1940–1962*, ed. Nicolas Bancel, Daniel Denis, and Youssef Fates (Éditions la Découverte, 2003), 16–18.
47. Janice N. Brownfoot, "'Healthy Bodies, Healthy Minds': Sport and Society in Colonial Malaya," *International Journal of the History of Sport* 19, no. 2–3 (2010): 129–56.

4. PHYSIQUE

48. Stewart, *For Health and Beauty*, 155; Anne Raffin, *Youth Mobilization in Vichy Indochina and Its Legacies, 1940–1970* (Lexington, 2005), 32; and Joan Tumblety, *Remaking the Male Body: Masculinity and the Uses of Physical Culture in Interwar and Vichy France* (Oxford University Press, 2012), 2–3.
49. Although Vietnamese were never officially barred from the Cercle Sportif, few frequented it. In 1922, attempts were made to organize an Indigenous Cercle Sportif, but the club never came to fruition. Agathe Larcher-Goscha, "Du Football au Vietnam (1905–1949): Colonialism, culture sportive et sociabilités en jeux," *Outre-Mers* 96, no. 364 (2009): 81.
50. Physical education became a key component of the Franco-Annamite curriculum, especially during the Popular Front years. Larcher-Goscha, "Du Football au Vietnam (1905–1949)," 68; and Raffin, *Youth Mobilization in Vichy Indochina and Its Legacies*, 41.
51. Physical education classes were introduced as part of the 1918 Code of Public Instruction that founded the colonial education system. "Lịch sử trường thể dục ở Hà Nội," *Nam Phong* 53 (1922): 286–90; and Trịnh Đình Báu, "Bàn về thể thao: Nên tập lối cử động đều và mạnh," *Hà Thành Ngọ Báo*, February 24, 1930.
52. "Thanh niên và thể dục của nước ta ngày nay," *Đông Pháp*, January 22, 1931; and Chu Xước Dư, "Vấn đề thể dục," *Nam Phong* 63 (n.d.), 21–38.
53. Larcher-Goscha, "Sports, colonialism et identiés nationales: première approaches du 'corps à corps colonial' en Indochine (1918–1945)," 13–31.
54. Advertisement, "Ovamaltine," *La Tribune Indochinoise*, July 30, 1937.
55. Advertisement, "Nguyễn Vân Trân," *Phụ Nữ Tân Văn*, May 9, 1929; Adveriesment, "Maison Giao Sports," *Công Luận Báo*, August 17, 1937.
56. Chu Xước Dư, "Vấn đề thể dục," *Nam Phong* 63 (n.d), 21–38; and "Tin thể thao," *Đông Pháp*, February 12, 1932.
57. Larcher-Goscha, "Du Football au Vietnam (1905–1949)," 82.
58. Trịnh Đình Bàu, "Bàn về thể thao: Nên tập lối cử động đều và mạnh," *Hà Thành Ngọ Báo*, February 24, 1930.
59. Chu Xước Dư, "Vấn đề thể dục," *Nam Phong* 63 (n.d.), 21–38; Trịnh Đình Báu, "Bàn cóp về việc: Phụ nữ nước ta có nên tập thể thao không?" *Hà Thành Ngọ Báo*, September 13, 1929; and "Phụ nữ và thể thao," *Đông Pháp*, December 6, 1936.
60. "Lịch sử trường thể dục ở Hà Nội," *Nam Phong* 53 (1922), 286–90; Chu Xước Dư, "Vấn đề thể dục," *Nam Phong* 63 (n.d.), 21–38; and Pierre Brocheux and Daniel Hémery, *Indochina: An Ambiguous Colonization, 1858–1954* (University of California Press, 2009), 39–40.
61. Larcher-Goscha, "Sports, colonialism et identiés nationales," 20; Agathe Larcher-Goscha, "La guerre des representations anthropometriques," in *La Colonisation des Corps: de l'Indochine au Viet Nam*, ed. François Guillemot and Agathe Larcher-Goscha (Vendémiaire, 2014), 104–5, 118.
62. "Lịch sử trường thể dục ở Hà Nội," *Nam Phong* 53 (1922), 286–90.
63. Hồng Nhân, "Thể thao," *Nam Phong* 175 (August 1932), 165–73.
64. Trân Vân K., "Cùng các chị em bạn gái," *Hà Thành Ngọ Báo*, October 22, 1930.
65. "Tin thể thao," *Đông Pháp*, February 12, 1932.
66. Hồng Nhân, "Thể thao," *Nam Phong* 175 (August 1932), 165–73; and Chu Xước Dư, "Vấn đề thể dục," *Nam Phong* 63 (n.d.), 21–38.

67. Vũ Trọng Phụng, *Dumb Luck: A Novel*, trans. Nguyệt Cầm Nguyễn, ed. Peter Zinoman (University of Michigan Press, 2002), 64–65, 74.
68. Judith A. N. Henchy, "Performing Modernity in the Writings of Nguyễn An Ninh and Phạm Văn Hùm" (PhD diss., University of Washington, 2005), 249.
69. Trịnh Đình Báu, "Bàn cóp về việc: Phụ nữ nước ta có nên tập thể thao không?," *Hà Thành Ngọ Báo*, September 13, 1929.
70. Vũ Trọng Phụng, *Dumb Luck*, 38–41.
71. Việt Bằng, "Dân thể thao Hà Thành đón cô Hồ Thị Lích," *Vịt Đực*, September 14, 1938.
72. Nguyễn Công Hoan, "Tinh thần thể dục [II]," in *Nguyễn Công Hoan Người ngựa ngựa người* (NXB văn học, 2016), 196–202.
73. Nguyễn Công Hoan, "Tinh thần thể dục [II]," 189–95.
74. Nguyễn Công Hoan, "Tinh thần thể dục [II]," 196–202.
75. "Phụ nữ với thể tháo: bà đốc nghĩa đã giựt chức vô địch ping pong," *Sài Thành*, May 11, 1932.
76. Kiều Oanh, "Phụ nữ với thể dục," *Phụ Nữ Tân Văn*, April 21, 1932; and Janice N. Brownfoot, "Emancipation, Exercise and Imperialism: Girls and the Games Ethic in Colonial Malaya," *International Journal of the History of Sport* 7, no. 3 (2007): 61–84.
77. Trương Quí Bình, "Phụ nữ nước ta có nên tập thể thao không?," *Hà Thành Ngọ Báo*, September 9, 1929; Mỹ Chân, "Phụ nữ với thể thao," *Hà Thành Ngọ Báo*, August 11, 1930; and "Le Meilleur sport féminin," *La Dépêche d'Indochine*, December 21, 1933.
78. Nguyễn Thị Thục Quyên, "Oanh vàng thỏ thẻ," *Đông Phương*, December 29, 1939.
79. See Yunxiang Gao, *Sporting Gender: Women Athletes and Celebrity-Making During China's National Crisis, 1931–1945* (University of British Columbia Press, 2013).
80. Việt Bằng, "Dân thể thao Hà Thành đón cô Hồ Thị Lích," *Vịt Đực*, September 14, 1938; and "Chuyện Đó, Đây," *Tràng An báo*, June 3, 1938.
81. "Phụ nữ với thể thao: bà đốc nghĩa đã giựt chức vô địch ping pong," *Sài Gòn*, May 11, 1932; and Brocheux and Hémery, *Indochina: An Ambiguous Colonization*, 240.
82. "Cô Hoàng Việt Nga nói về cuộc đi bộ Hanoi-Haiphong," *Hà Thành Ngọ Báo*, October 12, 1930; and Nguyễn Thị Kế, "Cô Việt Hoang Thị Kế nữ học sinh trường Cholon định xướng lên một cuộc đi xe đạp từ nam ra bắc," *Hà Thành Ngọ Báo*, April 2, 1931.
83. M. D., "Cô Phan Thị Nga lên diễn đàn," *Hà Thành Ngọ Báo*, September 13, 1934.
84. Larcher-Goscha, "Sports, colonialism et identiés nationales," 16–17.
85. Bích Thủy, "Mấy lời ngỏ cùng các chị em sính tập thể thao," *Hà Thành Ngọ Báo*, June 6, 1929.
86. Henriette Celarié, *Promenade en Indochine* (Éditions Baudinière, 1937), 176.
87. Bích Thủy, "Mấy lời ngỏ cùng các chị em sính tập thể thao," *Hà Thành Ngọ Báo*, June 6, 1929; and "Cùng các chị em bạn gái," *Hà Thành Ngọ Báo*, October 22, 1930.
88. Nguyễn Thị Kế, "Cô Việt Hoang Thị Kế nữ học sinh trường Cholon định xướng lên một cuộc đi xe đap từ nam ra bắc," *Hà Thành Ngọ Báo*, April 2, 1931.
89. Trân Vân K., "Cùng các chị em bạn gái," *Hà Thành Ngọ Báo*, October 22, 1930; and Bích Thủy, "Mấy lời ngỏ cùng các chị em sính tập thể thao," *Hà Thành Ngọ Báo*, June 6, 1929.

4. PHYSIQUE

90. Trương Quí Bình, "Phụ nữ nước ta có nên tập thể thao không?," *Hà Thành Ngọ Báo*, September 9, 1929.
91. H. S., "'Con ngựa sắt' chẳng còn là một thứ đồ dùng riêng của đàn ông: Chị em Hải Cảng đã nhiều người tập xe đạp để dùng đi cho tiện việc," *Hà Thành Ngọ Báo*, August 19, 1930. For interesting interpretations on the degree to which competitive sports led to women's emancipation in China, see Hong, *Footbinding, Feminism and Freedom*; Andrew Morris, *Marrow of the Nation: A History of Sports and Physical Culture in Republican China* (University of California Press, 2004), 141; and Gao, *Sporting Gender*.
92. VC An, "Thơ ở bên Paris gởi về biểu đồng tình với bài" vấn đề cải cách phụ nữ," *Phụ Nữ Tân Văn*, April 28, 1932.
93. Bích Thủy, "Mấy lời ngỏ cùng các chị em sính tập thể thao," *Hà Thành Ngọ Báo*, June 6, 1929.
94. Kiều Oanh, "Phụ nữ với thể dục," *Phụ Nữ Tân Văn*, April 21, 1932; and "Các cuộc diễn thuyết trong Hội chợ phụ nữ: dục anh, hôn nhân, và thể thao," *Phụ Nữ Tân Văn*, April 28, 1932.
95. "Phụ nữ với thể thao: bà đốc nghĩa đã giựt chức vô địch ping pong," *Sài Gòn*, May 11, 1932; Bích Thủy, "Mấy lời ngỏ cùng các chị em sính tập thể thao," *Hà Thành Ngọ Báo*, June 6, 1929; and "Bà đốc nghĩa đã giựt chức vô địch ping pong," *Sài Gòn*, May 4, 1932.
96. "Bà đốc nghĩa đã giựt chức vô địch ping pong," *Sài Gòn*, May 4, 1932; Trịnh Đình Báu, "Bàn cóp về việc: Phụ nữ nước ta có nên tập thể thao không?" *Hà Thành Ngọ Báo*, September 13, 1929; Trương Quí Bình, "Phụ nữ nước ta có nên tập thể thao không?," *Hà Thành Ngọ Báo*, September 9, 1929; "Cùng các chị em bạn gái," *Hà Thành Ngọ Báo*, October 22, 1930; "Phụ nữ và thể thao," *Đông Pháp*, December 6, 1936; M. D., "Cô Phan Thị Nga lên diễn đàn," *Hà Thành Ngọ Báo*, September 13, 1934; "Phụ nữ và thể thao," *Đông Pháp*, December 6, 1936; and Cô Duyên, "Đàn bà ngày nay," *Ngày Nay*, August 16, 1936.
97. "Cùng các chị em bạn gái," *Hà Thành Ngọ Báo*, October 22, 1930.
98. Mỹ Chân, "Phụ nữ với thể dục," *Hà Thành Ngọ Báo*, March 14, 1930.
99. Mme Nguyễn Đức Nhuận, "Phụ nữ ta nên lưu tâm đến vấn đề thể dục," *Phụ Nữ Tân Văn*, July 24, 1930.
100. H. S., "'Con ngựa sắt' chẳng còn là một thứ đồ dùng riêng của đàn ông: Chị em Hải Cảng đã nhiều người tập xe đạp để dùng đi cho tiện việc," *Hà Thành Ngọ Báo*, August 19, 1930.
101. "Cô Hoàng Việt Nga nói về cuộc đi bộ Hanoi-Haiphong," *Hà Thành Ngọ Báo*, October 12, 1930.
102. Mme Nguyễn Đức Nhuận, "Phụ nữ ta nên lưu tâm đến vấn đề thể dục," *Phụ Nữ Tân Văn*, July 24, 1930.
103. Nguyễn Thị Kế, "Cô Viết Hoang Thị Kế nữ học sinh trường Cholon định xướng lên một cuộc đi xe đạp từ nam ra bắc," *Hà Thành Ngọ Báo*, April 2, 1931.
104. Trịnh Đình Báu, "Bàn cóp về việc: Phụ nữ nước ta có nên tập thể thao không?," *Hà Thành Ngọ Báo*, September 13, 1929.
105. "Phụ nữ với thể thao: Phụ nữ Việt Nam ta nên đi xe máy đạp," *Trung Lập Báo*, February 3, 1932.
106. Pierre Bourdieu, "Sport and Social Class," *Social Science Information* 17 (1978): 819–40.

107. Caroline Herbelin, *Architectures du Vietnam Colonial: Repenser le métissage* (Institute National d'histoire d'art, 2016), 120.
108. Vũ Trọng Phụng, *Dumb Luck*, 38–41.
109. "???," *Phụ Nữ Tân Văn*, July 24, 1930; "Phụ nữ với thể tháo: bà đốc nghĩa đã giựt chức vô địch ping pong," *Sài Thành*, May 11, 1932.
110. Interview with Quy Ha, San Luis Obispo, California, March 1, 2022.
111. "Thanh niên và thể dục của nước ta ngày nay," *Đông Pháp*, January 22, 1931.
112. Nguyễn Thị Kế, "Cô Việt Hoang Thị Kế nữ học sinh trường Cholon định xướng lên một cuộc đi xe đạp từ nam ra bắc," *Hà Thành Ngọ Báo*, April 2, 1931.
113. "Cô Hoàng Việt Nga nói về cuộc đi bộ Hanoi-Haiphong," *Hà Thành Ngọ Báo*, October 12, 1930.
114. "Cô Hoàng Việt Nga nói về cuộc đi bộ Hanoi-Haiphong," *Hà Thành Ngọ Báo*, October 12, 1930; Nguyễn Thị Kế, "Cô Việt Hoang Thị Kế nữ học sinh trường Cholon định xướng lên một cuộc đi xe đạp từ nam ra bắc," *Hà Thành Ngọ Báo*, April 2, 1931; and "Về tin cô Lê Thị Thắm đến Hanôi," *Phụ Nữ Tân Văn*, June 25, 1931.
115. "Thanh niên và thể dục của nước ta ngày nay," *Đông Pháp*, January 22, 1931; "Cô Hồ Tố Quyên nhỏ của ta. Một bạn gái đi bộ từ Nam ra Bắc," *Phụ Nữ Tân Văn*, June 11, 1931; "Người đàn bà đi bộ vòng quanh Á-châu Cô Hồ Tố Quyên," *Phụ Nữ Tân Văn*, May 21, 1931; and David G. Marr, *Vietnamese Tradition on Trial, 1920–1945* (University of California Press, 1981).
116. Larcher-Goscha, "Du Football au Vietnam (1905–1949)," 66.
117. Tha Sơn, "Con gái đá bóng tròn," *Hà Thành Ngọ Báo*, July 20, 1933; and Brownfoot, "Emancipation, Exercise and Imperialism," 61–84.
118. M. D., "Cô Phan Thị Nga lên diễn đàn," *Hà Thành Ngọ Báo*, September 13, 1934; and Larcher-Goscha, "Du Football au Vietnam (1905–1949)," 67.
119. Vũ Tu-Thư giáo tọc, "Chị em nam Việt với quả bóng tròn," *Hà Thành Ngọ Báo*, September 6, 1933.
120. Tha Sơn, "Con gái đá bóng tròn," *Hà Thành Ngọ Báo*, July 20, 1933.
121. In the late nineteenth century, the "safety" bicycle with two equal-sized pneumatic tires and brakes was mass-produced. The new bicycle was marketed to women and became wildly popular. Sarah A. Gordon, "'Any Desired Length': Negotiating Gender Through Sports Clothing, 1870–1925," in *Beauty and Business: Commerce, Gender, and Culture in Modern America*, ed. Philip Scranton (Routledge, 2001), 36.
122. David Arnold and Erich DeWald, "Cycles of Empowerment? The Bicycle and Everyday Technology in Colonial India and Vietnam," *Comparative Studies in Society and History* 53, no. 4 (2011): 971–96.
123. Mlle D. Luông, "Phụ nữ với chiếc xe đạp," *Công Luận Báo*, September 1, 1938.
124. Advertisement, "Bécé," *La Tribune Indochinoise*, July 13, 1927.
125. For example, "Ý kiến bạn đọc báo: Về cuộc thi xe đạp của Ngọ báo tổ chức ngày 23 Février sắp tới," *Hà Thành Ngọ Báo*, February 15, 1930; "Saigon-Hanoi-Namquan-Camau-Saigon," *Trung Lập Báo*, March 4, 1931; "Vương-ngọc-Chánh người thanh niên Việt Nam cỡi xe đạp đi vòng quanh Đông Pháp, đã đến Saigon," *Trung Lập Báo*, October 30, 1931; "Trước khi đi dự vận động hội Huế, Võ Vĩnh Lợi thắng cuộc đua Vũng Tàu—Xuân Lộc-Saigon," *Sài Gòn*, Feburary 17, 1936; and "Chủ nhật 12 Avril, hơn 200 người dự cuộc đua xe đạp Hanoi-Tong lấy bằng cấp," *Đông Pháp*, April 14, 1936.

4. PHYSIQUE

126. For example, "Trên con ngựa sắt," *Hà Thành Ngọ Báo*, December 13, 1931; and "Với con ngựa sắt, anh Đoàn-quí-Thống đã đạt được mục đích một cách vẻ vang," *Sài Gòn*, December 7, 1938.
127. "Chuyện Đó, Đây," *Tràng An Báo*, June 3, 1938.
128. Nguyễn Thị Kế, "Cô Viêt Hoang Thị Kế nữ học sinh trường Cholon định xướng lên một cuộc đi xe đạp từ nam ra bắc," *Hà Thành Ngọ Báo*, April 2, 1931.
129. "Con ngựa sắt với bạn trai bạn gái," *Vịt Đực*, July 27, 1938; and "Phụ nữ với thể thao: Phụ nữ Việt Nam ta nên đi xe máy đạp," *Trung Lập Báo*, February 3, 1932.
130. "Con ngựa sắt với bạn trai bạn gái," *Vịt Đực*, July 27, 1938; "Phụ nữ với thể thao: Phụ nữ Việt Nam ta nên đi xe máy đạp," *Trung Lập Báo*, February 3, 1932; and Nguyễn Thị Kế, "Cô Viêt Hoang Thị Kế nữ học sinh trường Cholon định xướng lên một cuộc đi xe đạp từ nam ra bắc," *Hà Thành Ngọ Báo*, April 2, 1931.
131. Trần-thị-tý, "Dư Luận: Chị em việt nam thủ cựu," *Hà Thành Ngọ Báo*, September 4, 1928; and Nguyễn Thị Kế, "Cô Viêt Hoang Thị Kế nữ học sinh trường Cholon định xướng lên một cuộc đi xe đạp từ nam ra bắc," *Hà Thành Ngọ Báo*, April 2, 1931.
132. "Phụ nữ với thể thao: Phụ nữ Việt Nam ta nên đi xe máy đạp," *Trung Lập Báo*, February 3, 1932.
133. Mlle D. Luông, "Phụ nữ với chiếc xe đạp," *Công Luận Báo*, September 1, 1938.
134. Stewart, *For Health and Beauty*, 163.
135. Việt Bằng, "Dân thể thao Hà Thành đón cô Hồ Thị Lích," *Vịt Đực*, September 14, 1938.
136. "Phụ nữ với thể thao: Phụ nữ Việt Nam ta nên đi xe máy đạp," *Trung Lập Báo*, February 3, 1932; and "Chuyện Đó, Đây," *Tràng An Báo*, June 3, 1938.
137. Việt Bằng, "Dân thể thao Hà Thành đón cô Hồ Thị Lích," *Vịt Đực*, September 14, 1938.
138. Trần-Thị-Tý, "Dư Luận: Chị em việt nam thủ cựu," *Hà Thành Ngọ Báo*, September 4, 1928.
139. "Phụ nữ với thể thao: Phụ nữ Việt Nam ta nên đi xe máy đạp," *Trung Lập Báo*, February 3, 1932.
140. Nguyễn Thị Kế, "Cô Viêt Hoang Thị Kế nữ học sinh trường Cholon định xướng lên một cuộc đi xe đạp từ nam ra bắc," *Hà Thành Ngọ Báo*, April 2, 1931.
141. "Chuyện Đó, Đây," *Tràng An Báo*, June 3, 1938.
142. Celarié, *Promenade en Indochine*, 176.
143. For more information on dance halls, see Firpo, *Black Market Business*, 162–86.
144. Nguyễn Đình Lạp, "Thanh niên trụy lạc," in *Phóng Sự Việt Nam, 1932–1945*, Vol. 1, ed. Phan Trọng Thưởng, Nguyễn Cừ, and Nguyễn Hữu Sơn (NXB Văn Học, 2000), 205–6.
145. "Les décolletés du soir sont très profonds dans le dos," *La Dépêche d'Indochine*, May 15, 1930.
146. Mitchel Gray, *The Lingerie Book* (St. Martin's, 1980), 29.
147. "Chez Claudine," *La Dépêche d'Indochine*, January 19, 1939; "La Lingerie fine," *La Dépêche d'Indochine*, April 4, 1929; "La Mode," *La Dépêche d'Indochine*, December 21, 1933; "La lingerie simple et pratique," *La Dépêche d'Indochine*, September 15, 1934; C. Willet Cunnington and Phillis Cunnington, *The History of Underclothes* (Michael Joseph, 1951), 217, 236, 241; Jill Fields, *An Intimate Affair: Women, Lingerie, and Sexuality* (University of California Press, 2007), 90–99; Jill Fields,

"Fighting the Corsetless Evil: Shaping Corsets and Culture, 1900–1930," *Journal of Social History* 33, no. 2 (1999): 355–84; and Jane Farrell-Beck and Collen Gau, *Uplift: The Bra in America* (University of Pennsylvania Press, 2002).

148. "Một kiểu áo," *Ngày Nay*, November 13,1935; and Việt Sinh, "Quần áo mới," *Ngày Nay*, January 30, 1935.
149. Jason Gibbs, "Spoken Theatre, La Scene Tonkinoise, and the First Modern Vietnamese Songs," *Journal of the Study of Asian Music* 31, no. 1 (Spring/Summer 2000): 10.
150. Khải Hưng, *Trống Mái* (1936; repr. NXB Văn Nghệ TPHCM, 2000).
151. Advertisement, "Magasins Chaffanjon," *Hà Thành Ngọ Báo*, May 20, 1935; Advertisement, "Hãng Cư Chung," *Tiểu Thuyết Thứ Bảy*, July 8, 1939; and Claudia Brush Kidwell and Valerie Steele, *Men and Women: Dressing the Part* (Smithsonian Institution, 1989), 117.
152. "Đồ Sơn khai mùa tắm," *Vịt Đực*, June 22, 1938; and "Vờ vịt," *Vịt Đực*, June 29, 1933.
153. Nhi Linh, "Những bóng người . . . trên bãi biển," *Phong Hóa*, August 3, 1934.
154. Similar misogynistic humor was also being delivered through the medium of cartoons in China during the interwar years. See Roanna Yuk-Heng Cheung, "Embodying Modernity: Humor, Gender, and Popular Culture in Republican Guangzhou," (PhD diss., University of California Los Angeles, 2016).
155. *Tràng An Báo*, April 19, 1935.
156. *Trung Bắc Tân Văn*, June 23, 1940.
157. C L Jeunesse, "Đời tinh thần vật-chất và tình cảm của phụ-nữ Việt-Nam: Ăn mặc làm đỏm," *Đàn-Bà*, June 2, 1939.
158. "Phiên chợ thường xuân của Thương đoàn," *Hà Thành Ngọ Báo*, April 26, 1933.
159. Tha Sơn, "Con gái đá bóng tròn," *Hà Thành Ngọ Báo*, July 20, 1933; Cát Tường, "Một môn thể thao," *Phong Hóa*, March 30, 1934; "Một kiểu áo," *Ngày Nay*, November 13, 1935; "Xã Giao: Phục Sức," *Ngày Nay*, November 29, 1936; and "Mốt," *Vịt Đực*, September 7, 1938.
160. Sebastian Conrad, "Globalizing the Beautiful Body: Eugen Sandow, Bodybuilding, and the Idea of Muscular Manliness at the Turn of the 20th Century," *Journal of World History* 32, no. 1 (March 2021): 95–125.
161. Tumblety, *Remaking the Male Body*.
162. Advertisment, "Ovamaltine," *La Tribune Indochinoise*, December 29, 1939.
163. Khải Hưng, *Trống Mái*.
164. Kidwell and Steele, *Men and Women*, 20.
165. Mary Lynn Stewart, *Dressing Modern Frenchwomen: Marketing Haute Couture, 1919–1939* (Johns Hopkins University Press, 2008), 215.
166. In Japan, the slim, weak female figure was replaced with a stronger body that was expected to give birth to many healthy children. Ayuu Ishida, "The Wartime Modern Girl in Japan: Changes in Female Images in Cosmetic Advertisements of Housewife's Friend (Shufu No Tomo) from the 1930s to the 1940s," in *The East Asian Modern Girl: Women, Media, and Colonial Modernity During the Interwar Years*, ed. Sumei Wang (Brill, 2021); and I-Fen Chen and Hsiu-Hui Sun, "The Framed Female Image: A Pictorial Semiotic Analysis of Classic Shanghai Calendar Posters During the 1910s–1930s," in *The East Asian Modern Girl: Women, Media, and Colonial Modernity During the Interwar Years*, ed. Sumei Wang (Brill, 2021), 188.

4. PHYSIQUE

167. "Một môn thể thao," *Ngày Nay*, November 13, 1935.
168. Cát Tường, "Thế nào là đẹp," *Ngày Nay*, September 13, 1936.
169. Advertisement, "Institut de beauté Venus," *Đông Pháp*, December 6, 1935.
170. Ngọc Lang, "Phép sửa sắc đẹp," *Khoa Học Tập Chí*, January 15, 1933.
171. Nguyễn Cát Tường, "Thế nào là đẹp," *Ngày Nay*, September 13, 1936.
172. "Một môn thể thao," *Ngày Nay*, November 13, 1935; and Vũ Trọng Phụng, *Dumb Luck*, 37.
173. C. Đ., "Giữ vẻ đẹp," *Ngày Nay*, December 6, 1936.
174. Nguyễn Cát Tường, "Một môn thể thao," *Phong Hóa*, March 30, 1934.
175. Advertisement, "Institut de beauté Venus," *Đông Pháp*, December 6, 1935.
176. The protagonist does Müller exercises in Khái Hưng, *Trống Mái*.
177. "Thể thao phép thần hiệu để giữ vẻ đẹp," *Ngày Nay*, November 22, 1936; and Cô Duyên, "Đàn bà ngày nay," *Ngày Nay*, August 16, 1936; and "Quần phụ nữ," *Ngày Nay*, November 13, 1935.
178. Tha Sơn, "Con gái đá bóng tròn," *Hà Thành Ngọ Báo*, July 20, 1933; "Chị em Nam Việt với quả bóng tròn," *Hà Thành Ngọ Báo*, September 6, 1933; "Quần phụ nữ," *Ngày Nay*, November 13, 1935; and "Phụ nữ và thể thao," *Đông Pháp*, December 6, 1936.
179. Mĩ-Chân, "Thể thao của phụ nữ," *Hà Thành Ngọ Báo*, March 22, 1930; "Một ý kiến về môn thể thao đi bộ đường trường: có người hàng ngày đi bộ mà vẫn không biết rằng mình đã tập thể thao," *Hà Thành Ngọ Báo*, October 23, 1930; Tha Sơn, "Con gái đá bóng tròn," *Hà Thành Ngọ Báo*, July 20, 1933; "Thân hình mềm mại," *Ngày Nay*, November 15, 1936; and Cô Duyên, "Phái yếu," *Ngày Nay*, August 2, 1936.
180. "Tập thở," *Ngày Nay*, December 6, 1936; C. Đ., "Giữ vẻ đẹp," *Ngày Nay*, December 6, 1936; "Thể thao phép thần hiệu để giữ vẻ đẹp," *Ngày Nay*, November 22, 1936; "Người đàn bà nào cũng tập thể thao được," *Ngày Nay*, December 27, 1936; and Mộng Hoa, "Đẹp và đẹp," *Đàn-Bà*, July 28, 1939.
181. Impoverished mothers forewent meals in favor of feeding their hungry children.
182. Paula J. Martin, *Suzanne Noël: Cosmetic Surgery, Feminism and Beauty in Early Twentieth Century France* (Taylor and Francis, 2014), 47; and Stewart, *Dressing Modern Frenchwomen*, 218.
183. Phi Khanh, "Đẹp và đẹp," *Đàn-Bà*, June 9, 1939; and Mộng Hoa, "Đẹp và đẹp," *Đàn-Bà*, July 28, 1939.
184. Lệ Chi, "Có ai đi học giùm môn thuốc nầy," *Điển Tín*, February 20, 1937.
185. C. D., "Muốn thân thể được xinh xắn nên tập thở," *Ngày Nay*, September 6, 1936.
186. "Obecita Maigrir," *La Volonté Indochinoise*, December 21, 1932; and Lệ Chi, "Có ai đi học giùm môn thuốc nầy," *Điển Tín*, February 20, 1937.
187. "Studio Marianne," *La Dépêche d'Indochine*, February 12, 1934.
188. Electric treatment for weight loss was developed in the early 1920s by the French kinesiologist Jeanne Piaubert. See Martin, *Suzanne Noël*, 48; Vân-Hoàn, "Mỹ-nhơn viện" của cô Madeleine Bùi, lệnh-ái ông Bùi Quang Chiêu," *Hà Thành Ngọ Báo*, April 20, 1935; and Advertisement, "Mỹ viện Amy," *Đàn-Bà*, April 14, 1939.
189. "Mốt," *Vịt Đực*, September 7, 1938.
190. Beth Linker, *Slouch: Posture Panic in Modern America* (Princeton University Press, 2024).
191. Hão Huyền, "Đẹp và đẹp," *Đàn-Bà*, July 21, 1939.
192. In interwar France, bent spines and frail necks came to be seen as unmanly. See Tumblety, *Remaking the Male Body*, 167–204.

4. PHYSIQUE

193. Nguyễn Cát Tường, "Một môn thể thao," *Phong Hóa*, April 6, 1934; and Nguyễn Cát Tường, "Một môn thể thao," *Phong Hóa*, March 30, 1934.
194. Thông Reo, "Làm cho rõ mặt đàn bà nước Nam," *Trung Lập Báo*, March 21, 1931; Chung Anh, "Vệ sinh và thể dục: Cho được cao," *Khoa Học*, August 1, 1936; Chung Anh, "Vệ sinh và thể dục: Cho được cao," *Khoa Học*, August 11, 1936; Chung Anh, "Vệ sinh và thể dục: Cho được cao," *Khoa Học*, August 21, 1936; Chung Anh, "Vệ sinh và thể dục: Cho được cao," *Khoa Học*, September 1, 1936; Hão Huyền, "Đẹp và đẹp," *Đàn-Bà*, July 21, 1939; Advertisement, "Institut de beauté Venus," *Đông Pháp*, December 6, 1935; and Tha Sơn, "Con gái đá bóng tròn," *Hà Thành Ngọ Báo*, July 20, 1933.
195. Nguyễn Cát Tường, "Một môn thể thao," *Phong Hóa*, April 6, 1934.
196. Chung Anh, "Vệ sinh và thể dục: Cho được cao," *Khoa Học*, August 1, 1936; Chung Anh, "Vệ sinh và thể dục: Cho được cao," *Khoa Học*, August 11, 1936; Chung Anh, "Vệ sinh và thể dục: Cho được cao," *Khoa Học*, August 21, 1936; Chung Anh, "Vệ sinh và thể dục: Cho được cao," *Khoa Học*, September 1, 1936; and "Các bà nên biết cách nằm ngủ," *Ngày Nay*, December 27, 1936.
197. "Các bà nên biết cách nằm ngủ," *Ngày Nay*, December 27, 1936.
198. C. Đ., "Giữ vẻ đẹp," *Ngày Nay*, December 6, 1936, 521.
199. Advertisement, "Mỹ viện Amy," *Đàn-Bà*, April 14, 1939.
200. Cô Duyên, "Bộ Ngực Đàn Bà," *Ngày Nay*, November 29, 1936.
201. Y-sĩ Đ.T., "Nịt vú," *Hà Thành Ngọ Báo*, March 9, 1929.
202. Hữu Ngọc and Lady Borton, eds., *Áo dài: Women's Long Dress* (NXB Thế Giới, 2014), 23.
203. Cho Kyo and Kyoko Iriye Selden, *The Search for the Beautiful Woman: A Cultural History of Japanese and Chinese Beauty* (Rowman and Littlefield, 2012), 165–66, 216–17.
204. Marilyn Yalom, *A History of the Breast* (Knopf, 1998), 4.
205. Nguyễn Cát Tường, "Một môn thể thao 'cách luyện bộ ngực,'" *Phong Hóa*, June 15, 1934; and Y-sĩ Đ.T., "Nịt vú," *Hà Thành Ngọ Báo*, March 8, 1929.
206. Martina Thucnhi Nguyen, *On Our Own Strength*, 96–97.
207. Hyun Jeong Min, "New Women and Modern Girls: Consuming Foreign Goods in Colonial Seoul," *Journal of Historical Research in Marketing* 5, no. 4 (2013): 508; and Stewart, *Dressing Modern Frenchwomen*, 216.
208. "Một kỷ nguyên mới: Cuộc "thi vú" của phụ nữ," *Hà Thành Ngọ Báo*, September 14, 1928; and "Hội giải phóng bộ vú ở Luân-Đôn," *Đông Phương*, November 13, 1931.
209. Cô Duyên, "Bộ Ngực Đàn Bà," *Ngày Nay*, November 29, 1936; Kee-Sun Lung, "The Politics of Hair and the Issue of the Bob in Modern China," *Fashion Theory: The Journal of Dress, Body, and Culture* 4, no. 1 (1997): 353–66; and Dorothy Ko, *Cinderella's Sisters: A Revisionist History of Footbinding* (University of California Press, 2005).
210. Vũ Trọng Phụng, *Kỹ nghệ lấy tây & cơm thầy cơm cô* (NXB Văn Học, 2006), 50–52.
211. Y-sĩ Đ.T., "Nịt vú," *Hà Thành Ngọ Báo*, March 8, 1929; and Y-sĩ Đ.T., "Nịt vú," *Hà Thành Ngọ Báo*, March 9, 1929.
212. Ngọc Lang, "Phép sửa sắc đẹp," *Khoa Học Tập Chí*, January 15, 1933; and Tha Sơn, "Con gái đá bóng tròn," *Hà Thành Ngọ Báo*, July 20, 1933.
213. Advertisement, "Institut de beauté Venus," *Đông Pháp*, December 6, 1935.
214. Hoàng Thị Nhã, "Bộ ngực đàn bà," *Đông Pháp*, March 14, 1941.

5. BEAUTY CONTESTS

215. Cô Duyên, "Bộ ngực đàn bà," *Ngày Nay*, November 29, 1936.
216. Nguyễn Cát Tường, "Một môn thể thao," *Phong Hóa*, March 30, 1934.
217. Phạm Thảo Nguyên, *Áo dài Lemur và bối cảnh Phong Hóa và Ngày Nay* (NXB Hồng Đức, 2019), 27.
218. Hoàng Thị Nhã, "Bộ ngực đàn bà," *Đông Pháp*, March 14, 1941.
219. "Ý bạn," *Hà Thành Ngọ Báo*, October 5, 1934.
220. "Quan Toàn Quyền Robin đã về khánh thành cuộc đấu xảo tơ lụa tỉnh Hadong," *Hà Thành Ngọ Báo*, October 23, 1935.
221. Cô Duyên, "Bộ Ngực Đàn Bà," *Ngày Nay*, November 29, 1936.
222. Cát Tường, "Một môn thể thao 'cách luyện bộ ngực,'" *Phong Hóa*, June 15, 1934.
223. Cô Duyên, "Bộ Ngực Đàn Bà," *Ngày Nay*, November 29, 1936.
224. Cát Tường, "Một môn thể thao 'cách luyện bộ ngực,'" *Phong Hóa*, June 15, 1934.
225. Bà Đốc Kỳ, "Lại về vấn đề làm dáng," *Hà Thành Ngọ Báo*, March 22, 1929.
226. "Conseils de Beauté," La Dépêche d'Indochine, December 21, 1933; Cô Duyên, "Bộ Ngực Đàn Bà," *Ngày Nay*, November 29, 1936; Cát Tường, "Một môn thể thao 'cách luyện bộ ngực,'" *Phong Hóa*, June 15, 1934; "Muốn có bộ ngực nở nang," *Sài Gòn*, June 26, 1937; "Tập thở," *Ngày Nay*, December 6, 1936; and Hoàng Thị Nhã, "Bộ ngực đàn bà," *Đông Pháp*, March 14, 1941.
227. Advertisement, "Mỹ viện Amy," *Đàn-Bà*, April 14, 1939; Advertisement, "Mỹ viện Amy," *Đàn-Bà*, May 5, 1939; and Advertisement, "Mỹ viện Amy," *Đàn-Bà*, September 8, 1939.
228. For more information on padding for aesthetic purposes, see Yalom, *A History of the Breast*, 41; Kirsten E. Gardner, "Hiding the Scars: History of Breast Prostheses After Mastectomy Since 1945," in *Beauty and Business: Commerce, Gender, and Culture in Modern America*, ed. Philip Scranton (Routledge, 2000), 309–27; and Jill Fields, *An Intimate Affair: Women, Lingerie, and Sexuality* (University of California Press, 2007), 103.
229. Vũ Trọng Phụng, *Dumb Luck*, 90–91, 94.
230. Dinh Trong Hieu, "Le face, le ventre et autres symboliques du corps chez les Viets," in *La Colonisation des Corps: de l'Indochine au Viet Nam*, ed. François Guillemot and Agathe Larcher-Goscha (Vendémiaire, 2014), 54.
231. Cô Ngã, Mốt," *Vịt Đực*, November 9, 1938.
232. "Lông mày, nút ruồi, cặp vú," *Điễn Tín*, March 27, 1936.
233. Trọng Lang, *Hà Nội lầm than* (1938; repr. NXB Hội Nhà Văn, 2015), 33.

5. BEAUTY CONTESTS

1. Trang-Tử, "Ai báo *Công-Luận Báo* không có tri âm?," *Đông Pháp Thời Báo*, September 2, 1925.
2. Zhuang Zhou's premise was "A scabby person and the beautiful lady Xishi are the same in the eyes of Dao."
3. In the 1920s, trimming the eyelashes was believed to help the lashes grow back fuller.
4. Thông Reo, "Làm cho rõ mặt đàn bà nước Nam," *Trung Lập Báo*, March 21, 1931.
5. David Pomfret, "'A Use for the Masses': Gender, Age, and Nation in France, Fin de Siècle," *American Historical Review* 109, no. 5 (December 2004): 1439–74.

5. BEAUTY CONTESTS

6. Holly Grout, *The Force of Beauty: Transforming French Ideas of Femininity in the Third Republic* (Louisiana State University Press, 2015); Elizabeth Ezra, "Colonialism Exposed: Miss France d'Outre-mer, 1937," in *Identity Papers Contested Nationhood in Twentieth Century France*, ed. Steven Ungar and Tom Conley (University of Minnesota Press, 1996); and Aro Velmet, "Beauty and Big Business: Gender, Race, and Civilizational Decline at French Beauty Pageants, 1920-1937," *French History* 28, no. 2 (March 2014): 66-91.
7. Lois W. Banner, *American Beauty: A Social History . . . Through Two Centuries of the American Ideal* (Knopf, 1983), 260-69.
8. Ezra, "Colonialism Exposed."
9. Velmet, "Beauty and Big Business," 72.
10. RAM, "Về việc chơi bông giấy: Không lẽ?," *Công Luận Báo*, November 29, 1937; Elsbeth Locher-Scholten, "Morals, Harmony, and National Identity: 'Compassionate Feminism' in Colonial Indonesia in the 1930s," *Journal of Women's History* 14, no. 4 (Winter 2003): 38-58; Su Lin Lewis, "Cosmopolitanism and the Modern Girl: A Cross-Cultural Discourse in 1930s Penang," *Modern Asian Studies* 43, no. 6 (2009): 1385-1419; Penny Van Esterik, "The Politics of Beauty in Thailand," in *Beauty Queen on the Global Stage: Gender, Contests, Power*, ed. Coleen Ballerino Cohen, Richard Wilk, and Beverly Stoeltje (Routledge, 1995); and Genevieve Clutario, "Pageant Politics: Tensions of Power, Empire, and Nationalism in Manila Carnival Queen Contests," in *Gendering the Trans-Pacific World*, ed. Catherine Ceniza Choy and Judy Tzu-Chun Wen (Brill, 2017).
11. Shawn McHale, *Print and Power: Confucianism, Communism, and Buddhism in the Making of Modern Vietnam* (University of Hawaii Press, 2004); and Philippe Peycam, *The Birth of Vietnamese Political Journalism: Saigon, 1916-1930* (Columbia University Press, 2015).
12. Peycam, *The Birth of Vietnamese Political Journalism*, 105.
13. Trần Quang Đức, *Ngàn năm áo mũ: Lịch sử trang phục Việt Nam giai đoạn 1009-1945* (NXB Thế Giới, 2013), 237-38.
14. Holly Grout, "Between Venus and Mercury: The 1920s Beauty Contest in France and America," *French Politics, Culture, and Society* 31, no. 1 (Spring 2013): 51.
15. Ben Tran finds that presses generally benefited from the explosion of female literacy. See Ben Tran, *Post-Mandarin: Masculinity and Aesthetic Modernity in Colonial Vietnam* (Fordham University Press, 2017), 10.
16. *Công Luận Báo*'s mandate to use an Indigenous photographer may have been an effort to capture Indigenous beauty through local eyes, as opposed to subjecting the young women to sit for a French photographer. For more information on the politics of photographic representation, see Johann Le Guelte, "Photography, Identity and Migration: Controlling Colonial Migrants in Interwar France and Senegal," *French Politics Culture & Society* 37, no. 3 (Autumn 2019): 27-52.
17. "Người đờn bà đẹp nhất Sài Gòn," *Công Luận Báo*, July 1, 1925; B. B., "Cuộc đấu sắc đẹp của công luận báo," *Công Luận Báo*, July 4, 1925; and "Người đờn bà đẹp nhất Sài Gòn," *Công Luận Báo*, July 1, 1925.
18. Lieu-Nhự, "Cái sắc đẹp của đàn bà," *Công Luận Báo*, July 3, 1925.
19. Judith A. N. Henchy, "Performing Modernity in the Writings of Nguyễn An Ninh and Phạm Văn Hùm," (PhD diss., University of Washington, 2005), 208.

5. BEAUTY CONTESTS

20. Trang-Tử, "Ai bảo Công-Luận Báo không có tri âm?," *Đông Pháp Thời Báo*, September 2, 1925.
21. Eugene Weber, *Peasants Into Frenchmen* (Stanford University Press, 1979).
22. Thank you to Philippe Peycam for this discussion, August 19, 2021.
23. Peycam, *The Birth of Vietnamese Political Journalism*, 108–9.
24. "Lời cùng hồn Huệ Nhân," *Đông Pháp Thời Báo*, August 31, 1925.
25. "Ai bảo Công-Luận Báo không có tri âm?," *Đông Pháp Thời Báo*, September 2, 1925.
26. "Trái tai nên mới," *Đông Pháp Thời Báo*, September 11, 1925.
27. Mlle Đỗ Ngọc Kim, "Ngỏ cùng Huệ-Nhân Tiên Sanh," *Đông Pháp Thời Báo*, August 12, 1925.
28. Lê Thị H., "Nêu gương báu cho hàng Nữ lưu," *Công Luận Báo*, June 12, 1925.
29. Trung Tiên, "Dư luận: Có nên cản trở cuộc đấu sắc đẹp của CLB tổ chức đây chăng?," *Đông Pháp Thời Báo*, August 21, 1925.
30. "Đôi lời căm tạ," *Đông Pháp Thời Báo*, August 31, 1925.
31. "Hài đàm: Quả nổi ngặt nghèo," *Đông Pháp Thời Báo*, September 11, 1925. "Tú Bà" became a common name when referring to female pimps. See Nguyen Du, *The Tale of Kieu: A Bilingual Edition of Nguyen Du's Truyen Kieu*, trans. Huỳnh Sanh Thông (Yale University Press, 1983), 42–45.
32. "Nhàn Đàm: Ai lại éo dại mà đi phơi mặt!," *Trung Hoà Nhật Báo*, July 22, 1925.
33. Trang-Tử, "Ai bảo Công-Luận Báo không có tri âm?," *Đông Pháp Thời Báo*, September 2, 1925.
34. "Ngỏ cùng Huệ-Nhân Tiên Sanh," *Đông Pháp Thời Báo*, August 12, 1925.
35. Tự-Do, "Đấu sắc đẹp," *Công Luận Báo*, September 3, 1925.
36. "Tiếng súng nổ sau cùng!," *Đông Pháp Thời Báo*, September 16, 1925.
37. Nguyễn Thị Kiêm, "Trái tai nên mới," *Đông Pháp Thời Báo*, September 11, 1925; and "Ai bảo Công-Luận Báo không có tri âm?," *Đông Pháp Thời Báo*, September 2, 1925.
38. Madamoiselle Đ.O., "Dư luận: Có nên cản trở cuộc đấu sắc đẹp của CLB tổ chức đây chăng?," *Đông Pháp Thời Báo*, August 21, 1925.
39. Liêu-Nhự, "Cái sắc đẹp của đàn bà," *Công Luận Báo*, July 3, 1925.
40. Lê Thị H., "Nêu gương báu cho hàng Nữ lưu," *Công Luận Báo*, June 12, 1925.
41. Xiaorong Li, *Women's Poetry of Late Imperial China: Transforming the Inner Chambers* (University of Washington Press, 2012), 5–8; and Trang-Tử, "Ai bảo Công-Luận Báo không có tri âm?," *Đông Pháp Thời Báo*, September 2, 1925.
42. Nguyễn Thị Kiêm, "Trái tai nên mới" *Đông Pháp Thời Báo*, September 11, 1925. That this author draws from Nietzsche to make an argument in favor of Confucianism is not surprising considering that Trần Trọng Kim, who would have been writing *Nho giáo* at this time and publishing aspects of it in the newspaper, drew on Western philosophers himself. Trần Trọng Kim, *Nho giáo* (Song Moi, 1971); and McHale, *Print and Power*, 82.
43. Trang-Tử, "Ai bảo Công-Luận Báo không có tri âm?," *Đông Pháp Thời Báo*, September 2, 1925.
44. "Đáp từ," *Công Luận Báo*, June 12, 1925.
45. "Lời ra giùm Đ.P.T.B.," *Công Luận Báo*, July 28, 1925.
46. Tự-Do, "Đấu sắc đẹp," *Công Luận Báo*, September 3, 1925.
47. As quoted in Trang-Tử, "Ai bảo Công-Luận Báo không có tri âm?," *Đông Pháp Thời Báo*, September 2, 1925.

5. BEAUTY CONTESTS

48. Peycam, *The Birth of Vietnamese Political Journalism*, 133. Shortly after *Công Luận Báo* announced the beauty contest, the nationalist Phan Bội Châu was arrested in Shanghai and returned to Indochina for trial in late June. That same summer the famed nationalists Phan Châu Trinh and Nguyễn An Ninh returned to Saigon from France, and workers staged a strike at the Ba Son shipyard, temporarily crippling both maritime commerce and the colonial navy.
49. "Đáp từ," *Công Luận Báo*, June 12, 1925.
50. Liêu-Nhự, "Cái sắc đẹp của đàn bà," *Công Luận Báo*, July 3, 1925.
51. Minh Nguyệt, Phạm T. Đ., "Người một nước: Là anh em một nhà," *Đông Pháp Thời Báo*, September 23, 1925.
52. Nguyễn Thị Kiêm, "Trái tai nên mới," *Đông Pháp Thời Báo*, September 11, 1925.
53. Trang-Tử, "Ai bảo Công-Luận Báo không có tri âm?," *Đông Pháp Thời Báo*, September 2, 1925.
54. "Đôi lời căm tạ," *Đông Pháp Thời Báo*, August 31, 1925.
55. As quoted in Tự-Do, "Đấu sắc đẹp," *Công Luận Báo*, September 3, 1925.
56. "Dư luận: Có nên cản trở cuộc đấu sắc đẹp của CLB tổ chức đây chăng?," *Đông Pháp Thời Báo*, August 21, 1925.
57. As reprinted by Tự-Do, "Đấu sắc đẹp," *Công Luận Báo*, September 3, 1925.
58. Lão-kỹ-nữ tự Tú-Bà, "Hài đàm: Quả nỗi ngặt nghèo," *Đông Pháp Thời Báo*, September 11, 1925.
59. "Đôi lời căm tạ," *Đông Pháp Thời Báo*, August 31, 1925.
60. "Tiếng súng nổ sau cùng!," *Đông Pháp Thời Báo*, September 16, 1925.
61. "Dư luận: Có nên cản trở cuộc đấu sắc đẹp của CLB tổ chức đây chăng?," *Đông Pháp Thời Báo*, August 21, 1925.
62. "Nhàn Đàm: Ai lại éo dại mà đi phơi mặt!," *Trung Hoà Nhật Báo*, July 22, 1925.
63. "Ai bảo Công-Luận Báo không có tri âm?," *Đông Pháp Thời Báo*, September 2, 1925.
64. Trang-Tử, "Ai bảo Công-Luận Báo không có tri âm?"
65. Nguyễn Thị Kiêm, " "Trái tai nên mới," *Đông Pháp Thời Báo*, September 11, 1925.
66. "Dư luận: Có nên cản trở cuộc đấu sắc đẹp của CLB tổ chức đây chăng?," *Đông Pháp Thời Báo*, August 21, 1925.
67. Lê Thị H., "Nêu gương báu cho hàng Nữ lưu," *Công Luận Báo*, June 12, 1925.
68. Tự-Do, "Đấu sắc đẹp," *Công Luận Báo*, September 3, 1925.
69. "Người đờn bà đẹp nhất Sài Gòn," *Công Luận Báo*, July 1, 1925.
70. B. B., "Cuộc đấu sắc đệp của Công luận báo," *Công Luận Báo*, July 4, 1925; and Tự-Do, "Đấu sắc đẹp," *Công Luận Báo*, September 3, 1925.
71. Trung Tiên, "??," *Đông Pháp Thời Báo*, September 23, 1925.
72. "Cô thiếu nữ đẹp nhất Âu Châu," *Hà Thành Ngọ Báo*, April 17, 1931; and "Mấy người quốc sắc của các nước Âu châu cử đi dự cuộc thi tuyệt sắc thế giới," *Thanh Nghệ Tịnh Tân Văn*, May 15, 1931.
73. Untitled picture, *Sài Gòn*, December 29, 1938.
74. " . . . Rồi làm thành ngôi sao," *Hà Thành Ngọ Báo*, July 6, 1934; and C. L., "Nước Mỹ có nhiều hội thi con gái đẹp," *Hà Thành Ngọ Báo*, October 9, 1929.
75. Two examples are the 1930 Miss Europe contest, "Sắc đẹp khuynh thành: Người đàn bà đẹp nhất Âu-châu," *Hà Thành Ngọ Báo*, February 7, 1930, and the 1930 Miss Universe contest, A. B., "Cái hiếu kỳ của người đời: Cuộc thi sắc đẹp của toàn cầu," *Hà Thành Ngọ Báo*, May 9, 1930. This same newspaper was also particularly

5. BEAUTY CONTESTS

interested in the details of Hollywood, and it regularly published information about movies, gossip about starlets, and the business of Hollywood.

76. For example, in the 1932 Miss Universe contest: "Các danh họa thế giới," *Hà Thành Ngọ Báo*, July 20, 1932; Picture of Miss Russia, *Hà Thành Ngọ Báo*, July 21, 1932; "Các danh họa thế giới," *Hà Thành Ngọ Báo*, July 21, 1932; Picture of Miss Italy, *Hà Thành Ngọ Báo*, July 22, 1932; "Các danh họa thế giới," *Hà Thành Ngọ Báo*, July 23, 1932; Picture of Miss Germany, *Hà Thành Ngọ Báo*, July 24, 1932; "Une beauté britannique: Léonie Power," *L'Annam Nouveau*, December 8, 1932; and "Các danh họa thế giới," *Hà Thành Ngọ Báo*, July 24, 1932. In the 1933 Miss Europe contest: Picture of Miss Hungry *Hà Thành Ngọ Báo*, March 8, 1933; Picture of Miss Russia who won the Miss Europe contest, *Hà Thành Ngọ Báo*, July 9, 1933; Picture of Miss England, *Hà Thành Ngọ Báo*, August 4, 1933; Picture of Miss France 1933, *Hà Thành Ngọ Báo*, August 5, 1933; and Picture of Miss France, *Hà Thành Ngọ Báo*, August 5, 1933. In the 1934 Miss Universe contest: Picture of Miss Japan, *Hà Thành Ngọ Báo*, September 12, 1934; Picture of Miss Finland, *Hà Thành Ngọ Báo*, October 3, 1934; and Pictures of Miss France and Miss England, *Hà Thành Ngọ Báo*, October 24, 1934. In the 1935 Miss Universe competition: Picture of Charlotte Wassef, Miss Egypt, *Hà Thành Ngọ Báo*, November 2, 1935. The same picture of Miss Egypt was also printed in "Miss Universe," *La Tribune Indochinoise*, November 8, 1935.
77. Advertisement, "Lune-Fat," *Hà Thành Ngọ Báo*, May 31, 1933.
78. Advertisement, "Cadum soap," *Hà Thành Ngọ Báo*, May 12, 1936.
79. Advertisement, "Lux soap," *Công Luận Báo*, May 3, 1933.
80. Advertisement, "Quận Chúa," *Ngày Nay*, November 26, 1938.
81. Advertisement, "Tôi sẽ dự cuộc đấu sắc tại hội chợ Pháp Việt tới đây," *Công Luận Báo*, June 14, 1933.
82. The Confucian social order, which still had sway early in twentieth-century Vietnam, valued professions that produced essential goods, such as farmers or artisans. From this viewpoint, merchants were not productive contributors to society; instead, they fed on the productive capacity of others, and by selling goods they made a profit from the work of others.
83. R. M. Boeckel, "The Trend of Commodity Prices," *Editorial Research Reports*, vol. 2 (1930).
84. For more information on mutual aid groups, see Ngo Vinh Long, *Before the Revolution: The Vietnamese Peasants Under the French* (Columbia University Press, 1991).
85. "Thaibinh: Cuộc Chợ phiên giúp đồng bào bị lụt," *Hà Thành Ngọ Báo*, February 11, 1935.
86. "Cuộc chợ phiên ở Hội Khai Trí lấy tiền giúp dân bị nạn bão lụt, trung kỳ," *Hà Thành Ngọ Báo*, February 12, 1935.
87. "Chuyện đời," *Hà Thành Ngọ Báo*, December 17, 1931.
88. "Cuộc chợ phiên ở Hội Khai Trí lấy tiền giúp dân bị nạn bão lụt, trung kỳ," *Hà Thành Ngọ Báo*, February 12, 1935.
89. "Thaibinh: Cuộc Chợ phiên giúp đồng bào bị lụt," *Hà Thành Ngọ Báo*, February 11, 1935.
90. "Chuyện đời," *Hà Thành Ngọ Báo*, December 17, 1931; and "Typhoons of the Far East During September and October 1931," *Monthly Weather Review* 59, no. 11 (November 1, 1931): 442–43.

5. BEAUTY CONTESTS

91. "Thaibinh: Cuộc Chợ phiên giúp đồng bào bị lụt," *Hà Thành ngọ báo*, February 11, 1935; and "Cuộc chợ phiên ở Hội Khai Trí lấy tiền giúp dân bị nạn bão lụt, trung kỳ," *Hà Thành Ngọ Báo*, February 12, 1935.
92. "Un immense success," *La Tribune Indochinoise*, March 26, 1937; and "Chương trình chợ phiên Nam Định," *Đông Pháp*, October 27, 1937.
93. Minh Châu, "Thư Hà Thành," *Tràng An Báo*, November 25, 1938.
94. "Program de la Kermess organisée les 6, 7, mai 1939," *La Tribune Indochinoise*, April 12, 1939.
95. "Journée annuelle de l'Afisna," February 2, 1939.
96. Lauren M. E. Goodlad, " 'Making the Working Man Like Me': Charity, Pastorship, and Middle Class Identity in Nineteenth-Century Britain," *Victorian Studies* 43, no. 4 (Summer 2001): 591–617.
97. Van Nguyen-Marshall, "The Associational Life of the Vietnamese Middle Class in Saigon (1950s–1970s)," in *The Reinvention of Distinction: Modernity and the Middle Class in Urban Vietnam*, ed. Van Nguyen-Marshall, Lisa Drummond, and Danièle Bélanger (Springer, 2012).
98. For an excellent discussion of philanthropic activities, see Van Nguyen-Marshall, *In Search of Moral Authority: The Discourse on Poverty, Poor Relief, and Charity in French Colonial Vietnan* (Peter Lang, 2008), 6, 57.
99. Vũ Trọng Phụng, *Vỡ Đê* (1936; repr. NXB Văn Học, 2017), part 3, chap. 5.
100. "Hội chợ Huế kỳ thứ ba đã khai mạc rất long trọng," *Tràng An Báo*, April 19, 1938.
101. "Hôi chợ Huế 1937," *Công Luận Báo*, April 14, 1937.
102. "Hội chợ Faifoo đã khai mạc," *Sài Gòn*, May 29, 1936; and "Mây thua nước tóc tuyết nhường màu da," *Sài Gòn*, May 28, 1936.
103. Advertisement, "Quận Chúa," *Ngày Nay*, November 26, 1938.
104. "Tiếng dội trong hội chợ," *Sài Gòn*, April 17, 1935.
105. Phan Thị Nga, "Chị em Hội An với y phục Cát Tường," *Ngày Nay*, March 10, 1935; "Hội chợ Lạc thiện ở Huế," *Tràng An Báo*, November 15, 1935; and B. "Hội chợ Faifoo đã khai mạc," *Sài Gòn*, May 29, 1936.
106. "Phiên chợ thường xuân của Thương đoàn," *Hà Thành Ngọ Báo*, April 26, 1933.
107. Vũ Trọng Phụng, *Làm Đĩ* (1936; repr. NXB Văn Học, 2015), 175.
108. "Thaibinh: Cuộc Chợ phiên giúp đồng bào bị lụt," *Hà Thành Ngọ Báo*, February 11, 1935.
109. "Thaibinh: Khánh thành chùa Thái-phú," *Hà Thành Ngọ Báo*, April 11, 1936.
110. As recounted by Thông Reo, "Làm cho rỏ mặt đàn bà nước Nam," *Trung Lập Báo*, March 21, 1931.
111. "Miss Univers," *La Tribune Indochinoise*, November 8, 1935; "Hoa Khôi thế giới," *Tràng An Báo*, November 12, 1935; and "Ta thua Lào," *Loa*, November 21, 1935.
112. "En quelques mots," *La Tribune Indochinoise*, January 18, 1939.
113. Velmet, "Beauty and Big Business," 91; and Ezra, "Colonialism Exposed," 51–65.
114. Letter to M. Theis, January 3, 1938. French National Archives, F12-12258; Letter, Maurice de Waleffe to Governor Géraud, March 4, 1937, French National Archives, F12-12258; Photograph "Miss France D'outre-mer et ses concurrentes, jeunes beautés métisses de l'empire français sur une terrasse du centre colonial a l'exposition," in *L'Illustration*, August 7, 1937. Thank you to David Del Testa for sharing his sources.

5. BEAUTY CONTESTS

115. "Đi dự cuộc đấu xảo quốc tế ở Paris," *Sài Gòn*, April 30, 1937; and "Tin Paris gởi về: Hoa khôi Bắc kỳ nói trước máy vô tuyến truyền thanh," *Công Luận Báo*, August 14, 1937.
116. "Hanoi Đẹp 1938," *Ngày Nay*, November 5, 1938; and "Hanoi Đẹp," *Ngày Nay*, November 26, 1938.
117. The case of Vietnam contrasts with that of the American-colonized Philippines. Geneve Clutario shows that beauty contests functioned as both a tool of colonial domination and as an avenue for forming and expressing national identity in the Philippines. Genieve Clutario, *Beauty Regimes: A History of Power and Modern Empire in the Philippines, 1898–1941* (Duke University Press, 2023), 66.
118. For an excellent discussion on the case of Nigeria, see Oluwakemi M. Balogun, *Beauty Diplomacy: Embodying an Emerging Nation* (Stanford University Press, 2020).
119. B. Pinar Ozdemir, "Building a 'Modern' and 'Western' Image: Miss Turkey Beauty Contests from 1929–1933," *Public Relations Review* 42, no. 4 (December 2016): 759–65.
120. Phan Trần Chúc, "Thi Sắc đẹp," *Hà Thành Ngọ Báo*, February 19, 1935.
121. "Thi đẹp," *Loa*, January 2, 1936.
122. "Petites Nouvelles," *La Tribune Indochinoise*, April 2, 1937.
123. "Braderie de Cholon," *La Tribune Indochinoise*, March 29, 1935; and "Hai ngôi sao được trúng tuyển cuộc thi sắc đẹp tại hội chợ Cholon," *Sài Gòn*, April 16, 1935.
124. "Concours de beauté," *Sài Gòn*, December 12, 1940.
125. Christopher Goscha, *Vietnam or Indochina? Contesting Concepts of Space in Vietnamese Nationalism, 1887–1954* (NIAS, 1995).
126. "Phiên chợ thường xuân của Thương đoàn," *Hà Thành Ngọ Báo*, April 26, 1933.
127. "Thi đẹp," *Loa*, January 2, 1936.
128. Minh Châu, "Thư Hà Thành," *Tràng An Báo*, November 25, 1938.
129. "Cuộc chợ phiên ở Hội Khai Trí lấy tiền giúp dân bị nạn bão lụt, trung kỳ," *Hà Thành Ngọ Báo*, February 12, 1935.
130. See, for example, "Hội chợ Huế 1937," *Công Luận Báo*, April 14, 1937.
131. Dr. Trần Văn Lai was a member of Trần Trọng Kim's government during the Japanese invasion and would later be credited with tearing down the French statues and renaming the streets of Hanoi during the Japanese coup in 1945. He would go on to serve in the Democratic Republic of Vietnam (DRV) government.
132. "Cuộc chợ phiên ở Hội Khai Trí lấy tiền giúp dân bị nạn bão lụt, trung kỳ," *Hà Thành Ngọ Báo*, February 12, 1935.
133. Nghị Toét, "Câu chuyện hằng tuần: một cuộc tuyển cử ở ta," *Sông Hương*, June 19, 1937.
134. "Cuộc chợ phiên ở Hội Khai Trí lấy tiền giúp dân bị nạn bão lụt, trung kỳ," *Hà Thành Ngọ Báo*, February 12, 1935.
135. In the United States in 1929, winners often received $5,000 and travel around Europe. C. L., "Nước mỹ có nhiều hội thi con gái đẹp," *Hà Thành Ngọ Báo*, October 9, 1929. In 1934, Miss America won $2,000, a ten-horsepower car, or a dowry. The winner often received side perks, such as unlimited spending at a certain hat shop or a modeling contract. Wancaln, " . . . Rồi làm thành ngôi sao," *Hà Thành Ngọ Báo*, July 6, 1934.

136. Trung Tiên, "Dư luận: Có nên cản trở cuộc đấu sắc đẹp của CLB tổ chức đây chăng?," *Đông Pháp Thời Báo*, August 21, 1925.
137. "Cuộc chợ phiên ở Hội Khai Trí lấy tiền giúp dân bị nạn bão lụt, trung kỳ," *Hà Thành Ngọ Báo*, February 12, 1935.
138. In the US model, which was covered in the Vietnamese press, hat shops and tailors used the women for advertising, gave them unlimited spending, and hoped that the women would wear their products and other people would follow their lead. Wancaln, " . . . Rồi làm thành ngôi sao," *Hà Thành Ngọ Báo*, July 6, 1934.
139. "Hai ngôi sao được trúng tuyển cuộc thi sắc đẹp tại hội chợ Cholon," *Sài Gòn*, April 16, 1935.
140. "Phiên chợ thưởng xuân của Thương đoàn," *Hà Thành Ngọ Báo*, April 26, 1933.
141. "Phiên chợ thưởng xuân của Thương đoàn," *Hà Thành Ngọ Báo*, April 26, 1933.
142. Nguyễn văn Tuyên, who had grown up near the fairgrounds, had become a household name: he was the first Vietnamese musician appointed to the Saigon Philharmonic and is widely regarded today as the founder of "new music" (tân nhạc), the upbeat mixture of French and Vietnamese music that was spreading like wildfire in the mid-1930s. The Huế fair was just one stop in a highly publicized tour of Indochina commissioned by the governor of Cochinchina.
143. "Đi quanh hội chợ Huế," *Tràng An Báo*, April 19, 1938.
144. In 1933, the *Phụ Nữ Tân Văn* newspaper covered a pageant in Turkey where the audience rioted when they disagreed with the jury's choice of the winner. *Phụ Nữ Tân Văn*, June 8, 1933.
145. "Tại 'Hôtel La Pagode' tối thứ bảy 13 Avril," *Hà Thành Ngọ Báo*, April 16, 1935.
146. "Petites Nouvelles," *La Tribune Indochinoise*, April 2, 1937.
147. Nghị Toét, "Câu chuyện hằng tuần: một cuộc tuyển cử ở ta," *Sông Hương*, June 19, 1937.
148. N. N., "Xã Giao," *Ngày Nay*, August 23, 1936.
149. ẬT, "Tưởng Tượng: Hoa Khôi Nam Việt," *Khoa Học*, January 1, 1936.
150. Vũ Trọng Phụng, *Làm Đĩ*.
151. Công Thành Đinh, *Phụ nữ tân văn: Phấn son tô điểm sơn hà* (NXB Văn Hóa Sài Gòn, 2010); and Bùi Thị Thanh Hương, "Báo Phụ nữ tân văn: Những việc làm và tư tưởng mới," *Tư Liệu Tham Khảo* 46 (2013): 160–67.
152. "Ý kiến chúng tôi đối với thời sự," *Phụ Nữ Tân Văn*, August 27, 1931.
153. Trần Thị Bích, "Có nên bắt chước Âu-châu mở ra những cuộc thi sắc đẹp không?—Không!," *Phụ Nữ Tân Văn*, June 8, 1933.
154. "Phụ nữ ta nên bớt xa xỉ," *Phụ Nữ Tân Văn*, February 25, 1932; Shawn McHale, "Printing and Power: Vietnamese Debates Over Women's Place in Society, 1918–1934," in *Essays Into Vietnamese Pasts*, ed. Keith W. Taylor and John K. Whitmore (Cornell University Press, 1995), 189.
155. Trần Thị Bích,"Có nên bắt chước Âu-châu mở ra những cuộc thi sắc đẹp không?—Không!," *Phụ Nữ Tân Văn*, June 8, 1933.
156. Phan Trần Chúc, "Thi Sắc đẹp," *Hà Thành Ngọ Báo*, February 19, 1935.
157. "Paris Quarrels Over Milady Beautiful," *Washington Post*, July 8, 1928; and Grout, "Between Venus and Mercury," 51.
158. Phan Trần Chúc, "Thi Sắc đẹp," *Hà Thành Ngọ Báo*, February 19, 1935. For more information on networks that trafficked women to China, see Micheline Lessard, *Human Trafficking in Colonial Vietnam* (Routledge, 2015); and Christina Firpo,

Black Market Business: Selling Sex in Northern Vietnam, 1920–1945 (Cornell University Press, 2020), 98–108.
159. "Cuộc thi thanh," *Vịt Đực*, November 30, 1938.
160. Năm Nuôi, "Từ con," *Vịt Đực*, November 30, 1938. For more on cheap hotels, see Shaun Malarney, trans., "Introduction: Vũ Trọng Phụng and the Anxieties of 'Progress,'" in *Lục Xì: Prostitution and Venereal Disease in Colonial Hanoi*, by Vũ Trọng Phụng (University of Hawaii Press, 2011); and Firpo, *Black Market Business*, 33–36.

CONCLUSION

1. This was a strategy of many authors, but it is most evident in Nguyễn Công Hoan's 1933 short story *"Cô Kếu, gái tân thời"* and his 1938 novel *Cô Giáo Minh*. In both stories, the author uses cosmetics and new fashion to signal to the reader that young women from conservative families were testing "the new" (*cái mới*).
2. The first wartime economic changes occurred when Nazi forces invaded Poland in early September 1939, and the European economy contracted and pivoted to defense production. The following month France, now under the rule of the pro-German Vichy government, signed an armistice with Germany.
3. In August 1942, Allied forces began bombing industrial facilities, the ports of Hải Phòng and Cam Ranh, as well as airfields in Vietnam. Locals avoided railroads, bridges, and ferries because such spots were well-known targets for bombing.
4. Anne Raffin, *Youth Mobilization in Vichy Indochina and Its Legacies, 1940–1970* (Lexington, 2008).
5. David G. Marr, *Vietnam: State War and Revolution (1945–1946)* (University of California Press, 2013), 271–27.
6. Phạm Thảo Nguyên, *Áo dài Lemur và bối cảnh Phong Hoá và Ngày Nay* (NXB Hồng Đức, 2019), 60.
7. In September 1940, the group lost its license to publish the *Ngày Nay* newspaper. In 1940–41, the French police arrested some of the leaders of the movement. By 1945, the Self-Strengthening Movement was defunct. Martina Thucnhi Nguyen, *On Our Own Strength: The Self-Reliant Literary Group and Cosmopolitan Nationalism in Late Colonial Vietnam* (University of Hawaii Press, 2020); and Phạm Thảo Nguyên, *Áo dài Lemur và bối cảnh Phong Hoá và Ngày Nay*, 60.
8. A version of the dress first came into international focus during the US-Vietnam war when Trần Lệ Xuân, the de facto first lady of the Republic of Vietnam, appeared on camera with an update of the Lemur Tunic, which kept the curves but added a deep scoop or boat neck. But after the war, Trần Lệ Xuân and her dress became associated with the decadence of the failed southern regime.
9. The story of how the áo dài came to represent the nation is closely linked to the political and economic developments of the 1990s. In 1995, Vietnam enjoyed a flood of foreign investment after normalizing diplomatic and trade relations with the United States. As international and local businesses developed during the 1990s and early 2000s, the áo dài came to be worn as regular office attire, sometimes with a blazer. In the late 1990s, Vietnam embraced a tourist economy. In 1997, Vietnam relaxed its tourism policy to allow free travel throughout the

nation and began promoting itself as an international travel destination. As it turns out, the áo dài served as an ideal vehicle with which to tout the country's uniquely "exotic" character. Nhi T. Lieu, *The American Dream in Vietnamese* (University of Minnesota Press, 2011), 158, note 13.

10. Tran Thi Phuong Hoa, "Making the Vietnamese Áo Dài Tunic National Heritage: Fashion Travel Through Tradition, Colonialism, Modernity," *International Journal of Heritage Studies* 27, no. 8 (2021): 806–18; and "Ao Dai Displaying Vietnamese Cultural Heritage on Show in Hanoi," Vietnamnet.vn, June 29, 2020, https://vietnamnet.vn/en/ao-dai-displaying-vietnamese-cultural-heritage-on-show-in-hanoi-652624.html.

11. Le Huy, "Lịch sử áo dài Việt Nam từ thế kỷ 17 đến nay," *Harper's Bazaar Vietnam*, June 8, 2020, https://bazaarvietnam.vn/nhin-lai-lich-su-ao-dai-viet-nam-qua-cac-thoi-ky/.

12. Đức Thành, "Đi tìm phấn nụ Hoàng cung,", March 14, 2016. https://suckhoegiadinh.com.vn/lam-dep/di-tim-phan-nu-hoang-cung-21458/

BIBLIOGRAPHY

ARCHIVES

The Advertising Archives, www.advertisingarchives.co.uk
Amandahallay.com
Archives Nationales d'Outre Mer, Aix-en-Provence, France
Les entreprises coloniales françaises, www.entreprises-coloniales.fr
French National Archives, Paris (files consulted in 2004)
Makeup Museum, www.makeupmuseum.org
Radium Archives, www.lucyjanesantos.com
Vietnam National Archives, Center I, Hanoi
Vietnam National Archives, Center II, Ho Chi Minh City

NEWSPAPERS

Annam Nouveau
Bulletin de l'Agence Générale des colonies
Công Luận Báo
Cười
Đàn-Bà
Đàn Bà Mới
Điễn Tín
Đông Pháp
Đông Pháp Thời Báo
Đông Phương
Hà Thành Ngọ Báo
Khoa Học

Khoa Học Tập Chí
La Dépêche colonial illustrée
La Dépêche d'Indochine
La Tribune Indochinoise
L'Annam Nouveau
L'Avenir du Tonkin
Le Journal
L'Echo Annamite
Le Petit Écho de la mode
Le Petit Parisien
Les Nouvelliste d'Indochine
L'Éveil économique de l'Indochine
L'Illustration
Loa
Loa Tuần Báo
Lục Tỉnh Tân Văn
Nam Phong
Ngày Nay
Nhật Tân
Phong Hóa
Phụ Nữ Tân Văn
Sài Gòn
Sông Hương
Thanh Nghệ Tịnh Tân Văn
The Lewston Daily Sun
Thông Tin
Thời Vụ
Tiểu Thuyết Thứ Bảy
Tin Mới
Tràng An Báo
Trung Bắc Tân Văn
Trung Hòa Nhật Báo
Trung Lập Báo
Vịt Đực

PUBLISHED SOURCES

Aitchison, Madeleine E. "Who Holds the Mirror? The Creation of an Ideal Vietnamese Woman, 1918–1934." Master's thesis, University of Hawaii, 2018.

Ambaras, David. *Bad Youth: Juvenile Delinquency and the Politics of Everyday Life in Modern Japan*. University of California Press, 2006.

Anderson, Warwick. *Colonial Pathologies: American Tropical Medicine, Race, and Hygiene in the Philippines*. Duke University Press, 2006.

André-Pallois, Nadine. "École Supérieur des Beaux-Arts de l'Indochine." In *The Routledge Encyclopedia of Modernism*. Taylor and Francis, 2016.

BIBLIOGRAPHY

André-Pallois, Nadine. *L'Indochine: un lieu d'échange culturel. Les peintres français et indochinois (fin XIX-XXe siècle)*, EFEO, 1997.
Ariès, Philippe, and Georges Duby, eds. *A History of Private Life, Volume 4*. Harvard University Press, 1990.
Ariès, Philippe, and Georges Duby, eds. *A History of Private Life, Volume 5*. Harvard University Press, 1991.
Arnold, David, and Eric DeWald. "Cycles of Empowerment? The Bicycle and Everyday Technology in India and Vietnam." *Comparative Studies in Society and History* 53, no. 4 (2011): 971–96.
Arnold, Rebecca. *Fashion, Desire, and Anxiety: Image and Morality in Twentieth Century*. I. B. Tauris, 2011.
Ashikari, Mikiko. "The Memory of the Women's White Faces: Japaneseness and the Ideal Image of Women." *Japan Forum* 15, no. 1 (2003): 55–79.
Atkins, Taylor E. *Blue Nippon: Authenticating Jazz in Japan*. Duke University Press, 2001.
Balogun, Oluwakemi M. *Beauty Diplomacy: Embodying an Emerging Nation*. Stanford University Press, 2020.
Banner, Lois W. *American Beauty: A Social History . . . Through Two Centuries of the American Ideal*. Knopf, 1983.
Bao Dai, Sa Magesté. *Le dragon d'Annam*. Plon, 1979.
Bard, Christine. *Les femmes dans la société française au 20e siècle*. Armand Colin, 2004.
Barthes, Roland. *The Fashion System*, trans. Matthew Ward and Richard Howard. University of California Press, 1990.
Bayly, Christopher. "The Origins of Swadeshi (Home Industry): Cloth and Indian Society (1700–1930)." In *The Social Life of Things: Commodities in Cultural Perspective*, ed. A. Appadurai. Cambridge University Press, 1986.
Benet, Terry. *Early Photography in Vietnam*. Renaissance, 2020.
Berlanstein, Lenard R. "Selling Modern Feminity: Femina, a Forgotten Feminist Publishing Success in Belle Epoque France." *French Historical Studies* 30, no. 4 (Fall 2007): 623–49.
Berry, Sarah. *Screen Style: Fashion and Femininity in 1930s Hollywood*. University of Minnesota Press, 2000.
Bhabha, Homi. "Of Mimicry and Man: The Ambivalence of Colonial Discourse." *Discipleship: A Special Issue on Psychoanalysis* 28 (Spring 1984): 125–33.
Boeckel, R. M. "The Trend of Commodity Prices." *Editorial Research Reports*, vol. 2 (1930).
Boittin, Jennifer. *Colonial Metropolis: The Urban Grounds of Anti-Imperialism and Feminism in Interwar France*. University of Nebraska Press, 2010.
Boittin, Jennifer. *Undesirable: Passionate Mobility and Women's Defiance of French Colonial Policing 1919–1952*. University of Chicago Press, 2022.
Booth, Anne. "Crisis and Response: A Study of Foreign Trade and Exchange Rate Policies in Three Southeast Asian Colonies in the 1930s." In *Weathering the Storm*, ed. Pierre Brocheux. Brill, 2000.
Bourdieu, Pierre. *Distinction: A Social Critique of the Judgement of Taste*. Harvard University Press, 1984.
Bourdieu, Pierre. "Sport and Social Class." *Social Science Information* 17 (1978): 819–40.
Boussel, Patrice. *Histoire des Vacances*. Berger-Levrault, 1961.

Bradley, Mark Philip. "Becoming 'Van Minh': Civilizational Discourse and Visions of the Self in Twentieth-Century Vietnam." *Journal of World History* 15, no. 1 (March 2004): 65–83.
Brocheux, Pierre, and Daniel Hémery. *Indochina: An Ambiguous Colonization, 1858–1954.* University of California Press, 2009.
Brötel, Dieter. "French Economic Imperialism in China, 1885–1904/1906." *Itinerario* 23, no. 1 (1999): 52–61.
Brown, Ian. *Economic Change in Southeast Asia c. 1830–1980.* Oxford University Press, 1997.
Brownfoot, Janice N. "Emancipation, Exercise and Imperialism: Girls and the Games Ethic in Colonial Malaya." *International Journal of the History of Sport* 7, no. 3 (2007): 61–84.
Brownfoot, Janice N. "'Healthy Bodies, Healthy Minds': Sport and Society in Colonial Malaya." *International Journal of the History of Sport* 19, no. 2–3 (2010): 129–56.
Bùi Thị Thanh Hương. "Báo Phụ nữ tân văn: Những việc làm và tư tưởng mới." *Tư Liệu Tham Khảo* 46 (2013): 160–67.
Burton, Antoinette, ed. *Gender, Sexuality and Colonial Modernities.* Taylor and Francis, 1999.
Butler, Judith. *Gender Trouble: Feminism and the Subversion of Identity.* Routledge, 2015. First published in 1990.
Cadière, L. "Le changement de costume sous Vo-Vuong, ou une crise religieuse à Hue au XVIIIe siècle," *Bulletin des amis de vieux Hue* 4 (1915).
Callahan, William A. "The Ideology of Miss Thailand in National, Consumerist and Transnational Space." *Alternatives* 23 (1998).
Celarié, Henriette. *Promenade en Indochine.* Éditions Baudinière, 1937.
Chadwick, Whitney, and Tirza True Latimer, eds. *The Modern Woman Revisited: Paris Between the Wars.* Rutgers University Press, 2003.
Chaigneau, Michel Đức, *Souvenirs de Hué (Cochinchine).* L'Imprimerie Impériale, 1857.
Chan, Sylvia Li Wen. "Department Stores in Singapore: The History of Mass Consumption in Business Institution." Master's thesis, Nanyang Technological University, 2002.
Chen, I-Fen, and Hsiu-Hui Sun. "The Framed Female Image: A Pictorial Semiotic Analysis of Classic Shanghai Calendar Posters During the 1910s–1930s." In *East Asian Modern Girl: Women, Media, and Colonial Modernity During the Interwar Years*, ed. Sumei Wang. Brill, 2021.
Cheung, Roanna Yuk-Heng. "Embodying Modernity: Humor, Gender, and Popular Culture in Republican Guangzhou." PhD diss., University of California, Los Angeles, 2016.
Cheung, Han. "An 'Uplifting' Shopping Experience," *Taipei Times*, November 29, 2015.
Chiem, Kristen L. "Beauty Under the Willow Tree: Picturing Virtuous Women in 19th Century China." In *Modernity in the Arts of East Asia, 16th–20th Centuries*, ed. Kristen L. Chiem and Lara C. W. Blanchard. Brill, 2017.
Chō Kyō and Kyoko Iriye Selden. *The Search for the Beautiful Woman: A Cultural History of Japanese and Chinese Beauty.* Rowman and Littlefield, 2012.
Choi, Hyaeweol. *Gender and Mission Encounters in Korea: New Women, Old Ways: Seoul-California Series in Korean Studies*, vol. 1. University of California Press, 2009.
Choi, Hyaeweol. *New Women in Colonial Korea: A Sourcebook.* Routledge, 2013.

Choi, Hyaeweol. "'Wise Mother, Good Wife': A Transcultural Discursive Construct in Modern Korea." *Journal of Korean Studies* 14, no. 1 (Fall 2009) 1–33.

Chrisman-Campbell, Kimberly. *Skirts: Fashioning Modern Femininity in the Twentieth Century*. St. Martin's Press, 2022.

Chua Ai Lin. "Singapore's 'Cinema-Age' of the 1930s: Hollywood and the Shaping of Singapore Modernity." *Inter-Asia Cultural Studies* 13, no. 4 (December 2012): 592–604.

Clutario, Genevieve. *Beauty Regimes: A History of Power and Modern Empire in the Philippines, 1898–1941*. Duke University Press, 2023.

Clutario, Genevieve. "Pageant Politics: Tensions of Power, Empire, and Nationalism in Manila Carnival Queen Contests." In *Gendering the Trans-Pacific World*, ed. Catherine Ceniza Choi and Judy Tzu-Chun Wen. Brill, 2017.

Cohen, W. B. "The Colonial Policy of the Popular Front." *French Historical Studies* 7, no. 3 (1972): 368–93.

Cohn, Bernard. "Cloth, Clothes, and Colonialism." *Consumption: The History and Regional Development of Consumption* 2 (2001): 405.

Cook, Megan. *The Constitutionalist Party in Cochinchina: The Years of Decline, 1930–1942*. Monash University Center of Southeast Asian Studies, 1977.

Conrad, Sebastian. *What is Global History?*. Princeton University Press, 2017.

Công Thành Đinh. *Phụ nữ tân văn: Phấn son tô điểm sơn hà*. NXB Văn Hóa Sài Gòn, 2010.

Cooper, Nicola J. "Gendering the Colonial Enterprise: La Mère-Patrie and Maternalism in France and French Indochina." In *Empires and Boundaries: Rethinking Race, Class, and Gender in Colonial Settings*, ed. Harald Fischer-Tiné and Susanne Gehrmann. Routledge, 2008.

Cooper, Nicola. "Urban Planning and Architecture in Colonial Indochina." *French Cultural Studies* 11, no. 1 (2000): 75–99.

Conor, Liz. *The Spectacular Modern Woman: Feminine Visibility in the 1920s*. Indiana University Press, 2004.

Conrad, Sebastian. "Globalizing the Beautiful Body: Eugen Sandow, Bodybuilding, and the Idea of Muscular Manliness at the Turn of the 20th Century." *Journal of World History* 32, no. 1 (March 2021): 95–125.

Cott, Nancy F. "The Modern Woman of the 1920s, American Style." In *A History of Women in the West*, ed. Françoise Thébaud. ed Harvard University Press, 1994.

Craig, David. *Familiar Medicine: Everyday Health Knowledge and Practice in Today's Vietnam*. University of Hawaii Press, 2002.

Craik, Jennifer. *The Face of Fashion: Cultural Studies in Fashion*. Routledge, 1994.

Cross, Garry. "Vacations for All: The Leisure Question in the Era of the Popular Front." *Journal of Contemporary History* 24, no. 4 (1989): 599–621.

Crossick, Geoffrey, and Serge Jaumain, eds. *Cathedrals of Consumption: The European Department Store, 1850–1939*. Routledge, 2020.

Cunnington, C. Willet, and Phillis Cunnington. *The History of Underclothes*. Michael Joseph, 1951.

Dalby, Liz. *Kimono: Fashioning Culture*. Vintage, 1993.

Đặng Thị Vân Chi. *Vấn đề phụ nữ trên báo chí tiếng Việt trước năm 1945*. NXB Khoa Học Xã Hội, 2008.

Đào Duy Anh. *Việt Nam văn hóa sử cương*. NXB Văn Hóa-Thông Tin, 2000. First published in 1938.

Dau The Tuan. "La Transition agraire au Vietnam comme changement d'institutions." In *Développement et transition vers l'économie de marché: Ouvrage extrait des troisième journées*, ed. Agence francophone pour l'enseignement supérieur et la recherche, 457–71. Éditions de l'Agence, 1998.

Davis, Kathy. "Cosmetic Surgery in a Different Voice: The Case of Madame Noel/" *Women's Studies International Forum* 2, no. 5 (September-October 1999): 473–88.

De Grazia, Victoria, and Ellen Furlough, eds. *The Sex of Things: Gender and Consumption in Historical Perspective*. University of California Press, 1996.

Del Testa, David. "Workers, Culture, and the Railroads in French Colonial Indochina, 1905–1936." *French Colonial History* 2, no. 1 (2002): 181–98.

Del Testa, David. "Automobiles and Anomie in French Indochina." In *France and Indochina Cultural Representations*, ed. Kathryn Robinson and Jennifer Yee. Lexington, 2005.

Demay, Aline. *Tourism and Colonization in Indochina (1898–1939)*. Cambridge Scholars, 2014.

Demery, Monique Brinson. *Finding the Dragon Lady: The Mystery of Vietnam's Madame Nhu*. Public Affairs, 2013.

Dinh Trong Hieu, "Le face, le ventre et autres symboliques du corps chez les Viets." In *La Colonisation des Corps: de l'Indochine au Viet Nam*, ed. François Guillemot and Agathe Larcher-Goscha (Vendémiaire, 2014).

Đoàn Thị Tình. *Trang phục Việt Nam*. NXB Mỹ Thuật, 2006.

Dong, Madeleine Y. "Who Is Afraid of the Chinese Modern Girl?" In *The Modern Girl Around the World: Consumption, Modernity, and Globalization*, ed. Alys Eve Weinbaum, Lynn M. Thomas, Priti Ramamurthy, and Uta G. Poiger. Duke University Press, 2008.

Doumer, Paul. *L'Indo-Chine Française (Souvenirs)*. Vuibert, 1930.

Druesedow, Jean L. "Ready-to-Wear." In *Encyclopedia of Clothing and Fashion*, vol. 3, ed. Valerie Steele. Scribner, 2005.

Drummond, Lisa. "The Modern 'Vietnamese Woman': Socialization and Women's Magazines." In *Gender Practices in Contemporary Vietnam*, ed. L. Drummond and H. Rydstrøm. Singapore University Press, 2004.

Dumarest, André. "La formation de classes sociales en Pays Annamites." PhD diss., University of Lyon, 1935.

Durand, Maurice M., and Nguyen Tran Huan. *An Introduction to Vietnamese Literature*, trans. D. M. Hawke. Columbia University Press, 1985.

Dương Như Đức. "Education in Vietnam Under French Domination, 1862–1945." PhD diss., Southern Illinois University at Carbondale, 1978.

Edwards, Louise. "Policing the Modern Woman in Republican China." *Modern China* 26, no. 2 (April 2000): 115–47.

Edwards, Penny. "'Propagender': Marianne, Joan of Arc and the Export of French Gender Ideology to Colonial Cambodia (1863–1954)." In *Promoting the Colonial Idea: Propaganda and Visions of Empire in France*, ed. Tony Chafuer and Amanda Sackur. Palgrave Macmillan, 2002.

Edwards, Penny. "Restyling Colonial Cambodia (1860–1954): French Dressing, Indigenous Custom and National Costume." *Fashion Theory* 5, no. 4 (November 2021): 389–416.

Eiseman, Leatrice, and Keith Recker, eds. *Pantone the 20th Century in Color*. Chronicle, 2011.

BIBLIOGRAPHY

Elias, Norbert. *The Civilizing Process: Sociogenetic and Psychogenetic Investigations.* Blackwell, 2000.
Ezra, Elizabeth. "Colonialism Exposed: Miss France d'Outre-Mer, 1937." In *Identity Papers: Contested Nationhood in Twentieth Century France*, ed. Steven Ungar and Tom Conley. University of Minnesota Press, 1996.
Farrell-Beck, Jane, and Collen Gau. *Uplift: The Bra in America.* University of Pennsylvania Press, 2002.
Fay, Emma. "The Victims of Beauty: How Women Paid the Price of the Industrial Revolution, Science, and Hollywood." *The Forum: Journal of History* 15, no. 1 (2023): 1–25.
Fee, Annie. "Gender, Class, and Cinophilia: Parisian Cinema Cultures 1918–1925." PhD diss., University of Washington, 2015.
Field, Andrew David. *Shanghai's Dancing World: Cabaret Culture and Urban Politics, 1919–1954.* Chinese University Press, 2010.
Fields, Jill. "Fighting the Corsetless Evil: Shaping Corsets and Culture, 1900–1930." *Journal of Social History* 33, no. 2 (1999): 355–84.
Fields, Jill. *An Intimate Affair: Women, Lingerie, and Sexuality.* University of California Press, 2007.
Finnane, Antonia. *Changing Clothes in China: Fashion, History, Nation.* Columbia University Press, 2008.
Firpo, Christina. *Black Market Business: Selling Sex in Northern Vietnam, 1920–1945.* Cornell University Press, 2020.
Firpo, Christina. *The Uprooted: Race, Children, and Imperialism in French Indochina, 1890–1980.* University of Hawaii Press, 2016.
Formichi, Chiara. *Healthy Progress: Muslim Women as Modernizers in Twentieth Century Indonesia.* Stanford University Press, forthcoming.
Freedman, Alisa, Laura Miller, and Christine R. Yano, eds. *Modern Girl on the Go: Gender, Mobility, and Labor in Japan.* Stanford University Press, 2013.
Furlough, Ellen. *Consumer Cooperation in France: The Politics of Consumption, 1834–1930.* Cornell University Press, 1991.
Furlough, Ellen. "Making Mass Vacations: Tourism and Consumer Culture in France, 1930s to 1970s." *Comparative Studies in Society and History* 40, no. 2 (1998): 247–86.
Gao, Yunxiang. *Sporting Gender: Women Athletes and Celebrity-Making During China's National Crisis, 1931–1945.* University of British Columbia Press, 2013.
Gardner, Kirsten E. "Hiding the Scars: History of Breast Prostheses After Mastectomy Since 1945." In *Beauty and Business: Commerce, Gender, and Culture in Modern America*, ed. Philip Scranton. Routledge, 2000.
Gasch, Alice T. "Lash Lure and Paraphenylenediamine: Toxic Beauty Past and Present." *American Academy of Ophthalmology*, November 2, 2017. https://www.aao.org/senior-ophthalmologists/scope/article/lash-lure-paraphenylenediamine-toxic-beauty.
Gibbs, Jason. "Spoken Theatre, La Scene Tonkinoise, and the First Modern Vietnamese Songs." *Journal for the Society of Asian Music* 31, no. 2 (Spring/Summer 2000): 1–33.
Gibbs, Jason. "The West's Songs, Our Songs: The Introduction and Adaption of Western Popular Music in Vietnam Before 1940." *Asian Music* 35, no. 1 (2003): 57–84.
Goodlad, Lauren M. E. "'Making the Working Man Like Me': Charity, Pastorship, and Middle Class Identity in Nineteenth-Century Britain." *Victorian Studies* 43, no. 4 (Summer 2001): 591–617.

Gordon, Sarah A. "'Any Desired Length': Negotiating Gender Through Sports Clothing, 1870–1925." In *Beauty and Business: Commerce, Gender, and Culture in Modern America*, ed. Philip Scranton. Routledge, 2001.

Goscha, Christopher. "Bao Dai and Sihanouk: La fabrique Indochinoise des rois coloniaux." In *La colonization des corps: De l'Indochine au Viet Nam*, ed. François Guillemot and Agathe Larcher-Goscha. Vendémiaire, 2014.

Goscha, Christopher. "The Modern Barbarian: Nguyen Van Vinh and the Complexity of Colonial Modernity in Vietnam." *European Journal of East Asian Studies* 3, no.1 (2004) 135–69.

Goscha, Christopher. "Monarchies coloniales et décolonisations comparees dans l'Empire Français: Bao Dai, Norodom Sihanouk et Mohammed V." *Monde(s)* 2, no. 12 (2017): 41–69.

Goscha, Christopher. *Vietnam: A New History*. Basic Books, 2016.

Goscha, Christopher. *Vietnam or Indochina? Contesting Concepts of Space in Vietnamese Nationalism, 1887–1954*. NIAS, 1995.

Gray, Mitchel. *The Lingerie Book*. St. Martin's Press, 1980.

Greenhalgh, Paul. *Ephemeral Vistas: The Expositons Universelles, Great Exhibitions and World's Fairs 1851–1939*. Manchester University Press, 1998.

Grout, Holly. "Between Venus and Mercury: The 1920s Beauty Contest in France and America." *French Politics, Culture, and Society* 31, no. 1 (Spring 2013): 51.

Grout, Holly. *The Force of Beauty: Transforming French Ideas of Femininity in the Third Republic*. Louisiana State University Press, 2015.

Grout, Holly. "'Le Miracle et le Mirage': Beauty Institutes and the Making of the Modern French Woman." *Business History* 66, no. 1 (September 2020): 59–75.

Guénel, Annick. "The Creation of the First Overseas Pasteur Institute, or the Beginning of Albert Calmette's Pastorian Career." *Medical History* 43, no. 1 (1999): 1–25.

Guenther, Irine. *Nazi Chic? Fashioning Women in the Third Reich*. Berg, 2004.

Gulliver, Katrina. *Modern Women in China and Japan: Gender, Feminism and Global Modernity Between the Wars*. IB Tauris, 2012.

Ha, Mary-Paule. *French Women and the Empire: The Case of Indochina*. Oxford University Press, 2014.

Habermas, Jurgen. *The Structural Transformation of the Public Sphere: An Inquiry Into a Category of Bourgeois Society*. MIT Press, 1991.

Haiken, Elizabeth. *Venus Envy: A History of Cosmetic Surgery*. Johns Hopkins University Press, 1997.

Hale, Dana S. *Races on Display: French Representations of Colonized Peoples, 1886–1940*. Indiana University Press, 2008.

Healey, Lucy. "Modernity, Identity, and Constructions of Malay Womanhood." *Modernity and Identity: Asian Illustrations* (1994): 111–30.

Henchy, Judith A. N. "Performing Modernity in the Writings of Nguyễn An Ninh and Pham Văn Hùm." PhD diss., University of Washington, 2005.

Herbelin, Caroline. *Architectures du Vietnam Colonial: Repenser le métissage*. Institute National d'histoire d'art, 2016.

Herbert, James. *Paris 1937: Worlds on Exhibition*. Cornell University Press, 1998.

Hien, Nina. "Ho Chi Minh City's Beauty Regime: Haptic Technologies of the Self in the New Millennium." *Positions: Asia Critique* 20 (2012): 473–93.

BIBLIOGRAPHY

Hill, Sara, Christopher Rodeheffer, Kristina Durante, Vladas Griskevicius, and Andrew White. "Boosting Beauty in an Economic Decline: Mating, Spending, and the Lipstick Effect." *Journal of Personality and Social Psychology* 103, no. 2 (2012): 275–91.

Hoàng Đạo Thúy. *Phố phường Hà Nội xưa*. NXB Văn Hoa Thông Tin, 2000.

Hoàng Ngọc Phác. *Tố Tâm: Tâm-lý tiêu thuyết*. NXB Van Nghệ, 1988. First published in 1925.

Hoang Ngoc Thanh. *Vietnam's Social Development as Seen Through the Modern Novel*. Peter Lang, 1991.

Hobsbawm, Eric, and Terence Ranger, eds. *The Invention of Tradition*. Cambridge University Press, 1994.

Hội chợ Huế: Chương Trình. Imp. Tiếng Dân, 1936.

Hội Đồng Lịch Sử Hải Phòng, ed. *Lược Khảo Đường Phố Hải Phòng*. NXB Xí Nghiệp, 1990.

Hội Đồng Lịch Thành Phố, ed. *Địa Chí Hải Phòng*, vol. 1. NXB Hải Phòng, 1990.

Hội Đồng Lịch Thành Phố, ed. *Lược Khảo Đường Phố Hải Phòng*. NXB Hải Phòng, 1993.

Hong, Jeesoon. "Transcultural Politics of Department Stores: Colonialism and Mass Culture in East Asia, 1900–1945." *International Journal of Asian Studies* 13, no. 2 (2016): 123–50.

Hong, Fan. *Footbinding, Feminism and Freedom: The Liberation of Women's Bodies in Modern China*. Frank Cass, 1997.

Houy, Yvonne Barbara. "Of Course the German Woman Should Be Modern: The Modernization of Women's Appearance During National Socialism." PhD diss., Cornell University Press, 2002.

Huard, P. "Le noircissement des dents en Asie oriental et en Indochine," *France-Asie* 3 (July 1948): 808–12.

Huard, Philip, and Maurice Durand, *Connaissance du Viet-Nam*. EFEO, 1954.

Hue Tam Ho Tai. *Radicalism and the Origins of the Vietnamese Revolution*. Harvard University Press, 1992.

Huff, Gregg. "Causes and Consequences of the Great Vietnam Famine, 1944–5." *The Economic History Review* 72, no. 1 (2019): 286–316.

Hultquist, Clark. "The Price of Dreams: A History of Advertising in France, 1927–1968." PhD diss., Ohio State University, 1996.

Hữu Ngọc and Lady Borton, eds. *Áo dài: Women's Long Dress*. NXB Thế Giới, 2014.

Ikeya, Chie. "The Modern Burmese Woman and the Politics of Fashion in Colonial Burma." *Journal of Asian Studies* 67, no. 4 (November 2008): 1277–1308.

Ikeya, Chie. *Refiguring Women, Colonialism and Modernity in Burma*. University of Hawaii Press, 2011.

Ishida, Ayuu. "The Wartime Modern Girl in Japan: Changes in Female Images in Cosmetic Advertisements of Housewife's Friend (Shufu No Tomo) from the 1930s to the 1940s." In *The East Asian Modern Girl: Women, Media, and Colonial Modernity During the Intewar Years*, ed. Sumei Wang. Brill, 2021.

Jackson, Beverley. *Splendid Slipper: A Thousand Years of Erotic Tradition*. Ten Speed Press, 1997.

Jamieson, Neil. *Understanding Vietnam*. University of California Press, 1995.

Jaschok, Maria, and Suzanne Miers, eds. *Women and Chinese Patriarchy: Submission, Servitude, and Escape*. Hong Kong University Press, 1994.

Jennings, Eric. *Imperial Heights: Dalat and the Making and Undoing of French Indochina*. University of California Press, 2011.
Johnston, William. *A History of Tuberculosis in Japan*. Harvard University Press, 1995.
Jones, Geoffrey. *Beauty Imagined: A History of the Global Beauty Industry*. Oxford University Press, 2010.
Jones, Jennifer M. "Repackaging Rousseau: Femininity and Fashion in Old Regime France." *French Historical Studies* (1994): 939–67.
Jones, Stephen G. *Workers at Play: A Social and Economic History of Leisure, 1918–1939*. Routledge and Kegan Paul, 1986.
Jory, Patrick. *A History of Manners and Civility in Thailand*. Cambridge University Press, 2020.
Kelley, Liam C. *Beyond the Bronze Pillars: Envoy Poetry and the Sino-Vietnamese Relationship*. University of Hawaii Press, 2005.
Kelly, Gail P. "Colonial Schools in Vietnam, 1918–1938." *Proceedings of the Meeting of the French Colonial History Society* 2 (1977): 96–106.
Kelly, Gail. "Franco Vietnamese Schools, 1918–1938." PhD diss., University of Wisconsin, 1975.
Khải Hưng. *Trống Mái*. NXB Văn Nghệ TPHCM, 2000. First published in 1936.
Kidwell, Claudia Brush, and Valerie Steele. *Men and Women: Dressing the Part*. Smithsonian Institution, 1989.
Ko, Dorothy. *Cinderella's Sisters: A Revisionist History of Footbinding*. University of California Press, 2005.
Koehn, Nancy F. "Estee Lauder and the Market for Cosmetics." *Harvard Business School Cases* 801–362 (February 2001): 1–44.
Lancaster, Bill. *The Department Store: A Social History*. Leicester University Press, 1995.
Langlet, E. *Le Peuple Annamite: Ses moeurs, croyances et traditions*. Berger-Levrault, 1913.
Larcher-Goscha, Agathe. "Du Football au Vietnam (1905–1949): Colonialism, culture sportive et sociabilités en jeux." *Outre-Mers* 96, no. 364 (2009): 81.
Larcher-Goscha, Agathe. "La guerre des representations anthropométriques." In *La Colonisation des Corps: de l'Indochine au Viet Nam*, ed. François Guillemot and Agathe Larcher-Goscha. Vendémiaire, 2014.
Larcher-Goscha, Agathe. "Sports, colonialism et identiés nationales: première approches du 'corps à corps colonial' en Indochine (1918–1945)." In *De l'Indochine à l'Algerie: la jeunesse en movement des deux côtés du miroir colonial, 1940–1962*, ed. Nicolas Bancel, Daniel Denis, and Youssef Fates. Éditions la Découverte, 2003.
Le Guelte, Johann. "Photography, Identity and Migration: Controlling Colonial Migrants in Interwar France and Senegal." *French Politics Culture & Society* 37, no. 3 (Autumn 2019): 27–52.
Le Manh Hung. *The Impact of World War II on the Economy of Vietnam, 1939–1945*. Eastern Universities Press, 2004.
Le Quang Ninh and Stéphane Dovert, eds. *Saigon 1698–1998 Kiến Trúc/Architectures, Quy hoạch/Urbanisme*. NXB Thành Phố Hồ Chí Minh, 1998.
Lê Thị Kinh. *Phan Châu Trinh qua những tài liệu mới*. NXB Đà Nẵng, 2001.
Lê Thước, Vũ Tuân Sán, Vũ Văn Tín, Trần Huy Bá, and Nguyễn Văn Minh. *Lược Sử Hà Nội*. NXB Văn Hoá Thông Tin, 1964.
Lê Trung Hoa. *Từ Điển Địa Danh Thành phố Sài Gòn-Hồ Chí Minh*. NXB Bản Trẻ, 2003.

BIBLIOGRAPHY

Lean, Eugenia. *Vernacular Industrialism in China: Local Innovation and Translated Technologies in the Making of a Cosmetics Empire, 1900–1940.* Columbia University Press, 2020.

Lee, Haiyan. "The Cult of Qing." In *Revolution of the Heart: A Genealogy of Love in China, 1900–1950.* Stanford University Press, 2007.

Lee, Jong-Chan. "Hygienic Governance and Military Hygiene in the Making of Imperial Japan, 1868–1912." *Historia Scientiarum: International Journal of the History of Science Society of Japan* 18, no. 1 (2008): 1–23.

Leow, Rachel. "Age as a Category of Gender Analysis: Servant Girls, Modern Girls, and Gender in Southeast Asia." *Journal of Asian Studies* 71, no. 4 (2012): 975–90.

Leshkowich, Ann Marie. "Fashioning the Field in Vietnam: An Intersectional Tale of Clothing, Femininities, and the Pedagogy of Appropriateness." In *Fashion and Beauty in the Time of Asia*, ed. S. Heijin Lee, Christina H. Moon, and Thuy Linh Nguyen Tu. New York University Press, 2019.

Lessard, Micheline. *Human Trafficking in Colonial Vietnam.* Routledge, 2015.

Levy, Roger. "Indo-China in 1931–1932." *Pacific Affairs* 5, no. 3 (1932): 205–17.

Lewis, Su Lin. *Cities in Motion: Urban Life and Cosmopolitanism in Southeast Asia, 1920–1940.* Cambridge University Press, 2016.

Lewis, Su Lin. "Cosmopolitanism and the Modern Girl: A Cross-Cultural Discourse in 1930s Penang." *Modern Asian Studies* 43, no. 6 (2009): 1385–1419.

Li, Cong Huilang. "TMC in Skin Whitening and Lightening: The Eternal Pursuit in East Asia." *Cosmetics and Toiletries* 128 (2013): 104–9.

Li, Huiliang. "Traditional Chinese Medicine in Cosmetics." *Cosmetics and Toiletries*, October 17, 2013.

Li, Xiaorong. *Women's Poetry of Late Imperial China: Transforming the Inner Chambers.* University of Washington Press, 2012.

Liên, Tran Thi. "Henriette Bui: The Narrative of Vietnam's First Woman Doctor." In *Viêt Nam Exposé: French Scholarship on 20th Century Vietnamese Society*, ed. Gisele Bousquet and Pierre Brocheux. University of Michigan Press, 2002.

Lieu, Nhi T. "Remembering the Nation Through Pageantry: Femininity and the Politics of Vietnamese Womanhood in the 'Hoa Hau Ao Dai' Contest." *Frontiers: A Journal of Women Studies* 21, no. 1–2 (2000): 127–51.

Lieu, Nhi T. *The American Dream in Vietnamese.* University of Minnesota Press, 2011.

Lipovetsky, Gilles. *The Empire of Fashion: Dressing Modern Democracy.* Princeton University Press, 1994.

Lin, Chua Ai. "Singapore's 'Cinema-Age' of the 1930s: Hollywood and the Shaping of Singapore Modernity." *Inter-Asia Cultural Studies* 13, no. 4 (2012): 592–604.

Ling, Wessie. "Chinese Clothes for Chinese Women: Fashioning the Qipao in 1930s China." In *Fashion Forward*, ed. Alissa de Witt-Paul and Mira Crouch. Inter-Disciplinary, 2011.

Linker, Beth. *Slouch: Posture Panic in Modern America.* Princeton University Press, 2024.

Locher-Scholten, Elsbeth. "Morals, Harmony, and National Identity: 'Compassionate Feminism' in Colonial Indonesia in the 1930s." *Journal of Women's History* 14, no. 4 (Winter 2003): 38–58.

Lockhart, Bruce McFarland. *The End of the Vietnamese Monarchy.* Council on Southeast Asian Studies. Yale University, 1993.

Lockhart, Greg, and Monique Lockhart, eds. *The Light of the Capital: Three Vietnamese Classics*. Oxford University Press, 1996.

Lopatkova, Marta. "Vần quốc ngữ: Teaching Modernity Through Classics." In *Southeast Asian Education in Modern History: Schools, Manipulation, and Contest*, ed. Pia Jolliffe and Thomas Bruce. Routledge, 2018.

Lowy, Dina. *The Japanese "New Woman": Images of Gender and Modernity*. Rutgers University Press, 2014.

Lung, Kee-Sun. "The Politics of Hair and the Issue of the Bob in Modern China." *Fashion Theory: The Journal of Dress, Body, and Culture* 4, no. 1 (December 1997): 353–66.

Lurie, A. *The Language of Clothes*. Bloomsbury, 1992.

Lwin, Tinzar. *The Mission: Colonial Discourse on Gender and the Politics of Burma*. Working paper no. 3. Australian National University, 1994.

Lý Tùng Hiếu. *Lương Văn Can và Phong Trào Duy Tân Đông Du*. NXB Văn Hóa Sài Gòn, 2005.

Mackerras, Colin. "Theatre in Vietnam." *Asian Theatre Journal* 4, no. 1 (1987): 1–28.

Macpherson, Kerrie L., ed. *Asian Department Stores*. University of Hawaii Press, 1998.

Maître, Claude Eugène. "L'enseignement indigène dans l'Indo-Chine Annamite." *La revue pédagogique* 52 (January–June 1908): 144–60.

Malarney, Shaun, trans. "Introduction: Vũ Trọng Phụng and the Anxieties of 'Progress.'" In *Lúc Xì: Prostitution and Venereal Disease in Colonial Hanoi*, by Vũ Trọng Phụng. University of Hawaii Press, 2011.

Marr, David G. "Concept of 'Individual' and 'Self' in Twentieth-Century Vietnam." *Modern Asian Studies* 34, no. 4 (2000): 769–96.

Marr, David G. "The Passion for Modernity: Intellectuals and the Media." In *Postwar Vietnam: Dynamics of a Transforming Society*, ed. Hy Van Luong. Singapore Institute of Southeast Asian Studies, 2003.

Marr, David G. *Vietnamese Tradition on Trial, 1920–1945*. University of California Press, 1981.

Marr, David G. *Vietnam: State War and Revolution (1945–1946)*. University of California Press, 2013.

Martin, Paula. *Suzanne Noël: Cosmetic Surgery, Feminism and Beauty in Early Twentieth-Century France*. Taylor and Francis, 2014.

Martin, Phyllis M. *Leisure and Society in Colonial Brazzaville*. Cambridge University Press, 1995.

Martin, Richard, and Harold Koda. *Orientalism: Visions of the East in Western Dress*. Metropolitan Museum of Art, 1996.

McClintock, Anne. *Imperial Leather: Race, Gender and Sexuality in the Colonial Contest*. Routledge, 1995.

McConnell, Scott. *Leftward Journey: The Education of Vietnamese Students in France 1919–1939*. Transaction, 1989.

McHale, Shawn. *Print and Power: Confucianism, Communism, and Buddhism in the Making of Modern Vietnam*. University of Hawaii Press, 2004.

McHale, Shawn. "Printing and Power: Vietnamese Debates Over Women's Place in Society, 1918–1934." In *Essays Into Vietnamese Pasts*, ed. Keith W. Taylor and John K. Whitmore. Cornell University Press, 1995.

McLeod, Mark W., and Nguyen Thi Dieu. *Culture and Customs of Vietnam*. Greenwood, 2001.

Meleau, Marc. *Des pionniers en Extrême-Orient: Histoire de la Banque de l'Indochine, 1875–1975*. Fayard, 1990.

BIBLIOGRAPHY

Méneux, Catherine. "'Initier nos colonies d'Indo-Chine à l'art Français': La section Beaux-Arts à l'exposition international de Hanoi (1902–1903)." In *Sociétés, expositions et revues dans l'empire français, 1851–1940*, ed. Dominique Jarrassé and Laurent Houssais. Editions Esthétiques du Divers, 2015.

Miller, Michael B. *The Bon Marche: Bourgeois Culture and the Department Store, 1869–1920*. Princeton University Press, 1981.

Miller, E. Willard. "Industrial Resources of Indochina." *The Far Eastern Quarterly* 6, no. 4 (1947): 396–408.

Min, Hyun Jeong. "New Woman and Modern Girls: Consuming Foreign Goods in Colonial Seoul." *Journal of Historical Research in Marketing* 5, no. 4 (2013): 494–520.

Monnais, Laurence, and Noémi Tousignant. "The Colonial Life of Pharmaceuticals: Accessibility to Healthcare, Consumption of Medicines, and Medical Pluralism in French Vietnam, 1905–1945." *Journal of Vietnamese Studies* 1, no. 1–2 (February/August 2006): 131–66.

Monnais, Laurence. *Médecine et colonization. L'aventure Indochinois*. CRNS Editions, 1999.

Morris, Andrew. *Marrow of the Nation: A History of Sports and Physical Culture in Republican China*. University of California Press, 2004.

Morton, Patricia. *Hybrid Modernities: Architecture and Representation at the 1931 Colonial Exposition, Paris*. MIT Press, 2003.

Morton, Patricia. "National and Colonial: The Musée des Colonies at the Colonial Exposition, Paris, 1931." *The Art Bulletin* 80, no. 2 (June 1998): 357–77.

Murray, Martin. *The Development of Capitalism in Colonial Indochina, 1870–1940*. University of California Press, 1980.

Nelson, Ryan. "South Vietnam: A Social, Cultural, Political History, 1963 to 1967." PhD diss., University of California, Berkeley, 2020.

Ngô Đức Thịnh. *Trang phục cổ truyền các dân tộc Việt Nam*. NXB Tri Thức, 2018.

Ngo Vinh Long. *Before the Revolution: The Vietnamese Peasants Under the French*. Columbia University Press, 1991.

Nguyễn Công Hoan. "Cô Kếu, gái tân thời." In *Truyện ngắn hay chọn lọc*. NXB Văn Học, 2018.

Nguyễn Công Hoan, "Tinh thần thể dục [II]." In *Nguyễn Công Hoan Người ngựa ngựa người*. NXB Văn Học, 2016.

Nguyen Du. *The Tale of Kieu: A Bilingual Edition of Nguyen Du's Truyen Kieu*, trans. Huỳnh Sanh Thông. Yale University Press, 1983.

Nguyen, Hong-Kong T. "Beauty Culture in Post-Reform Vietnam: Glocalization or Homogenization?" SocArXiv, January 30, 2020. https://doi.org/10.31235/osf.io/pkny6.

Nguyen, Hương. "Vietnamese Women Writers During the French Colonial Period." *Journal of Vietnamese Studies* 8 (May 1995): 62–82.

Nguyen, Khai Thu. "Personal Sorrow: *Cải Lương* and the Politics of North and South Vietnam." *Asian Theatre Journal* 29, no. 1 (2012): 255–75.

Nguyen, Martina Thucnhi. "Wearing Modernity: Lemur Nguyễn Cát Tường, Fashion, and the Origins of the Vietnamese National Costume." *Journal of Vietnamese Studies* 11, no. 1 (Winter 2016): 76–128.

Nguyen, Martina Thucnhi. *On Our Own Strength: The Self-Reliant Literary Group and Cosmopolitan Nationalism in Late Colonial Vietnam*. University of Hawaii Press, 2021.

Nguyễn Ngạc and Nguyễn Văn Luận. *Un Siècle d'Histoire de la Robe des Vietnamiennes.* Ministère de la Culture de l'Éducation et de la Jeunesse, n.d.

Nguyễn Q. Thắng. *Phong Trào Duy Tân: Các khuôn mặt tiêu biểu.* NXB Văn Hóa Thông Tin, 2006.

Nguyen, Thi Thanh Nga. "Émergence et développement du tourisme en Annam (1910–c.1945). Histoire." PhD diss., Université de La Rochelle, 2019.

Nguyen, Thuy Linh. *Childbirth, Maternity, and Medical Pluralism in French Colonial Vietnam, 1880–1945.* University of Rochester Press, 2016.

Nguyen, Thuy Linh. "Overpopulation, Racial Degeneracy and Birth Control in French Colonial Vietnam." *Journal of Colonialism and Colonial History* 19 no. 3 (Winter 2018).

Nguyễn Văn Ký. *La Société Vietnamienne face à la modernité: Le Tonkin de la fin du XIXe siècle à la seconde guerre mondiale.* L'Harmattan, 1995.

Nguyễn Van Ký. "Rethinking the Status of Vietnamese Women in Folklore and Oral History." In *Việt-Nam Exposé: French Scholarship on Twentieth-Century Vietnamese Society.* University of Michigan Press, 2002.

Nguyễn Vinh Phúc. *Phố và Đường Hà Nội.* NXB Giao Thông Vận Tải, 2010.

Nguyễn Xuân Hiên. "Betel-Chewing in Vietnam: Its Past and Current Importance." *Anthropos* 101 (2006): 499–518.

Nguyen-Marshall, Van. "The Associational Life of the Vietnamese Middle Class in Saigon (1950s–1970s)." In *The Reinvention of Distinction: Modernity and the Middle Class in Urban Vietnam*, ed. Van Nguyen-Marshall, Lisa Drummond, and Danièle Bélanger. Springer, 2012.

Nguyen-Marshall, Van. "Poverty, Gender and Nation in Modern Vietnamese Literature During the French Colonial Period." In *Asia in Europe, Europe in Asia*, ed. Srilata Ravi, Mario Rutten, and Beng-Lan Goh. ISEAS-Yusof Ishak Institute, 2004.

Nguyen-Marshall, Van. *In Search of Moral Authority: The Discourse on Poverty, Poor Relief, and Charity in French Colonial Vietnam.* Peter Lang, 2008.

Nguyen-Marshall, Van, Lisa Drummond, and Danièle Bélanger, eds. *The Reinvention of Distinction: Modernity and the Middle Class in Urban Vietnam.* Springer, 2012.

Nguyễn Thanh Thảo. "Công Luận Báo và phong trào Thơ Mới." *Nghiên cứu Khoa học* 4 (2014): 79–83.

Nguyễn Thanh Trừng, *Vision de la femme dans la littérature du Sud-Vietnam (de 1858 à 1945).* L'Harmattan, 2012.

Nhất Linh. *Đoạn Tuyệt.* NXB Hội Nhà Văn, 2016. First published in 1934.

Nhất Thanh. *Đất lề quê thói: Phong tục Việt Nam.* NXB Hồng Đức, 2016. First published in 1970.

Nhiếp ảnh hiện thực và Việt Nam, cuối thế kỷ 19 đầu thế kỷ 20. NXB Thế Giới, 2015.

Ninh, Kim. *A World Transformed: The Politics of Culture in Revolutionary Vietnam 1945–1965.* University of Michigan Press, 2002.

Nicols, Nancy A. *Women Behind the Wheel: An Unexpected and Personal History of the Car.* Pegasus, 2024.

Nordholt, H. Schulte, ed. *Outward Appearances: Dressing State and Society in Indonesia.* KITLV, 1993.

Norindr, Panivong. *Phantasmatic Indochina: French Colonial Ideology in Architecture, Film, and Literature.* Duke University Press, 1996.

Óbriain, Lonán. *Voices of Vietnam: A Century of Radio, Red Music, and Revolution.* Oxford University Press, 2021.

BIBLIOGRAPHY

Oger, Henri Joseph. *Introduction Générale à l'étude de la technique du people annamites: Essai sur la vie matérielle, les arts et industries du peuple d'Annam.* Geuthner, 1908.
Oger, Henri. *Technique du peuple annamite.* EFEO, 2009.
Oh, Jin-Seok, and Howard Kahm. "Colonial Consumerism: Capitalist Development and the Internal Management of Department Stores in Late Colonial Korea." accessed July 9, 2022. http://www.worldbhc.org/files/full%20program/A8_B8_OhKahm ColonialConsumerism.pdf.
Ozdemir, B. Pinar. "Building a 'Modern' and 'Western' Image: Miss Turkey Beauty Contests from 1929–1933." *Public Relations Review* 42, no. 4 (December 2016): 759–65.
Pairaudeau, Natasha. *Mobile Citizens: French Indians in Indochina, 1858–1954.* Nordic Institute of Asian Studies, 2016.
Paliard, Pierre. *Un Art Vietnamien: Penser d'autres modernités. Le Projet de Victor Tardieu pour l'École des Beaux Arts de l'Indochine à Hanoi en 1924.* L'Harmattan, 2014.
Pallingston, Jessica. *Lipstick: A Celebration of the World's Favorite Cosmetic.* Macmillan, 1999.
Peer, Shanny. *France on Display: Peasants, Provincials, and Folklore in the 1937 Paris World's Fair.* State University of New York Press, 1998.
Peiss, Kathy. *Hope in a Jar: The Making of America's Beauty Culture.* University of Pennsylvania Press, 1998.
Peiss, Kathy. "On Beauty ... and the History of Business." *Enterprise & Society* 1, no. 3 (September 2000): 485–506.
Peiss, Kathy. "On Beauty ... and the History of Business." In *Beauty and Business: Commerce, Gender, and Culture in Modern America,* ed. Philip Scranton. Routledge, 2001.
Peters, Erica. *Appetites and Aspirations in Vietnam: Food and Drink in the Long 19th Century.* Rowman and Littlefield, 2012.
Peycam, Philippe M. *The Birth of Vietnamese Political Journalism: Saigon, 1916–1930.* Columbia University Press, 2012.
Peycam, Philippe M. "From the Social to the Political: 1920s Colonial Saigon as a 'Space of Possibilities' in the Vietnamese Consciousness." *Positions: Asia Critique* 21, no. 3 (2013): 496–546.
Peyvel, Emmanuelle. "From Cap Saint-Jacques to Vũng Tàu: The Spatial Path of a Vietnamese Seaside Resort." In *Resorting to the Coast.* Blackpool, 2009.
Pham Cao Duong. *Vietnamese Peasants Under French Domination, 1861–1945.* University of California Press, 1985.
Pham Ngọc Lân. *Unknown Father: A Vietnamese Eurasian Life Spanning Colonialism, Independence, and Communism.* L'Harmattan, 2022.
Phạm Thảo Nguyên. *Áo dài Lemur và bối cảnh Phong Hoá và Ngày Nay.* NXB Hồng Đức, 2019.
Phan Bội Châu. *Nữ quốc dân tu tri.* NXB KNXB, 1926.
Phan Kế Bính. *Việt Nam phong tục (Moeurs et coutumes du Vietnam),* vol. 2, trans. Nicole Louis-Hénard. École Française d'Extrême-Orient, 1980.
Phan Thứ Lang. *Bảo Đại: Vua cuối cùng Triều Nguyễn.* NXB Văn Nghệ, 2009.
Phan Trọng Thưởng, Nguyễn Cừ, and Nguyễn Hữu Sơn, eds. *Phóng Sự Việt Nam, 1932–1945,* vol 1. NXB Văn Học, 2000.
Phinney, Harriet M. "Objects of Affection: Vietnamese Discourses on Love and Emancipation." *Positions: East Asia Cultures Critique* 16, no. 2 (2008): 329–58.

Ping, Wang. *Aching for Beauty: Footbinding in China*. Knopf Doubleday, 2002.
Pomfret, David. "'A Use for the Masses': Gender, Age, and Nation in France, Fin de Siècle." *American Historical Review* 109, no. 5 (December 2004): 1439–74.
Popkin, Samuel. *The Rational Peasant: The Political Economy of Rural Society in Vietnam*. University of California Press, 1979.
Pulju, Rebecca. *Women and Mass Consumer Society in Postwar France*. Cambridge University Press, 2011.
Raffin, Anne. *Youth Mobilization in Vichy Indochina and Its Legacies 1940–1970*. Lexington, 2008.
Reitan, Richard. "Claiming Personality: Reassessing the Dangers of the 'New Woman' in Early Taishō Japan." *Positions: East Asia Cultures and Critique* 19, no.1 (Spring 2011): 83–107.
Robequain, Charles. *The Economic Development of French Indo-China*. Oxford University Press, 1944.
Roberts, Mary Louise. *Civilization Without Sexes: Reconstructing Gender in Postwar France, 1917–1927*. University of Chicago Press, 1994.
Roberts, Mary Louise. "Gender, Consumption, and Commodity Culture." *American Historical Review* 103, no. 3 (June 1998): 817–44.
Roces, Mina. "Gender, Nation, and the Politics of Dress in 20th Century Philippines." *Gender and History* 17, no. 2 (August 2005): 354–77.
Roces, Mina, and Louise Edwards, eds. *The Politics of Dress in Asia and the Americas*. Sussex Academic Press, 2007.
Rogaski, Ruth. *Hygienic Modernity: Meanings of Health and Disease in Treaty-Port China*. University of California Press, 2004.
Rosenlee, Li-Hsiang Lisa. *Confucianism and Women: A Philosophical Interpretation*. State University of New York Press, 2006.
Ruscio, Alain. "Nous avons débarqué au milieu du people le plus étrange." In *La Colonisation des Corps: de l'Indochine au Viet Nam*, ed. François Guillemot and Agathe Larcher-Goscha. Vendémiaire, 2014.
Santos, Lucy Jane. *Half Lives: The Unlikely History of Radium*. Pegasus, 2021.
Sato, Barbara. *The New Japanese Woman: Modernity, Media, and Women in Interwar Japan*. Duke University Press, 2003.
Scanlon, Jennifer, ed. *The Gender and Consumer Culture Reader*. NYU Press, 2000.
Schaffer, Sarah. "Reading Our Lips: The History of Lipstick Regulation in Western Seats of Power." *Food and Drug Law Journal* 62, no. 1 (2007): 165–225.
Scranton, Philip, ed. *Beauty and Business: Commerce, Gender, and Culture in Modern America*. Routledge, 2001.
Schwenkel, Christina. "The Things They Carried (and Kept): Revisiting Ostalgie in the Global South." *Comparative Studies in Society and History* 64, no. 2 (2022): 478–509.
Shi, Xia. *At Home in the World: Women and Charity in Late Qing and Early Republican China*. Columbia University Press, 2018.
Siegel, Mona L. "The Dangers of Feminism in Colonial Indochina." *French Historical Studies* 38, no. 4 (October 2015): 661–90.
Silverberg, Miriam. "The Modern Girl as Militant." In *Recreating Japanese Women, 1600–1945*, ed. Gail Lee Bernstein. University of California Press, 1991.
Simonetti, Marie Agathe. "The Ecole des Beaux-Arts de l'Indochine: Victor Tardieu and French Art Between the Wars." PhD diss., University of Illinois at Chicago, 2016.

BIBLIOGRAPHY

Slade, Toby. *Japanese Fashion: A Cultural History*. Berg, 2009.
Smith, Ralph B. "Bui Quang Chiêu and the Constitutionalist Party in French Cochinchina, 1917–1930." *Modern Asian Studies* 3, no. 2 (1969): 131–50.
Sokolsky, Anne. "Reading the Bodies and Voices of 'Naichi' Women in Japanese-Ruled Taiwan." *US-Japan Women's Journal* 46 (2014): 51–78.
Stanley, Adam. "Hearth, Home, and Steering Wheel." *The Historian* 66, no. 2 (Summer 2004): 249.
Statler, Kathryn C. *Replacing France: The Origins of American Intervention in Vietnam*. University Press of Kentucky, 2007.
Stauth, Georg. "'Elias in Singapore': Civilizing Processes in a Tropical City." *Thesis Eleven* 50, no. 1 (1997): 51–70.
Steele, Valerie, ed. *Encyclopedia of Clothing and Fashion*, vol. 1. Scribner, 2005.
Steele, Valerie, ed. *Encyclopedia of Clothing and Fashion*, vol. 2. Scribner, 2005.
Steele, Valerie, ed. *Encyclopedia of Clothing and Fashion*, vol. 3. Scribner, 2005.
Steele, Valerie. *Fashion and Eroticism: Ideals of Feminine Beauty from the Victorian Era to the Jazz Age*. Oxford University Press, 1985.
Stevens, Sarah E. "Figuring Modernity: The New Woman and the Modern Girl in Republican China." *NWSA Journal* 15, no. 3 (2003): 82–103.
Stewart, Mary Lynn. *Dressing Modern Frenchwomen: Marketing Haute Couture, 1919–1939*. Johns Hopkins University Press, 2008.
Stewart, Mary Lynn. *For Health and Beauty: Physical Culture for Frenchwomen, 1880s–1930s*. Johns Hopkins University Press, 2001.
Suh, Jiyoung. "The Flâneuse and the Landscape of Colonial Seoul in the 1920s–1930s." *Sociétés: Revue des sciences humaines et sociales* 135 (2017): 63–72.
Suh, Jiyoung. "The 'New Woman' and the Topography of Modernity in Colonial Korea." *Korean Studies* 37 (2013): 11–43.
Sullivan, Charles. "Years of Dressing Dangerously: Modern Women, National Identity and Moral Crisis in Sukarno's Indonesia, 1945–1966." PhD diss., University of Michigan, 2020.
Sun, Lung-Kee. "The Politics of Hair and the Issue of the Bob in Modern China." *Fashion Theory* 1, no 4. (1997): 353–65.
Swinbank, John Michael. "Girl with Lotus and M-16: the Equivocal Legacy of the École des Beaux-arts de l'Indochine 1924–1945." *World History Connected* 17, no. 3 (2020).
Tạ Thị Thúy. *Việc nhượng đất, khẩn hoang ở bắc kỳ từ 1919 đến 1945*. NXB Thế Giới, 2001.
Tai, Hue Tam Ho. *Radicalism and the Origins of the Vietnamese Revolution*. Harvard University Press, 1992.
Tamari, Tomoko. "The Department Store in Early Twentieth-Century Japan: Luxury, Aestheticization and Modern Life." *Luxury* 3, no. 1–2 (2016): 85–106.
Tamari, Tomoko. "Rise of the Department Store and the Aestheticization of Everyday Life in Early 20th Century Japan." *International Journal of Japanese Sociology* 15, no. 1 (2006): 99–118.
Tanizaki, Jun'ichiro. *Naomi*. Vintage, 2001. First published in 1924.
Taylor, Jean Gelman. "Costume and Gender in Colonial Java, 1800–1940." In *Outward Appearances: Dressing State and Society in Indonesia*, ed. Henk Schulte Nordholt. KITLV Press, 1998.
Taylor, Nora Annesley. "The Artist and the State: The Politics of Painting and National Identity in Hanoi, Vietnam, 1925–1995." PhD diss., Cornell University, 1997.

Taylor, Nora Annesley. *Painters in Hanoi: An Ethnography of Vietnamese Art.* University of Hawaii Press, 2009.
Tejapira, Kasian. "Pigtail: A Pre-History of Chineseness in Siam." *Sojourn* 7, no. 1 (1992): 96–121.
Testa, David Del. "Automobiles and Anomie in French Indochina." In *France and Indochina Cultural Representations*, ed. Kathryn Robinson and Jennifer Yee. Lexington, 2005.
Thạch Lam. *Hà Nội 36 phố phường.* NXB Văn Học, 1943.
Thạch Phương and Lê Trung Hoa, eds. *Từ Điển Thành phố Sàigòn-Hồ Chí Minh.* NXB Bản Trẻ, 1999.
Thomas, Martin. *The French Empire Between the Wars.* Manchester University Press, 2017.
Thompson, C. Michele. "French Colonial Medicine and Pharmacology in Indo-China, 1802–1954." In *Science Across the Empires, 1800–1950*, ed. Benedikt Stuchtey. Oxford University Press, 2005.
Tran, Ben. *Masculinity and Aesthetic Modernity in Colonial Vietnam.* Fordham University Press, 2017.
Tran, Ben. *Post-Mandarin: Masculinity and Aesthetic Modernity in Colonial Vietnam.* Fordham University Press, 2017.
Trần Huy Liệu, ed. *Lịch sử thủ đô Hà Nội.* NXB Sử Học, 1960.
Tran, Nhung Tuyet. *Familial Properties: Gender, State, and Society in Early Modern Vietnam, 1463–1778.* University of Hawaii Press, 2019.
Tran, Quang Anh Richard. "From Red Lights to Red Flags: A History of Gender in Colonial and Contemporary Vietnam." PhD diss., University of California, Berkeley, 2011.
Trần Quang Đức. *Ngàn năm áo mũ: Lịch sử trang phục Việt Nam giai đoạn 1009–1945.* NXB Thế Giới, 2013.
Trần Thanh Hương. "Tìm hiểu quá trình hình thành giai cấp tư sản Việt Nam." *Nghiên cứu Lịch sử* 11+12 (2008): 93–97.
Trần Thị Phương Hoa. "Franco-Vietnamese Schools for Girls in Tonkin at the Beginning of the Twentieth Century," Harvard-Yenching Institute Working Paper Series, 2010.
Trần Thị Phương Hoa. "Making the Vietnamese Áo Dài Tunic National Heritage: Fashion Travel Through Tradition, Colonialism, Modernity." *International Journal of Heritage Studies* 27, no. 8 (2021): 806–18.
Trần Trọng Kim. *Nho Giáo.* Song Moi, 1971.
Trần Trọng Kim. *Nho Giáo.* NXB Văn Hóa Thông Tin, 2001/1932.
Trần Văn Giàu and Trần Bạch Đằng, eds. *Địa chí văn hóa thành phố Hồ Chí Minh, Tập I: Lịch sử.* Nhà xuất bản Thành phố Hồ Chí Minh, 1998.
Trentmann, Frank, ed. *The Oxford Handbook of the History of Consumption.* Oxford University Press, 2012.
Trinh Van Thao. *L'ecole Française en Indochine.* Karthala, 1995.
Trinh Van Thao. *Vietnam: Du Confucianisme au Communisme.* L'Harmattan, 1990.
Trọng Lang. *Hà Nội lầm than.* NXB Hội Nhà Văn, 2015. First published in 1938.
Trivedi, Lisa. *Clothing Ghandi's Nation: Homespun and Modern India.* Indiana University Press, 2007.
Tu, Thuy Linh Nguyen. *Experiments in Skin: Race and Beauty in the Shadows of Vietnam.* Duke University Press, 2021.

BIBLIOGRAPHY

Tumblety, Joan. *Remaking the Male Body: Masculinity and the Uses of Physical Culture in Interwar and Vichy France*. Oxford University Press, 2012.
Turcot, Laurent. *Sports et Loisirs: Une histoire des origins à nos jours*. Folio, 2016.
"Typhoons of the Far East During September and October 1931." *Monthly Weather Review* 59, no. 11 (November 1, 1931): 442-43.
Van Der Meer, Arnout. *Performing Power: Cultural Hegemony, Identity, and Resistance in Colonial Indonesia*. Cornell University Press, 2021.
Van Esterik, Penny. "The Politics of Beauty in Thailand." In *Beauty Queen on the Global Stage: Gender, Contests, Power*, ed. Coleen Ballerino Cohen, Richard Wilk, and Beverly Stoeltje. Routledge, 1995.
Vann, Michael G. "White City on the Red River: Race, Power, and Culture in French Colonial Hanoi, 1872-1954." PhD diss., University of California, Santa Cruz, 1999.
Veblen, Thorstein. *The Theory of the Leisure Class*. Sage, 1970. Originally published in 1899.
Velmet, Aro. "Beauty and Big Business: Gender, Race and Civilizational Decline in French Beauty Pageants, 1920-1937." *French History* 28, no. 1 (2014): 66-91.
Vinh Sinh. "Nguyen-Truong-To and the Quest for Modernization in Vietnam." *Japan Review* 11 (1999): 55-74.
Von Hirschhausen, Ulrike. "International Architecture as a Tool of National Emancipation." *Hungarian Historical Review* 7, no. 2 (2018): 331-47.
Vũ Đức Bằng. "The Đông Kinh Free School, 1907-1908." In *Aspects of Vietnamese History*, ed. Walter F. Vella. University of Hawaii Press, 1973.
Vu, Linh. "Careless and Carless Natives: Automobile Accidents and the Project of Modernity in French Indochina." *Sojourn: Journal of Social Issues in Southeast Asia* 27, no. 2 (October 2012): 328-41.
Vu, Linh. "Drowned in Romance, Tears, and Rivers: Young Women's Suicide in Early Twentieth Century Vietnam." *Explorations* 9 (Spring 2009).
Vũ Huy Phúc. *Lịch sử Việt Nam, 1858-1896*. NXB Khoa Học Xã Hội, 2003.
Vũ Trọng Phụng. *Dumb Luck, A Novel*, trans. Nguyen Nguyet Cam, ed. Peter Zinoman. University of Michigan Press, 2002.
Vũ Trọng Phụng. *Kỹ nghệ lấy tây & cơm thầy cơm cô*. NXB Văn Học, 2006.
Vũ Trọng Phụng. *Làm Đĩ*. NXB Văn Hoa, 2010. First published in 1936.
Vũ Trọng Phụng. *Làm Đĩ*. NXB Văn Học, 2015. First published in 1936.
Vũ Trọng Phụng. *Lúc Xì: Prostitution and Venereal Disease in Colonial Hanoi*, trans. Shaun Kingsley Malarney. University of Hawaii Press, 2011.
Vũ Trọng Phụng. *Vỡ Đê*. NXB Văn Học, 2017. First published in 1936.
Vu-Hill, Kimloan. *Coolies Into Rebels: Impact of World War I on French Indochina*. Les Indes Savantes, 2011.
Wakeman, Frederic. *Policing Shanghai, 1927-1937*. University of California Press, 1996.
Wang, Sumei, ed. *The East Asian Modern Girl: Women, Media, and Colonial Modernity During the Interwar Years*. Brill, 2021.
Warsh, Cheryl Krasnick, and Dan Malleck, eds. *Consuming Modernity: Gendered Behavior and Consumerism Before the Baby Boom*. University of British Columbia Press, 2013.
Weber, Eugene. *Peasants Into Frenchmen*. Stanford University Press, 1979.
Weinbaum, Alys Eve, Lynn Thomas, Priti Ramamurthy, and Uta G. Poiger, eds. *The Modern Girl Around the World*. Duke University Press, 2008.

White, Jenny B. "State Feminism, Modernization, and the Turkish Republican Woman." *NWSA Journal* 15, no. 3 (2003): 145–59.

Williams, Rosalind. *Dream Worlds: Mass Consumption in Late 19th Century France.* University of California Press, 1991.

Wilson, Donald Dean, Jr. "Colonial Việt Nam on Film: 1896 to 1926." PhD diss., City University of New York, 2007.

Wolf, Naomi, *The Beauty Myth: How Images of Beauty Are Used Against Women.* Harper Perennial, 2002.

Woodside, Alexander. *Community and Revolution in Modern Vietnam.* Harvard University Press, 1976.

Woodside, Alexander. "The Development of Social Organizations in Vietnamese Cities in the Late Colonial Period." *Pacific Affairs* 44, no.1 (Spring 1971): 39–64.

Woodside, Alexander. "History, Structure and Revolution in Vietnam." *International Political Science Review/Revue Internationale des Sciences Politiques* 10, no. 2 (1989): 143–57.

Woodside, Alexander. *Vietnam and the Chinese Model: A Comparative Study of Vietnamese and Chinese Government in the First Half of the Nineteenth Century.* Harvard University Press, 1988.

Wright, Gwendolyn. *The Politics of Design in French Colonial Urbanism.* University of Chicago Press, 1991.

Wu, Yongmei. "Colonial Modernity, Beauty, Health, and Hygiene: Centering on Japanese Cosmetics, Cleaning Supplies, and Medicine Advertisements in Shengjing Times (Shengjing Shibao)." In *The East Asian Modern Girl: Women, Media, and Colonial Modernity During the Interwar Years*, ed. Sumei Wang. Brill, 2021.

Xu Xiaoqun. *Cosmopolitanism, Nationalism, and Individualism in Modern China: The Chenbao Fukan and the New Culture Era, 1918-1928.* Lexington, 2014.

Yang Nianqun. "The Rise and Fall of 'Individualism' Before and After the May Fourth Movement." *Chinese Studies in History* 52, no. 3-4 (2019): 209–22.

Yalom, Marilyn. *A History of the Breast.* Knopf, 1998.

Ying, Hu. *Tales of Translation: Composing the New Woman in China, 1899-1918.* Stanford University Press, 2000.

Zeldin, Theodore. *A History of French Passions 1848-1945.*: Vol. 2, *Intellect, Taste and Anxiety.* Oxford: Clarendon Press, 1993.

Zdatny, Steven. *Fashion, Work, and Politics in Modern France.* Springer Nature, 2006.

INDEX

Page numbers in *italics* indicate illustrations.

advertisements, *86*, *88*, 93–94, 109; for beauty pageants, 204–5; cosmetics, 54, 123–24, *124*, 134–35, 137, 261n19; by Nguyễn Đức Nhuận, 248n106
aesthetics: aesthetic reforms, interwar period, 93–96; beauty culture as break from past, 226; Western, 18, 84–90
l'AFINA, 207
Agents L. Rondon Company Limited, 37
aging, cosmetics and, 135–39
Ái Liên, 48, 54–55, *73*, 74, 188, 227; stardom of, 72–73, 251n144
Alain, Raymonde, 220
Albert Sarraut School, 172
"Amapola," 52
Annam, 12, 37, 48, 52, 78, 82, 214
anthropology, 29–30
áo dài dress, 291n8; history of, 230–31; as national dress, 291n9. *See also* Lemur Tunic
archetypes, fashion and beauty trends and, 59–67
Art Deco, 68, 93–95, 120, 123–24, *125*, 256n84
automobiles, 173, 181, 224, 245n69; cars, 58, 170

Bạch Liên, 62, 72, 143, *144*
Banner, Louis K., 28–29
Banque d'Indochine, 104
Bảo Đại (Emperor), 19, 49, 53, 68–71, 168, 229; on marriage, 118; marriage of, 70–72, *71*; return of, 249n128
Bảo Long (Prince), 19
Barnum, P. T., 196
Barthes, Roland, 87
Basty, 87
Bà Triệu, 272n22
beautification rituals, 136
beauty contests, 10; advertisements for, 204–5; audiences of, 217–18; Confucianism and, 192–93; contestants at, 215; criteria in, 216–17; critiques of, 27–28; Faifoo Fair, *215*; at fairs, 208–9; fashion in, 216; as global phenomenon, 195; during Great Depression, 193–94, 203; history of, 195–96; identity and, 214; kiss auctions at, 216; middle class and, 205, 208; modernity linked with, 208–10; multiethnic, 213; nationalism and, 200–202, 212–13; norms contested by, 194–203; operation of, 212–21;

beauty contests (*Continued*)
  photographic, 196, 202; popularity of, 210, 217; prizes at, 217, 289n135; public opinion on, 193; redemption of, 203–12; venues, 208; *Vịt Đực* on, 220–21; Vũ Trọng Phụng on, 210
beauty culture and trends: archetypes and, 59–67; as art movement, 225; as break from past aesthetics, 226; cinema and, 56–58; commodification of, 201–2; Confucianist objections to, 197; criteria for, 216–17; dissemination of, 36; hygiene and, 160; icons and, 67–73; in interwar period, 11–26, 43–44, 156–57; of *khuê các* maiden ideal, 156; leisure activities and, 44–53; me tây adopting, 60–61; morality and, 197, 199; print media and, 53–67; social class and, 4; as source of expression, 6–7; subversive power of, 231; tutorials, 5–6
beauty industry, 26; in China, 127; colonialism and, 36–44; growth of, 23–24
beauty institutes, 125, 148–49
beauty technology, 128–46
Bhabha, Homi, 14, 96
bicycles: introduction of, 169–70; New Women and, 170–71; public opposition to, 171; safety, 278n121; form of liberation, 144, 221, sport, 155, 164; physique, 179
Bình Tây market, 44
blush, 141
bob haircut, 268n170
bodybuilding, male, 179–80
body ideals, 153–54; bodies on display, 172–79; breasts and, 185–89; colonialism and, 155–58; dieting and, 182–83; Europeanization and, 190–91; gait and, 184–85; hygiene and, 158–60, 181; in Japan, 280n166; modernity and, 181; new physique, 179–90; posture and, 184; traditional, 155–58
Bombay shops, 43, 82

Bourdieu, Pierre, 25, 168
boycotts, 256n72
Branchet, Francois, 165
Brazzaville, 45
breasts, female, 157; binding of, 186–88; body ideals and, 185–89; fetishizing of, 187; padding of, 189–90
British colonies, 165
Buddhism, 208
Bùi, Madeleine, 72, 125, 126; See Institute de beauté Madeleine
Bùi Quang Chiêu, 72, 125
Burma, 91; colonialism in, 256
Butil, 135

Cadium soap, 123, 159
Cải Lương (Reform Theater), 18, 72, 73, 104, 225, 227, 236n39
calisthenics, 54, 61, 165, *166*, 182, 205
Cambodia, 214
Cam Ranh, 291n3
Cần Thơ, 210
Cantonese Assembly, 206
Cần Vương movement, 12–13
Cap Saint Jacques, 52
Caravelle, 46
cartoons, 176–77; misogyny in, 280n154; in newspapers, 55; on sports, *164*
Catholic Church, 20, 70
Cécé, 122, 146
Cercle Sportif, 59, 275n49
Chanel, 82–83, 173
charity, 206–8
Charles, Jean, 68
chastity, 22, 194, 234n12
Chez Claudine, 173
chiffon, 87
China, 147; beauty industry in, 127; hygiene in, 160; national dress in, 257n97; skin care in, 265n101, 266n124
Cho Kyo, 185–86
Chợ Lớn, 43, 210
Chợ Lợn Girls' School, 165
Chung Võ Diệm, 197
Chương Mỹ, 48

INDEX

cinema: beauty trends and, 56–58; fashion trends and, 56–58; print media and, 53–67
city planning, 243n37
clothing reform campaign (*cuộc vận động canh cải y phục*), 90, 95, 107–8, 111–12; Nguyễn Cát Tường in, 97–100
Clutario, Geneveve, 289
Cochinchina, 11, 14, 78, 82, 91–92, 169, 214; land ownership in, 20; newspapers in, 195
cockfighting, 206
Coco Chanel, 173
Cô Giáo Minh (Nguyễn Công Hoan), 291n1
"Cô Kếu, gái tân thời" (Nguyễn Công Hoan), 291n1
Colbert, Claudette, 85
colonialism, 7, 14, 90–91, 111; beauty industry and, 36–44; in Burma, 256; education and, 61; female body ideals and, 155–58; modernism and, 48; Neo-Confucianism resisting, 237n50; Vietnamese identity and, 214; wage labor before, 235n29. *See also specific topics*
colonial modernity, 36–37, 48, 73–74
comedy, 236n39
Communist Party, 53, 164; Confucianism and, 230
Compassionate Marriage movement, 237n49, 260n8
Comptoire Commercial, 37
Confucianism, 4–7, 33, 167, 174; beauty contests and, 192–93; beauty trends critiqued by, 197; Communist Party and, 230; *Công Luận Báo* contest and, 200; defining, 233n6; education and, 176–77; modernism and, 8; public influence of, 238n62; social order of, 287n82
Công Luận Báo (newspaper), 211
Công Luận Báo contest: Confucianism and, 200; critiques of, 198–99, 202; failure of, 203; photography in, 284n16; success of, 195–96; underlying motivations for, 202; winner of, 203

Connor, Liz, 23
Conrad, Sebastian, 26
Côn Sinh, 106
Constitutionalist Party, 19, 125–26, 258n129
construction, in interwar years, 224
consumerism, 15–16, 22–23, 64, 212; critiques of, 220; gender and, 23; women and, 23, 25–26; after World War I, 223
cosmetics, 4, 5, 10, 116, 122–23, 136; advertisements, 54, 123–24, *124*, 134–35, 137, 261n19; aging and, 135–39; costs of, 150; critiques of, 146–52; *Đàn-Bà* on, 264n70; at department stores, 42–43; for eyes, 129–30; in Great Depression, 117, 119; hair styles and, 141–44; hands and, 144–45; importing of, 37; instruction articles, 137–38; in Japan, 262n36; for mouth, 130–33; nails and, 144–45; Peiss on, 260n2; powder, 139–41; sexuality and, 148–49; social anxiety about, 149–50; social class and, 24
Cott, Nancy F., 57
Coty, 42, 47, 54, 94, 113, *121*, 137, 146
Coupe Trịnh Đình Thảo, 169
crane neck, 156–57, 184
Crème Siamoise, 39, 123, 124, 134, 135
cultural capital, 25
Cường Để (Prince), 12, 234n17
Curie, Alfred, 123, 262n41
Curie, Marie, 262n41

Đại Việt kingdom, 252n7
Đà Lạt, 68–69
Đà Nẵng women's union, 143
Đàn-Bà (newspaper), 54, 131, 150, 179; columns in, 125; on cosmetics, 264n70
dance halls, fashion trends in, 46
Darrieux, Danielle, 57
Debeaux Frères, 38, 39
debt bondage, 24, 92, 119, 164, 233n4
Dekobra, Maurice, 58, 246n90
Delalande, Lemanson, 126

Democratic Republic of Vietnam (DRV), 198, 289n131
department stores, 23–24; cosmetics at, 42–43; in interwar period, 39, 40–42; middle-class marketing of, 42; transnationality of, 39; window displays of, 40
Depraved Youth (Nguyễn Đình Lạp), 67
Điển Tín (newspaper), 130
dieting, body ideals and, 182–83
diet pills, 183
Dietrich, Marlene, 67, 129, 158
Dinh Trong Hieu, 30
Đoàn Thị Tình, 30
Đổi Mới reforms, 31
Đông Ba, 44
Đông Du movement, 13, 235n26
Đỗ Ngọc Kim, 199
Đông Pháp (newspaper), 122; female readership of, 198–99; newspaper rivalries, 198
Đông Pháp Thời Báo, 199
Đồng Xuân market, 44
Đồ Sơn, 153, *154*, 173
Drummond, Lisa, 31
DRV. *See* Democratic Republic of Vietnam
Đức Chaigneau, Michel, 247n94
Dumail, Félix, 104
Dumb Luck (Vũ Trọng Phụng), 87, 95, 101, 136–37
Duy Tân Hội movement, 12, 13, 234n19, 235n26

Eastern Jin Dynasty, 266n124
École des Beaux Arts de l'Indochine, 70, 93, 97, 104–5, 119–20, 216, 225; opening of, 236n40
economic reforms, interwar period, 91–92
Eden Center Theater, 58
education, 16–17; in French colonial schools, 237n54; of New Women, 61–62; physical, 275n50; of women, 8–9, 15
Edwards, Penny, 96

Elias, Norbert, 106
Elizabeth Arden Institute, 127
eugenics, 155; hygiene and, 159–60; sports and, 167
Europeanization, 7–8, 14, 19, 93; body ideals and, 190–91; critiques of, 200, 220; individualism and, 19–20; nationalism and, 231; Neo-Confucianism and, 197; Neo-Confucianism as reaction to, 21; *Vịt Đực* on, 220; Vũ Trọng Phụng on, 190
evening dresses, 83, *85*
Exposition Colonial, 211
Exposition Universelle, 195
eyelashes, 264n70
eyes, cosmetics for, 129–30
Ezra, Elizabeth, 29

fabrics, 43–44; production of, 251n5
Faifoo Fair, 48, 209; beauty contest winner, 215
fairs: beauty contests at, 208–10; opening ceremonies of, 244n55
fascism, 212–13
fashion industry, 43
fashion prescriptions, 105–11
fashion reform campaign, 76–77
fashion trends, 2–3, 10, 30; archetypes and, 59–67; in beauty contests, 216; cinema and, 56–58; in dance halls, 46; dissemination of, 36; icons and, 67–73; individualism and, 83–84; leisure activities and, 44–53; me tây, 81; of Modern Girls, 35–36, 90; modernization of, 79; nationalism and, 96; in newspapers, 54; of New Women, 35–36; print media and, 53–56; sartorial history, 77–80; sports and, 45–46; Vietnamese modernism and, 14–15, 79. *See also* beauty culture and trends
fasting, 183
Felix, Genevieve, 204
Femina (magazine), 54, 103
femininity, 84–85, 87; ideals, 217

INDEX

feminism, 33, 155, 171–72; of New Women, 182
fertility rates, 261n13
finances, familial, 151
Finanne, Antonia, 29
Finot Museum, 104
fishing, 173–74
"Fitness Mentality, The" (Nguyễn Công Hoan), 163
flapper fashion, 187
Food, Drug, and Cosmetics Act of 1938, US, 264n70
food, "hot" and "cold," 265n106
foot binding, 156–57
foreign soldiers, relationships with, 234n12
Formichi, Chiara, 29
Forvil, 122
Fourié, A., 158
Four Virtues (Tứ Đức), 2–3, 9, 22, 171, 192, 219; appearance, 194; financial management, 151; nationalism and, 201
foxtrot, 46
fragrances, 270n194
France, 11–12, 16; hygiene in, 273n26; Popular Front government, 244n67, 275n51; vacations in culture of, 51
Franco-Prussian War, 158
Free Love movement, 237n49
French Colonial Exposition, 157–58
French Foreign Legion, 11
fur, 89–90

gait, body ideals and, 184–85
Gandhi, Mahatma, 182–83
Garbo, Greta, 67
Gellé Frères, 42, 146
gender, 10–11; consumerism and, 23; individualism and, 165–66; nationalism and, 257n97; Neo-Confucianism and, 21–22; social norms and, 1–3
germ theory, 158
glycerin, 189
Golden Gate Exposition of 1939, 211

golden teeth, 217
Goodlad, Lauren, 208
Goscha, Christopher, 14
Grands Magasins Charner, 40, *41*
Grands Magasins de la Société Bordelaise Indochinoise, 40
Grands Magasins Réunis, 39, 40, 41
Great Depression, 4, 65, 92, 115, 181, 219, 223; beauty contests during, 193–94, 203; beginning of, 206; cosmetics in, 117, 119; middle class during, 205–6
Grout, Holly, 29, 42, 160
Guilla, Jeanne, 204
Gulf of Tonkin, 153

Hà Đông fair, 48, 218
Hải Phòng, 38, 40, 45–46, 291n3
Hải Phòng pageant, 215–16
haircare products, 123
hair styles, 13, 80; cosmetics and, 141–44; of New Women, 142–44; Nguyễn Cát Tường on, 143; short, 142–44, 219
Hale, Dana, 47
hands, cosmetics and, 144–45
Hàng Đậu, 43
Hàng Than Street, 126
Hanoi, 37, 40, 157–58
Hanoi Fair of 1938, 210
Hanoi Municipal People's Committee, 230
Hanoi School of Physical Education, 162–63
Harper's Bazaar Vietnam, 231
Hà Thành Ngọ Báo (newspaper), 58, 66–67, 82–83, 92, 122, 149, 166
Haussmann renovations, Paris, 274n26
health initiatives, public, 158–59
Hébrard, Ernest, 104
Henchy, Judith, 197
Herbelin, Caroline, 104
Hien, Nina, 31
high heels, 185
Hoàng Đạo, 149
Hoàng Thị Nhã, 188
Hoàng Việt Nga, 62, 165, 167, 169
Hoàn Kiếm Lake, 38, 206
Hồ Biểu Chánh, 62, 63–64

INDEX

Ho Chi Minh City Women's Museum, 230
Hội Khai Trí Tiến Đức, 217
Hollywood, sexuality and, 57
Hotel de Paix, 46
Hồ Thị Lích, 62, 165, 171
Hồ Tố Quyên, 169
Houbigant, 42, 43
Huard, Pierre, 30
Huế, 38, 81–82
Huế Fair of 1938, 208
Huilian Li, 266n124
human trafficking, 290n158
Hundred Days Reform movement, 13
hunger strikes, 182–83
Huỳnh Thị Bảo Hoà, 62, 142–43
Huỳnh Văn Chính, 195
hydrotherapy, 184
hygiene, 83, 99, 188–89; beauty trends and, 160; body ideals and, 158–60, 181; in China, 160; eugenics and, 159–60; in France, 273n26; health associated with, 159–60

icons, fashion and beauty trends and, 67–73
identity, Vietnamese, 26; beauty contests and, 214; colonialism and, 214; Lemur Tunic as symbol of, 230; modernity and, 209–10
India, nationalism in, 257n97
Indigenous Cercle Sportif, 275n49
individualism, 32, 136–37; Europeanization and, 19–20; fashion trends and, 83–84; gender and, 165–66
Indochina identity, 214
Indochine Import Agent C. Huchet, 37
industrialization, in interwar period, 16–17
Industrial Revolution, 6–7, 76, 116, 270n194
Institute de Beauté Madeleine, 43, 72, 125–126, 137, see Madeleine Bùi
international expositions, 47–48
International Pageant of Pulchritude, 195
interwar period, Vietnam, 6–7, 35–36; aesthetic reforms in, 93–96; beauty culture in, 11–26, 43–44, 156–57; construction in, 224; department stores in, 39, 40–42; economic reforms in, 91–92; industrialization in, 16–17; middle-class in, 17–18; political reforms in, 96–105; rejection of marriage in, 117–18; social class in, 17; technological developments in, 19; tourism in, 51; tunics in, 79–80; urban infrastructure in, 16
Italy, 147
It Happened One Night (film), 85

Japan, 39; body ideals in, 280n166; chemicals industry in, 262n36; cosmetics in, 262n36; Modern Girls in, 64–65, 142; modernization in, 235n26
Jeanne, Mariette. *See* Nam Phương
jewelry, 89
Jones, Geoffrey, 29, 145–46
Jory, Patrick, 259n134
journalism, realism, 236n41

Kang Youwei, 15
karma, 208
Kéva Institute, 43, 134, 137, 138, *138*
Khái Hưng, 67, 174, 180
Khoa Học (journal), 128
khuê các maiden, 2–3, 9, 22, 33, 199–200, 221, 271n4; beauty culture of, 156; critiques of, 63, 167–68
Khương-bình Tịnh, 44
Kim Hue Oil, 123
Klytia Beauty Institute, 72, 125
KMT Party, 147
Kolynos, 131–32
Korea, 9

Lachevrotière, Henry Chavigny de, 245n76
Lạc Thiên fair, 210, 216
Làm Đĩ (Vũ Trọng Phụng), 210, 219
Lăm Quang Sĩ, 204
land ownership, in Cochinchina, 20
Langlet, Eugène, 29
Lang-Quê, 75, 76, 95, 97, 108

INDEX

Laos, 211
Larcher-Goscha, Agathe, 162
League of Light, 160
Lean, Eugenia, 127, 265n101
Lệ Chi, 55, 183
leisure activities, 5; beauty trends and, 44–53; city planning and, 243n37; development of, 45; fashion trends and, 44–53
Lemur Tunic, 27–28, 30, 31, 35, 46, 66, 83, 99; controversy around, 101–2, 104; debut of, 49–51, 210, 216; design of, 56, 77, 99–100; nationalism and, 88–89; as Vietnamese symbol, 230
Lê Phát Đạt, 69
Lê Phổ, 55, 56, 93, 216, 226, 227
leprosy, 159
Leshkowich, Ann Marie, 30, 31
Lê Sĩ Hoàng, 230
Lê Thanh Cảnh, 218
Lê Thị H., 202
Liang Qichao, 15
Lieu Như, 199, 200–201
Ligit, Mireille, 204
linen, 253n28
lingerie, 87, 88, 172–73
Linh Vu, 118
lipstick, 37, 132
Lipstick Effect, 24, 119
liquid nail polish, 144–45
Loa Tuần Báo, 102
Loire Valley, 38
Long, Gia, 79, 117
looms, 79, 251n5
Loy, Myrna, 57
lust, 201
Lux soap, 122–3, 204
Lý-Trần period, 77

Ma Beauté Institute, 126
Magasin Chaffanjon, 40
Maison Giao Sports, 86, 162
Maison Godard, 39–40
Maron, Rochat, and Company, 37
marriage, 22, 152; arranged, 237n49; Bảo Đại on, 118; choice in, 237n49; Compassionate Marriage movement, 237n49, 260n8; rejection of, in interwar period, 117–18
Marseille soap, 273n26
Martin, Phyllis, 45
massage, 184
mass media, 53
materialism, 25
May Fourth Movement, 20, 237n49
McHale, Shawn, 195
Meiji Restoration, 12, 158, 160
Mekong Delta, 63
me tây, 131, 187; beauty trends adopted by, 60–61; classes of, 59–60; fashion style of, 81; Modern Girls and, 66–67
middle class, 33, 172; beauty contests and, 205, 208; department stores marketing to, 42; emergence of, 22–23; during Great Depression, 205–6; in interwar period, 17–18; origins of, 235n30, 235n33; philanthropic efforts of, 206–8
Middle Kingdom, 13
Ming Mang, 79
misogyny, 280n154
Miss America contest, 204
Miss Côte d'Azur contest, 204
Miss Europe contest, 195, 204
Miss France d'Outre Mer pageant, 195, 211
Miss Germaine Saraghi, 218
Mission Civilisatrice, La, 7, 11, 48
Miss Ất, 62, 165, 169
Miss Tonkin contest, 211–12
Miss Universe contest, 204, 212, 219, 287n76
Miss Vietnam contest, 213; nationalism and, 214
Mlle Mộng Khanh, 181
modeling, 217
Modern Girls, 25, 49, 76, 111, 175, 196; characteristics of, 64; fashion trends of, 35–36, 90; in Japan, 64–65, 142; me tây and, 66–67; *Phụ Nữ Tân Văn* on, 219–2120; trend of, in Vietnam, 65

modernism, Vietnamese, 7, 25, 65, 97, 103–4, 111, 234n16; beauty contests and, 208–10; body ideals and, 181; colonialism and, 48; Confucianism and, 8; critiques of, 220; fashion trends and, 14–15, 79; identity and, 209–10
modesty, 26
monarchy, 8–9
Mộng Khanh, 188
morality, beauty trends and, 197, 199
Morin Frères, 52, 57
Morin Hotels, 52
"Mốt" (newspaper column), 1
motherhood, 4–5
mouth, cosmetics for, 130–33
movie theaters, 246n787
Müller, J. P., 182
multiethnicity, 213–14
Muscular Christianity movement, 179
Mussolini, Benito, 147
Mỹ Chân (journalist), 62, 92, 167
Mỹ Viện Amy, 120

nails, cosmetics and, 144–45
Nam Định, 43, 44, 53, 206, 246n787
Nam Giao festival, 168
nằm lửa, 269n186
Nam Phong, 162
Nam Phương (Empress), 35–36, 49, 54–55, 67, 69, 100; marriage of, 70–72, 71
Naomi (Tanizaki), 65
nationalism, 25–26, 151–52; beauty contests and, 200–202, 212–13; Europeanization and, 231; fashion trends and, 96; Four Virtues and, 201; gender and, 257n97; in India, 257n97; Lemur Tunic and, 88–89; Miss Vietnam contest and, 214; in Philippines, 257n97; sports and, 162; Threefold Dependencies and, 201
Nazi Party, 146–47
Neo-Confucianism, 7, 9, 168, 233n8; colonialism resisted by, 237n50; Europeanization and, 197; gender and, 21–22; as reaction to Europeanization, 21; traditional values promoted by, 224

New Arts, 73, 104, 225–6
New Life Movement, 147
New Literature movement, 105, 225, 227
New Music (Tân Nhạc), 18, 73, 104, 173, 218, 225, 227, 290n142
New Poetry (Thơ Mới), 18, 104, 225
newspapers, 25–26, 27; fashion trends in, 54; French, 245n76. *See also specific topics*
New Theater (Cải Lương), 72, 104
New Women, 15, 27–28, 219; bicycles and, 170–71; education of, 61–62; fashion trends of, 35–36; feminism of, 182; hair styles of, 142–44; media portrayals of, 62
Ngày Nay (newspaper), 35, 49, 54, 72, 106–7, 181–82; cartoons in, 55; publishing license, 291n7
Nghệ Tĩnh, 96, 152
Ngọc Lang, 181
Ngọc Minh, 149
Ngô Đức Thịnh, 30
Ngũ Vọng, 164
Nguyen, Hong-Kong, 31
Nguyen, Martina, 30, 55–56
Nguyễn An Ninh, 20, 286n48
Nguyễn Cảnh line, 234n17
Nguyễn Cát Tường, 30, 35, 49, 54, 83, 89; in clothing reform movement, 97–100; on hair styles, 143; influence of, 55–56, 110; on nail polish, 144–45; on powder use, 140–41; swimsuit designs of, 175
Nguyễn Công Hoan, 67, 114–15, 163, 291n1
Nguyễn Đình Lạp, 67, 172
Nguyễn Du, 199
Nguyễn Đức Nhuận, 62, 167; advertising by, 248n106
Nguyen-Marshall, Van, 208
Nguyễn Nam Sơn, 236n40
Nguyễn Ngạc, 30
Nguyễn Qui Toàn, 162
Nguyễn Quyền, 80
Nguyễn Thiến Lăng, 216
Nguyễn Thị Kế, 168, 171
Nguyễn Thị Thanh Vân, 147, 151
Nguyễn Thị Thục Quyên, 165

INDEX

Nguyễn Văn Ký, 30, 118
Nguyễn Văn Luận, 30
Nguyễn Văn Tuyên, 218, 290n142
Nguyễn Văn Vĩnh, 14
Nhà Thuốc Phùng Gia Viên, 4
Nhất Linh, 93, 105, 271n230
Nha Trang, 173
Nhất Thanh, 30
Nhi Linh, 174
Nietzsche, Friedrich, 200, 285n42
Nihalchand Bros., 82
nịt vú, 186–88, 252n8
Noël, Suzanne, 126
Norindr, Panivong, 47
nudity, in art, 157–58

Oeuvres de Guerre de la Lạc Thiện, 207
Oger, Henri Joseph, 29
Orientalist studies, 29–30
Ottoman Empire, 213
Ovamaltine, 162, 179

Pajamas (sleeping), 75, 107–8, 231
palazzo pants, 52, 75–76
pants: palazzo, 52, 75–76; white, 81–84
Paraphenylenediamine, 264n70
Paris, 194–95; city planning, 243n37; Haussmann renovations, 274n26
Paris Soir, 194–95
Paul Bert Square, 44
Peers, Shanny, 47
Peiss, Kathy, 6, 29, 121–22; on cosmetics, 260n2
perfume, 145–46, 270n194
Peycam, Philippe, 195
Phạm Quỳnh, 22, 160
Phạm Thảo Nguyên, 30
Phan Bội Châu, 12, 62, 149, 151, 235n26, 286n48
Phan Châu Trinh, 13–15, 80, 234n19, 286n48
Phan Kế Bính, 30, 97
Phan Khôi, 13, 62, 234n19
Phan Thị Bạch Vân, 54
Phan Thiết, 173
Phan Thị Nga, 79, 101,165
Phan Trần Chúc, 220
Phan Văn Gia, 167

Phibun administration, 255n67, 259n134
philanthropy, 221; middle-class engaging in, 206–8; Vũ Trọng Phụng on, 208
Philippines, 91; nationalism in, 257n97
Phong Hóa (newspaper), 98, 101; cartoons in, 55
photographs, 211; of swimsuits, 177–78
photography: in beauty contests, 196, 202; in *Công Luận Báo* contest, 284n16
Phúc Thịnh, 43
Phùng Thị Phát, 67, 209
Phụ Nữ Tân Văn (newspaper), 45, 67, 70, 72, 143, 147, 151; on Modern Girls, 219–2120; sales of, 248n103; on textile industry, 91–92; on women in sports, 166–67
physical education, 33, 155, 161–2, 165, 275n50, 275m51
Piaubert, Jeanne, 281n188
plaque d'identitie, 89
Plus Belle Femme de France pageant, La, 194, 212
Po, Pauline, 204
Pohoomull Frères, 82
Poland, 291n2
political reforms, interwar period, 96–105
Pomfret, David, 29
Popular Front government, France, 244n67, 275n50
posture, body ideals and, 184
poverty, 193–94
powder: cosmetic use of, 139–41; Nguyễn Cát Tường on, 140–41
Press Latine d'Europe et d'Amerique, 194
Printemps, 40
print media: beauty trends and, 53–56; fashion trends and, 53–56. See also *specific topics*
prostitution, 202
Prussian Army, 161
public health initiatives, 158–59

Qing dynasty, 160
Quận Chúa, 204

Quảng Hưng Long, 43
quốc ngữ script, 15, 16, 18, 20, 21, 23, 54, 61, 94, 224

Rạch Kiến, 165, 169
rail lines, 240n2
rayon, 87
realism journalism, 236n41
Red River Delta, 24
Reform Theater (cải lương), 225
Republic of Turkey, 213
Republic of Vietnam, 31
Roces, Mina, 257n97
Rochat et Beaumont, 37
Rossi, Tino, 52
rubber, vulcanized, 254n46
Rue Catinat, Saigon, 38, 221, 248n106
Rue de France, 38
Rue Paul Bert, 38, 127
rural women, 3

safety bicycles, 278n121
Saigon, 35, 82, 87, 110, 195
Saigon Philharmonic, 290n142
Sài Thành (newspaper), 165
Salon de Coiffure Michel Phu, 142
Sầm Sơn, 52, 53, 173, 174, *178*, 178–79
Sandow, Eugen, 179
Sarraut, Albert, 17, 103
Sát Market, 44
Sato, Barbara, 29, 64
Sauzé, 123, 146
science, 123
seaside resorts, 173–74
seduction, 146
Self-Reliant Literary movement, 20, 25, 54, 55–56, 98, 160
sexuality, 102; cosmetics and, 148–49; Hollywood and, 57
shoes, 254n46, 259n148
"Silhouettes at the Beach, The" (Nhi Linh), 174
silk, 87
skin care, 116, 133, 140; in China, 265n101, 266n124
Slade, Tobe, 45
slippers, house, 259n148

snake skin, 89–90
sneakers, 86–87
soap, 273n26
social anxiety, about cosmetics, 149–50
social class, 3; beauty trends and, 4; cosmetics and, 24; in interwar period, 17. *See also* middle class
Social Darwinism, 162, 167
social media, 31
social norms, gender and, 1–3
Société Poinsard et Veyret, 40
Sông Hương (newspaper), 218
Song Nguyệt, 95–96
Song Nguyệt Phạm thị Lan Khanh Mỹ-Chânall, 54
Souret, Agnes, 67
sports, 27, 35, 44, 161–64; cartoons on, *164*; eugenics and, 167; fashion trends and, 45–46; nationalism and, 162; sporting movement, 85–86; Vũ Trọng Phụng on, 163; women in, 165–72
Stewart, Mary Lynn, 29, 180
stock market crash, 1929, 206
Studio Marianne, 183–84, *184*
Style-Republik (magazine), 31
suicide, 107, 118, 261n11
Swadeshi Movement, 256n72
swimsuits, 174; Nguyễn Cát Tường designing, *175*; photographs of, 177–78

tailoring, 43
Tale of Kiều (Nguyễn Du), 199
Tamari, Tomoko, 39
tango, 46
Tanizaki, Jun'ichiro, 65
Tân Nhạc (New Music), 18, 104, 173, 218, 225, 27, 290n142
tanning, 135; popularization of, 173–74
Tân Phong nữ sĩ (Hồ Biểu Chánh), 63–64
Tardieu, Victor, 104, 236n40
Taxi Girls, 23, 65, 92, 190, 218, 228
Taylor, Nora, 236n40
Tây Sơn Rebellion, 78
tennis jumpers, 86
tennis movement, 168
textiles, 91–92; British, 255n72

INDEX

Thái Bình, 210
Thanh Lâm, 102–3
Thành Thái (Emperor), 12, 80; abusiveness of, 234n16
Third Republic, 158
Thơ Mới (New Poetry), 18, 20, 62, 104, 117–118 225, 227
Tho Radia, 123, *124*, 125, 137
Threefold Dependencies (Tam Tòng), 2–3, 9, 22, 192, 219; nationalism and, 201
three-piece suit, 13–14, 17
Tokalon, *120*, 120–21, 123, 134, 135, 137, 138, *139*, 140
tomboys, 169
Tô Ngọc Vân, 55, 93, 104, 216, 227
Tonkin, 12, 72, 87, 173, 213
Tonkin Free School, 15, 91, 131, 160
tooth blackening, 30, 32, 130–31, 217
toothpaste, 131–32
Toshiko, 54
Tosika brand cosmetics, 119–140
Tố Tâm, 118
Tourane, 37, 46
tourism, 230; in interwar period, 51
To Whore (Vũ Trọng Phụng), 58, 84, 148
traditionalism, 9
Tran, Richard, 10
Tràng An Báo (newspaper), 49, 66–67, 176, 217
Trang-Tử, 199
Trần Huy Liệu, 198
Trần Lệ Xuân, 291n8
Trần Quang Đức, 30
Trần Quang Trân, 104
Transindochinois rail, 240n2
Trần Thị Bích, 219
Trần Thị Phương Hoa, 30
Trần-Thị-Tý, 171
Trần Trọng Kim, 285n42, 289n131
Trần Văn Lai, 216, 289n131
Trịnh Thục Oanh, 62, 72, 253n26
Trọng Lang, 190
Trống Mái (Khái Hưng), 67, 174, 180
Trung Bắc Tân Văn (newspaper), 153, 177
Trung Hòa Nhật Báo, 147
Trung Lập Báo (newspaper), 65

Trưng Sisters, 62
Trường Xuân Milk, 54, 134
T. T. (journalist), 92
Tự-Do (Huỳnh Văn Chính), 195, 199
Tự Đức (Emperor), 234
Tùng-Hiệp, 53
tunics: colorful, 81–84; designs of, 78–79; in interwar period, 79–80. *See also* Lemur Tunic
Tuyên Quang, 37

United States, 6–7
urban infrastructure, in interwar period, 16

vacationing: in French culture, 51; guaranteed vacation time, 244n67
Veblen, Thostein, 17, 45
Velment, Aro, 195
Viễn Đệ, 123
Việt Hoa Nguyễn Thị Kế, 168
Vịt Đực (newspaper), 1, *50*, 55, 107–9, 148; on beauty contests, 220–21; on Europeanization, 220
Vỡ Đê (Vũ Trọng Phụng), 50
Võ Đức Diên, 104
Võ Vương, 78
Vu-Hill, Kimoloan, 235n29
Vũ Trọng Phụng, 50, 58, 84, 87, 95, 101, 136–37, 148; on beauty contests, 210; on Europeanization, 190; on philanthropy, 208; on sports, 163

wage labor, 15–16, 17; before colonialism, 235n29
Waleffe, Maurice de, 194–95, 196, 211, 214
WanCaln, 58, 204
Wang, Sumei, 65, 121
Want to Be Beautiful (Mlle Mộng Khanh), 55, 181, 188
water, running, 159
weight loss, electric treatment for, 281n188
West, Mae, 180–81
white pants, 81–84
Wild, Laura, 204

willow leaf body, 33, 35, 153, 156, 166, 167, 179, 180, 181, 227
Wilson, Donald Dean, 246n787
witch hazel, 189
women: artistic agency of, 231; bodies of, 33; as consumers, 23, 25–26; images of, 27, 54–55; physiques of, 153–54; in sports, 165–72. *See also specific topics*
Woodside, Alexander, 79
World Fair, 47, 161, 211
World War I, 7–8, 15–16, 32, 79, 80, 114, 173; consumerism after, 223
World War II, 33–34
Wretched Hanoi (Trọng Lang), 149, 190

Yalom, Marilyn, 186–87
Yên Bái, 96

GPSR Authorized Representative: Easy Access System Europe, Mustamäe tee 50, 10621 Tallinn, Estonia, gpsr.requests@easproject.com

www.ingramcontent.com/pod-product-compliance
Lightning Source LLC
Chambersburg PA
CBHW022030290426
44109CB00014B/811